The Spiritual Journey of St. Philip's Church

Charleston, S.C.
1906 - 2012

William McIntosh, III

Copyright © 2013 William McIntosh, III
All rights reserved.
ISBN-10: 148122476X
EAN-13: 9781481224765
Library of Congress Control Number: 2012923689
CreateSpace Independent Publishing Platform, North Charleston, SC

RECTORS AND INTERIM RECTORS OF ST. PHILIP'S FROM 1906 THROUGH 2012

Rev. Samuel Cary Beckwith
April 1, 1906 – March 4, 1935
Emeritus 1935 – 1939

Rev. Merritt Francis Williams
October 1, 1935 – September 1, 1941

Rev. John E. Reilly
Interim November 1941 – January 1, 1942

Rev. W. Herbert Mayers
Interim February 1942 – December 1, 1942

Rev. Marshall Edward Travers
December 1, 1942 – October 15, 1956

Rev. Waddell F. Robey
Interim October 16, 1956 – May 3, 1957

Rev. Roderick J. Hobart
Interim June & July 1957

Rev. Sidney Grayson Clary
August 1, 1957 – August 31, 1964

Rev. Frank Coventry
August 7, 1962 – August 31, 1963
while Clary was in England

Rev. Charles L. Widney
Interim September 1, 1964 – June 1, 1965

Rev. Canon Samuel Thompson Cobb
June 1, 1965 – May 31, 1982
Emeritus 1982 – 2003

Rev. Canon Knud A. Larsen
Interim June 1, 1982 – September 9, 1983

Rev. Henry Lawrence Scott Jr.
September 10, 1983 – May 18, 1986

Rt. Rev. Moultrie Moore
Interim May 19, 1986 – September 1986

Canon Peter Gillingham
Interim October 10, 1986 – May 31, 1987

Rev. Terrell Lyle Glenn, Jr.
Interim June 1, 1987 – October 3, 1987

Rev. James Eugene Hampson
October 4, 1987 – September 1, 1999

Rev. John Haden McCormick
Hired as associate June 1996
Assistant to Rector
September 22, 1997
Priest in charge and vicar
September 2, 1999 – June 10, 2000
Rector
June 11, 2000 – to present and beyond

DEDICATED
TO THE GLORY OF GOD

This book would not be possible without guidance from my tough editor and loving wife, Suzanne V. McIntosh. She said sometimes I get carried away.

Many thanks to Charles DeAntonio for giving his permission to use his beautiful painting of the "Presentation in the Temple" as the cover of this book. The portrait hangs in the narthex.

I thank Carol Burk, who is in charge of the church's communications, for keeping the manuscript safe on the church's hard drive and teaching me how to use our kinky copiers. I thank St. Philippian Grace Creel for copying hundreds of vestry minute pages. At the request of our rector J. Haden McCormick, the project also included copying all of the vestry minute pages on archival paper from 1945 through 2012. Every vestry minute page from 1906 into 2012 has been read by this author to obtain the information needed to make this book possible.

I apologize in advance for misspelled names. There are hundreds of names in this book, and a tremendous effort has been made to double check these names. Poor Dorothy Bollwinkle, former organist, had her name misspelled in the vestry minutes for twenty years. Fortunately, she probably never knew that. Many names in the vestry minutes have been spelled in many different ways.

Cities without a state behind the name are within South Carolina or they are large well known cities such as Atlanta.

The book begins in 1906 when the Rev. Cary Beckwith was the first rector to be called to St. Philip's in the twentieth century. This author chose the twentieth century so that living people could share input and memories. Those who shared are: Mrs. Fleetwood Albrecht, Mrs. Rhett Barrett, Clarence (Hank) Bauer, Dan Beaman, Dubose Blakeney, Mrs. Jo Ann Booker, Mrs. Robert Bowles (Elizabeth), C.B. Branan, Mrs. Grayson Clary, Mrs. Grace Creel, Mrs. Lydia Evans, Mrs. Frances Geer, George Greene III, Mrs. Mary Anne Hanckel, Ed Holt, Miss Langhorne Howard, Mrs. Catherine Jones, Mrs. Philip Kassebaum, John Kerr, Dr. George Orvin, Dr. and Mrs. James Ravenel, Ms. Beverly Schroder, James M. Stelling, Mrs. Patience Walker, Mrs. Emily Whipple, Arthur M. Wilcox and Mrs. Harriet Travers Yarborough.

Clergy who shared: Rt. Rev. FitzSimons Allison, Rev. Ralph Byrd, Jr., Rev. Jay Fowler, Bishop Terrell Glenn, Rev. Peter Larsen, Rev. Maurice Lee, Rev. William P. Rhett, Rev. Renny Scott, Rev. Frederick S. Sosnowski, Rev. Benjamin W. Turnage, Jr. and Rev. A. Kenneth Weldon.

Be aware. This is just not a history book but much more. It consists of scandals, blessings and miracles. Tears have been shed at St. Philip's, anger has been expressed and joyous voices have praised the Lord through the centuries. The Holy Spirit lives within our ancient walls.

St. Philip's has not touched just its members but others from all over the world. This is not a book only for St. Philippians but those who have done such physical work as repairing and rebuilding the church, for those who found Christ here and spread His word everywhere, for those who need comforting, for those searching for the narrow gate and for those who have found it. God bless you all.

This book is the property of St. Philip's Church. All proceeds will be given to St. Philip's.

WELCOME TO ST. PHILIP'S

A good way to begin this book is to learn something about St. Philip's church buildings. Charles Town was founded in 1670 on a site west of the Ashley now called Old Town. A few years later, the settlers realized "oyster point" was a better location and a plat was made by 1672 marking off the lots that would be sold. The first site slowly withered away. One lot at the southeast corner of what is now Broad and Meeting streets was left open so that a church could be built there. The Lords Proprietors, founders of South Carolina, inserted a clause that parliament would build the Church of England edifices and that they would also pay the clergy, "which being the only true and orthodox religion of all the King's dominions," including South Carolina. Therefore, only Church of England churches would be allowed to receive public maintenance.

Historian Edward McCrady said it was not certain when the first St. Philip's was built. He said it could have been built between 1682 and 1690. The church was built of wood over a brick foundation and was said to be "large and stately." Rev. Frederick Dalcho[1] said the workmen burned heaps of oyster shells, producing lime. The lime was hydrated and mixed with hair or fibers as a binding agent to make plaster to cover the interior walls and ceiling.

By March 1706 St. Philip's had a bell. Thomas Booth was paid £2 and fifteen shillings to ring the bell. It was required the bell be rung at eight in the morning when the assembly was in session in Charles Town.[2]

---

1   Dalcho, who was Bishop Nathaniel Bowen's assistant from 1819 -1835 and assistant at St. Michael's, wrote a history of the Episcopal Church in South Carolina 1663 -1820. Bishop Albert Sidney Thomas continued the history from 1820 to 1957.

2   In the *1702 Journals of the Common House of Assembly* there was a reference that Augustine Smith was paid twenty shillings for ringing the bell for the assembly but there was no reference to a church bell.

The first known donors were Original and Millicent Jackson, who arrived in South Carolina on the first fleet in 1670. In 1672, they were granted 100 acres and later purchased ninety-two acres between the Ashley and Wando (now Cooper) rivers on the Charleston neck.

The Jackson's donation was not made to the church but to its rector, Rev. Atkin Williamson. On January 14, 1681, "Original Jackson of Carolina, carpenter, and Milicent, his wife, being excited with a pious zeale for the propagation of the true Christian religion" gave Williamson four acres adjacent to their property so that he could perform the Church of England liturgy "in a church or house of worship" that would be built on those four acres. The boundaries of the property were marked by four trees, each marked with three notches and a cross. It is not known what happened to the property.

Original Jackson died by May 6, 1684.

The first St. Philip's building was torn down in the 1720s because it was rotten and too small. Later, St. Michael's was built on the then empty lot. The second St. Philip's building was completed on Church Street in 1723 and it burned to the ground in 1835 with only one small table and a roof shingle surviving. There are two paintings of the interior of the second church that hang in the narthex of the third church. There were two bells in the second church.

McCrady wrote that the congregation so loved the second building that they wanted the third building to be a complete reproduction of the second. After a year passed, other ideas prevailed. One presentation was to build a pagoda.

The third St. Philip's building was completed on the site of the second church in 1838, and the steeple was completed in 1850. The interior of the third church is in a "Corinthian order" of architecture with the columns mostly covered with stucco but the capitals of the columns are carved wood. The church is 114 feet long and forty-two feet at its highest interior measurement. Eight-hundred people can be seated in the church and close to 1,000 with folding chairs in the aisles. In July 1839, it was reported the cost of building, not including the steeple, was $84,206.01. The height of the church from sidewalk to the top of the steeple is 195 feet, 5 inches.

Please come into St. Philip's. We begin in 1906.

St. Philip's in the early 20th century - courtesy of Gini Steele at antiquepix@aol.com

THE REV. SAMUEL CARY BECKWITH

RECTOR

APRIL 1, 1906 - MARCH 4, 1935

RECTOR EMERITUS 1935 – 1939

Prior to the War Between the States, Petersburg, Virginia, was a prosperous town of 18,000 people. Conditions of the town rapidly deteriorated during the Federal siege that began on June 9, 1864, and ended March 25, 1865, when Petersburg fell. It is no exaggeration to compare the intensive damage of Petersburg in 1865 with Berlin, Germany, in 1945.

It was in this shattered town where Samuel Cary Beckwith was born, the son of Thomas Stanly Beckwith and Emma Cary Beckwith on November 17, 1870, the same year Virginia was readmitted to the Union. The citizens of Petersburg were struggling to rebuild. Reconstruction did not end until 1876.

Beckwith's parents somehow sent him to good schools. He attended Col. W. Gordon McCabe's University School and afterwards the Davis Military School in La Grange, North Carolina. At the age of nineteen, he entered into business in Petersburg. He was also a member in the state militia in the Petersburg Grays and, on one occasion, Beckwith was sent with a detail to prevent a lynching of two African-Americans in Mecklenberg County.

Beckwith entered the University of the South at Sewanee, Tennessee, in 1890 and he was recognized for his scholastics as well as athletics. He was captain of the "scrub" football team from 1891 to 1894 and was a letterman on the football squad. He won a medal for winning the one mile race. Beckwith was the director of the college chapel choir and a member of the banjo, mandolin and guitar clubs. He was involved in other interests as well. In 1894 he joined the faculty there and earned his bachelor's and masters' degrees. From 1896 to 1900 Beckwith studied at the University of the South's theological department and on November 26, 1899, he was ordained a deacon in the Episcopal Church. He was ordained priest on May 31, 1900.

On December 11, 1900, Beckwith married Miss Videau Marion Yeadon Legare of Aiken. They had five children: Thomas Stanly Beckwith, Eliza Polmer Beckwith, Videau Marion Legare Beckwith, Keith Legare Beckwith and Samuel Cary Beckwith, Jr.

From 1902 to 1904 Beckwith was rector of St. Luke's at Hot Springs, Virginia, and Christ Church at Warm Springs, Virginia, and he also served as assistant in charge of educational work at St. Andrew's in Richmond. Following a summer abroad, Beckwith moved to Aiken where he became rector of the Holy Apostles Church in Barnwell and of St. Albans in Blackville. Soon after, he also had charge of the Church of the Holy Communion at Allendale and the missions in Bamberg and Graniteville. Beckwith began his rectorship at St. Philip's on April 1, 1906.

Beckwith's predecessor, the Reverend John Johnson, who was the engineer at Fort Sumter during its siege, was born December 25, 1829, and was rector of St. Philip's from 1872 to 1906. On May 22, 1905, Walter Pringle, chairman, of the vestry, reported that Johnson wanted to take his vacation during July. The chairman suggested the vacation time should also include August so that the rector would not have to return during the heat. Because of the rector's recent illness, his seemingly impaired health and his advanced years, the chairman wanted the vestry to hire a permanent assistant rector.

There have been many assistant rectors at St. Philip's. Between 1700 and 1872 there were thirty assistant rectors although there were dry periods without assistants: 1820 – 1834; 1841 – 1851; 1860 – 1871. Johnson was the assistant rector from 1871 until 1872. The next assistant rector was A. Campbell Tucker in 1947.

Apparently Johnson agreed with Pringle as the rector wrote the vestry that the time had come for him to be provided with an assistant, and he suggested several names including Albert S. Thomas—later Bishop Thomas. Beckwith was not on his list. Johnson wrote, "We certainly want a man of at least as much ability as the rectors of St. Michael's and of Grace Church." Johnson was willing to fall back on a yearly salary of $1,200, "being just half of what I once received."

At the same meeting, the vestry agreed to contact clergymen who would be willing to preach during Johnson's vacation. Beckwith was one of those men on the list.

Beckwith must have preached a great sermon because on October 7, 1905, the vestry called Beckwith as assistant rector. The vestry minutes show that no one else was called. His annual salary would be $1,500. Beckwith wrote on October 19, 1905, to Walter Pringle, "Since I left you in Charleston I have had the call to be the assistant rector at St. Philip's Church continually on my mind, & I regret more than I can tell you that I find that I cannot accept it. In taking this action I have been guided solely by a sense of duty for while it would be a privilege & pleasure to work among you, I find that conditions & circumstances force me to decline.

> Again thanking you &wishing you every blessing in your work, I am
> Very truly yours,
> S. Cary Beckwith"

Nothing happened until January 26, 1906, when Johnson sent the vestry a letter of resignation. Johnson wrote, "By some effects of age, to avoid what may amount to inefficiency in the Sacred Office of Rector of your Parish, to which I was called, more than thirty years ago – Therefore, I hereby respectfully tender my resignation, as your Rector, to take effect on the first day on next March trusting that you will be guided from above in the right choice of my successor ..." The same day the vestry elected Beckwith as the new rector and Johnson was elected as rector emeritus with a salary of $1,200 annually.

Beckwith accepted immediately with an annual salary of $2,000. Bishop William T. Capers advised Beckwith not to leave his present charges for at least two months. On March 14, Walter Pringle advised the vestry that Beckwith would start on April 1, 1906.

The vestry that called Beckwith in 1906 was elected April 24, 1905. Walter Pringle was chairman and Isaac Mazyck was vice-chairman. The vestry members were: E. M. Moreland, Henry C. Cheves, W. H. Warley, Theo. D. Jervey, Huger Sinkler, F. L. Green, and Jas. P. Gibbs. Also elected were Arthur Mazyck as secretary treasurer and John. J. Whitney was elected sexton.

Johnson died April 7, 1907, at age 77. On May 8 the vestry received a thank you letter from Rev. James Willis Cantey Johnson, Rev. John Johnson's son, for the money St. Philip's sent during his father's illness. The widow Johnson also sent a thank you note to the vestry for paying her husband's full April salary. At the same meeting the vestry voted to pay C. Floride Johnson, the rector's widow, $25.00 a month during the term of office of "this vestry" and to also pay J. M. Connelley $204 for Johnson's funeral. Mrs. Johnson was thrilled. The vestry wrote a three page memoriam for the vestry records and the Johnson family. The vestry extended the monthly $25.00 payment year by year until her death. According to the records of the St. Philip's church home, Mrs. Johnson also received a stipend of $8.00 a month from May 1906 to her death. Floride Johnson was born May 29, 1838, and died May 27, 1913. Rev. and Mrs. Johnson are buried in the eastern churchyard.

Four of Johnson's six children survived their father. In March 1910, they made known their wish to offer a memorial to their father including a memorial window in the chancel. The 1916 vestry approved the window but it was rescinded in 1918. The vestry explained that in the past the custom was to erect memorial tablets to former clergy in the nave of St. Philip's as evidenced by the existing memorials to former clergy.[3] The vestry added, that experience proved memorial tablets erected in the body of the church lasted longer and were more enduring.

Beckwith reported on January 13, 1926, that Dr. Johnson's memorial table was installed on the church's south wall and the dedication would be on January 31. The tablet was paid for by friends, relatives and compatriots. The vestry paid the $97.48 that was needed to complete the fund. Rev. Johnson's memorial tablet, the only memorial that has a Confederate flag on it, still looks good in the 21st century.

OVERVIEW

When the Reverend S. Carey Beckwith became rector of St. Philip's at age thirty-five in 1906, Theodore Roosevelt was president of the United States and there were forty-five states. In the final decade of the nineteenth century the eight leading denominations in order of membership were: eight million Roman Catholics, five and a half million Methodists, four million Baptists, one million Presbyterians, almost one million Lutherans and nearly a million Disciples of Christ. The Episcopal and Congregational churches each had around six hundred thousand. In 1900 the population of the United States was just under seventy-six million. Of that number, church membership stood at twenty-six million.

Beckwith served under three bishops of the diocese of South Carolina: The Rt. Rev. Ellison Caper, the Rt. Rev. William Alexander Guerry and the Rt. Rev. Albert S. Thomas.

The Rt. Rev. Ellison Capers was elected bishop coadjutor on May 4, 1893. A bishop coadjutor is a bishop who is elected to assist the bishop of a diocese and upon his resignation or death the coadjutor succeeds him in office. After his predecessor The Rt. Rev. William Bell White Howe[4] resigned, Capers was consecrated as bishop on July 20, 1893, at Trinity Church in Columbia.

On May 15, 1907, the Rev. William Alexander Guerry, then chaplain of the University of the South and professor of its theological department, was elected bishop coadjutor

---

3   Actually not all the memorials in the nave are to clergy.
4   Howe became rector at St. Philip's in 1859 and was consecrated bishop of the diocese of South Carolina on October 8, 1871. Howe resigned as rector of St. Philip's on January 1, 1873, ending the diocesan custom of the bishop also holding a rectorship. Howe died November 25, 1894, and is buried in the western churchyard.

of the diocese of South Carolina. Bishop Capers resigned in 1907 and Guerry was consecrated bishop on September 15, 1907, at Trinity Church in Columbia. Bishop Capers died April 22, 1908. Guerry was murdered in June 1928.

The Rev. Albert Sidney Thomas, rector of St. Michael's, who succeeded Guerry, was elected bishop on September 16, 1928, and was consecrated on November 30, 1928, at St. Michael's. Thomas resigned his office effective December 31, 1943.

CHURCH SERVICES, MEMBERSHIP & CLERGY

In 1901 there were 312 communicants at St. Philip's.

In 1906, Walter Pringle, who was again elected chairman of the vestry, presented a proposal for combining the services with St. Michael's church during August and September. The vestry approved. St. Michael's would be closed during August and Beckwith would be in charge of both parishes. In return, St. Philip's would close in September with the rector of St. Michael's, Rev. John Kershaw, in charge of both parishes. In 1910, there was a suggestion that St. Philip's would remain open in September but the rector seemed to discourage it. He advised that St. Michael's would probably be glad to resume the old arrangement. Theodore Jervey moved the church remain closed in September so the rector and choir could enjoy vacations. The motion passed.

The three-day annual council (later called 'convention') of the diocese of South Carolina met at St. Philip's on May 12 -14, 1908. In preparation for the council meeting, Henry C. Cheves on April 21 made a motion that the rector and chairman, Walter Pringle, should be authorized to appoint the committees. Apparently the committees, including the railroad committee, did well on short notice for no complaints were made to the members. The diocese of South Carolina then encompassed the entire state. All the arrangements went well and the entertainment committee arranged for an excursion to the Charleston Navy Yard. Cars would leave the Commercial Club promptly at 4:30 p.m. There would also be a smoker at St. Michael's parish house at 9:00 p.m.

In addition to all the other events, there was a business meeting. The council adopted a seal and amended a canon by striking out the word "male" to allow women to vote in parochial elections. It was approved in the 1909 council. Women were voting in local elections in a few states but they did not win "the vote" until 1920. Also in 1909, the council moved the Church Home Orphanage from Charleston to York.

In past years, it was a tradition that the Christmas offering would be added to the communion alms. In 1910 it was decided to split the offering between the communion alms and the paupers in the parish. Communion alms were simply the offerings collected at special services such as Holy Communion, Christmas and other such authorized services. Communion alms were generally given to the rector and or the bishop as a discretionary fund.

Beckwith on December 10, 1909, sent a letter to the vestry suggesting the purchase of a number of the 1892 or 1893 Books of Common Prayer and hymnals to be placed in the church pews. On the motion of Isaac Mazyck, $30.00 was to be appropriated for the purchase and labeling of the books. This may have been something new. Since everyone purchased a pew, it would seem they would be expected to come with a Book of Common Prayer, a hymnal and a Bible.

In 1914, there were 271 families in the church and 142 individuals for a total of 1,016 baptized persons. There was one morning service at 11:00 am with communion on the first and third Sundays. There was no mention of the occasional fifth Sunday. Evening prayer was on Sunday at 6 p.m. Services on Friday and Saint's days were at 6:00 p.m.

St. Philip's revised its by-laws in April 1916. A member was defined as a baptized, white person who was a member of the Protestant Episcopal Church in the United States. Also to be a member, one must own a pew or part of a pew. In order for a member to vote at congregational meetings, he or she must have paid not less than $10.00 during the year to support the church and his or her pew fees must have been paid in full.

In November 1917, on motion of Thomas E. Myers and E. G. Guerard, the vestry thanked W. G. Mazyck for donating a processional cross. At the same time Mrs. Henry Augustus Middleton (H.A.M.) Smith, mother of J. J. Pringle Smith, who was soon to be on the vestry, donated a cross to the church that arrived by April 1918. Beckwith suggested the pulpit and the lectern be moved ahead one pew. The cost was $203.60. The vestry approved that the flag be used in the procession.

The vestry voted August 14, 1924, that the church remain open during September and that Beckwith make the possible arrangements for providing clergy during that time.

The *News and Courier* printed a large article on November 23, 1924, on the service held the evening before at St. Philip's with four headlines. Two of the headlines were, "CALLS ON MASONS TO LEAD MANKIND TO A HIGHER LIFE" and "Big Congregation in 'Westminster of the South' to hear the Clergyman."

Rev. L. E. McNair, D.D. spoke. He quoted the inscription on the tomb of General Gordon in St. Paul's Cathedral: "Who at all times and everywhere gave his strength to the weak, his substance to the poor, his sympathy to the suffering and his heart to God." McNair also said, "It is a great thing to go forth lovingly into the territory of benevolence; to have part in the mighty expansion of sociology; to carry skill and fine training into the moral movements of the day."

Beckwith, who received the thirty-third degree in 1919, was appointed Deputy of the Supreme Council in South Carolina.

The Great War ended November 11, 1918. Soon after, a flag was placed in the vestibule by the Honor Roll. Unfortunately, the St. Philip's World War I Honor Roll was not kept. The Carolina Yacht Club does have a memorial plaque with the names of its fifty-nine members who served. Two St. Philippians are known to have fought in the war: Langdon McCord Cheves and Captain Edward Lawrence Wells. Wells has a memorial in the "vestibule."

CAPTAIN EDWARD LAWRENCE WELLS

Wells, who was born in Charleston on August 7, 1886, just prior to the earthquake, was the youngest of five children. By 1913, he was a civil engineer living with his parents at 2 Water Street. Wells was active in the Charleston Light Dragoons which he saved from being disbanded and for that he was made First Lieutenant and its local commanding officer. He served on the Mexican border with the Dragoons in 1916 when General John Pershing and 12,000 troops entered Mexico to capture Pancho Villa who killed Americans in New Mexico.

Wells enlisted in the army soon after the outbreak of World War I and was trained in the cavalry. He arrived in France in the early fall of 1917 and was switched to the Second Machine Gun Battalion where he made Second Lieutenant by September 1918. He distinguished himself during desperate fighting in the second battle of the Marne. "He gave evidence of splendid courage under fire." After fighting in other battles, he was sent in September 1918 to the St. Mihiel front and then on to the Meuse-Argonne offensive where he was mortally wounded leading a fierce attack against German machine guns near the town of Exermount. He was shot after capturing many prisoners but with his last breath he was able to disclose the location of the hostile position. He was thirty-two when he died on October 4, 1918.

Captain Edward Lawrence Wells was awarded the French Croix de Guerre, the Distinguished Service Cross and the Oak Leaf Cluster. President Wilson posthumously promoted Wells to Captain. He was cited for extraordinary heroism.

In 1930, a service was held at St. Philip's to commemorate the 250th anniversary of the 1680 founding of Charleston on its present site. Beckwith was so enthused about the commemoration that he invited President Herbert Hoover to attend the church service and that the church would pay up to $37.50 to defray the cost of the float to be entered into the parade commemorating the festivities. Hoover replied that because of "pressing business" he was unable to leave Washington, D. C.

THE YOUTH, THE LAYMAN'S LEAGUE AND THE LADIES

The Woman's Auxiliary was formed in the diocese of South Carolina at its council in 1884 under Bishop Howe. At the 1885 council, Bishop Howe reported there were sixteen parochial branches of the Woman's Auxiliary with about 600 members. The ladies had furnished boxes valued at $1,200 to missionaries in various parts of the country. They also contributed $1,300 in cash to the missionary work of the church.

Bishop Albert Thomas in his book *The Episcopal Church in South Carolina* states there was a chapter of the Woman's Auxiliary in 1890 at St. Philip's. But the *St. Philip's Parish Letter* of May 1914 stated the St. Philip's chapter of the Woman's Auxiliary was established in 1910. Perhaps, the Woman's Auxiliary at St. Philip's faded away for a while. In 1914, the officers of the Woman's Auxiliary were: the rector was president, vice-president, Miss M. B. Washington and the secretary Mrs. J. S. Heyward.

The fifty-three women of the auxiliary were busy as the following notes indicate. "A most successful Lenten study was given to the Auxiliary by Miss Elise F. Hayne." The women's last year's pledges went to: the Mary E. Pinckney Bible Woman in "Tokio," the Nana Shand Wilson School fund in Hankow, China, and other locations such as Puerto Rico and Shanghai. As late as 1930, $66.30 was sent from St. Philip's to help support "Tokio Hospital."

The Woman's Auxiliary on May 1, 1914, sent a box to Miss Gwendolyn Brown of Fairbault, Minnesota, providing her with a summer outfit. Members of the auxiliary generously contributed $33.00 in cash and articles valued at $13.00. A grateful letter of acknowledgement has been received.

In addition to the Woman's Auxiliary, Miss Hayne was chairman of the Church Home Orphanage Association and Miss Minnie Pringle was president of the City Mission Society. Mrs. J. North Smith was the secretary.

Miss Hayne wrote about Sunday schools in the February 1914 issue of the *St. Philip's Parish Letter*. One of the reports put out at the last general convention stated that Sunday school attendance during the last three years has shown a marked drop. That was not necessarily the case at St. Philip's. Miss Hayne wrote "The Sunday School is the nursery of the church ... Not only is it incumbent on parents to send their children, but the obligation of members of the congregation to fit themselves for teaching cannot be shirked. It is a great responsibility, but it is also a great opportunity." When you hear a baby crying in church, do not get annoyed, but thank God that St. Philip's is growing.

After the Sunday school had been operating for some time, James Campbell Bissell was made superintendent. He was elected to the vestry in 1915.

Bissell was born in 1875 in Charleston. His wife, Floride Peyre H. Johnson Bissell, was the daughter of the Rev. John Johnson. The Bissells, who lived at 10 Trumbo Street, had three sons and a daughter. Bissell was a member of the Charleston County Assessment Board and he served on city council. The vestry accepted his resignation in 1927with great regret and extended to him the privilege of occupying his pew "so long as he may desire." He died after a long illness on August 19, 1949. He was buried in the eastern churchyard with The Rev. Travers Marshall and the Rev. A. Campbell officiating..

In 1912, James P. Gibbs, a member of the Church and Grounds Committee, received an estimate from the Hazelhurst Electric Co. for installing lights in the Sunday school building.

In 1914, during certain Sunday afternoons Bissell would take different classes of the Sunday school "to provide service" for the inmates of the City Alms House. "The inmates showed a most touching interest in them and expressed much gratitude."

The Sunday school closed for the summer on June 14, 1914. Bissell had previously announced that prizes would be awarded for perfect attendance. Those receiving prizes were: Arthur Pinckney, Floride Bissell, Somers Pringle, Stanly Beckwith and Margaret Pringle.

The annual Sunday school picnic in 1914 was held May 2 at Faber Place, Col. A. C. Kaufman's country home near Summerville. "The cool day, ample provisions and kindly spirit made a very happy combination for the enjoyment of the beautiful country place." In April 1915, the vestry voted an amount not to exceed $100 to be given annually for the Sunday school picnic. The $100 for the picnic was approved every year through 1923 and in 1924 an additional $35.00 was added to the cost.

Kaufman died in 1918 and left a bequest to St. Philip's. The executor of the Kaufman Trust Fund did not release the fund to the trustee, the South Carolina Security Company, until November 18, 1927. There is no explanation why the transfer took such a long time, but it was a source of frustration to the vestry. By 1928, the bequest was worth $46,022.44 consisting of $13,022.44 in bonds, some cash and $33,000 in two pieces of real estate. Faber Place Plantation was worth $15,000 and 198 East Bay Street, located on the northeast corner of East Bay and Cumberland streets, was worth $18,000.

On February 11, 1930, the wardens and vestrymen consented to sell Faber Place for $18,500 to the South Carolina Power Company.

The vestry rented 198 East Bay Street until 1943 when the church sold the building for $6,200 to Norman L. Cannon on May 4.

From January 1 through July 31, 1931, the Kaufman Fund brought in a net income of $1,285.73.

The vestry purchased the land north of the church which would provide a playground and a remodeled Sunday school building. An appeal was made from church members to donate joggling boards, swings and rings.

In November 1914, Bissell asked permission to form a committee of young men to act as ushers and to invite "strangers" to attend services while visiting Charleston. The vestry agreed.

In June 1916, the vestry voted that on Sunday June 25th the general collection be given toward defraying the expenses of the "Sunday School Convention" recently held in Charleston and that the rector should give such notice on the previous Sunday. Only $5.45 was raised from the general collection (not including pledges put in the collection) because of the "very inclement" weather. In December, the vestry agreed to add $50.

MRS. ISABEL A. SMITH

James Campbell Bissell reported in June 1916 that a tablet had been proposed to Mrs. Isabel A. Smith (1839 – 1915). Frederick Griffith Davies said permission was granted, but it would be in the vestibule (narthex) and not in the church (nave). Location would be subject to the approval of the vestry.

Anyone who enters from the narthex into the middle aisle passes the tablet or memorial on the right just prior to entering through the doors. Mrs. Smith ran the Mrs. Isabel Smith School from 1872 to 1903. The tablet was "erected by her former pupils as a loving tribute to the memory of a generous and cultured teacher." Mrs. Smith believed there must be "variety in education instead of uniform prescription."

One former pupil wrote, "hundreds of women in South Carolina rise up and call her blessed …"

Mrs. Smith was baptized at St. Philip's in 1854. She lost her father, Major James Alexander Ashby, when she was seven. She married her husband, William Edward Smith, when she was fourteen. Before she was twenty-one, she lost her husband and two of her children. Her third child, James Mongin Smith, who attended the College of Charleston, died in 1892 at age thirty-six.

Her quarterly payments for her pew, number eighty-nine, were paid up until just prior to her death. With all her tragedies, she did not turn from God. In 1934, nineteen years after her death, the vestry gave pew eighty-nine to the Ashley Hall students. Perhaps, Mrs. Smith would have liked that.

In 1942, the vestry offered the use of the church to Ashley Hall for their annual Christmas pageant. The offer was subject to the approval of the bishop. Once again, the young ladies were invited to worship at St. Philip's. The Ashley Hall students were invited in 1950 specifically to take part in the church's teenage discussion group. They were also invited sing in the choir at the 11:15 a.m. service.

The music committee was empowered to hire a musician to play piano or organ for the Sunday school. They hired an organist, Miss Dorothy Bollwinkle for $100 per year. Hymnals were ordered for the Sunday school. By 1927, the Sunday school's annual budget was up to $200 and the annual picnic then cost $158.

THEOLOGY, EVANGELISM AND MISSIONS

It is difficult to know what the theology of St. Philip's was at this time. None of Beckwith's sermons exist. We do have a slight clue of the theology of Bishop Guerry from an article he wrote circa 1915 called "Progress, a Permanent Element in Religion." Guerry stated "There are three permanent elements in religion: the sense of dependence on God; the desire for fellowship with God; and the necessity of progress. These three elements find their truest expression respectively in the Christian doctrine of the fatherhood of God, of the incarnation, and of the mission of the Holy Ghost. It has been the glory of Christianity that from the beginning it has assimilated new truths and shown itself capable of change and development, while other religions have become hopelessly archaic and stereotyped. The church has no more dangerous foe to combat than that spirit of ultra-conservatism which allows her leaders and members to get out of touch with their times so that they stick to a vocabulary which is a relic of a bygone age."

Guerry continued, "On the other hand, we should avoid the rashness with which some men have proclaimed a so-called 'new theology' divorced from historic and generic Christianity. This process of reinterpretation and restatement in language and philosophy of the day is as old as the New Testament, since the Gospel of John is a restatement of Christianity in terms of Greek philosophy. The author appropriated the language of a disciple of Plato and applied it to the person and work of Christ. It was the time when Christianity threw off the swaddling clothes of an effete Judaism and entered upon its world-wide career. John did a work for Christianity that needs to be repeated in every age of the church."

In 1914, St. Philip's paid diocesan missions $389.21, general missions $536.31, Church Home and orphanage $95.16 and communion alms and other charities $978.55.

In 1916, the vestry agreed to pay the diocesan council's 5% levy to support religious education at Sewanee, Porter Academy and St. Mary's School in Raleigh. The total paid was $171.02. York asked for funds so their church could be enlarged. Beckwith made an appeal to the congregation and $27.94 was raised and the vestry sent an additional $12.06 for a total of $40.00. At the same time $25.00 was taken from mission funds to cover a shortage promised to diocesan convention delegates. Vestry members, who discussed purchasing the proper Sunday school equipment, also agreed to replace windows and do necessary repairs. In 1919, Beckwith requested, and received a request that $100 per year be made for the use of the Sunday school.

At the October 1923 vestry meeting, Beckwith stated that in his opinion he did not consider it wise for the parish as an organization to become identified with the "Billy Sunday" revival.

According to Christian Biography Resources, William Ashley Sunday, Sr. was born in Ames, Iowa, in 1862 and died in Chicago in 1935. He was called the 'baseball evangelists" from his ball playing days. He was licensed to preach by the Presbyterian Church in 1898 and was ordained by the Presbyterian Church in 1903. Large scale evangelistic campaigns were very popular before World War I and Sunday was in the forefront. He used colorful, slangy language, impersonations and anecdotes among other things and he was strongly against alcohol. His message strongly emphasized that every person needed personal salvation through Jesus Christ and he emphasized the authority and reliability of the Bible. Sunday was involved in the management of the Winona Bible Conference, later called Winona Institutions, and in 1935 he received a Doctor of Divinity degree from Bob Jones College.

The rector and Thomas E. Myers on April 9, 1924, received permission from the vestry to have suitable cards printed featuring a photo of the church with an invitation inviting "strangers" to services. The cards would be displayed in hotels and other such appropriate places.

FINANCES & VESTRY

In 1905, the vestry secretary said he had been called by Messrs. Butts, and Phillips, solicitors of claims of Washington, D.C. They advised the secretary that under a recent act of Congress, compensation was being made to Southern churches for injuries and losses during "The War." The matter was turned over to the committee on church and grounds to investigate what steps should be taken. By January 1906, the secretary and treasurer reported progress was being made but they would need to pay $10.00 to architect J. H. Devereux for records. The vestry agreed to pay. In September 1906, it was announced the claim agent and a representative of the government would be in Charleston on the nineteenth to take testimony concerning war damages to the church. Nine years later in 1915, the issue of compensation popped up again. A letter was read from Mr. A. R. Serven wanting to know who would represent the claims before the United States government. The issue was never mentioned again.

From March 1, 1906, to February 28, 1907, the church's income totaled $5,002.95. The two largest receipts were $2,424.58 from pew rentals and $2,729.00 from house rents on the glebe land. Expenditures totaled $4,965.02.

On January 8, 1908, vestry chairman, Huger Sinkler, informed the vestry that a movement had begun to make very necessary repairs to the church and organ. Two members had already donated $1,050 toward the estimated cost of $4,000 for painting the interior and exterior of the church. The vestry would send a letter to the members detailing the urgent need of funds. A pledge card was enclosed in the letter and in it asked each member to enclose what amount would be given. Monthly or quarterly payments were offered but it was asked that all be paid on or before January 1909.

Sinkler wrote in his letter "Our forefathers, who have worshipped in this church, have given generously in the past for its support, maintenance and adornment, and today we feel assured that the same generous spirit is not lacking, although incomes have been greatly reduced. Let us give according to our means ..."

JAMES S. MURDOCK

Vestry chairman Walter Pringle in May 1908, announced that James S. Murdoch had left St. Philip's 100 shares, valued at $100 per share, of the American Manufacturing Company of which Murdoch had been a director.

He made this bequest on April 16, 1908, and died one week later. Murdoch wrote he "wished to show my interest in St. Philip's ... and to promote and contribute to its welfare." Murdoch desired there should be no published testimonials of his gifts to this or any other institutions. Theodore D. Jervey and Arthur Mazyck, vestry secretary, were asked to prepare a suitable acknowledgement to immediate family members..

Murdock was a very interesting man and perhaps one of the few members of St. Philip's to have been born in Ireland. He was born in County Tryon in 1835 and was brought with his parents to Pennsylvania in 1842. Two years later they moved to Asheville where Murdoch spent his childhood. Among his school mates at Col. Stephen Lee's school were Governor Vance and Chief Justice Merriman of North Carolina. In 1853 he moved to Charleston where his older brother Robert had already established himself and James was later associated with two businesses.

He took part in the first bombardment of Ft. Sumter serving in the Marion Artillery. John Fraser & Co. sent Murdoch to England and France to sell Confederate bonds and to also send goods and supplies through the blockade to Charleston.

In the summer of 1865, James Murdoch returned to Charleston and he and his brother Robert formed a co-partnership with W.C. Courtney that operated a cotton and commission business that lasted several years. In about 1876, Charleston Bagging Manufacturing Co. was formed largely through the efforts of James Murdoch and under his management "this most flourishing industry" in Charleston lasted until his death.

Murdoch was very active in Charleston organizations including the St. Andrew's Society. Being Scottish was not a requirement for membership. He also joined the Charleston Club, the Carolina Yacht Club and he was particularly active in the Carolina Art Association now called the Gibbes Museum of Art.

"Murdoch shunned notoriety and shrank from the public eye … no one knew what he did in kindly care for his neighbors because what he did was not for the purpose of exciting the applause of men, but for the purpose of doing good … There have been very few men like him; there is none to take his place" reported the *News and Courier.*

His last illness was lengthy and painful. His funeral was on Sunday April 24, 1908, the day after he died, at St. Philip's.

Murdoch requested that the 100 shares of the American Manufacturing Co. remain intact as long as it benefited St. Philip's. In November 1910, Huger Sinkler made a motion to sell the stock that it might be invested in safe and convenient securities. The motion passed. The price of the stock had risen from $100 per share to $115 per share bringing a total of $11,500. Vestryman E. M. Moreland, who was the broker, made no charge for commissions.

Moreland, who was first elected to the vestry in 1898, resigned on April 7, 1915. His resignation was accepted with regret from the vestry.

Moreland was with a group of vestrymen who served as long as he did. These men were: James Campbell Bissell; Walter and Ernest Pringle, Arthur and Isaac Mazyck, Henry C. Cheves, Theodore Jervey, Huger Sinkler, James Gibbs and a few others. These men ruled St. Philip's for more than sixteen years. The rector attended vestry meetings only on invitation. There were no term limits although each vestryman, the organist and the sexton had to run for office each year at the congregational meeting.

By 1917 Henry C. Cheves and Huger Sinkler were still on the vestry but there were new names added: Frederick. G. Davies, Thomas E. Myers, Dr. McMillan K. Mazyck, J. J. Pringle Smith, William F. Gray and Edward Percival Guerard II.

F.G. DAVIES

One of the new names, Frederick Griffith Davies, was unusual in two ways: he was not born in Charleston, but in Buffalo, New York, on February 19, 1865, and he was actively affiliated with the Republican Party. He may have been the first vestryman who was not born in Charleston. Very few white South Carolinians were Republican.

When Davies was two his parents moved to Tonawanda, New York, where his father was engaged in shipbuilding. After he graduated from school, he went into the lumber business but by 1900 it became obvious that timber was becoming exhausted in that area. After surveying many areas, he decided to relocate in the South Atlantic and became interested in a large timber tract near Charleston. Davies came to Charleston in 1905 and he and A. C. Tuxbury acquired valuable timber tracts nearby.

After three months of wading through swamps and camping in tents at night, he decided to locate a sawmill on the Shipyard River. A double band sawmill was built on the river and an extensive railroad system was constructed. The Tuxbury mill cut 715,000,000 feet of timber and at its height hired 400 to 500 employees.

In 1924, their mill, the A.C. Tuxbury Lumber Co., where Davis was vice-president was Charleston County's largest lumber plant. Davies was a member of the Port Utilities Commission and after three years resigned his chairmanship to become collector of customs, appointed by Republican President Herbert Hoover. Davies was a trustee of the Bank of South Carolina when it was closed during the 1933 bank holiday. These trustees received high praise because after the bank holiday all depositors received their money which was not the case in many instances. He was described, "as sympathetic with all Charleston aspirations and his usefulness as a citizen was revealed in the quality of service rendered as chairman of the Ports Utilities Commission."

Davies' granddaughter, Patience D. Walker, née Davies, shared the story that when President Howard Taft came to Charleston in 1909, Davies was asked to drive Taft because Davies was the only Republican in Charleston. He drove Taft in his Packard touring car and Penny's then young father, Carlton Davies, sat in the rumble seat.

Davies joined St. Philip's as soon as he arrived in 1905 and was on the vestry in 1917. He contributed much to the church until he died in December 1940. There is more on Davies in THE CHOIR section.

St. Philippians found an unusual way to raise money. They rented its steeple to the United States sixth district "Light House Board" from 1893 to 1915. A petition had recently been sent by certain Charleston shipmasters asking that the new jetty channel, or the swash as it was called, be illuminated with a range that would enable their vessels to enter and leave the port at night. A "Locomotive Head Light Reflector" was installed on the steeple. If the church desired, the sexton would, during good behavior, be employed as keeper of the light with a monthly salary from ten to fifteen dollars. In 1908, the rent received for the steeple was $300. The beacon was to have been taken down from the steeple by June 30, 1915, but was there was a delay. The beacon was temporarily replaced in 1921.

Even though the "Locomotive Head Light Reflector" is long gone, the church remains a beacon. Miss Elise F. Hayne could not have expressed it better "For many years St. Philip's has stood as a beacon to ships far out at sea. Is it not fitting that she (St. Philip's) shall also illume the lives of them 'that are nigh?' " Let us warmly greet those who are searching.

An update in 2012 – When the steeple was being restored from 1992 to 1994, two greenish reflectors (range markers) that were convex and two and a half inches in diameter were found on the river side of the steeple. They were at a height of 160 feet. It is not known if these were the original reflectors.

In March 1911, Beckwith explained to the vestry a method of collecting money on Sundays by using the Duplex Envelope System generally used in other churches.

The vestry finally did approve the use of the envelopes on November, 11, 1914. *St. Philip's Parish Letter* praised the system highly. It was reported that 140 members had taken the envelopes and the offerings from those envelopes exceeded those offerings from the remainder of the congregation. The majority of those not using the Duplex Envelope System only put in twenty-five cents each Sunday. "These results seem to be a sufficient argument for the value of the system."

The diocesan council announced in 1917 that the Duplex Envelope System was very generally being adopted in the diocese. At the same time, the envelopes had a new innovation – a division down the middle. On one side you were to put the money for the church and property upkeep, the development of the Sunday school, music, the bishop's fund, council dues and current expenses. Money placed on the other side was for missions – general, diocesan and communion alms.

Apparently in 1920, the issue was still not resolved. Davies was going to ask the congregation "regarding their wishes using the Duplex Envelopes." No resolution of the nine year process was recorded in the vestry minutes.

Income in 1914 was $14,849.55. The largest receipts were: offerings at church services $2,567.32, pew rentals $2,919.34, interest $887.97, Church Home $1,842.95 and the glebe $4,801.69. Expenditures totaled $12,412.45.

On June 29, 1914, W.H. Warley was selected as temporary secretary/treasurer because Arthur Mazyck had a serious and quick illness, dying July 17 at his residence 133 Broad Street.

The vestry had an interesting custom that was to note in their minutes the deaths of certain people. They could be sextons, a member of the vestry or others.

The vestry placed the following resolution in the minutes:

"Arthur Mazyck was for many years Secretary & Treasurer of St. Philip's Church. The intimate relations which had existed between him and the Wardens and Vestry of the Church have ended,

Be it resolved.

That we record our appreciation of the many estimable qualities of our late Secretary. Punctual and exact, courteous and patient, careful and considerate, a man of the strictest integrity, he was guided through life by the finest instincts of a true gentleman and lived as free from blame as far as humanly possible.

Without shrinking from the expression of his opinions, when necessary, he thrust his views upon no one: and has passed away affectionately regretted by his associates in the care of the old Parish so dear to him …

W. H. Warley, Sect'y"

The funeral was at St. Philip's on Saturday, July 18 and Mazyck was buried in the eastern churchyard. He was vice-president of the Huguenot Society and secretary and treasurer of the board of trustees of the College Charleston. He was member of the South Carolina Society and a member of Camp Sumter 250 of the United Confederate Veterans. Mazyck would have been thirteen in 1861. All of these organizations posted a notice in the newspaper inviting their members to attend the funeral.

Isaac Mazyck died January 29, 1915, less than a year after Arthur. He, too, is buried in the eastern churchyard. His successor was W.W. Shackelford.

In 1916, the diocesan council approved and formerly entered into the newly proposed clergy pension fund. In 1917, the rector made a vigorous appeal for subscriptions to the church pension fund and through St. Philippian vestryman, J. C. Bissell, $25,000 was raised.

After a lengthy discussion on October 29, 1919, the vestry approved raising $43,000 over a three-year period for necessary maintenance and improvements. The breakdown was: rectory $700, inside of church $1,000, outside of church $2,000, renovating pews $2,500, new organ $15,000, lights $1,500, heating $200, and current expenses $18,400.

During the March 8, 1922, vestry meeting, "Beckwith mentioned the recent gift of a pair of vases for use on the altar as a memorial to Miss Henrietta Murdoch, and also the gift of two exceedingly beautiful silver vases given by Miss Lowben of Philadelphia." The secretary was instructed to make suitable acknowledgement.

On April 18, 1922, the vestry authorized that a person suitable to act as clerk to the parish be hired at a salary not to exceed $1,000 per year. That would be about $83.00 per month. This may be the first time at St. Philip's that a lay person was sought as a clerk or assistant. The duties of this clerk were to keep the books and records of the parish and glebe but other duties could be requested by the rector. The first attempt at hiring a clerk did not work.

An entire page in the vestry minutes was dedicated to Robert Bacot:

> "In Memoriam
> Robert Dewar Bacot
> Born in Charleston, SC Jany 31, 1878
> Died in Charleston, SC April 18, 1924
> Served as a vestryman of St. Philip's Church
> From Easter Monday 1922
> To Good Friday morning 1924
>
> Father in thy gracious keeping,
> Leave we now thy Servant Sleeping"

In 1927, two new men came on the vestry: Simeon Hyde, Jr., attorney, and John Laurens. They replaced J.C. Bissell and McMillan K. Mazyck.

Robert L. Sinkler was elected sexton.

In March 1927, Beckwith proposed a junior vestry to consist of nine men. It was requested that the existing vestry would at all times welcome junior vestry suggestions which, in their opinion, would be in the best interest of the parish. The vestry approved the motion.

There was a balanced budget in 1928 at $13,926.77.

In 1928, the insurance coverage included: church building, $100,000; church home, $8,000; Sunday school building, $1,500; parish house $18,000; and the sexton's house, $1,200. That is total of $133,700. Bequests totaled $95,451 and the churchyard trust had $2,625.

The total assets in 1928 including glebe land, other properties, bequests and churchyard trust fund came to approximately $289,765.

A. H. Von Kolnitz and J. Stanyarne Stevens were elected in 1929 to the vestry. This vestry voted to look in to the matter of compiling a pamphlet of the historic facts about St. Philip's. That did not happen.

In 1930, John Laurens resigned from the vestry and was replaced by J. Heyward Furman. John E. Gibbs served as secretary from 1922 and was going strong in 1935. For much of that time he was also treasurer.

In February 1931, the treasurer reported a balance of $892.94 cash in the bank and all current bills were paid. J.W. Bartell was awarded the contract to repair the church roof. New radiators were to be installed in the church and vestibule.

GREAT DEPRESSION

Reading the vestry minutes through 1931, there were seemingly no effects of the Great Depression on St. Philip's. The year 1932 would tell a different story.

On June 8, 1932, the "Treasurer reported the finances of the Church were in serious shape, with the income curtailed from a drop in receipts from pew rents to $552 from $3,009.65 in 1929." There was also a big drop in pledges in 1929 from $4,467.03 to $1,600.00 in 1932.

There was not a quorum present at the April congregational meeting and there were no recorded vestry meetings from July 1932 to January 1934. The vestry reduced the salaries of all church employees by 20%. The semiannual income of $1,285.73 received from the Kaufman Trust in 1929, was reduced to $332.79 in 1932. Also in 1932, Miss Henrietta Heyward left an unrestricted bequest of $1,000 to St. Philip's. The vestry used that money to reduce the amount owed to the South Carolina Public Service Company for the "heating plant in the Parish House." The money was "to be restored to the church when funds are in hand." Fortunately, it only cost $5.50 to repair the church roof.

In October 1934, there was an urgent necessity to repair the leaks and paint the roofs of the church, the parish house and the exterior woodwork of the parish house. The heating of the church was inadequate. It was recommended that three gas-steam radiators that were then "in surplus" in the parish house and also four similar units then in the Kaufman building, 198 East Bay, be installed in the church.

It was an extremely difficult time for St. Philip's and the entire country.

PROPERTY & MAINTENANCE

The fire that burned the chancel in 1920 has been forgotten. The chancel that rises up from the nave through the choir is the part of a church that contains the sanctuary where the altar is located. There are seats in the sanctuary for the bishop In addition, the value of the glebe land properties was $43,500. The net income from these properties was $1,945.57 for a per cent return of .044. The glebe land properties had other values such as selling property and borrowing money from the glebe land for other purposes and the clergy.

St. Philip's chancel burned on Tuesday night April 27. Vestryman J. Campbell Bissell wrote it was a conflagration but that seems to be a great exaggeration. There were no articles in the newspapers about the fire and the fire chief did not list the St. Philip's fire in his annual report as one of the most serious fires of 1920. Perhaps, it was not a serious fire because of the "prompt and efficient service rendered and for the carefulness and consideration" of the fire chief, L. Behrens, and his firemen. Thus wrote Bissell in the thank you letter he sent the fire chief to show the vestry's appreciation. On May 3, 1920, the vestry went so far as to say, after a long discussion, that there was now the opportunity "for the long desired enlargement of the chancel."

Negotiations began with the insurance companies and the vestry voted not to take a settlement of less than $5,000. Albert Simons of Simons & Samuel Lapham, who were members of the church, were hired as the architects. The congregation was encouraged to offer suggestions for the design of the chancel. By June, McCrady Brothers Engineers and Contractors and the architects were at the vestry meeting by invitation. Plans for the proposed extension of the chancel were submitted. After much discussion, it was agreed that with the counsel of the architect, plans and photographs of the interior of the church should be submitted to an architect with "wider experience for an expression of his judgment."

They found Ralph Adams Cram (1863 – 1942) of Cram and Ferguson of Boston, who was consulted about the chancel window and probably about the entire chancel. His father was a Unitarian minister and Cram described his youth as being agnostic but in 1887 during a Christmas Eve Mass in Rome he had a dramatic conversion experience. He remained a fervent Anglo-Catholic who self-identified himself as a High Church Anglican. Cram was on the December 13, 1926, cover of *Time Magazine* identified as the most prominent Episcopal layman in the country. He was a prolific and influential architect of collegiate and ecclesiastical buildings.

In November 1920, Cram's recommendations for placing the choir stalls were approved by the vestry. The choir stalls cost $802.88 and were installed by April. Bissell made a request at the congregational meeting to approve borrowing the necessary money to finish the ongoing repairs. The chancel expenses were exceeding original estimates.

While St. Philip's was going through repairs and modifications, St. Philippian's worshiped part of the time in the Seaman's Chapel of the Redeemer. At some point, St. Michael's offered the pulpit there to Beckwith until October 1, 1921. Beckwith would serve both congregations.

In 1921, a sketch of the proposed chancel changes was presented to the congregation. During the vestry meeting of January 10, 1923, it was reported that a bill of $500 due to Simons and Lapham had not been paid. The vestry agreed they would not settle for more than $250. At the next vestry meeting, February 20, "Simons and Lapham graciously agreed to accept $250 in settlement for fees in connection with the chancel extension and said they would donate the remaining $250 to the church. The secretary was instructed to write thanking them for their generosity.

In February 1923, the music committee was authorized to sell the old organ "at such price as to them seemed sufficient."

THE NEW CHANCEL WINDOW AND ALTAR

As chairman of the vestry, Davies wanted the contractors to provide a temporary chancel window made of ground glass. The cost would be $80.00. Bissell asked to be recorded he voted against this proposition.

Plans for the new chancel window began as early as August 1920 and the window design would be approved by the vestry. A committee consisting of Mrs. Henry C. Cheves and Miss Mary O. Marshall was formed to raise funds for a memorial window to be dedicated to "All Saints." They had collected $3,200 by 1925 and they needed another $1,000 before the work could proceed. It was 1926 before the window was installed on All Saints Sunday.

The window was designed by Clement J. Heaton the younger (1861 – 1940) who started with his father's stain glass company in London. Heaton left there to move to Switzerland where he became famous for his cloisonné enamel and in 1914 he moved to New York where he once again made stain glass windows. In addition to St. Philip's, some of Heaton's other windows were placed in Rockefeller Center and the Cleveland Museum of Art.

The new chancel c. 1922

There is neither a written nor oral description of the symbolism of St. Philip's stained glass window. An English priest, Rev. Andrew Hayler, who was at St. Philip's in 2004 and 2005, studied the window carefully and offered the following explanation of the symbolism.

At the bottom of the window are ten figures. Hayler suggests this scene is based on John: 20-22 when certain Greeks asked Philip, "Sir, we would see Jesus." Philip told Andrew and the two of them told Jesus. There are two figures with gold halos – one possibly Christ and one possibly Mary. On the left, Philip may be speaking to Christ with the Greeks standing by holding scrolls. Andrew, perhaps with no scroll or book is on the far left. To the right of Christ, presumably are some of the disciples with possibly two female figures. One of whom, as stated, may be Mary.

As one's eyes move upward into the panels above, there is the root of a tree that leads our eyes further upward to a banner announcing "Ecce Agnus Dei" (Behold the Lamb of God) symbol of the risen Christ. The tree is surely the root of Jesse, the father of King David, reminding us that this Lamb of God is fulfillment of God's promise. Six daises that grow at the foot of the tree are a symbol commonly used since medieval times in Christian art to represent innocence – particularly the innocence of a spotless lamb.

Surrounding this central theme are five angels – two on each side and one above. The angel at the top appears to be in Heaven and is crowning the Lamb "who sits upon the throne." On either side of the Lamb, angels swing thuribles offering incense symbolic of unceasing prayer. Two angels, standing on firm ground on either side of the tree, gesture as if to bring the message of the Christ to those below. The angels and other figures are all standing before a large structure. Hayler said the structure might suggest heaven and that this chancel window therefore connects heaven and earth.

Another addition to the chancel was the donation of the beautiful marble altar from Henry C. Cheves in honor of his deceased son. The inscription reads:

> "Marble altar
> Gift of Henry C. Cheves
> To The Glory of God and in Memory of Langdon McCord Cheves
> April 27, 1898 – May 8, 1923
> Ensign U.S. Naval Aviation 1917 – 1919"

GLEBE LAND

JOHN COMING AND HIS WIFE, MRS. AFFRA HARLESTON COMING

John Coming and Affra Harleston arrived in South Carolina in 1670 in the first fleet. Affra came with three indentured servants – John Chambers, Michael Lovell and Philip

Orrill. John Coming, who was a mariner and ship captain, married Affra Harleston by July 27, 1672.

At the same time, Affra Coming brought complaints to the Grand Council about the disobedience of her three indentured servants who refused to obey her lawful commands. According to Mrs. Coming, Philip Orrill was the worst of the group threatening to turn over the boat when she was in it "or words to that effect." Orrill also gave provisions to the dogs that were meant for him and the other servants and he threatened to run away to the Indians. There were divers[5] other gross abuses and destructive practices. Orrill was found guilty and it was ordered he be tied to a tree to receive twenty one lashes on his naked back. The two other servants received warnings.[6]

Historian David D. Wallace wrote indentured servants were subjected to strict discipline, including lashings, to enforce labor and discipline until the time of their servitude expired. An indentureship of five to seven years was common and after that time the former indenture servant would receive their allotments of land, tools and clothes.

Seven years after arriving in South Carolina, Orrill was granted his due – seventy acres of land. In 1678, Orrill was listed as a planter living on the peninsula near the Wando (Cooper) River.[7] Chambers received his seventy acres in only three years and by 1680 he had acquired more than 305 acres in addition to the original seventy acres. There was no mention of Lovell.

In July 1672, Mr. and Mrs. Coming were granted 150 acres on the peninsula. Between then and November 1678, they were allotted an additional 1,373 acres.

John Coming wrote his will in August 1694 and he died by June 1696.

In 1698, Mrs. Affra Harleston Coming donated seventeen acres to St. Philip's to be used as glebe land where a rectory might be built and room enough for growing food and perhaps a barn.

Mrs. Coming's desire was to promote and encourage such "good, charitable and pious work" so that the Church of England minister in Charles Town would have the same lifestyle advantages as a minister in England. After the Revolution, St. Michael's claimed and received half of this glebe land.

By 1698 and 1699, smallpox and yellow fever arrived in South Carolina for the first time. Many people died. Mrs. Affra Coming wrote to her sister in 1699 that "smallpox had taken many lives, especially among the Indians. She stated a

---

5 Divers is an 18th century word for "various."
6 A.S. Salley, Jr. editor *Journal of the Grand Council 1671-1680* p. 33
7 Editors Susan Baldwin Bates & Harriott Cheves Leland *Abstracts of the Records of Register of the Province 1675 – 1696 Vol. II* p. 37

whole neighboring nation, which could mean a town or a village, was destroyed by smallpox except for five or six survivors who fled without burying the dead."[8]

Affra wrote her will on December 28, 1698, affirming she was the relic (widow) of John Coming of "Berkly" County which then went from the ocean to many, many miles inland and from the Santee River to the Edisto River. There was no Charleston County. Her brother, John Harleston, who was deceased, had property in Dublin and in Essex County in "Malling" (perhaps Maldon) England.

She left her nephew, John Harleston, all her lands, tenements, woods and pastures. She also left to John Harleston and Elias Ball, son of William Ball, half-brother of John Harleston, deceased, in tenancy all her "Negroes," Indian servants, cattle, furniture, goods, debts and chattels to be equally divided.

Affra's will was signed by witnesses including the Rev. Samuel Marshall, rector of St. Philip's, who died shortly after Affra's death. Her will was recorded on March 9, 1700. In 1702, there was a reference of John Harleston and Elias Ball owning the land left by Affra. Ball went on to acquire much more land – mentioned as late as 1706.

The glebe land that Mrs. Coming so generously donated was located in the country. Glebe Street, located between Wentworth and George Streets, was the general area of the glebe land. There is a monument to Affra Coming next to Grace Episcopal Church on the Glebe Street side. Mrs. Coming had no children but her name lives on in 2012 with St. Philippian Coming Ball Gibbs and Gendron and Helen Gibbs' daughter, Affra Gibbs.

Over a period of time as Charleston grew, St. Philip's decided to build houses on the glebe land and rent them. The income did not go directly to the rector but to the income of the church. The glebe houses consumed much time at many vestry meetings as members discussed repairs, and the possibility of renting or selling some of the houses. Sometimes the vestry would mortgage a glebe property or borrow money from the glebe account and use the money for a needed project.

In 1901 there was an inventory of the glebe houses: 30 Coming St., 114 Wentworth St., 75 George St. with shop, 24 & 26 Coming St., 14 Glebe St. with outhouse, 6 Glebe St. with stable and 77 George Street.

By 1905, some of the properties in the 1901 inventory were no longer listed. Theo. Jervey moved that $4,500, less 2½ % commission, be accepted for 2 Glebe Street. The motion was adopted. The price was reduced to $4,200 and the property was purchased

---

[8] Waring, J.I. *History of Medicine in South Carolina 1670 – 1825* p. 19

by Mrs. Julia I. Gadsden. In 1906, lots 14 and 15, with buildings on them (located on the on east side of Coming Street between George and Wentworth Streets) were purchased by Mrs. Bluhma Cohoeb for $2,500.

In 1918, the committee on glebe lands consisted of Henry C. Cheves, Huger Sinkler, who was a warden, and E. P. Guerard. A lot on the corner of George and St. Philips streets was purchased by the Board of School Commissioners for $2,500. In old Charleston, with a few remaining in the 21st century, many of the water pipes went up the buildings on the outside walls. When a hard freeze was coming, everyone drained the pipes and turned off the water so the pipes would not burst. Messrs. Sinkler and Guerard in November 1918 sent a notice to the occupants of the glebe land houses stating they were responsible for turning the water off from the street and "failing to do so," the tenants would be charged one tenth of all repairs.

In 1928 the value of the glebe land properties was $43,500. The net income from these properties was $1,945.57 for a per cent return of .044. The glebe land properties had other values such as selling property and borrowing money from the glebe land for other purposes.

PEWS

If you wanted to join a church, a person had to purchase or rent a pew in that church. Pews were property owned by the church. The tradition began centuries ago and the practice was continued in England even after the Church of England broke ties with the Roman Catholic Church. From there the practice came to America and St. Philip's among other churches.

Pews were another ongoing issue for the vestry. In 1915, Cheves reported that because some members were in arrears, a bill collector, who was paid a commission whether he collected the fees or not, was hired. One in arrears was Miss Anne M. Hanckel who asked the vestry "to accept her notice of giving up her pew and asked that a bill be sent for her pew rent for July and August."

Apparently, Hanckel stayed at St. Philip's, because the rector, Merritt Williams, stated on May 12, 1937, that under the terms of her will, she left specific pieces of silver and $100 for the purpose of having an alms basin made and inscribed in the memory of her parents, Mr. and Mrs. C.F. Hanckel. Her sister asked the vestry if she could purchase certain pieces of the silver. It was the consensus of the vestry that such permission could not be granted. Miss Anne Hanckel lived at 26 Church Street by 1929 with at least one sister.

Some typical pew transactions were – E.N. Chisolm wanted pew 26 and W.W. Wagner wanted pew 82. Each paid $40.00 per year. There was a stipulation that if an assessment of the pews was made later and the value was greater than $40.00, then they would have to pay the higher fee or relinquish the pews. Not all of the pews were occupied.

In 1916, the vestry asked that a committee be formed to discuss "Pew Renters" with the rector and the treasurer.

In 1917, on motion of F. G Davies, a committee was formed to work out a system for ushering "strangers" into pews. At the same time, pew renters were warned if their rents were not paid in full by Easter, those pews would be declared vacant. On Easter 1918, Messrs. Bissell and Guerard proposed "purchasing markers to show what pews are vacant, and what pews have vacant seats in them, and to label each pew." The motion passed. On August 14, Bissell reported the pew name tags had been ordered.

In 1918, the finance committee came up with a plan to increase income. They said the large increase in Charleston's population presented a great opportunity to increase the number of pew holders. Members were encouraged to greet strangers who attended services and even to greet strangers with whom they may make contact with from time to time to encourage them to come to St. Philip's. Hopefully some of these strangers would buy a pew.

The vestry on April 15, 1920, approved a motion about people in arrears, "Any pewholder or pewholders that shall be six months in arrears that his or her pew shall automatically be forfeited and declared vacant." In January 1923, the vestry extended the deadline to one year. A short time later, the vestry ordered a review of the prices of the pews.

On March 29, 1921, E. P. Guerard, executor of the late Dr. William H. Prioleau, begged to quote the following from Prioleau's will: "I give, devise and bequeath to the corporation known as St. Philip's Church … its successors and assigns, my family pew NO. 30 and hereby request that my daughter, Annie P. Dent, be allowed the use of half said pew free of rent so long as she shall live." Guerard added that Dr. Prioleau and his forebears, as far as he was aware, had been members of St. Philip's. He requested the vestry's approval.

The matter was turned over to church solicitor, Thomas W. Bacot, who said it was not a legal matter but it was actually a request solely left to the discretion of the vestry. There was no further mention of this of this matter.

Davies suggested on June 8, 1921, "that a meeting of pew holders should be called to consider the upholstery of the pews, but after lengthy discussion it was deemed inappropriate and inadvisable." In April 1925, a committee of two was formed to again consider some way of collecting pew rents that were in arrears.

The plat of the pews was drawn in 1922 by Arthur Wilcox's grandfather, Arthur Middleton Manigault. Guv Gottshalk in 2012 re-formated the plat for the book and added the names of the pew owners which can be seen in the appendix.

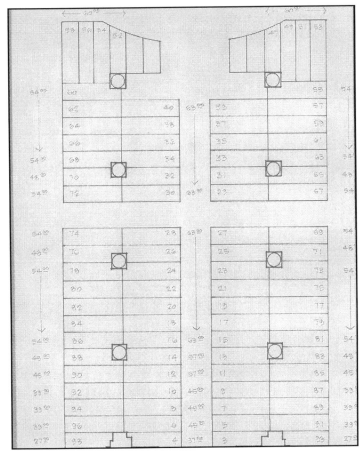
The pews c. 1922

CONTINUATION OF PROPERTY & MAINTENANCE

In Exodus 35:29, God gave explicit instructions on building the tabernacle. "The children of Israel brought a freewill offering to the Lord, all the men and women whose hearts were willing to bring material for all kinds of work which the Lord, by the hand of Moses, had commanded to be done." That is the way it was done then and that has remained true at St. Philip's in 1906 and even today in 2012. St. Philippians always provide so that God's church may be maintained in a way that honors God.

Maintenance is ongoing. St. Philip's was damaged by Federal bombardment from November 1863 until the fall of Charleston in February 1865. There were at least ten cannon balls that hit the church. In 1885 there was a cyclone and the next year there was an earthquake and there were other storms such as hurricane Hugo in 1989.

Maintaining small items are as important as the large projects. In October 1906, the "Committee on Church & Grounds" was asked to obtain a proper ladder for use in the interior of the church and to repair the fences in the rear of the Sunday school building. The same committee was authorized to purchase mats for the doors and to have the worn or broken places repaired in the church steps. A fence was being built between the Congregational Church and the west end of the western churchyard. In May 1926, the vestry received an estimate from N.I. Ball for $140 for painting the western churchyard's iron fence. Ball lost out to a Mr. McBride's $120 estimate.

It takes a vestry and members to keep an eye out for maintenance problems. In 1915, vestry member, J.J. Pringle Smith, reported that the gas meter located in the vestry room occupied valuable space. He also reported that some of St. Philip's valuable records were stored in an unsafe place. Perhaps we owe Pringle Smith's father, Henry Augustus Middleton (H.A.M.) Smith, who was one of South Carolina's most respected historians, a debt of gratitude for teaching Pringle Smith to respect valuable and historical documents.

Pringle Smith, a lawyer, inherited Middleton Place from a cousin in 1913. In 1916 he married Heningham Ellet from Richmond and they began a grandiose restoration of the house and the gardens. Mrs. Smith described Middleton Place "as a wilderness overgrown … First, the house must be made livable … Sore knees and a tired back meant nothing … No ice, as there were no electric lines … For a refrigerator we used the spring house … Heavens, what I couldn't do with a kettle of hot water …" By 1921 the Smiths were living at Middleton except in the summer. By 1925 the Smiths were advertising for the public to visit their beautiful gardens. Their town house was 21 East Battery.

In February 1916, the vestry requested that the treasurer, W. W. Shackelford, and Beckwith look into the possibility of moving the rector's valuable books from the vestry room to the "Charleston Library." They hoped the library could construct suitable boxes or cases and provide two keys – one for the rector and one for the treasurer. Perhaps, the gas meter had been moved by that time as well.

CHURCH HOME

In 1952, Coming Ball Gibbs wrote how the Rev. William Bell W. Howe (later bishop) established the St. Philip's Church Home. Howe was assistant rector 1859 – 1863 and rector 1863 – 1873 or as Gibbs said, "Howe served St. Philip's before during and after the Confederate War." In 1869, Howe conceived the idea for a church home for the poor ladies of St. Philip's. One moonlight night as he walked down Church Street, he pondered how to bring about the church home's existence and as he reached the three story brick building on the northeast corner of Church and Queen streets he saw a for rent sign. The building was then called the Commercial House, a former hotel that may have been empty since the War Between the States. Howe realized this was the place for the church home but felt it would be better to purchase the building and not rent.

On December 19 of that year he preached a quite remarkable sermon on the subject. That was the impetus needed to raise $10,000 to purchase the property. Gibbs wrote, "This achievement, under the circumstances, in which our people found themselves so soon after the Confederate War, surely should be an inspiration to us at St. Philip's now when we are faced with our present challenging problems." Even Howe admitted it was a bold move to purchase the building.

The owner of the building, Jane M. Rudulph, agreed to sell the building. The vestry and congregation reacted favorably and the vestry approved the sale price of $10,000 on January 12, 1870. H.D. Lesesne, chairman, and C. Williman, secretary signed the papers.

The St. Philip's Church Home was dedicated and opened in June 1870.

In her will of June 4, 1887, Miss Sarah A. Andrews left $20,000 to the wardens and vestry of St. Philip's for the support and maintenance of the "inmates" of the St. Philip's Church Home. Because of a codicil, it was not until 1903 that St. Philip's received $10,000 and it is not known if the church ever received the other $10,000.

Mrs. Ellen Porcher (née Barker) left the church home $1,000 on May 29, 1909.

As can best be determined from the disbursement book, the ladies paid no rent and their medicines and heat were provided. Some of the expenses paid by the church home in 1906 were: Julius Smith plumber $3.40, E. L. Lonck for work on the home $15.00, Lakeside Drug Store $6.35 for medicine, the March gas bill $4.48 and parlor furniture from Cowperthwait & Co. at 235 King Street $60.00. On January 22, 1907, Beckwith ordered the annual appropriation of $34.00 for fuel for the "Inmates" of the home. In 1917, Robert Bee Lebby and Pringle Smith were on the church home committee.

On November 8, 1922, the executive council of the diocese of South Carolina thanked St. Philip's for giving Bishop Guerry a room in the church home as a headquarters for the diocese. In 2012, the archives are approximately located on the former site of Bishop Guerry's office.

THE MURDER OF BISHOP GUERRY

On Saturday, June 2, 1928, The Rev. James Herbert Woodward arrived from Georgia and checked in at the YMCA. The next day he attended service at St. Michael's and on Monday morning June 4 he checked out of the YMCA where he asked if they would keep his suitcase until he returned.

Woodward had served small churches in the Bluffton area until 1925 when he moved to Georgia. Woodward was described by members of St. Michael and all Angels Church in Savannah, where he was rector for a short time, as having a nervous temperament but he was well liked and was known as a scholarly man. Woodward was currently serving a small church in Darien.

Woodward arrived at the diocesan headquarters at 9:30 a.m. June 4 and was greeted by the bishop's secretary, Miss Henrietta Jervey. Woodward asked to see Bishop Guerry. He wanted to ascertain the retirement age for ministers. Miss Jervey told Woodward the bishop was not in yet, but she called the bishop who told her to tell Woodward he was welcome to come to his house on Broad Street since it would be an hour before he arrived at the office. Miss Jervey relayed that to Woodward who hesitated as though he had not heard. She told him again and he agreed to go. Miss Jervey called the bishop about something else and Guerry said to tell Woodward he was leaving his house now and to wait for him at the office. While waiting, the Rev. Albert S. Thomas stopped by Guerry's office and Woodward asked him about the church pension fund and said he wanted to see the bishop about it. Miss Jervey said Woodward did not seem irritated or out of his mind or look nervous while he was waiting other than looking at his pocket watch several times.

After Bishop Guerry arrived, he spoke to Woodward and made a phone call to the Rev. William Way, who was rector of Grace Church from 1902 to 1946, then invited Woodward into his office. The bishop closed the door behind Woodward and told Miss Jervey, "I want you to stay in this office. This man is half crazy, and there is no telling what he'll do." Miss Jervey said, "They were in conference for some time and then the bishop came into my office and dictated several routine letters that he signed with a steady hand." The bishop returned to his office and within five minutes she heard a shot fired in the office and the bishop called out, "Miss Etta!" She immediately headed for the phone at the end of the hall when she heard a second shot. After calling for help, she ran into the office and found the two men on the floor and a $50.00 check lying on the desk. The bishop later said from the hospital, that he had been standing up pleading with Woodward not to shoot him. Chairs in the office were found overturned but that may have been caused by the reeling bodies of the two men. Guerry was shot in the right breast and Woodward shot himself with his own pistol, causing a self-inflicted wound in the right temple. There had been only two cartridges in the pistol.

The second person to reach the room in which the shooting took place was Frederick G. Davies, who was leaving the building when he heard the shots. Davies was quoted in the paper, "I rushed back and found the men lying gasping on the floor. I realized immediately that there was nothing I could do so I hastened to call for help."

Both men were rushed to the Thompson Memorial Infirmary and Guerry was later transferred to the Riverside Infirmary. Woodward died that evening. Guerry was unconscious and had lost a lot blood. The bullet passed through his entire body. The surgeon was St. Philippian Dr. Robert S. Cathcart, assisted by Dr. Robert Wilson and Dr. J.J. LaRoach. Guerry reacted very favorably to the surgery.

The *News and Courier* wrote that Woodward was a minister in the South Carolina diocese for twenty years. "He was known as a man with fixed opinions on the negro question, in particular." During 1911 to 1914, Bishop Guerry sought a "Negro" suffragan bishop, (assistant), for African-Americans in the diocese of South Carolina. Woodward, who despised Guerry's plan, made a number of public attacks on Guerry through public statements and speeches. Bishop Albert S. Thomas wrote that the entire diocese was agitated during that time by the question of a "Negro suffragan." Woodward never forgave Guerry. One source states the only reason Woodward shot Guerry was because of the issue of having a suffragan bishop for African-Americans, but there was more than that.

Woodward had a very mixed religious background. For eight years he was a Methodist minister for which he felt he was unsuited. He took a great interest in the Greek Orthodox Church where he studied Greek liturgy and later moved to the Roman Catholic Church. He read deeply into its history and tenets. He finally decided to join the Episcopal Church and studied at the University of the South. He served various Episcopal churches in the South.

Other situations made it worse. When Woodward was serving in the Bluffton area, he shot and killed an African-American burglar and was acquitted but residents said he never fully recovered from the nervous shock. June 4 was the second anniversary of the death of his sixteen-year-old daughter who was his favorite child. From that date to June 4, 1928, Woodward lost three other members of his family. His mother died and two other daughters were left as widows. There were financial problems. At the time of his death, Woodward was living alone in McIntosh County, Georgia, near Darien. His youngest child, a son, was twelve.

It would seem that Woodward was so angry and frustrated by so many issues, including the issue of an African-American suffragan bishop, that he went over the edge and murdered Guerry, the man he hated.

The *News and Courier* wrote long daily reports on the facts of the shooting, Woodward's family and on Guerry's health. On Tuesday June 5, the headline said

"Night Brings No Especial Change - Bishop Guerry Resting Comfortably." An inquest into Woodward's death was to be held at "Connelley's establishment" on Meeting Street. Miss Jervey and the chief of detectives, John J. Healy, were the only people who testified. Connelley's funeral home had the reputation that its services were for the "elite." It was turned into condominiums in the late 20th century.

Woodward's family arrived in Charleston on June 5 and took his body from Connelley's, and as he requested, Woodward was buried at sea off the Georgia coast near Darien.

The paper reported on Wednesday June 6 that "the bishop holds his own throughout the night, but his condition was grave." Mrs. Guerry had been in Lexington, Virginia, for a commencement. When she arrived at her husband's bedside, he smiled.

On June 7, a service of intercession was held for the recovery of Bishop William A. Guerry at 11 o'clock at St. Paul's on the corner of Coming and Vanderhorst streets. A prayer service was held the day before at St. Michael's. Guerry's vitals were: temperature 100 degrees, pulse 120 and respiration 32. He was composed with few signs of shock except for heavy breathing. His nourishment was orange juice and buttermilk. Messages of condolence from clergy and laity poured in from all parts of the country, including a telegram from Adolph Ochs, publisher of the *New York Times*.

On Friday June 8, the doctors reported Guerry "seems better." On Saturday June 9, it was reported "Bishop Steadily Gaining Ground" and when he learned of Woodward's death, the bishop said, "poor fellow" and asked people to pray for Woodward. However, during the afternoon of June 9, Guerry took a turn for the worst and declined rapidly. He died at 9:35 p.m. from pneumonia at age sixty-seven. His wife, daughter, three sons, three doctors and Rev. Albert S. Thomas were at his bedside. Two of his sons, Moultrie and Sumner, were clergy.

The funeral for the Right Rev. William Alexander Guerry D.D., eighth bishop of the diocese of South Carolina, was held at St. Michael's on Tuesday, June 12, 1928.

Four bishops read the ritual and the Rev. Thomas, who was rector of St. Michael's, led the procession followed by thirty clergymen, including, Beckwith. Following behind the clergymen were a large number of honorary pallbearers and senior wardens from many parishes. The active pallbearers, who carried the casket, were: Thomas E. Myers, O.T. Waring and Dr. Robert Wilson from Charleston, Walter Hazard from Georgetown, Dr. William Egleston from Hartsville and W.R. Boykin and R.W. Sharkey from Florence. Many who could not get into the church, stood outside the church with their hats removed.

Even though Guerry always considered St. Michael's his home church, he was interred at St. Philip's.

The diocesan standing committee, of which Beckwith was a member, assumed control and arranged for an election for the next bishop who would be Guerry's good friend, the Rev. Thomas.

Those appointed to the church home finance committee in 1930 were Davies, Dr. Josiah Smith, J.S. Stevens, C.P. Means and J. H. Furman. Those appointed to the committee on church home advice. were J.G. Ball, W. deBryn Kops, A.W. Newton, J.D. Matthew and G.S. deForest.

In 1934, the offices of the rector and his secretary were on the first floor of the church home and the ladies lived on the second and third floors. Caspar A. Chisolm, treasurer, made a report of all income received in 1934. Virtually all of it came from bonds and interest with the exception of a few "sundry" items. Miss Belle Tucker paid $16.58 for telephone expenses. Miss Palmer had to pay fifty cents for electricity for using her fan. DuBose Heyward made two payments on behalf of his relative, Miss Lulie Heyward, for unknown expenses. In May he paid $8.00 "to July" and in October he paid to January 1, 1935, $11.90.

Miss Mary Geddings in April 1935 left $671.82 to St. Philip's and "expressed a wish that this money be used to put water in the rooms of the (church) house." At the 1936 congregation meeting, it was announced that a new hot water system had been installed in the church home which was made possible by a legacy from Miss Geddings, a devoted member of "the Home" and church for a number of years.

Scaffolding on the steeple late 1990's

THE RECTORY

The old rectory at 6 Glebe Street had not been used as such for many years. Huger Sinkler at the October 14, 1908, vestry meeting stated "that a piece of property, 92 Church Street, was offered for sale which he considered very important for the church to purchase." Coincidentally, Miss Dorothy Bollwinkle, who would be St. Philip's long time organist, was born in that house on October 14, 1903. On October 26, 1904, Dorothy's father George C. Bollwinkle and his sister, Meta Buggeln, sold 92 Church Street to Peter J. Petersen for $3,075.

Petersen lived in and owned 86 Church and owned a wholesale and retail fish company at Boyce's North Wharf. He rented 92 from 1906 to 1908.

Several members of the vestry agreed that $5,000 was a reasonable price for 92 Church Street. Theodore Jervey wanted to be recorded as opposing the purchase. Even so, at the same meeting, a committee of three: Huger Sinkler, Arthur Mazyck and Henry C. Cheves, plus the chairman, Walter Pringle, were empowered to purchase the residence from Peter J. Petersen not to exceed $5,000. The sum of $1,000 was paid upfront in cash, $500 the next year and a final payment of $3,500 two years later. Interest was 6%. The deed was recorded on November 25, 1908.

The vestry asked Beckwith to move into the rectory as soon as possible and asked him to pay the water bill. He billed the church for $20.21 for cleaning up the rectory.

An article on the rectory appeared in *Do You Know Your Charleston?* on February 5, 1977, by Robert P. Stockton who wrote, "Alexander Christie, a merchant of Scottish descent, acquired the lot from Henry W. DeSaussure and Timothy Ford, and built now what is 92 Church Street sometime after 1805. The house is a 3 ½ story structure of Charleston "grey" brick laid in Flemish bond.

On April 11, 1911, Theodore Jervey made a motion that effective April 1 Beckwith would no longer have to pay rent while living in the rectory as an appreciation of his services. The motion passed.

OTHER PROPERTY

During the majority of the time St. Philip's has been in existence, there had been no heat in the three church buildings. People could only bring iron boxes with hot coals burning within them to keep feet warm. Gas radiators were finally installed in 1906 and later were repaired by M. Bartel for $18.00. In 1910 the gas system was upgraded for $190.

On November 22, 1913, Mr. F.J.H. Haesloop purchased a lot on the northwest corner of Philadelphia Alley in the rear of 148 Church Street for $1,300 from F. Q. O'Neil. Haesloop was the proprietor of the Palace Stables at 224 Calhoun Street. Beckwith urged the vestry to purchase Haesloop's lot for $1,500 because he thought "it very important as well as desirable that the church own the property as a protection from undesirable neighbors and for extension of the grounds." Some members of the congregation offered financial help. The church did purchase the lot in 1914 for $1,500, including brokerage fees. On October 13, 1915, the vestry authorized repairs to 148 Church Street where the sexton, J.J. Whitney, lived.

In April 1922, Beckwith formally presented to the congregation a deed given as a gift for the land north of the church, now between the church and the parish house. By May 9, a committee was formed to make plans for the layout of a playground.

The vestry on March 29, 1921, thanked Miss J. Heyward for the beautiful silver ewer, a wide mouthed pitcher that Beckwith showed to the vestry. On March 8, 1922, Mr. Heyward requested permission to put up a memorial tablet on the wall of the vestibule (narthex). It is located on the left side as you enter the center aisle.

> IN MEMORY OF
> ELIZABETH MIDDLETON HEYWARD
> BELOVED WIFE OF
> JULIUS H. HEYWARD
> AND ONLY DAUGHTER OF
> WILLIAMS MIDDLETON AND
> SUSAN SMITH HIS WIFE
> BORN NOVEMBER 7, 1849
> DIED JUNE 15, 1915
> DEVOTED MEMBER OF THIS CHURCH
> "BLESSED ARE THE PURE IN HEART"

One of the purchases the vestry made in 1922 was a Remington typewriter for $12.50. The vestry minutes did not record what the price of a "tech support contract" was.

WILLIAM RUSSELL DeHON

In January 1926, Beckwith reported that Russell Dehon of Summerville gave the church a painting of "Old St. Philip's." Dehon, who was born in 1849, was the son the Rev. William Dehon and Anne Manigault Middleton. Russell's father was rector of St. Philip's from 1859 until his death in 1862. His grandfather, the Right Rev. Theodore Dehon, was the second bishop of the diocese of South Carolina who served from 1812 to 1817.

Dehon married Margaret Mabus in 1872 and they had at least five children. Dehon, although not clergy, was active in the Episcopal Church. He served faithfully on the vestry of St. Philip's from 1876 to 1884. He was immediately made chairman of the "Committee on back Pew Rents and Assessments at St. Philip's Church." Serving with Dehon were H.P. Archer and C.A. Chisolm.

The committee reported on November 1, 1876, that the debt from non-payment for pews amounted to $4,302.05 and the chances of recovering more than 8% to 10% were slim. After Dehon recommended the pew rents be reduced by 25%, it may have been a coincidence that he was moved to the music committee and later the grounds committee.

By 1884, Dehon and his family moved to Summerville and they immediately became involved with St. Paul's Church in Summerville. He died September 26, 1927.

In February 1927, the vestry asked that McMillan K. Mazyck confer with surveyor R.C. Rhett to see if the building built by Adolphus B. Bennett next to the western churchyard encroached on St. Philip's property. It was found that Bennett had indeed encroached by one foot. The vestry decided to draw up a lease in which Bennett would agree that he would pay an annual rental of $1.00.

At the vestry meeting of March 9, 1927, Beckwith spoke at length about the great need for a parish house that would be suitable for the work of the church. On August 29, the vestry read the estimates, decided all were too high and rejected them. They decided the construction would be supervised by members of the building committee.

By September, the remaining $15,000 needed to complete the parish house work would be financed by issuing "Serial Bonds" bearing interest of 6% payable semi-annually. On September 23, 1927, R. S. Small, president of The South Carolina National Bank, wrote a letter to Davies confirming the details of the bonds. Small added, "we would like very much to secure from you any of these bonds which are not subscribed for by members of the congregation ... We regard the bonds exceptionally well secured and will be very glad indeed to take the entire $15,000, par value, or any part thereof which may be available."

The newly remodeled two-story parish house, that was dedicated on October 7, 1928, had a kitchen with three cabinets and windows. Screens were put in the locker rooms, probably adjacent to the gymnasium. There were accordion doors that could be moved to different locations and wiring for moving pictures. Three hundred chairs were ordered for the auditorium in which there was an organ pit and a stage above the level of the floor. The panel wainscoting must have added a nice touch. The lumber came from the A.C. Tuxbury Lumber Company.

MUSIC AND THE CHOIR

THE ORGANS

The first pipe organ in South Carolina was installed in the second St. Philip's building in 1728. It was an English organ with sixteen stops which had been first played at the coronation of George II in 1727. It was replaced in 1833 by a new instrument built by Henry Erben of New York. Two years later the new organ burned in the 1835 fire.

The first organ in the third, or present church building, was installed in 1840 in the west gallery by Gray of London. It was badly damaged during the Federal bombardment of Charleston. J.T. Welsman donated the money for the rebuilding of the organ and the order for the needed parts was approved by the vestry on March 17, 1868. Welsman wrote on February 27, 1869, that at last the work done by John Baker, who was the only organ builder in Charleston, had been completed. Some of the delay was due to Baker's health and because he had to order the pipes "in a Northern City." As much of the old case was used as possible but it was enlarged in width and height and its style altered to correspond with the architecture of the interior of the church. Everything furnished by Baker was new and many improvements in organ building were introduced in its reconstruction. There were thirty-four stops, 1,332 pipes, three sets of banks of keys and a set of two octave pedals. The principal organists in Charleston were invited to test the organ and all agreed it was a fine and complete instrument. Baker was given much praise and credit and it was believed it was the most superior organ in the city or state.

The organ was restored again in 1909 and was used until it burned on April 27, 1920.

About six weeks prior to the 1920 fire, the vestry approved an appropriation of $14,000 for a new organ. Blueprints of proposals on how to best situate the new organ were shown at the vestry meeting twelve days before the fire. In June after the fire, Mr. Stanley, the organ repair man, said the $400 the insurance money was not enough money to restore the organ. No decision was made.

The second organ was installed in the newly constructed north chancel organ chamber in 1921 by the Austin Organ Co. of Hartford, Connecticut. This three manual twenty-six stop instrument was used for more than fifty years until it was removed to make room for the organ installed in 1978.

That organ, built by Casavant Freres of St. Hyacinthe, Quebec, in 1978 was located in the north chancel and the antiphonal division in the west gallery. Still in use in 2012, it features thirty-eight stops and fifty-one ranks consisting of twenty-six hundred and forty pipes plus chimes. The horizontal trumpets or trompette en chamade, a part of the antiphonal organ, with its eight foot open rank was used most effectively in triumphal processions. The then choirmaster/organist John Sanders and his mother in 1969 purchased the trumpet pipes for future use. They were installed in 1978.

The trompette was invented in the 16th century in Spain and were reserved for royal appearances and certain feast days. Many churches have the trompette including the National Cathedral in Washington, D.C., St. John the Devine in New York, St. Paul's in London and others.

Shortly after Beckwith arrived, the organist, Miss Dauer, giving no reason, tendered her resignation effective July 1, 1906. At the same time, the sexton, John J. Whitney, asked the vestry to relieve him from his duties as bellows blower even though he was paid a fee of $5.00 during Lent. The vestry referred his request to the music committee.

Mr. A.H. Mole had replaced Miss Dauer as organist but by January 1907 he had, according to the vestry, proven to be unsatisfactory. Henry C. Cheves made a motion to fire him. The motion passed. At the March vestry meeting Huger Sinkler reported that Mole had made a claim through an attorney for a balance of salary. The vestry authorized Sinkler "to make such composition of the claim of Mr. Mole as he may find most advantageous."

MISS ELISE (ELIZA) FROST HAYNE
& HER SISTERS – ALICE, ELLEN & HENRIETTA

Miss Elise (Eliza) Frost Hayne was chosen as organist to replace Mole. Her annual salary was $250 with $25 for extra services at Lent and $1.00 for each funeral attended.

In 1909 Elise lived at 26 New Street with her father, Henry F. Hayne, her mother, Nellie, and her three sisters Alice Pauline Trapier Hayne, Ellen F. Hayne, and the youngest, Henrietta, who married Mr. Gadsden when she was fifty. None of the three other sisters married. Alice was one of the very first women to work as a stenographer on Broad Street where she was employed by at Mitchell & Horlbeck. Ellen was a teacher.

At some point, the Gadsden's lived in the back house with the other sisters in the front. Mr. and Mrs. C. F. Middleton, parents of Dorothy M. Anderson and her siblings, lived at 28 New Street next door to the Haynes. Henry F. Hayne died by early 1924. The Midddletons went to the funeral and took their very young daughter, Dot, who vividly remembers someone asking her if she wanted to pat Mr. Hayne's cheek. Dot said she was horrified and nearly died of fright.

In April 1908, it was decided that St. Philip's would no longer hire singers for the choir. With the upcoming renovation of the organ and the church, the money saved from hiring paid singers would be applied to the renovation. The vestry felt the volunteer choir that sang during Lent and Easter was quite satisfactory.

Miss Hayne was re-elected organist from 1908 to 1911 and in 1911 she received an annual salary of $500. Later she was granted permission to take her vacation starting after the fourth Sunday in July. Then Miss Hayne had bad news. Because of her health, her doctor required that she not work for a year. She tendered her resignation effective Easter 1912.

The new organist, Mrs. William G. Locke (Julia W.) who lived at 105 Tradd St., took over after Easter. In 1913, Mrs. Locke was re-elected at an annual salary of $500 and re-elected through 1922. The tenors were Julia's husband and W.G. Hopke. In 1915, J. C. Bissell was authorized to remove the bellows from the organ loft.

Several volumes of the 1914 *St. Philip's Parish Letter* were saved. They were "Published in the interest of the work of St. Philip's Parish. Annual subscription fifty cents. Address all communications and send all subscriptions to Miss E. F. Hayne, Business Manager, 26 New Street." Subscribers to the *Letter* would always find their paper in their pew. Should they wish them delivered otherwise, they were asked to leave a stamped and addressed envelope with the sexton or with the manager.

Miss Hayne wrote that one of the reasons the *Letter* was being published was to keep its large congregation in touch with the active work of the church. Some were unaware of the variety and number its many organizations in the church. On December 23, 1914, the vestry agreed to pay a bill of $11.08 for the printing of 300 copies of *St. Philip's Parish Letter*. They added a cravat – that it was paid without in anyway recognizing any responsibility to pay it, and that they do not desire to convey the idea such would be paid in the future.

In 1936, the vestry agreed to pay for a monthly parish bulletin. The records do not tell if Elise Hayne was involved in that.

Elise, who died October 14, 1963, and her sister, Alice, who died December 9, 1966, are buried in the western churchyard. Henrietta, the last sister, died at 26 New Street around 1970. The sisters left a bequest to St. Philip's that amounted to more than $30,000. No mention of Ellen.

CONTINUATION OF MUSIC AND THE CHOIR

Remember, that in April 1908 the vestry called for an all-volunteer choir. By 1924, the volunteer choir had imploded and a special vestry meeting was called to consider the situation. That night the music committee, consisting of Thomas E. Myers, R. Dewar Bacot and Edward Chisolm, made their case. They said after the 1921 enlargement of the church and the installation of "our beautiful organ, conceded to be one of the handsomest … in the South," the volunteer choir greatly increased. The committee wrote that the beautiful music and singing were the reason the services, particularly the night service, were well attended. However, they said the recent music had not been very attractive and many of the volunteers seemed to have lost heart and dropped out entirely or only dropped by occasionally because there was a lack of leadership.

The music committee said it was essential to have a paid quartet to keep the choir together and the committee asked for a 1924 – 1925 budget of $1,860 to provide the organist and the quartet. The organist would receive $30.00 per month or $360 per year. To provide leadership, either the tenor or the soprano or both would be in charge of music selection with and under the supervision of the committee and the rector.

The vestry also had a report on the cost of performing The Messiah at the church and found that after all bills were paid $17.63 remained which the vestry unanimously agreed to give to Mrs. Locke in recognition of her untiring efforts towards its success.

On January 31, 1924, Thomas E. Myers, chairman of the music committee, wrote a letter to Mrs. Locke stating that there had been a re-organization. For financial reasons, they asked that she remain only through Easter, April 20. Myers expressed thanks for what she had done and wished her the best. He also assured her that she should have no problem in finding a job. Mrs. Locke sent a handwritten reply to Myers by hand on February 10, 1924, stating that it was impossible for her to continue until Easter and tendered her resignation to take effect on March 7.

The city directories did not list Mrs. Locke as an organist in another church or that she worked anywhere. In 1927, her husband was selling real estate and they had a son, Walter M. Locke, who was a student living with his parents at 1 Lenwood.

The vestry on February 13, 1924, ordered the final payment of $1,000 on the organ provided the chairman, Davies, investigate the contract to see if the $1,000 was "justly due." The contract was "justly due." At the same time, vestments were ordered for the choir.

St. Philippian Patience D. Walker née Davies shared information about her grandfather, Fred G. Davies. Penny wrote that once a year in the spring, Davies took the St. Philip's choir on a picnic in the country. They crossed the Cooper River on a barge owned by Tuxbury Lumber Company and landed where the lumber company had a railway spur. They then boarded a flat-bed rail car that had been outfitted with enough chairs and off they went singing their way to the picnic until they arrived at the company's mill camp in Awendaw. As the train approached the camp, the engineer let out a loud whistle to alert the cook that is was time to put the biscuits in the oven. When the choir disembarked, they dined on shrimp and hominy with hot biscuits. Everyone loved the outing and each year would ask "When is Mr. Fred going to have his next picnic?"

The land later was incorporated into the Francis Marion National Forest.

THE CHURCHYARDS

Our churchyards alone bring many visitors to St. Philip's. People love to walk through the churchyards, but they refer to them as "cemeteries" instead of the correct term, "churchyards." Unfortunately, the sign on the western churchyard says "western cemetery." In the Anglican world, members are buried in their churchyards.

The vestry records are filled with transactions concerning tombstones, memorials and grave sites. For example, on April 21, 1908, the treasurer, Arthur Mazyck, received $100 from Mrs. Eliza S. Cox of Philadelphia for the perpetual care of the graves of Rev. Milward Pogson (died 1836) and Mrs. Pogson Smith in the eastern churchyard. The money was deposited in a St. Philip's savings account in the Miner's & Merchants Bank for its cemetery (churchyard) fund. Pogson's grave site has received perpetual care, based on the $100 payment, for 104 years from 1908 to 2012 at a cost of ninety-six cents per year so far, not including interest.

Governor Robert Daniell, who died in 1718, was a fascinating personality. He was fighting Indians during the Yemassee Indian War when he was seventy and he served, actually as deputy governor, from April 22, 1716, to August 10, 1717. He had purchased Daniell Island, now misspelled Daniel Island, in 1699. In 1908, workmen on Rutledge Street[9] dug up Governor Daniell's tombstone. It was turned over to the Colonial Dames and Vestryman Theodore Jervey requested permission to place the tombstone permanently against the outer wall, preferably in the south porch. That is where it is in 2012, on the right side of the south door as you enter the church. Daniell may have been buried in the churchyard of the first St. Philip's where St. Michael's was established in 1751.

Everyone who comes to St. Philip's wants to see the graves of famous people such as John C. Calhoun, Charles Pinckney, Edward Rutledge and many others.

There are many, many other forgotten and humble souls who need to be remembered. Very few of these people would have a tombstone.

The first recorded burial in the St. Philip's register was Mortimer, a child, on May 10, 1720. A high percentage of the burials were children and there were many drowned

---
9   Rutledge Street is from Tradd Street to Murray Blvd.

sailors. Many people that were listed in the St. Philip's register were buried in the Huguenot churchyard. There were two souls registered at St. Philip's who were buried at the First (Scots) Presbyterian churchyard and even an Anabaptist, Mrs. Axtel.

The second St. Philip's opened in 1723 but the first recorded burial in its "New Church Yard" was of Joseph Monk in 1725. Also in 1725, Elizabeth Foster, a child was buried in the "Old Church Yard." It was quite likely that many listed in the St. Philip's register were buried on the site of the first church up until St. Michael's began construction in 1751.

Here are some burial entries from 1720 through 1754: Philip Pilpot, a sailor; Mary Newman, a poor woman; Anne Smith, a servant; John Pert, a soldier; William Williams, a Negro; William Tattle, a mulatto; Samuel Smith, a barber, Thomas Garrett, no minister;[10] John and Thomas Wright, twins; Margaret Smith, a school mistress; Nathaniel Cox from the workhouse; William Winderas, an old mathematician; John Cray, the barber; William Purnell, a convict lately brought from Bristol by Capt. McKenzie; Thomas Delaney, a fencing master; Mary Dale and her child one coffin; Edward Horn and Mr. Forest, out of prison; Vertue, a Negro woman; William Wilsford, a shoemaker; Prudence Miller at the charge of the parish and William Barns, mariner – he murdered himself. In May 1742, John, the illegitimate son of Capt. Edward Lightwood, was buried. In 1743, John the supposed son of Edward Lightwood was buried. Three days later, Harriot the supposed daughter of Edward Lightwood, was buried. Then was buried Mary Craig, belonging to the Royal Regiment; John Vaughan, a bricklayer; John Coleman, bred a Quaker and baptized one day before his death; Charles Carroll, a perukemaker (wig maker); Antonia Reggia, a Spaniard, a woman from the barracks; and Edmond Larken, organist.

The 1916 by-laws included funeral rules. Those who were white Episcopalians and who lived with a member of the church would be buried without any fee. Nonmember white Episcopalians who lived in South Carolina could be buried at St. Philip's for $18.00 while a white Episcopalian, who lived outside of the United States, had to pay $30.00. Burial plots were included in all three categories. The sexton had to keep the burial records in the register.

All tombstones had to be approved by the vestry. They were installed for $1.00 and the charge was $2.00 for opening of the church for deposit of body at night and keeping the body there until the funeral. It cost $3.00 to remove a body from the churchyard when permitted by the vestry.

Edward Percival Guerard II offered to pay for his burial site even though under the 1916 by-laws he was entitled to a free burial plot and funeral. The vestry voted on April 10, 1917, that he would not be charged for his burial site. Guerard died on September 15, 1924. "Percy" was put on his tombstone and not "Percival."

---

10 He could not afford a minister.

In 1918, Bishop Guerry had asked for a burial lot in the churchyard. The vestry wanted to consult with the solicitor concerning the legality "of giving such a lot by the vestry." The vestry decided to charge him $2.00 for his lot in the western church yard. The vestry minutes do not explain why Guerry had to pay.

On January 11, 1925, the vestry granted free grave sites to vestrymen W. W. Shackelford and F. G. Davies. Shackelford wanted his site to be just north of E. P. Guerard's grave.

On July 9, 1925, the vestry voted to start a trust fund of $30,000, the interest of which would be used to keep up the churchyards. At the same time, they also ended free grave sites, charging $25.00 per site. Miss Leila Waring's application for a grave was received and read at the same vestry meeting. She was told she had to pay the $25.00 fee and she may have been the first to pay. She purchased four burial sites.

CHARLESTON ARTISTS

Leila and her sister, Mary Ann (May) Waring, who is also buried at St. Philip's, lived at 2 Atlantic Street. Leila died in 1964 and May in 1960. During the second and third decades of the twentieth century, Atlantic Street was a hot bed of artists. Anna Heyward Rutledge lived at 6 Atlantic. Alice Ravenel Huger Smith and her sister, Caroline Ravenel Huger Smith, purchased 8 Atlantic Street as a studio while they lived around the corner at 69 Church Street. Noted artist Elizabeth O'Neil Verner and her family lived at 3 Atlantic Street. Leila made beautiful small portraits on ivory in the tradition of the early miniaturist, Malbone, who was her ancestor. She had many patrons who came from all over the country to sit for her. Leila's cousins were the DuPonts of Wilmington, Delaware, where she also had many patrons. "Leila had a lovely soft voice and a delicious sense of the ridiculous."

On Sundays during March and April, the four artists would be "At Home" serving tea from silver tea pots. Such favorites as benne biscuits or wafers, cheese straws and peach leather were served. Sometimes there was music at the Smiths. Nothing was offered for sale on Sunday. To read the entire article on the artists written by Elizabeth Verner Hamilton see the South Carolina Historical Society's *Carologue* Vol. 25 NO. 1 Summer 2009.

In 1927, the vestry decided to close accounts amounting to $2,425 held in several banks to form one account for the sole use of the St. Philip's Church Cemetery Trust Fund. This was the first time this had been done. The sole purpose of the fund was to provide the perpetual care of the churchyards. The chairman of the vestry was in charge of the trust but no funds could be invested without the agreement of the entire committee.

At the vestry meeting of June 12, 1929, its members had a lengthy discussion about the proposed passageway from the Circular Church through the western churchyard leading to Church Street. The request was defeated with only Davies and Myers voting yes. No reason was given why it was defeated. Then von Kolnitz made a motion to pass the proposal if the vestry had the power to rescind the permission at any time. Those who previously voted yes voted no and those who previously voted no then voted yes. The motion passed.

St. Philippian Mrs. Clelia Peronneau McGowan of 5 St. Michael's "Place" was inspired during a trip to Paris by its charming small walkways. As the first civic project of the Garden Club of Charleston, its president, Mrs. McGowan, was determined to replicate such a walkway as she saw in Paris. Because the Charleston Gateway Walk would stretch three blocks from Archdale Street to Church Street, it was requested that St. Philip's vestry open the gate between St. Philip's and the Circular Church. The Gateway Walk opened on April 10, 1930, during the celebration of the 250th anniversary of Charleston on its present site. In 1955, Palmer Gaillard reported that even though there were objections, the vestry decided to lock the churchyard gates at 5 p.m. because of vandalism. The gate between the Congregational church's churchyard and St. Philip's western churchyard continues to be closed.

THE REV. S. CARY BECKWITH

In 1925, The Porter Military Academy called Beckwith to come as permanent rector and chaplain of the school. Beckwith was fifty-five and had been at St. Philip's nineteen years. Beckwith wrote in declining Porter Military Academy, "I am answering a new call to St. Philip's and my earnest prayer is that God will give to your Rector a new power and a greater zeal in doing with you His great work in the field of service that he has entrusted to us.

Beckwith was a busy man and a joiner. In addition to organizations already mentioned, he joined the Lions Club as a charter member, the Washington Light Infantry, serving as chaplain and as a member of its reserve company, Camp Sumter, the United Confederate Veterans as chaplain, the Army of Northern Virginia as assistant chaplain general and with the rank of lieutenant colonel, the St. Cecilia Society and the South Carolina Society.

As stated, Beckwith was active over a long period of time in Masonry. He served as commander of South Carolina Company No. 1 Knights Templar and was a member of the Omar Temple. He also belonged to the Royal Order of Scotland, a masonic organization in Washington, D.C.

He was a member of the diocesan executive committee and was president of its standing committee. In 1922, 1925 and 1928 he was a delegate to the general convention of the "Protestant Episcopal Church."

In 1923, and probably other years as well, Beckwith took part in the celebration of the May 10 Confederate Memorial Day where he read an ode. School children were asked to bring flowers and many King Street stores closed at 1 p.m.

Because of bad health, Beckwith sent a letter of resignation dated March 4, 1935, to the vestry. The vestry hoped he could stay until a replacement could be found, but Beckwith had to resign right away. The letter was read to the congregation at the morning service on Sunday March 10 Robert L. Sinkler was elected sexton.

He had served virtually twenty-nine years. He died in Aiken on January 2, 1939.

REV. MERRITT FRANCIS WILLIAMS

RECTOR

OCTOBER 1, 1935 – SEPTEMBER 1, 1941

The first rector of St. Philip's, Atkin Williamson, allegedly baptized a bear.[11] The Rev. Merritt F. Williams did better with animals for he used them for a good purpose. As a minister in Alaska, he had dogs pull the sled to visit his parishioners who were Eskimos – now called Intuits.

Williams was born 1898 in Wakefield a suburb of Boston. He received early training in Texas. After graduating from Washington University in St. Louis in 1924, he took postgraduate courses at his alma mater. From there he studied at the marine biological laboratories at Woods Hole, Massachusetts, which led him to teach in the department of biology at the University of Iowa. In 1926 he entered the General Theological Seminary in New York and while there he spent two summers in England. Graduating

---

11 The "bear story" is often told, but told out of context. Atkin Williamson did conduct Anglican services at St. Philip's from circa 1681 to 1696, but his credentials were skimpy at best. He was accused of being a lover of strong liquor and the Rev. Francis LeJau hoped Williamson could totally overcome his "fault." His baptism of a cub bear took place circa 1690. One source said two men, about whom Williamson gave unflattering testimony in court, encouraged him to get drunk and baptize a cub bear out of revenge for "reporting their faults." In 1709, Williamson petitioned the South Carolina General Assembly for a pension. And he was given £30 per year. He said that he had grown so disabled with age, sickness and other infirmities that he could no longer attend to his ministerial functions and was so poor he could not maintain himself.

from seminary in 1929, Williams was ordained deacon in the same year by Bishop William T. Manning of New York.

Williams served three years at St. Stephen's Mission at Port Yukon, Alaska. He served as a deacon his first year and in 1930 he was ordained a priest by Bishop Peter T. Rowe of Alaska.

Williams was interviewed by the *News and Courier* on October 1, 1935, about his time in Alaska. Asked about the marked changes in localities he said that he was entirely "thawed out now," but that when he first returned from the great open spaces of Alaska, he was nearly run over by automobiles. His parish there was 12,000 square miles and he covered it by dog sled, preaching to the Eskimos in a combination of English and an Eskimo dialect. He ministered to their needs in many other ways. On the whole, he said, the Eskimos were as receptive to the Gospel as other people, and he said that some of the finest Christians he had known were Eskimos.

In 1932 Williams married Lucy Ogden Cornell the daughter of Mrs. William P. Cornell and the late Dr. W.P. Cornell of Charleston. From 1932 to 1935 Williams served as chaplain to Episcopal students at the University of Florida in Gainesville, Florida.

While the church was searching for someone to replace Beckwith, the vestry minutes of March 13, 1935, indicate Williams already had some association with St. Philip's because J. Stanyarne Stevens was asked to secure Williams as supply rector for the period from Palm Sunday through Easter Sunday.

On April 18, after consulting with Bishop Thomas, the vestry extended an invitation to Williams to accept the rectorship of St. Philip's at a salary of $2,400 per year and also agreed to provide him with a furnished residence. He must have been an outstanding speaker.

On September 26, the vestry offered to up William's salary to $2,700 annually and agreed to provide a suitable residence and pay his moving costs from Gainesville to Charleston. Williams accepted and became rector on October 1, 1935, at age thirty-six. His salary was increased by $300 on July 1, 1938, and on January 1, 1940, his salary was increased to $4,000.

The Williams arrived in Charleston with two small children, Jeannie Ogden Williams, age two, and Merritt Francis Williams, Jr. age one. A third child, Richard Cornell Williams, would be born later.

The vestry had agreed Beckwith, as rector emeritus, could continue to live in the rectory at 92 Church Street during their stay in Charleston, Williams, his wife and young children, had to move four times. Upon their arrival in Charleston, the Williams family were guests of Mr. and Mrs. Arthur Grimball at 139 Broad St. The Williams then rented an apartment at 33 New St. in a house owned by Miss Harriet (Hallie) Coffin who worked for Bishop Thomas in his office at St. Philip's. By 1938 they had rented 64 Tradd Street next to Mr. and Mrs. J. Stanyarne Stevens and their daughter Mary Louis Stevens Webb.

Mary Louis greatly admired Williams because he was energetic and that he led many young people into the ministry. Williams was to perform the marriage of Mary Louis and her husband, Rutledge Webb, until they found out Willliam's son chose to be married the same day. Later, Rutledge and Mary Louis visited Williams on their honeymoon in Springfield, Massachusetts, where he and his family had moved.

Beckwith continued in bad health after his retirement and in April 1938, his thirty-seven year old son died of a heart attack at 92 Church Street. At the 1938 congregational meeting, Davies explained that the Williams family was growing and it was necessary to ask Beckwith to leave 92 Church Street. Beckwith was paid $1,000 a year as rector emeritus and $60.00 a month would be added to that. The Beckwiths had to move in October 1938 because a tornado had damaged the rectory. As previously written, he died in Aiken in 1939, and was buried on January 4 at St. Philip's, with arrangements by Connelley's. Williams presided.

MERRITT WILLIAMS' BUSY SCHEDULE

Williams kept a busy schedule. He served at times as a member of the diocesan standing committee, chairman of the department of Christian education, chairman of the department of Christian social service, trustee of the Harriott Pinckney Home for Seamen, trustee of the church home and orphanage for children, dean of the Charleston convocation and a member of the executive council. In February 1940, Williams replaced Beckwith as chaplain of the Washington Light Infantry of Company B of the 118th infantry. The Washington Light Infantry held special memorial services at St. Philip's for many years, including an observance of George Washington's birthday. As a first lieutenant in the naval chaplain's reserve, Williams spent two weeks yearly on active duty in Norfolk.

By 1938, interest spread in having an Episcopal camp for the diocese. Rev. A. R. Stuart had held previous conferences with Episcopal layman Victor Morawetz who owned Seabrook Island. Morawetz gave the diocese a ten-year lease on six acres at Seabrook. A committee including reverends Merritt Williams, L.A Taylor and W.W. Lumpkin met with Bishop Thomas on the beach on April 18, 1938, to survey the ground and determine a site under the lease. Thus began Camp St. Christopher.

CHURCH SERVICES AND MEMBERS

Williams entered more than just numbers in the Church Services Records book. He would make notes about the weather like "rain – bad day" or "day fine weather" or "cold snap, windy." On January 1, 1937, after only four people showed up for the Feast of the Circumcision, Williams wrote, "Don't do this again." He noted that he preached at the Citadel at 9 a.m. on Sundays at least twice. On Tuesday January 28, 1936, 400 attended an 8 p.m. memorial service for King George. Williams noted, "cold night."

Williams also kept exact church attendance numbers in the Church Services Records book from December 1935 to August 1, 1941, that included the 8:00 a.m. service, the 11:15 a.m. service and all special services showed the annual attendance ranged from a high of 18,000 in 1937 to a low of 16,072 in 1940. A total of 750 people attended the 1938 Thanksgiving service.

Even though attendance declined during 1940, the last full year of Williams' tenure, he said in August 1941 that communicants (as opposed to attendees) had increased 21%, church school attendance increased 125%, and the number of teachers, officers and chairmen of committees in the parish organization increased by more than 300%.

In 1937, due to low summer attendance during July and August, St. Philip's and St. Michael's once again combined their services at St. Philip's. Attendance varied from 120 to 180. The Rev. Albert R. Stuart, who became rector of St. Michael's on July 1, 1937, preached at St. Philip's. On April 24, 1938, 700 attended a special concert held during the Azalea Festival that featured Bach. Williams directed the chorus.

National Geographic was given permission in 1938 to take photographs of St. Philip's during the Easter service for an article about Charleston that was written by St. Philippian DuBose Heyward. The article appeared in the magazine in March 1939. There was no interior picture but two exterior photographs, including one taken from the balcony of the Dock Street Theater, and the other showing St. Philippians exiting from the south door after the service ended.

Then on January 5, 1941, Williams wrote, "I learned today of the death of Robert L. Shuler for twenty-one years the faithful sexton of this church." For most of those twenty-one years his name was written as Shuler and sometimes as Sinkler. The city directory verifies his name was "Sinkler." He and his wife, Ella, lived a 9 Cumberland Street in a house St. Philip's owned. The vestry agreed to pay his widow her late husband's salary for the entire month of January and that she could stay in the house until March 10.

THE YOUTH, LAYMAN'S LEAGUE AND THE LADIES

In March 1936, the parish house was being abused by a number of boys playing there and that caused the building to be closed "until further notice." Early in 1937, Williams reported to the vestry that he had engaged an athletic director, Edwin Rogers, at $20.00 per month for four months. Rogers would supervise the junior Porter Academy cadets on Tuesday and Thursday afternoons in the gymnasium.

Williams advised the vestry on May 12, 1937, that Miss Mary Pressley Walsh of Walterboro was coming to St. Philip's as director of religious education. Miss Walsh studied at St. Mary's in Raleigh and Winthrop College. Her other duties were to reside in the church home and to have general oversight of the welfare of its "inmates" and serve as general secretary to the rector. She would be paid $500 from the parish and $300 by the church home. In October of 1937, Williams said, "he was much gratified at the services being rendered by Miss Walsh." By 1941 her salary had increased to $1,200.

In Williams' letter to the congregation at the annual meeting held on March 14, 1937, several paragraphs about the youth were read.

"The Sunday school has made progress this year, though in point of effectiveness it is not yet up to the level that it should be. He was not criticizing any faculty but pointed out the school needed trained leadership."

There were sixty members of the Young People's Service League (YPSL) with an average attendance for the past year of more than fifty. He said they were a splendid group of youngsters and that they were doing good work. He hoped the group would grow into a well-rounded program of supervised recreation for our young people. Williams added that, "With our splendid plant with its basketball court, tennis courts, playground and shower rooms, we can fill a real need in the community."

The athletic program was sponsored by the church's newly formed "The Layman's League." Already there had been three well attended and enthusiastic meetings. Williams said, "There is much for the men of the parish to do and we have a right to expect much of them in the future." In May 1937, the vestry authorized the replacement of some window panes that had been broken by tennis players.

Also in his letter to the congregation of March 1937 he spoke of the work the ladies were doing at St. Philip's. He said, "This past year has seen a fine growth in the activity of the parish. Presently there were more than twenty organizations, guilds and committees – all actively engaged in the church's work. The work of the women in the parish has been reorganized." He pointed out that at least 50% more women of the parish are active in the organized work of parish than a year ago.

Williams went on to mention some of the guilds and committees. The church yard guild, one of the youngest organizations, was attempting to repair the monuments in the churchyard and to beautify its grounds. The York orphanage committee raised $271.75 as a special gift for the children. Williams was especially grateful for the pilgrimage committee for renovating his office. The entertainment committee had provided bountifully for the various suppers and communion breakfasts and had added considerably to the kitchen equipment.

Williams closed his 1937 letter to the congregation by saying, "May I express my gratitude for the fine cooperation I have received from the Wardens and Vestry and from the congregation? In everything I have attempted, I have met with the highest consideration and most loyal response. I am conscious that I am still serving my novitiate and that much remains for me to learn and to do. But Please God and with your help, we shall go forward in our work for Christ and His Kingdom in an ever finer and more noble way."

Gifts, fancy work and home made delicacies were being sold at the bazaar. Mrs. David Maybank was the general chairman of the bazaar and Miss Eugenia C. Frost was chairman of the of the cake booth. Mrs. Henry F. Walker was in charge of the doll booth and Miss Julia Rees was in charge of the canned goods. Mrs. Edward K. Pritchard and Mrs. John T. Jenkins were in charge of grab bags for children and adults. Mrs. Charles Cuthbert, Mrs. Norman S. Welch, and Mrs. Dwight H. Gadsden were members of the tea committee.

THEOLOGY, EVANGELISM AND MISSIONS

None of Williams' sermons survive. Perhaps some hint of his theology may be gleamed from what he was taught at seminary. He attended the General Theological Seminary (GTS) in New York City from 1924 to 1929.

After the American Revolution, there were no Episcopal seminaries in this country. Bishops would instruct candidates but it was not a requirement and there was always a shortage of clergy. During Bishop Theodore Dehon's episcopate, he ordained one priest, four deacons and at Dehon's death there were six candidates for holy orders. But Dehon knew the answer was to open a seminary and he was the first person to bring up this idea. He proposed such a project at the general convention in May 1814 and the idea was approved in 1817. The GTS opened on September 13, 1820, in New Haven but it was moved to New York and reopened on February 13, 1822.

In January 1917, Hughell Edgar Woodall Fosbroke, born in England, became the new dean of the GTS. He was at GTS when Williams was there. Comments about Fosbroke: "To men who penetrated his shield of reticence and found behind it the deep springs of Christian affection. Nothing, however, could conceal his dedication to the will and purposes of God. To listen to his lectures on the Prophets was to experience the moment of truth of God's reign over history and creation. To hear him read the Holy Week gospels was to encounter Christ in his passion." In 1924, Fosbroke resisted all pressure to appoint a man whose specialty was the popular presentation of the Christian faith.

While Fosbroke wrote very little at that time, his staff members did write. Marshall Bowyer Stewart in 1925 published *God and Reality* as part of his Paddock Lectures.

Professor Burton Scott Easton wrote a commentary in 1926 on the *Gospel of Luke* and Leonard Hodgson wrote *And Was Made Man and Essays in Christian Philosophy*.

Returning to activities in Charleston, Williams in February 1936 requested permission to order engraved cards and place them in the various hotels to invite visitors to St. Philip's. The vestry agreed. The program, apparently, was ongoing because in 1939 E. H. Pringle offered to assume $50.00 of the cost of printing the engraved cards.

St. Philippian's in 1941 gave $253.75 for British missions.

FINANCES AND THE VESTRY

The meeting of the 1936 congregation meeting was called to order with J. Campbell Bissell as chairman and Miss Ellen Hayne as secretary. It was decided that the quarterly financial reports would be left in the vestibule so that members of the congregation could be made aware of the church's financial condition at all times. During the meeting, Williams said he "deemed it most important that the Church be self-supporting, especially in its current expenses and not borrow from funds which had been legacies to the Church and intended for specific purposes."

Comparing the budget from 1934, the year before Williams arrived, with the budget from 1941, the year Williams left St. Philip's, it is clear that the Great Depression was loosening its grip.

In 1934, total income was $11,327.29. The largest sources of money were: pledges and subscriptions, $3,478.82; pew rentals, $2,422.07; Easter collection, $856.47 and glebe property, $2,017.68.

In 1934, expenditures were $11,327.29. The largest expenditures were: salaries, $3,679.99; music, $1,674.15; glebe expense, $853.09; operating expenses, $906.55; parish house debt payment, $832.47; repairs, $486.03 and diocese of general church, $1,212.42.

In 1941, total income was $22,059.83. The largest sources of money were: plate collection, $1,692.48; pledges, $7,930.44; pew rents, $3,068.33; Kaufman trust, $763.90 and glebe properties, $2,867.53.

In 1941, expenditures were $20,302.39. The largest expenditures were: salaries, $5,715.59; organist, music and choir, $1,986.50; operating expenses, $1,671.16; assessment, $1,181.00; glebe property, $980.50; and payment on debt, $1,900.

In 1939, the vestry decided to hire a certified public accountant to audit the treasurer's books for 1938, 1939 and 1940 and have the treasurer ask for suggestions to improve the current system. In 1941, they hired G.G. McKnight.

There is no indication that the vestry denied any request made by Williams or Beckwith, but the rector, then as now, had to have the vestry authorize any expenditure the rector requested.

Some examples of these expenditures were:

Williams was authorized in 1936 to send out letters giving the Lenten services schedule and he was allowed to purchase an addressograph for $10.00. In 1937, Williams was reimbursed $2.50 for plumbing repairs he had incurred and two months later he was given permission to purchase a typewriter for his office. In June 1940, the vestry authorized installation of an electrical outlet in Miss Walsh's office. Miss Walsh had worked in her office for three years without an electrical outlet.

Williams reported on May 13, 1940, that Miss Sophia Thurston had made a bequest of $1,000. Her bequest was temporarily borrowed from the operating account and used toward the restoration.

By the late 1930s and early 1940s, more new faces were on the vestry. Thomas Engelhard Myers, junior warden, died prior to January 8, 1936. The vestry wrote, "Whereas Thomas Engelhard Myers for more than a quarter of a century, a loyal and devoted member of St. Philip's Church and for many years a member of the Vestry and a Warden of the Parish …St. Philip's has lost a member interested in every department of its work true to the faith and the teachings of the Church …"

In 1938, Daniel E. Huger, J. H. Furman and J.E. Smith were on the vestry.

On January 26, 1940, John Ernest Gibbs Sr. retired from the vestry of which he had been secretary for eighteen years. Gibbs and his wife, Annie S. Ball Gibbs, lived at 10 Logan Street. He died on May 30, 1945, at the Riverside Infirmary after a week's illness and was buried at St. Philip's with funeral arrangements by Connelley's. Gibbs, long a leading figure in the fertilizer business in Charleston, was president-treasurer of the Etiwan Fertilizer Company and vice-president of the Cooper River Terminal Company and the Shipyard River Terminal Company.

Gibbs was survived by his widow, one brother, Benjamin P. Gibbs and four sons including John E. Gibbs Jr., who taught English at the High School Charleston. Many still fondly remember Mr. Gibbs who died in 1992. Also, Surviving were Coming Ball Gibbs Sr., Captain James Gendron Gibbs of the United States Army and Lt. Charles H. Gibbs of the United States Navy.

Edward K. Pritchard Sr. was elected interim secretary until R. Baron Munnerlyn was elected February 2, 1940. Charles S. Dwight joined the vestry in 1940. In 1941,

Dr. Henry C. Robertson Jr. and Lewis deB. McCrady resigned from the vestry. They were replaced by Coming B. Gibbs and Dr. Frank G. Cain.

F. G. Davies' granddaughter, Patience D. Walker née Davies related that when her grandfather was seventy or more and not in good health there was one day when he could not be found. He was later located at the top of St. Philip's steeple and he said, "I just wanted to climb up one more time." Penny also remembered what a distinguished man her grandfather was with his gray hair.

Davies had been on the vestry twenty-two years as senior warden and simultaneously as treasurer for eleven years. On February 2, 1940, Mrs. Davies (Margaret) was elected assistant treasurer and served for one year.

Davies died on the morning of Saturday December 28, 1940, in his home at 11 Legare Street. The funeral, arranged by Connelley's, was held the next day at 3:30 p.m. at St. Philip's where he was buried. Rev. Williams officiated. "Mr. Davies was retiring by nature but had a keen sense of humor. His smile was described by a friend as lighting up his entire countenance and often it was accompanied by a merry twinkle of the eye." Surviving were his wife, Margaret Neff Davies, a son Carlton Davies and two daughters, Mrs. Katherine Neff Guy and Mrs. E. Lloyd Willcox. When Willcox went off to school, his parents would address envelopes to "Student" Willcox and that name stuck for the rest of his long life. Student was a member of Grace Episcopal Church.

PROPERTY AND MAINTENANCE

In addition to the glebe land property, other property also owned in 1941 included the church building and the chapel, the parish house, the rectory and the sexton's house at 9 Cumberland Street.

In 1936, Mrs. G.D. Canfield gave a gift to St. Philip's of seven branch candle sticks with the provision that their use be allowed for nuptials of any member of the Canfield family. Miss Riley of Orangeburg made a gift in 1939 of the lights on the altar in memory of Francis Marion Riley.

In 1937, Williams suggested it would be proper to plan something to observe the centennial of the completion of the church building during 1938. He proposed removing the old organ from the rear of the church and restoring the rear gallery to the way it looked in 1838. The newspaper stated the organ dated from circa 1880. Williams also had taken steps to replace the tablets in the chancel. Neither project was completed by 1938. The *Charleston Evening Post* on April 6, 1939, reported that the work was well under way with the restoration of the rear gallery.

In 1939, while the interior of the church was being painted, it was discovered that damage had been caused to a number of columns and pilasters because vines had been hung from them for weddings, etc. That practice was ended. In the same year, shields were placed around the radiators at a cost of $65.00. Hand rails were placed on the steps leading up to the narthex. Vestryman, John Laurens, requested that a vacuum cleaner be purchased for cleaning the interior of the church. He explained, "At that time, the dust and dirt was merely moved from one place to another within the building and that a vacuum cleaner was the only feasible manner of handling the situation." Laurens said the Electrolux Cleaner only cost $69.25. The vestry approved.

Archie Baker Myers, who was a construction engineer and architect, was hired in 1939 to design the reconstruction of the rear balcony, the west wall, the old Sunday school building and to oversee the work of all the contractors. In January 1940, it was reported that a crack had developed between the addition to the chancel and the old portion of the church building. The vestry asked Myers to make an examination and recommendations.

At another time, Myers was asked to check a steeple window that supposedly had been repaired. One morning, he left his house to check the window without telling his wife because he knew he would be swung around the steeple "so high off the ground." It had not been fixed. When the contractor went to Myers asking for his payment, Myers looked at him and said, "You didn't fix the window." The man went off sputtering and surprised that Myers had checked his work. There was a picture of Myers in the *Charleston Evening Post* being swung around the steeple and that is how Mrs. Myers found out what transpired. Myers loved to tell this story to his children who laughed hilariously.[12]

Two tornadoes that struck Charleston on September 29, 1938, appeared without warning killing twenty-six people and injuring scores. About 8 a.m. the tornado tore off the roof of St. Michael's and made shambles along Market Street. The French Huguenot Church and St. Philip's, both located between Broad and Market streets, suffered less damage with the exception of St. Philip's old Sunday school. The *News and Courier* reported damage to the city would be at least two million dollars.

Ironically, the vestry met the night before the tornado struck. The vestry voted that senior warden, Davies, would have $34,000 in serial bonds printed to be used for the purpose of refinancing the current indebtedness and make necessary repairs on the parish house. The bonds would bear 5% interest per annum.

---

12 Thanks to Myers' daughters for this vignette – Rose Marie Smith, Helen Tatum, Elisabeth Hall and Jean Boos.

The vestry met five days later and asked for a loan of $10,000 or $15,000 for rebuilding from the Disaster Finance Corporation which later approved $10,000. A congregational meeting was called for 8 p.m. October 6 to report the tornado damages and to ask for donations for restoration. The congregation raised $3,663.95 and Henry Cheves donated $1,000.

Because of St. Michael's roof damage, its congregation worshipped at St. Philip's on October 2, 9 and 16. During that time, the attendance was 550 – double the average number.

On December 9, 1938, the Dawson Engineering Company submitted the low bid of $7,584 to repair the tornado damage. H.S. Barden and Archie B. Myers Associate were hired as supervising architects with a remuneration of 2% ($151.68) in consultation with the firm of Cram and Ferguson of Boston.

The vestry in January 1939, decided to purchase fire and tornado insurance for the church and it property. In 1940, the vestry authorized the purchase of a $5,000 windstorm policy on the organ.

At the church's annual meeting, it was reported that the finances of the church were in excellent condition considering the large amount of repairs and construction work necessary due to the tornado. By April 1939, approximately $27,000 had been spent on the work. The debt would be paid in full by 1945.

Bishop Thomas wrote that the old Sunday school building was rebuilt as a chapel by Miss Eugenia C. Frost in memory of her parents, Thomas and Martha Calhoun Frost, but many others also donated to the building. Miss Frost kept her eyes on the chapel through the years. In 1946, she placed iron railings on the steps of the chapel, "electric lights" on the chapel steps and more lights in the chapel at her expense. In 1955, she had the roof painted. The old communion table that was saved from the fire of 1835 was placed in the chapel where it remains in 2012. The restored building was consecrated by Bishop Thomas as "The Chapel of the Good Shepherd" on Ascension Day 1941.

In February 1941, three years after Williams mentioned they were looking into new tablets in the chancel, the vestry approved the design of the Canfield Memorial as submitted by Cram and Ferguson. The tablets, executed by Irving, Casson and Davenport of Boston, appear to be marble but are wood. The tablet bearing the Ten Commandments was surmounted with Moses. The tablet with the Lord's Prayer was surmounted by a figure symbolical of Christ. Each figure was decorated in several colors. At some point, the Moses and Christ figures were removed – no one seems to know when or why that happened.

Damage to the Sunday school building in the 1938 tornado. The building became the Chapel of the Good Shepherd. Also, notice the tennis courts.

MUSIC AND THE CHOIR

In 1939, when choir member Mr. Matthew died, three new singers were hired: Mrs. Deveaux, Mrs. Cone and Franklin E. Robson.

Cotesworth Means wanted to increase Miss Dorothy Bollwinkle's salary from $40.00 to $50.00 per month because he knew organists at other churches were paid $50.00 to $75.00 per month. In addition, Miss Bollwinkle volunteered to handle the children's choir and she was having great success. Means said Miss Bollwinkle deserved a raise not only because she earned it, but because the strain of meeting her living expenses "under the present inadequate basis is telling upon her, and the church will feel her loss if she breaks down."

Because there had been no budget for purchasing music, the choir and organist had been purchasing music out of their salaries. Means had paid $50.00 out of his pocket during 1939. He requested a new budget of $100 to purchase music.

Means wrote, "Like all human endeavors, our efforts have not always been completely successful, and I know there have been days when the music was not only bad, but rotten. Throughout all these years, however, there has never been a word of complaint by the congregation, and I would be totally ungrateful if I closed this statement without acknowledging the considerate regard and warm friendship for the choir on the part of the rector, the vestry and the entire congregation."

The vestry approved Means' proposed budget, including the $100 for music.

THE CHURCHYARDS

During the mid-1930s, local ladies were hired by the Works Progress Administration (WPA) to transcribe the tombstones in our churchyards and in several others. The work they did was wonderful since more of St. Philip's tombstones were becoming less legible. Time flies and in 2008 St. Philip's archives recognized more than seventy years had passed since any tombstones had been transcribed. The church hired Erin Smith, then a student at the College of Charleston, to undertake the job with Frances Frost providing professional forms for Smith to use for the transcriptions. All tombstones are transcribed through the summer of 2008. Smith did a very thorough job.

On April 14, 1936, the vestry authorized the rector and the senior warden to allot burial lots. For the first time, a majority of the vestry did not have to approve the purchase of burial lots.

DEPARTURE

The first hint that Williams might leave St. Philip's was given at the vestry meeting of January 21, 1941. Williams announced he had accepted an appointment as chaplain in the Naval Reserve.

Williams tendered his resignation soon after his return from Norfolk. He wrote on June 14, I received a communication from the secretary of the National Cathedral, Washington, D.C., formally notifying me that I had been duly elected a member of the Cathedral Chapter, a canon of the Washington Cathedral and Acting Almoner, (an official distributor of alms).

"It is nearly six years since I came to the Parish. I count them the happiest period of my life. The prospect of severing our relationship is most painful. Believe me when I say that no severance of official ties can alter the ties of love and friendship which Bind me very close to every person in the Parish.

"For the loyal and generous support given me without fail by the Wards and Vestrymen, past and present, I am deeply grateful. May the dear Lord bless and keep every one of you." He resigned September 1, 1941.

LIFE AFTER ST. PHILIP'S

Williams remained at the Washington National Cathedral until he was called to active duty on the *Wasp* that was torpedoed by Japanese submarines in the Pacific Ocean on June 5, 1942, at 2:50 p.m., The *Wasp*, with other escort ships, was protecting transport and supply ships bringing American reinforcements to the Solomon Islands. Three Japanese torpedoes plunged into the ship starting fires near the stores where five inch shells were kept. Williams bravely stood on the bridge and broadcast over the loudspeakers a running report to the men below of any action above. He was the only naval chaplain whose battle duty station was not at a medical dressing station. Williams said his predecessor had thought of the idea.

After the torpedoing, the last of the wounded had been taken from the ship by 3:50 p.m. Captain Sherman was the last man to leave the ship but before he could leave he had to physically force some enlisted men off the ship who did not like the idea of giving it up.

As Williams went down the ship's side and neared the water, he became entangled in cordage and he later said, "All I remember is how mad it made me." At last he freed himself and "found the sea rather choppy." He was in the water two and a half hours with hundreds of men. Ninety per cent of the crew survived. Williams said, "The only time I was really terrified was when a shark made a pass at me. I saw the dorsal fin and I remember yelling 'shark.' Then I was ashamed of myself."

Williams received the Purple Heart in 1943 and the Bronze Star in 1945 for his conduct on the *Wasp*.

He returned to Charleston at least three or four times. A headline in the *News and Courier* on January 9, 1943, read, "Lieut. Williams will speak here." He was quoted as saying, "I still feel that I belong here." He stayed at 62 Tradd Street, the home of J.S. Stanyarne. The newspaper reported that Williams had written a series of articles for the *Philadelphia Enquirer* entitled *The Life and Death of the Wasp*, later published as a book. Williams preached the next day at St. Philip's at the 11:15 a.m. service.

In January 1943, Williams, who was the chief of chaplains, went on speaking tours to seminary students about service as a chaplain. Toward the end of the war, he was back on sea duty on the *West Virginia* and was wounded while serving on that ship. He participated in landings at Leyte, Mindanoa, Iwo Jima and others.

After the war, he was elected dean of the Cathedral of Springfield, Massachusetts, where he remained until his retirement in 1967. He died in 1977 in a nursing home near his daughter in Stratford, Connecticut. He was survived by his wife, three children and eight grandchildren. Reverend and Mrs. Williams are buried at the National Cathedral in Washington, D.C.

Canon Sam Cobb, later rector of St. Philip's, wanted it noted in the vestry minutes of June 27, 1977, that a former rector of St. Philip's, Merritt Williams, had died the previous week. Cobb said Williams was warm, witty and a gentle person. The vestry sent an invitation to the widow to visit Charleston.

Williams wrote one last comment in the St. Philip's Church Service Records Book that was probably never seen by the congregation:

"August 1, 1941

Here ends my ministry in St. Philip's Parish. It has been a happy ministry and I take leave of it with deep regret. No man was ever treated with greater kindness and affection. I owe the many men and women and children of this parish far more than they owe me. May the dear Lord bless them in the years to come with a full measure of His Grace.

Merritt F. Williams"

POSTSCRIPT

The Rev. Dr. William Rhett, a member of St. Philip's, remembers hearing a story about Williams conducting a funeral. The ground was wet, there were no boards around the empty grave and Williams slipped and fell into the grave. Rhett said to this day when he is conducting a funeral he will not get too close to the edge.

INTERMINS

SEPTEMBER 1, 1941 – DECEMBER 1, 1942

By November, the search committee had two ministers reject their offers. In the meantime, the vestry agreed to pay Dr. John E. Reilly $200 per month as acting rector and asked him to stay through January. Reilly said he could not stay after January 1 unless he was allowed to live in that part of the rectory that was furnished. His request was rejected but he was paid an extra $100 for December.

The vestry did attend to some other items. The use of the assembly room and showers by enlisted men was approved providing there were no extra costs to the church and that they did not interfere with the church school. W. Gordon McCabe offered the use of his pew for visitors. Miss Walsh was paid a $100 bonus for the extra work she was doing because there was no rector.

On February 16, 1942, the Rev. W. Herbert Mayers expressed his pleasure in temporarily being at St. Philip's and asked the vestry to suggest the work they desired him to do. After Mayers served at churches in the 1920s at Marion, Mullins and Conway, he then went to Florida. Initially, Mayers was asked to stay until May 1 but that was extended.

MARY MANIGAULT

In the middle of this, Miss Mary Huger Manigault, the daughter of Confederate Brigadier General Arthur Middleton Manigault, requested permission to erect a tablet in the church to honor her Manigault ancestors. That was refused because there were only two suitable places remaining in the church where tablets could be erected and those spaces were to be saved for deceased clergy. The senior warden, Daniel Huger, was requested to advise Miss Manigault.

Coming Gibbs and Tom Myers met with Miss Manigault. All agreed that she could place a marble memorial on the floor of the nave located just in front of the steps that lead up to the chancel. Five Manigaults are honored on this memorial.

In addition, Miss Manigault asked that a brass memorial plaque be placed on pew 20 that was granted Peter Manigault on August 17, 1724. From a certified copy provided by Arthur Manigault Wilcox, "Know ye therefore that we the said Vestry and church commissioners in consideration of the generous benefaction of Mr. Peter Manigault to the said church and of his paying the sum of Eighty pounds ... have given and granted by these present, to give and grant unto the said Peter Manigault and to his heirs and assigned forever a pew in the said church," ... distinguished by the number 20 and its location on the middle aisle on the north side.

Some of the distinguished commissioners and vestry who signed Manigault's grant were: Governor Francis Nicholson, Commissary Alexander Garden, who was rector of St. Philip's, Chief Justice Thomas Hepworth, who was buried at St. Philip's in 1728, and South Carolina treasurer Alexander Parris.

Coming Gibbs wrote to Miss Manigault on April 7, 1944, stating that although Peter Manigault had been granted pew 20 in the St. Philip's in the second church, he said they could not guarantee that pew 20 in the current church building would be in the exact location as the original. Gibbs closed the letter by saying he advised the Davies family of this intended action because prior to January 1, 1944, pew 20 was owned by the Davies family.

On April 8, 1944, Miss Manigault wrote to her nephew, Robbie who was Robert Smith Manigault. He called her "Annie." "To-day has been particularly happy for me, not only because it is Easter, but because a life-long desire of father, your father and mine has been realized ... My father, and your father twice tried during their lifetime to do what I have succeeded in doing, not for myself alone, but for you and others who come after. Robbie died the next year and was added to the memorial making the fifth Manigault.

The plaque reads:

MANIGAULT
Pew No. 20 was granted to the first
Ancestor of the family in this country
By the vestry and church commissioners of
St. Philip's church August 17, 1724

INTERMINS

> To have and to hold the said pew
> No. (20) twenty in the said church
> To him, his heirs and associates forever.

On June 1, 1942, the vestry decided that an honor roll for men in the armed forces should be secured and they requested that J. Heyward Furman inscribe the names of the members of the parish then in service. There were two ladies on the list – Ellen Hume Jervey and Gwynn Wilson.

At some point, the honor roll wound up in the hands of Beverly "Bevo" Howard, who was a noted aviator. He tried to sign up but the draft board would not let him because he was needed to train pilots. Bevo made a great contribution in World War II by training pilots under a government contract. His daughter, Langhorne Howard, came across the honor roll in her house in 2008 and generously gave it to St. Philip's where it is now protected in the archives. Thank you Langhorne. The honor roll did not list the names alphabetically because they possibly were listed as they enlisted. This list is alphabetical. The top of the honor roll reads:

> OUR PRAYERS ARE ASKED
> FOR THOSE WHO HAVE GONE
> TO SERVE OUR FLAG AND COUNTRY
> BY LAND, SEA AND AIR

> OUR ROLL OF HONOR

The eighty people listed are: Edward Simons Allston Jr., Walter Rhett Bacot, F. Macnaughton Ball M.D., Robert Thomson Ball, George Hammond Bamberg Jr., John McCrady Barnwell Jr., William Hazard Barnwell, John Rutherford Bennett Jr., Edward Stanley Bullock, Burgh Smith Burnet M.D., Edward Milby Burton, Francis Gendron Cain Jr., Albert Cannon, Thomas Heyward Carter, Hugh Cathcart M.D., John Cameron Clark, Charles Pinckney Cuthbert Jr., Daniel Elliott Jr., Reginald Cain Fitzsimons, Graham Moses Forshee, Irvine Keith Furman M.D., John Palmer Gaillard, Benjamin Owen Geer, Donald Roller Gesterfeld, Charles Haskell Gibbs, James Gendron Gibbs, John Ernest Gibbs Jr., Harold Godin Guerard Jr., Russell Bogert Guerard, Alexander Ritchie Haig, Alfred Huger, Daniel Huger, David Cullen Humphries, William Wirt Humphries, Harry Colcock Hutson, Richard Woodward Hutson, William Elliott Hutson, Arthur Postell Jervey, Charles Heyward Jervey, Ellen Hume Jervey, James Trapier Jervey Jr., Edwin Heriot Kerrison Jr., John Thomas Leonard, Edward Huguenin Lesesne, James Petigru Lesesne, John Mitchell Lesesne, William Mason Smith Lesesne Jr., Grange Simons Lucas Jr., Pringle McColl, John Cox Minott, William Butler Minott Jr., John North Moore, John Hamilton Murdock Jr. M.D., Andrew Murray, DeRossett Myers, John Henry Nixon,

James O'Hear M.D., Robert Lovell Oliveros, Paul Trapier Palmer, Edward Hall Pinckney Jr., Cleveland Forsythe Pratt, James Whitehead Pringle, Robert Alexander Pringle, Walter Pringle III, Robert Barnwell Rhett Jr., Henry Clay Robertson Jr. M.D., Donald Deane Sams Jr., Theodore Jervey Simons III, William Sinkler, Wilson Walker Small, John Thomas Smith, Daniel Somers Jr., Robert Charles Sproule, Francis Bergh Taylor Jr., Joseph Robertson Trott Jr., Simons Vanderhorst Waring Jr., Charles Caldwell Warley, Charles Webb Jr., Charles Wilson Jr., Gwynn Wilson, and Walter LeRoy Wooten Jr.

There have been many members of St. Philip's who fought in World War II who were not members of the church at the time the honor roll was completed or were simply left off the honor roll. Five who were not listed are: Craig M. Bennett, Sr., James Alva Burkette, Louis Y. Dawson, Alston Deas, Malcolm D Haven and Arthur Manigault Wilcox.

ELLEN JERVEY

Ellen Hume Jervey, one of the two ladies listed on the honor roll, was a native Charlestonian who graduated from Boston University. From there she taught physical training at the University of Texas. Returning to Charleston, she taught physical education at the YWCA, Ashley Hall and other schools. She was a member of the national basketball committee. In 1935, Jervey and Mrs. Paul Allen of Charlotte established a record as the first women to climb Clingman's Dome in the Great Smokies unaccompanied by men. From 1939 to 1942, Jervey was associate director of Eastbrook Camp in Brevard, North Carolina.

Jervey was commissioned a lieutenant (jg) in the WAVEs on October 7, 1942, and she was sent to Northampton, Massachusetts, for a month's training at Smith College. By 1943, Jervey wound up in Memphis as chief woman executive at the air station. Both men and women were trained as aviation mechanics and metal smiths as well as other duties. After the war ended she was one of five WAVE officers to close the various camps throughout the country.

In 1946, Jervey, who was back in Charleston, was an ancillary administratrix c.t.a. of the estate of Charles H. Haig. The Haig Fund was established on June 8, 1947. In 1948, Jervey, who was the College of Charleston's librarian, was living at 71 Rutledge Avenue with her two sisters. Miss Elizabeth H. Jervey was the secretary-treasurer at the South Carolina Historical Society and Miss Frances Jervey was the assistant librarian at Charleston Library Society. In the same year, the vestry approved Jervey's request for two lots in the "Church burial ground." Jervey was the chapter chairman in 1973 of the ECW. In 1991, a check to St. Philip's was received for $72,420 from the estate of Ellen Hume Jervey with no restrictions.

INTERMINS

On July 28, Rev. Mayers announced he had received a call and that he had to leave St. Philip's. The vestry asked him to stay until October 1. Finally, Mayers agreed to stay until December 1, 1942, and the vestry paid him an extra $25.00 to cover the cost of his return to Florida.

In August, the vestry extended a call to Rev. Charles C. Fishburne who declined the offer as did Rev. George Purnell Gunn from Norfolk.

However, Gunn sent Daniel Huger a very favorable letter of recommendation praising Rev. Marshall Travers of Prescott, Arizona, who was then visiting in Alexandria, Virginia. He wrote, "Travers is one of the finest fellows I have ever known. He is genuine, and his character is appealing, sincere, and truly Christian … He is a good preacher, and an exceptional pastor. He has been greatly beloved wherever he has been …His family consists of one child, a lovely little girl, and his wife is not only pretty, but also a very interested and helpful Minister's wife."

Since Travers was in Virginia, it was decided to call Travers "over long distance" and explain they could not at this time extend a call but wanted to invite him to come to Charleston to meet with the vestry. It so happened that his brother-in-law was Vestryman Charles S. Dwight who spoke with him on the phone. Travers agreed to come. Remember St. Philip's had not had a full time rector since August, 1941.

In October 1942, Ben Scott Whaley accepted the chairmanship of the Every Man Canvass and he also extended a call to Travers. Travers accepted and would start on December 1. The wardens asked Travers if he could arrive in time to perform the loyalty Sunday service on November 29 because it was the kickoff date of the Every Man Canvas. Travers agreed to come. The vestry than asked if he would also do the 8:00 a.m. service as well.

The vestry decided to purchase 2000 series G war bonds for the churchyard fund.

REV. MARSHALL EDWARD TRAVERS

RECTOR OF ST. PHILIP'S

DECEMBER 1, 1942 – OCTOBER 15, 1956

We thank Mrs. Harriet Travers Yarborough, the daughter of Rev. Marshall Travers and his wife, Harriet Dwight Travers, for sharing newspaper clippings, letters and other items concerning her family. Harriet and her husband, Joseph, in 2012, live on the Isle of Palms.

The Rev. Marshall E. Travers was born May 16, 1904, in Alexandria. In 1922, when he was eighteen he trained for one month with the Citizens Military Training under the auspices of the War Department at Camp Meade, Maryland. He successfully completed the "RED" course of instruction that made him a member of the reserves. He received his A.B. degree from William and Mary College and his B.D. degree from the Virginia Theological Seminary. In 1930, Travers married Miss Harriet Singleton Dwight, the daughter of Mr. and Mrs. Francis Marion Dwight, Jr. of Stateburg. The same year, Travers, who was ordained by the Rt. Rev. A.C. Thompson, bishop of the southern diocese of Virginia, began serving churches in that state. He also studied at Oxford University in England in the spring of 1952.

In 1936, Travers went on a visit to Arizona with the idea of doing mission work. The members of St. Luke's Episcopal Church in Prescott became interested in him and a call came forth that he accepted. He began on January 1, 1937.

Travers made a list, "In case you have not heard of the various calamities which befell us upon our advent into Arizona." Because of severe weather and the heaviest snow on record, they had to spend several days in Phoenix. Travers had to take the train to Prescott to make Sunday service and take the train back to Phoenix to drive Harriet and little Harriet to Prescott. They experienced a temperature of 21 degrees below zero and all got sick. Travers slipped on ice and wrenched his back which kept him out of action for a few days. Because of work on the rectory and the severe cold, they were delayed moving into the rectory for a month. During that month, they had to share an apartment including the bathroom, living room and dining room with two men. On their first Sunday when the three of them went to services, the church nearly "burnt up." Then some of their belongings were ruined when a record breaking twenty-four hour, four-inch rain flooded the basement of their living quarters.

Travers joined the Prescott Rotary Club and when he was departing in 1942 the president of the club wrote a nice letter, "I am sure that if each member of our club had the opportunity to voice individual feelings, you would know that the fellows will long remember Marshall Travers and the contribution which he has made, not alone to our club but to all religious and civic matters of our community."

While Travers was in Prescott organizing his departure, he received many letters welcoming him to St. Philip's and offering advice. A letter written before he accepted the St. Philip's call was sent from the wardens, John Laurens and J. Stanyarne Stevens, hoping that he would accept the call. They also advised him the salary was $4,000 per year and that the rector and his family also had use of the rectory. Travers had seen the rectory. They added that St. Philip's did not provide furniture for the rectory nor were utilities provided.

"JCG" who lived in Tucson wrote Travers, "you have told us with a southern accent, that you always wanted to return to the South, but we will surely miss you Mr. Travers … We miss the rationality and human-ness which you invariably give your sermons … thanks for being such a swell egg with the youth and the guidance you have given us since the war started, and for everything else …If you see Joe Trott tell him hello for us." Joe Trott was Harriet Travers first cousin.

Susanna Mazyck wrote that a stranger is not coming to St. Philip's because we know Ida Dwight and Harriet (Travers) who probably wouldn't remember me from Confederate College days. She wanted to tell Travers they were ready to give him a very warm welcome.

St. Philip's organist, Miss Bollwinkle, wrote a letter of welcome stating that "the choir is a fine group and they love to sing. I know you will enjoy working with them. Our choir rehearses every Friday evening at 8 o'clock in the parish hall but please come whenever you wish and please add any suggestions you have."

The Charleston clergy, as suggested by Mayers, sent a letter of welcome to Travers.

Miss Pressley Walsh wrote to Travers that even though Mayers was employed as interim rector, she had felt the responsibility of having to run the church. She was very glad that Travers was coming and was looking forward to having a new boss. She felt God was sending him to St. Philip's. She did have one request and that was if she could leave some of her furniture in the rectory because she had no other place to store it. Rev. Mayers, who was living in the rectory, also had some furniture in the rectory which Travers was welcome to have. She said, "Tell Mrs. Travers I think she will like living in the Rectory in spite of its size."

Later, Miss Walsh wrote Travers that the people who loaned Mayers furniture would take it back but Mrs. Stevens will be leaving a living room table, some chairs and pictures. There is another lady, who was in hospital, who left some furniture in the living room but they had not been able to find out what she would do with it. Miss Walsh was also leaving some chairs and bedroom furniture. There was a bed but her mother had taken the mattress, so Travers would have to purchase a mattress to use the bed. Miss Walsh also had an ivory bureau and there was a very nice dining room table and secretary in the rectory that was owned by the parish, leaving them with the dining room table and a mixture of furniture which could be removed whenever by whomever.

Miss Walsh, who waited for her fiancée to return from the war, would leave St. Philip's in July 1946 because they were getting married. The vestry wrote a nice thank you saying she had been at St. Philip's since September 1, 1937, and had served the church, the Sunday school, the church home and the parish at large faithfully and devotedly. The church gave her a $100 wedding present.

CHURCH SERVICES, MEMBERSHIP & CLERGY

In 1943, there were 720 members of St. Philip's. Travers at St. Philip's would serve under two bishops: Rt. Rev. Albert Sidney Thomas who resigned on December 31, 1943, and Thomas Neely Carruthers who was consecrated as bishop of the diocese of South Carolina on May 4, 1944, at St. Philip's. Carruthers died in 1960.

In May 1943, men were being trained as ushers under the guidance of I. Mayo Read, Sr. who was chairman of that committee. In 1945, there was an early mention of a lay reader, Lawrence W. Barrett, who received a letter thanking him for having recently read.

DICK REEVES

Harold Sloane Reeves, who had been elected to the vestry in January, was known to everyone as "Dick." Everyone loved his Gullah talks and his thirty three and a third records were filled with wonderful stories. He autographed his 1963 record, *Gullah: A Breath of the Carolina Low Country,* at Legertons on King Street. Reeves gave a sample of the Gullah language, "Uh too glad yuh kin yeddy wha uh hab fo' say." Translation: "I'm so glad you can hear what I have to say."

At that time, Gullah was beginning to fade into the past. Dick Reeves and the Society for the Preservation of Spirituals, part of its membership being

St. Philippian's, led the way to keep the language from dying. In 2012, the term Gullah now encompasses people, as well as the language and a Gullah festival is held annually in Beaufort and at nearby Penn Center on St. Helena's Island.

Reeves and his wife, Roberta, lived at 24 New Street and his work title was "Manager, United States Department of Health Education and Welfare and Social Security Administration." Dick, a member of the St. Cecelia Society, died in 1972 and was buried in the western churchyard.

REV. A. CAMPBELL TUCKER

ASSISTANT RECTOR

APRIL 21 1947 – SEPTEMBER 1, 1950

In 1947, the vestry discussed having an assistant and they invited the Rev. A. Campbell Tucker to preach at St. Philip's on April 20. The next day the vestry called him and offered him an annual salary of $3,000 and residency in 14 Glebe Street which was owned by St. Philip's. Tucker accepted. In June, they offered to pay Tucker his moving expenses. They soon changed their minds and told Tucker that because 14 Glebe Street had been abandoned there would be "excessive costs" to restore the property. They said the property was not particularly desirable for residential purposes.

The vestry then decided to investigate the legal right to convert certain rooms on the lower floor of the church home into an apartment for the use of the assistant minister and his family. That idea did not come up again.

The vestry secretary wrote a thank you letter to Ernest Pringle for his kindness and generosity for furnishing quarters for the Tucker family while they waited for their new home. The vestry authorized paying a monthly rent of $85.00 to Rudolph F. Momeier for the Tuckers new home at 67 South Battery. The vestry paid $210 to have the upstairs painted.

Tucker was from Ashland, Virginia, and graduated from the Episcopal Theological Seminary on May 23, 1923. He was probably close in age to Travers. From 1923 to 1947 we only know two of his assignments: Johns Memorial Episcopal Church in

Farmville, Virginia, from 1934 to 1941 and St. John's Episcopal Church in Halifax, Virginia, from 1945 to 1946. He may have served missions as well.

As stated, Tucker was the first assistant minister at St. Philip's since 1871.

✛ ✛ ✛

The annual report showed attendance at congregational meetings ranging from sixty-five to eighty-five. Then attendance in December 1948 dropped further because of a conflict with the annual meeting of the St. Andrew's Society. "In this connection, there is a large reservoir of men who if they would make up their minds to attend the congregational meeting – could and would do so. An attendance of 100 to 125 would not be out of line with the present membership of the church."

The St. Andrew's Society, Charleston's oldest society (1732), was founded to help Scottish immigrants who were in need. The St. Andrew's Society which proudly leads the annual June 28 Carolina Day parade, does not require a member to be Scottish, but there is a waiting list of about twenty years. The annual meeting is held on St. Andrew's Day, November 30, unless that is a Sunday.

In 1946, the vestry minutes reported that the processional cross fell and it was bent and otherwise damaged. It was to be repaired. It was not the only time. St. Philippian E. DuBose Blakeney III remembers dropping the processional cross as an altar boy when he was twelve in 1949. Blakeney left Charleston for many years and when he returned he noticed the cross had the same dent in it.

In 1948, there were forty-four baptisms, 132 communion services, 163 services without communion, fifty-one confirmations, ten marriages and fourteen burials. There were more than 200 enrolled in the church school. Tucker recommended strong support for the church school. In 1949, there were 1,016 communicants at St. Philip's.

Thomas Huguenin asked what could be done to prevent the interruption of services by tours and tourists. Travers, the senior warden and Carlton Davies reported they had spoken to the Gray Line authorities.

Robert Lovell Oliveros was certified for the deaconate on May 22, 1949.

Because the vestry decided the congregations of St. Philip's and St. Michael's were too large for joint services, they decided on June 27, 1949 to end the old system of combining worship with St. Michael's for two months during the summer.

Some new ideas were discussed in 1950. Senior Warden Dr. Henry Clay Robertson, Jr., proposed to the boys or men after taking up the collection in the balconies that they walk up the aisle and present the offering. It was approved. There was a discussion of obtaining additional ushers, other than vestrymen. In November 1951, Robertson responded to a letter from Peter Haidet, chairman of the YPSL, who volunteered a dozen members of the YPSL as junior ushers and Mrs. J. Heyward Furman also had a list of twelve junior ushers.

TUCKER DEPARTS

Although Tucker announced his resignation on June 28, 1950, he was paid for August as a vacation month. He officially left St. Philip's on September 1. The vestry passed a resolution stating that he had served faithfully and that he had endeared himself to the congregation and the community. He had accepted a call from Woodstock, Virginia.

On August 5, 1950, Tucker wrote Senior Warden Ben Scott Whaley thanking the people of St. Philip's for their kindness. He wrote, "You all have been grand to us right from the day of our arrival in Charleston and we appreciate it more than you ever realize. You have always been more than generous and your gifts and good wishes lavished upon us at our departure are evidence of your natural graciousness. The vestry gave him a "handsome pitcher" with appropriate engraving and a wallet with a hundred dollar bill enclosed. William Porter Cart of Cart Jewelry Store on King Street engraved the pitcher at no charge and he donated the wallet. There was also a farewell reception.

Tucker added they had arrived safely and had found the work quite interesting. The weather was chilly and they were sleeping under blankets. They felt a bit strange to be back in Virginia for they had all come to love Charleston and St. Philip's. "Yours is the friendliest parish we have ever lived in." He signed "Yours faithfully, A. Campbell Tucker."

The letterhead was from Shrine Mont in Orkney Springs, Virginia.

REV. JAMES STONEY

ASSISTANT RECTOR

SEPTEMBER 25, 1950 – SEPTEMBER 6, 1952

In September, Travers said there was general satisfaction throughout the parish with the work of the Rev. Mr. James Stoney, who had been acting as supply minister.

Travers nominated him as assistant rector. J. Ross Hanahan moved that Stoney be hired at an annual salary of $3,000, a $300 yearly automobile allowance plus expenses for living quarters. Thirty dollars were also given to Stoney for moving expenses. He began his job as assistant rector on September 25, 1950. Stoney was invited to vestry meetings and he would often give the opening prayer and benediction. He received a raise of $30.00 per month that was effective June 1, 1951. Rev. James Stoney resigned effective September 6, 1952. The vestry accepted his resignation with regret and with appreciation for the work he did at St. Philip's.

The 161st annual diocesan convention was held at St. Philip's on April 10, 1951. At the convention, Bishop Carruthers wanted the delegates to give serious consideration to clergy stipends by distributing his talk to churches throughout the diocese.

Carruthers said, "The clergy are expected to maintain a certain standard of living. They are expected to support every worthy community cause and are obliged to operate a car that in-it-self is a terrific expense, almost the equivalent of an average clergy salary twenty-five years ago. Yet, they are called 'materialistic' and 'mercenary' if they bring up the matter of money."

Carruthers continued that a clergyman, who in 1940 made $2,000, should make $3,600 in 1950. He said the clergyman who made $4,000 in 1940 should make $7,200 in 1950. Clergy salaries generally have not been advanced in anything like this proportion and he said that salaries have not been increased to meet the rising cost of living. Carruthers wanted to lay this whole problem upon the vestries and the department of Missions of the diocese. As previously stated, Travers' salary was $5,000 in 1946.

In November 1952, Travers asked, "that when possible the seats in the rear of the Church be saved for late comers." An anonymous letter writer suggested something be done about the excess noise caused by people leaving the balcony during communion service. The congregation decided the balcony should not be used by people intending to take communion or to leave the service early. The problem was finally solved in 1977 when anonymous donors carpeted the balcony steps and aisles. It was said, "The entrance into and the exodus out of the balcony was unbelievably calm."

Mrs. Charlotte Dozier Valdiva remembers that in the early 1950s Travers would sometimes visit with her Catholic grandparents, Mr. and Mrs. Jesse Murphy (Alfrieda), at 129 Church Street and have a glass of wine. Jesse Murphy was a night watchman at the States Ports Authority. Valdiva and her mother, Mrs. Mary A. Dozier's, lived with the Murphy's. Valdiva's mother, who was a faithful member of St. Philip's, was a sales woman at W.T. Grant.

Valdiva remembers that at that time the neighborhood children were allowed to play in the Dock Street Theater. Its janitor, Joe Freeman, would hire one or two horse carriages twice a year to take the children for a ride and buy them ice cream. Freeman's wife, Alice, had the Freeman Grocery on Drake Street.

There was a movement in the congregation that a new assistant minister should not be hired. Tom Myers and Travers received a number of letters and phone calls – most of which were against hiring a new assistant. Even so, the vestry continued to attempt to find and call an assistant.

Cotesworth Means weighed in with his opinion that he was against hiring an assistant. He wrote, "Our vestry regularly cries poor mouth these days and tell us no money is available for improvements. We began running into debt when we indulged in the luxury of an Assistant Rector and we have spent between $20,000 and $30,000 for this purpose in the last five or six years." Means believed there were enough members of St. Philip's to lovingly do the work that an assistant would do and do it far more effectively than any paid employee could.

Means wrote, "Can it be possible that St. Philip's – mother church of the Carolinas – which has the most dilapidated, run-down, inadequate, makeshift, obsolete, 'poor-white trash' accommodations for housing, (the choir)[13] ... It is discouraging and depressing to watch all the financial benefits of the good work contributed by choirs and music disappearing down the rat hole of an unnecessary position."

---

13 Means wanted rooms where the clergy could put on their robes.

REV. WADDELL F. ROBEY

ASSISTANT RECTOR

MARCH 2, 1953 – MAY 3, 1957

Tom Myers and Heyward Furman flew to Atlanta in September or October 1952 to meet and hear the Reverend Waddell F. Robey at the Church of the Epiphany. The plane was late and they missed Robey's sermon but they spoke with church members at the coffee afterwards and found he had built up the membership and that he was especially good with the youth. Myers and Furman were favorably impressed with Robey. Other candidates were considered including the Rev. Robert L. Oliveros who was in Cheraw.

On January 5, 1953, Travers announced to the vestry that Robey had accepted the call as associate rector. The vestry offered him an annual salary of $3,700 and then the vestry voted to give Travers and Robey each a $400 automobile allowance. They also agreed to spend $328 to paint the inside of the South Battery rectory prior to Robey's arrival. Robey was on the job by March 2, 1953, when he attended the vestry meeting and gave the opening prayer.

The vestry in September 1953 voted to pay an additional $1,250 from the Haig Fund for Mrs. Robey's medical expenses. Because Mrs. Robey could not climb steps, the vestry decided to build a bathroom onto the back of the ground floor of 67 South Battery. G.M. Canady of the Canady Construction Co. did the work for $1,155. Momeier donated $400, Robey paid $377.50 and St. Philip's paid up to $380.

At the annual congregational meeting that was held on Wednesday, January 13, 1954, Travers reported there had been 322 services held in 1953. He reminded the members that in the last ten years St. Philip's had sent seven men into the ministry and he challenged the congregation with the responsibility of bringing new people to St. Philip's.

Mrs. F. Bartow Culp supervised the Sunday school and J. North Moore was in charge of the men. Ben Scott Whaley spoke of the desperate need Porter Military Academy had for funds. He asked the congregation to appropriate $1,200 for Porter and for each communicant to pledge $2.00 for the next five years. The motion passed unanimously.

F. Bartow Culp, who was a chemistry professor at the Medical College of South Carolina, requested his fellow vestrymen to attend a service Tuesday, May 4, 1954, at 8:00 p.m. to commemorate the tenth anniversary of Bishop Carruthers' episcopate.

The vestry in June 1955 notified Travers that upon his return to Charleston he would be granted a thirty day leave of absence effective June 9. The vestry wanted Travers to go to the Duke University clinic immediately to undergo physical examinations to determine if he could perform his duties. The vestry would pay up to $500 to cover the medical bills. Travers did have a heart attack prior to his departure from St. Philip's.

The vestry on May 1, 1956, gave Travers a $400 salary increase and $1,000 to Robey. In August 1955, the vestry voted to give Travers $100 to help him meet his expenses while attending a convention in Hawaii.

THE YOUTH, LAYMAN'S LEAGUE AND THE LADIES

Mrs. Christopher G. Howe in 1943 received permission to write a brief history of the church providing there was no cost to the parish. It was suggested there be a pre-publishing subscription offer. In 1948, the vestry changed its decision and paid $145 for 600 copies of Mrs. Howe's 2 ½ page *A History of St. Philip's Church*.

Mrs. Howe wrote that John Quincy of Boston, who worshipped at St. Philip's, was very surprised that the sermon was only twenty minutes. Mrs. Howe ended her history, "It has been said that the History of Rome was written from gravestones, and should all other records of Charleston be lost, the history of Charleston might be written from the inscriptions on the tombs in old St. Philip's." In 1963, Rufus Barkley wanted to have Mrs. Howe's history reprinted. In 2012, there is a framed copy of part of her history in the narthex under Mrs. Heyward's memorial.

In the same year, the vestry agreed to rent the gymnasium to Porter Military Academy for basketball practice for a period of sixty days at a rental of $100 per month.

Senior Warden Stanyarne Stevens read the 1943 annual report to the congregation. He could not say too much for the Women's Auxiliary … and that there would not be a St.

Philip's without the auxiliary … he would strike out the word auxiliary entirely. "They were not an auxiliary of the church, they are the church."

Stanyarne said Sunday school enrollment shrank from 200 to 127 blaming the parents for not wanting to make the effort to bring their children. He also took on the men, urging them to take an interest in the work of the parish. He believed that if the church got its manpower behind it, this old parish would again take the lead and top place in the diocese that rightfully belongs to her.

Former vestryman Dr. Robertson in 1944 was in the military and his wife, Elizabeth, "Lib," wanted to rent the St. Philip's gymnasium for a dancing school. Even though Mrs. Robertson's request was declined, her dancing school was established in 1947 using the ground floor of the Hiberian Hall. St. Philippian Llewellyn Kassebaum was in that first class. Mrs. Robertson became partners with Mrs. Emily Whaley, wife of Vestryman Ben Scott Whaley and they taught fourth through eighth graders. By 1950, they were teaching at the South Carolina Society Hall where the classes remain in 2012. It was first called the Junior Cotillion and later The Cotillion where ball room dancing, square dancing and the shag were taught. The girls still wear white gloves and the young men wear a blazer and tie. Later, Mrs. Whaley's daughter, Mrs. Grant D. Whipple (Emily or Miss Em) took over. Mrs. James M. Ravenel (Elizabeth), Mrs. Robertson's niece, and Mrs. William C. Helm (Moonee), Mrs. Whaley's niece, assisted. Many of their current students are third generation attendees.

Vestry secretary, J. Heyward Furman, Jr. wrote a thank you letter in 1945 to Miss Caroline L. Porcher, who lived in Columbia, for a gift of pictures and records entitled *"A History of St. Philip's Church and its Silver."*

The vestry permitted the youth of Holy Communion Church to use the parish house's basketball court from 3:00 p.m. for an hour at no charge. St. Philip's agreed to sponsor a Cub Pack of Boy Scouts that Mrs. McCullough had been assisting.

In February 1949, the idea of a week day Sunday school was approved and the name changed to the "Daily Bible School." The Women's Auxiliary sent a letter to the vestry supporting the idea – Mrs. Walter Pringle, Jr. offered to teach for free.

Mrs. Coming B. Gibbs, president of the Women's Auxiliary, requested the vestry hire a hostess to be in charge of certain activities in the parish house and playground. Gibbs said the salary should be $100 per month for the next five months and the auxiliary would pay half of the salary. In September 1950, Miss Sarah Bailey Hood was hired as secretary-hostess at $125 per month of which the Colonial Dames would pay $30.00 per month.

In 1948, the ladies were very active and had a large membership of 453 members. Eighty-three were members of St. Martha's chapter, composed of the youngest women, and forty-three were members of the business women's group, St. Columba's chapter. The remainder, 327 members, belonged to the auxiliary. Their money was raised from voluntary contributions from all the women in the church and from money making projects such as tours. They raised $2,386.30 for the year and spent $2,251.30 for missions, York orphanage and other causes. They prepared and served the men's monthly suppers with an average attendance of ninety men.

The ladies distributed clothing and shoes to some thirty individuals, including Europeans in three countries. They sent Thanksgiving and Christmas baskets to the church home, the city home on Columbus Street and made visits to the women in the county jail where the "inmates" were given gifts of clothing, cigarettes and magazines. From winter through spring, volunteers would visit the "inmates" at the Florence Crittenton Home where they taught to sew. Fifty-four garments were completed. One member made monthly visits to the "colored female" ward at Pinehaven, the tuberculosis sanatorium, and gave gifts of clothing, toilet articles and materials for "fancy work." The report was given by Mrs. Thomas P. White, Jr.

The Young Couples Group, headed by Cadwallader Jones, had a twofold purpose: to provide Christian fellowship and to make friends with newcomers. Although there was no charge for the monthly covered dish meals, a fifteen cent donation was requested to cover expenses. After each meeting ping pong, shuffleboard, billiards and bridge kept members entertained until around 10 p.m.

On January 10, 1949, Mrs. E. DuBose Blakeney, Jr. (Frances) who was the chairman of the altar guild, wrote a letter to vestry about acquiring a competent sexton.

She said that the ladies of the guild were well aware of the situation because each day one or two of the members were in the church polishing brass and silver, "preparing Holy Communion" or arranging flowers for the Sunday service. "Most of you are not possibly aware that the aged sexton's mind is gone. He wanders through the church and grounds, wants to light the heaters when there is no service, and apparently has no idea of the day or time – and certainly remembers none of us."

The sexton's fourteen-year old son helped out after school. Because of the size of the church, the guild felt the young man did the best he could but what was needed was a full time reliable sexton. Blakeney wrote, "The brass litany bench has not been polished for weeks; I personally scrubbed the floor of the sanctuary two weeks ago, as I could bear the dirt no longer." She said there was no one to help with the heavy lifting that was required for decorating the church for weddings and other duties.

The letter continued, "In view of the fact that the sexton's condition is mental as well as physical, we do not think he should be discharged without some arrangement whereby he could be assisted in obtaining support, possibly in part from St. Philip's funds, and/or in conjunction with aid from some charitable institution" … "we hope that a satisfactory arrangement will be found in a short time in order that the present condition will not exist for an indefinite length of time, as it did in a similar situation some ten years ago."

On April 3, 1950, almost a year and half after Mrs. Blakeney wrote her letter, senior warden Whaley read a report about the sexton's problems to the vestry. Dr. Robertson also reported the state hospital said the sexton's condition was poor and he needed to stay longer in that institution. John E. Gibbs, secretary, was instructed to write to the sexton's wife to inform her the church needed to hire a "new and efficient sexton."

After three people were interviewed for the sexton's job, Joseph Kinloch was chosen for a temporary ninety-day trial period, but only a month later he was working out satisfactorily. The wife of the former sexton found a new house in July.

Kinloch quit by December 1950 and James Hamilton was hired at the same salary. The vestry voted to give the sexton $10.00 extra for Christmas and $5.00 to each of the other "colored help." The senior warden said he thought Hamilton was leaving because no self-respecting "colored man" was going to live in the current accommodations under extremely poor conditions. They decided to offer the sexton a raise to $125 a month. The vestry in March 1951 wanted two estimates to repair the sexton's house – one for bare essentials and one for a complete first class repair. They chose the first class repair.

In September 1951, the repair work was completed at a cost of $1,663.90 and the house at 9 Cumberland Street was ready for occupancy. They repaired the buckling brick wall on Philadelphia "Street," and broken windows and doors. Floors, windows, doors and locks were replaced. Gas outlets were placed in each room and the wiring was replaced. The door and window screens were made with copper. There were twenty-three items on the list to be fixed. The remodeling placated James Hamilton and he and his wife, Agnes, moved into 9 Cumberland Street. Hamilton remained St. Philip's sexton until the vestry notified him on February 12, 1962, they were actively looking for a replacement.

In 1950, the vestry allowed H.L. Matthews (Matty) to use the gymnasium for boxing lessons for eighteen sessions providing he would pay for upkeep, hot water and wear and tear. In 1953, Matthews gave the church $30.00. The vestry renewed Matty's contract every year until 1955 when he chose to move to a different location. In February 1967, the vestry approved Matty's request to use the small building on the Cumberland Street lot for boxing classes.

The Women's Auxiliary owed $500 from the 1950 budget. Vestryman Douglas Wilkinson suggested "the problem be solved on the best possible basis consistent with peace and harmony." Vestryman Thomas A. Huguenin suggested that the vestry set fixed expenses for linens, wine, wafers, laundry, vestments, etc. Wilkinson felt that giving the auxiliary a fixed sum would result in "fewer petty irritations and less confusion."

In February 1951, Miss Carolyn Carpenter of 96 South Battery asked for a raise. She said she was most privileged to have worked for the last four years as a secretary at St. Philip's with such a fine group of people but her $125 per month salary had not been raised in the entire time she had been there. In August, she gave her letter of resignation effective October 1. It was pointed out that since Miss Carpenter had not had a vacation, she would be paid until October 15.

Roy Wooten received permission from the vestry in February 1952 to rent the parish house one night a week for the Civil Air Patrol. They could not conflict with any other activity and had to pay $3.00 per night to cover utilities, etc.

The vestry approved having a book display in the vestibule (narthex) but nothing could be sold in the church. However, order blanks were available.

THE SHELL SHOP

By 1934, Mr. and Mrs. William Pringle Hume (Millicent B.) had moved into the little building on Queen Street just east of the church home where they lived and sold shells hence the name of the building – the Shell Shop. They stayed there at least sixteen years and by 1950 they moved into the Confederate Home at 62 Broad Street but Mrs. Hume still sold shells from the Shell Shop. In 1951, their annual rent was $120.

The Women's Auxiliary asked Mrs. Hume in May 1952 to vacate the building because the ladies were going to use the Shell Shop for the work of the church. The vestry agreed and the vestry secretary was instructed to wait a reasonable length of time before giving Mrs. Hume notice because of the recent death of her husband. Even though Tom Myers did not give Mrs. Hume notice until September 20, Mrs. Hume had not moved by February 1953. Vestryman W.I. Holt was asked to notify Mrs. Hume that she had to move by the end of February because the ladies were going to start renovating the building in March. The women would pay a rent of $10.00 per month to the vestry and they agreed to keep the building in good condition and make any necessary repairs. In April 1953, Travers reported that the Shell Shop had been vacated and the auxiliary should begin paying the same rent

as the Humes paid. The ladies got the vestry to pay for repairing the roof and gutters and painting the outside.

At some time, George DeMerell sold handsome three panel screens decorated with classic Audubon prints and other similar motifs from this small building.

Later, the name of the building was changed to the tea garden where in 2012 photographs of the church's rectors and assistant rectors hang on the paneled walls.

The women of the auxiliary put together a house tour that took place on Saturday March 14, 1953. Those who were going on the tour assembled at the church and would travel in five groups of ten cars each. The ladies asked the police to keep ten parking places free in front of these houses: the rectory at 92 Church Street, 83 Church Street, 39 Church Street, 19 Archdale Street, 83 East Bay Street, 15 Meeting Street and 32 South Battery, the home of Ashmead and Helen Pringle, where tea was served.

In October 1953, the young ladies of Ashley Hall were once again invited to worship at St. Philip's. They were specifically invited to take part in the teenage discussion group that began at 10:20 a.m. on Sunday mornings. They were also invited to sing in the choir at the 11:45 a.m. service.

F. Bartow Culp was appointed parish keyman in December 1953 replacing Edward S. Bullock. Culp resigned his position in 1956. He said his greatest efforts were directed towards the attendance at the "Men's Advent Corporate Communion and Breakfast." The attendance was the largest ever. He also enjoyed establishing a schedule for parish boys ushering at the family service at 9:30 a.m. James Gibbs replaced Culp.

In December 1953, Miss Catherine Oliver, who was a student at the High School of Charleston, was chairman of a committee to raise funds for scholarships to send young men to the Youth Festival that was held in the parish house on December 5. Later, she would be better known as Madame Jones because she taught French at Ashley Hall. In 2012, she remains a member of the choir, the vestry, the Church Street Mission and many other church activities. Catherine married Harry D. Jones and they had three lovely daughters.

Mrs. W.A. Dotterer received permission in 1954 from the vestry to open a kindergarten at St. Philip's. She required a minimum of twenty children and no more than thirty. The registration fee was $6.00 and the monthly fee $12.50. Children of St. Philippian's would be contacted first.

Senior Warden William B. Ellison in October 4, 1954, gave Mrs. Dotterer guidelines for the new kindergarten. The vestry declared that the rectors and wardens were trustees of the kindergarten and that religious instruction would be taught daily. Other requirements were: no more than thirty-five children, Mrs. Dotterer had to obtain liability insurance and pay $40.00 per month rent that did not include utilities or use of the "icebox." Janitor service was not included. In November, Travers reported that the new kindergarten seemed to be doing very well.

The vestry continued to renew Mrs. Dotterer's contract each year through the 1964/65 school year when there were thirty-two children.

In 1955, Mrs. Bartow Culp was in charge of the Sunday school, Mrs. David Maybank was head of the Women's Auxiliary, Wallace Walker was head of the YPSL and J. North Moore headed the men.

St. Philippian's visting Kanuga c. late 1990's

THEOLOGY, EVANGELISM AND MISSIONS

Again, one should not draw too many conclusions about one's theology from one article and one sermon. When Travers lived in Prescott, Arizona, he wrote an article for its newspaper. The headline read:

**Prescott Rector Tells Traditions
Of the Protestant Episcopal Church
By Rev. Marshall E. Travers**

"The Episcopal Church is an extremely broad church. It embodies within its bounds individuals whose beliefs range from Methodism to Roman Catholicism ...Today, the church emphasizes that there are only two sacraments that are necessary for salvation, they are Baptism and Holy Communion. In its teachings the Episcopal Church sets forth, through the guidance of the Holy Spirit that which it thinks best for the spiritual growth of its people. It does not say you have to conform to these moral values, but for your richest and best development you will wish to obey."

Travers continued, "In keeping with our Lord's command: 'Go ye, therefore, and teach all the nations,' the church has placed a great deal of emphasis on the missionary work … Believing that all events in the life of Christ should be emphasized and not just one or two important ones, the church through the Prayer Book observes the Christian year … Believing that true knowledge can never run counter to true religion, the church welcomes every sincere effort of science and learning … The church stresses the words, 'I am the Resurrection and the Life' this comforting the sorrowful and the bereaved, painting the way to spiritual fellowship in the Great Beyond."

He closed, "The churchman realizes his own shortcomings, therefore he seeks the teaching of the church that he might be strengthened and comforted through the sacraments. He realizes still further, that the 'Good news' as stressed by the church, is not only to be emphasized in home and community but in the nation and the world."

The *News and Courier* had a series called *Sunday's Sermons*. On November 1, 1944, the paper covered Travers' previous day sermon. The headline read, "Man Needs Redemptive Power of God, Mr. Travers Asserts." Travers urged his listeners to consider the questions of why the need of God and what God has to offer them.

He said, "We need God because he is our Creator, the omnipotent authority … we cannot live without him … He holds within his hands the very destinies of our lives. We need God because of our multitudinous sins … When we take inventory we really discover that we have fallen short of the Christ-like life. However, as long as we have not turned our backs on Him, as the source of all goodness, there is pardon for us … sin not only hurts us, it hurts God as well. Yet, His very nature is to forgive the penitent soul … If we would be all that He has created us to be, we certainly need Him to fulfill that destiny."

"In our creed, we learn that God created us, redeemed and sanctified us … man was made in God's image and God has not only supplied man with his physical needs but enabled him to know the difference between good and evil. He has called us His own children."

Travers continued, "… it was necessary for God to send His own son into the world to redeem man. Through His teachings, miracles, parables and examples, Jesus showed us how to become the sons of God. Once departed from earth, Christ did not leave man defenseless but sent us the power of the Holy Spirit which sanctifies us and enables us to live as children of God. It is the invisible power of the Holy Spirit which enables us to prepare ourselves for life beyond the grave."

"Jesus died for all mankind," Travers said, "and that means freedom from sin and the beginning of a new life. As one goes from historical and theological aspects and thinks from an existential fact, he obtains the essence of The Gospels. The important fact is that he died for me. The cross is not only an event of the past but something I experience now. Paul said 'I die daily' and 'I am risen with Christ.'"

Travers concluded, "We cannot redeem ourselves by our own efforts but through the effectual working of the Cross of Christ. Salvation comes from outside ourselves. The Gospel is the Cross plus resurrection … As we journey through life, may we realize that we do need the redemptive power of God and that He has revealed that power in Christ and once we have comprehended that fundamental truth, endeavor to live in the spirit of the Christ."

Prior to entering St. Philip's, two candid comments were made to Travers.

The first was a letter written by Cotesworth P. Means to Travers on November 16, 1942, while Travers was still in Prescott.

Means said "they were pleased that a man 'of your type' was coming to St. Philip's and that they had missed not having a regular rector for a year and a half. You are coming to St. Philip's with a favorable psychological condition because the congregation will be so glad to have a regular rector again and they will be more disposed to help you succeed than they would normally be."

Means continued, "Our parish has one splendid fact in its favor, which is that there is no division of sentiment or feeling on any subject such as too often spoils the effectiveness of a congregation. There are no cliques or factions and no particular controversial factors."

"On the other side of the ledger," Means wrote, "you will find a great deal of ignorance and indifference, amounting almost to lethargy, and your hardest problem will be to arouse and maintain living interest in the facts and affairs of our Church. Even the vestry know little about the Bible and church history, but everyone is quite honest and frank about our ignorance and taken all together the atmosphere of the parish is wholesome and pleasant even though it may not be intellectual or spiritually inspired."

Note: C. FitzSimons Allison, bishop of the diocese of South Carolina from 1980 to 1990, said at that time Rev. Richard Dority, rector of St. James on James Island, had an early Bible study. Dority ran into opposition by some of the congregation so he left the church and took part of the congregation with him. But in 1955 there was a successful adult Bible class St. Philip's that was led by Cadwallader (Quaddy) Jones at St. Philip's.

The second candid view of St. Philip's was from Alexander C. Zabriskie, dean of the Virginia Theological Seminary and a friend of FitzSimons Allison. Zabriskie wrote a letter to Travers while he was still in Prescott congratulating him on his appointment.

Zabriskie stated, "I have twice visited Charleston and have gotten some impression of St. Philip's, that the rector of that parish could do a great work. I don't mean to imply that I have preached there and know it from that angle, but simply that I have gone there as a visitor. The Church building impressed me. There seem to be folk in the congregation of intelligence and force. It looked like a group which, given proper leadership, could really make Christianity count for something in their community."

In 1943, Travers read a letter to the vestry from the rector of "Pawley's Island Holy Cross and Faith Memorial Colored Church" soliciting funds to rebuild a church which had been recently destroyed by fire.

Sometime later, the Pawley's Island congregation raised $4,000 toward rebuilding.

Other funds came from the diocese and the national church that enabled a new church to be built in 1953. Bishop Thomas wrote, "a great step forward was taken in the Archdeaconry when Bishop Carruthers notified the national council that the diocese of South Carolina would financially aid black churches in the future and would no longer need help from the national church."

During World War II, St. Philippians tried to accommodate the needs of the military personnel. In April 1943, the vestry gave approval for the use of the service room by naval officer's wives. At the same time, the receipts from the collection of "The Crucifixion," after the payment of expenses, were $129.91 that was donated to the Army and Navy Relief. In September 1943, the vestry granted permission to the Charleston County Board of Public Welfare to operate the service men's room in the parish house where the committee placed envelopes in that room for contributions to maintain its operation.

In 1944, the vestry requested the Recreation Department of the Charleston County Board of Public Welfare to pay the additional bills for electricity, gas, etc. used by the service men's room. The vestry also requested from the same board that they pay the entire cost of the use of electricity and heat rather than the 5/7 basis proposed by the board for the reading room. In April 1945, the church agreed to place envelopes in the church for the benefit of the Army and Navy Commission at an upcoming service. After the County Recreation Center advised they would cease funding the St. Philip's service men's room as of July 1, the vestry decided to close the room for the summer but the telephone would be kept.

The Junior League of Charleston in 1947 received permission from the vestry to use a section of the parish house to run a school for deaf and mute children five days a week and that the playground was available for the children as well. In return, the Junior League would pay the church $25.00 a month to cover utilities. By December 1952, the Junior League was preparing to move their school. In June 1953, Mrs. John T. Welch wrote to the vestry expressing the appreciation of the Junior League for use of the parish house by the speech school.

Robey reported in September 1953 that our parish had been asked to host people from Florence who would be here for the Bryan Green Mission in February. Rev. Bryan Green (1901 – 1993) was one of the most effective evangelists in England and in New York, 6,000 people would go each night to hear him. Malcolm Haven in March 1954 reported that the first follow up meeting by the Bryan Green Mission was scheduled for 8:00 p.m. on Friday March 12.

By the end of 1953 the vestry discussed mailing out a weekly bulletin to all members of the parish. The bulletin was mailed in 1954, but was discontinued in 1956 and replaced with a monthly bulletin with the exception of Easter and Christmas.

FINANCES & VESTRY

Recent additions to the vestry in 1943 were: I. Mayo Read Sr., Coming B. Gibbs, R. Baron Munnerlyn and Dr. Frank G. Cain. Travers was elected chairman of the vestry.

Cotesworth Means, who was a prolific letter writer, had been promoting the choir to the vestry since 1924. Not everyone wanted to hear what he had to say, but it was always interesting.

In early 1943, the idea of hiring an assistant minister was again popping up. Means opposed an assistant because he felt that the more urgent need was for adequate and proper facilities for the more than 100 volunteer members of the three choirs of the church. They needed space where the choir could rehearse and store their robes. "It was a matter of moral and financial obligation."

He said the vestry had made a big mistake when they agreed to make Merritt Williams, at his own suggestion, chairman of the vestry because an unnecessary and unnatural burden was placed upon him. Means said, "Very few fine ministers are also experts in business administration and commercial matters, and Mr. Travers is no exception. In fact, the better the minister is in his chosen field, the worse he is apt to be as a business man … Travers' finer talents are infinitely more valuable to the Parish when devoted exclusively to the spiritual life of the parish."

Means was in favor of using the untapped source of laymen rather than having an assistant. He said that little has been done to promote the talents of the laymen when there were easily fifteen to twenty talented men in the congregation who could take turns reading. Means pointed out there was a shortage of clergy, "Just what kind of talent can we expect to secure for the shabby pay and half-boy job we are offering at St. Philip's if the market for real men at decent pay is so critically lacking in available material?"

Ernest H. Pringle was chosen as chairman of the 1943 Every Man Canvas. On February 3, 1944, Pringle was congratulated on the most successful Canvass in the church's history.

In 1944, I'On L. Rhett was chosen as the head of the 1945 Every Member Canvas. The vestry gave the treasurer, W.S. Stevens, a gift of $50.00 in appreciation of the excellent work he did during the past year.

Outgoing senior warden, J. Stanyarne Stevens, ended his 1943 year-end report saying it was a privilege to have served as senior warden and as a vestryman for sixteen years. He hoped, in his humble way, he had contributed something worthwhile to the parish. "I don't mean to be presumptuous but I am not offering for re-election to the vestry and I would appreciate you not voting for me."

In 1945, Coming Ball Gibbs was given a unanimous rising vote of thanks for his splendid services during the year 1944.

Isaac Motte Haig, who died prior to February 25, 1942, left property and stock to St. Philip's. Thomas E. Myers was elected treasurer of the Mary Maham Haig memorial fund that was under the will of Isaac Haig. The fund had $3,000. Myers, who was putting that money in Series G government funds, would be remunerated once it was seen how much work would be involved. Coming B. Gibbs, attorney for the church, was asked to secure possession of a large number of shares that were in the name of Charles H. Haig, as trustee, under the will of Isaac Motte Haig.

Gibbs found a shortfall of $1,250 from the estate but there was a $1,000 surety.

The attorneys for the Haig estate notified the vestry in October 1946 that under the will of Isaac Motte Haig he had left the church half of 330 acres in Fairfield County – appraised at $8,500. By April 1947, the only offer made was $6,000 and it was accepted.

Haig also left an interest in 30 Meeting Street to the church. In May, Mrs. Marjorie Nolt Morawetz was the high bidder and purchased 30 Meeting Street for $30,025. In October, Myers reported they had received $17,000 from property sold from the trust. Some money was paid to Haig's debtors.

The vestry thanked Charles S. Dwight for his splendid work as the 1946 chairman of the Every Member Canvass. Travers' salary was increased to $5,000. Three new vestry members in 1947 were David Maybank, Carlton G. Davies and Chester N. Perry. James Gendron Gibbs was secretary. John Laurens resigned from the vestry in January 1948 after serving since 1935. At the same time, the vestry expressed its appreciation to Dr. Robertson for his splendid service as senior warden. Cornelius (Buster) Huguenin was appointed chairman of the 1949 of the Every Member Canvas and Cadwallader

Jones was vice-chairman. In January 1949, the vestry wrote letters of congratulations to Buster Huguenin and Cadwallader Jones for their splendid work.

The rector, assistant rector and the two wardens were to investigate a way the rector and assistant rector could be reimbursed for their automobile expenses incurred in the work of the parish. They voted to pay Travers and Tucker car expenses at $50.00 a month for the two of them to share.

Travers opened the vestry meeting with a prayer. Opening and closing prayers may have been said at previous vestry meeting, but the first time it was recorded was on January 18, 1949.

In 1950, J. Ross Hanahan and two Hugueins, who were first cousins, were on the vestry. They were Buster and Thomas A. who was the father of Mrs. Richard Coen, (Vereen). Vestrymen Robert M. Hitt, chairman, E. H. McIver and Douglas Wilkinson were on the music committee. Hitt was on the committee for some time.

In 1950, Edward K. Pritchard agreed to head the Every Man Canvas.

The tentative 1951 budget was $38,000: Salaries, $11,800; organist and choir, $2,700; boys' choir, $300; operating expenses, $5,500; rector's discretionary fund, $300; church yard upkeep, $500; general repairs, $2,000; major improvements, $5,000; religious education director, $600; estimated diocesan assessment, $3,300; and general church apportionment, $6,000.

Two new faces on the vestry in 1952 were Thomas P. White and William B. Ellison. Tom Myers was senior warden and J. Heyward Furman Jr. was junior warden. In an anonymous letter to the vestry it was suggested that vestry nominations be made through the "Parish Council" and be published in the bulletin prior to the annual meeting. In 1953, John Palmer Gaillard, William I. Holt, DeRosset Myers and Chester N. Perry were elected to the vestry.

When Mrs. Carl E. Millford, church secretary, was not able to work full time, Travers hired Miss Patsy Pigott so between the two there would be full time help. The vestry gave Travers permission to do this provided the cost was not increased.

Mrs. Coming Gibbs suggested the sexton's fee for weddings be increased from $5.00 to $10.00 per wedding. It was pointed out that this would require a change in the by-laws at a congregational meeting.

Dick Reeves reported in April 1953 that Miss Nathalie Dotterer bequeathed $1,000 to St. Philip's and that Owen Geer Sr. had left $50.00. Travers said were no strings attached either on this bequest or the $1,000 bequest left by Mrs. Hertz. At the same time, Miss Annabelle Bruns left a bequest of $2,000.

The vestry decided to use Miss Dotterer's bequest and Miss Bruns' bequest to purchase kneeling benches, which cost about $25.00 each. The regular users of the pews were asked if there were any objections. There were. In a number of cases, kneeling benches were omitted on the request of the principal users of certain pews (This was ten years after the ending of pew rentals).

Douglas H. Wilkinson, vestryman and Sunday school superintendent, moved to Sanford, North Carolina, in the fall of 1953 because he purchased the Oldsmobile-Cadillac dealership. He said that his small endeavors at St. Philip's had been most enjoyable and the love he had for St. Philip's made it extremely difficult to move.

THE ROYAL-LIVERPOOL INSURANCE GROUP OF RICHMOND

Joseph S. Brown, regional manager of the Royal-Liverpool Insurance Group of Richmond, wrote Travers on July 27, 1954, to advise him the insurance company was canceling two perpetual policies. They were policy 933 in the amount of $4,561.90 for fire insurance on the church building and policy 1104 in the amount of $8,000 for fire insurance on the church building. Brown said these policies were issued in 1869 and 1870 respectively and were perpetual policies by nature.

Brown said policies such as these had not been issued since about 1890 and the number of these policies in effect had dwindled to twenty-five. The insurance company had to maintain separate premium reserves and had to make an addition to the annual statement with the various states. Brown wrote, "… our senior management has determined … that we should ask for the return of these policies. We, of course, will return the entire premium to you."

On August 2, 1954, Senior Warden William B. Ellison sent a return letter to Brown pointing out first that policy 933 was on the organ. Ellison said he was "extremely concerned over the contents of your letter." The policies were purchased by the Church in all good faith and it is our sincere hope you will reverse this decision. "St. Philip's Church has, for a number of years, been quite proud to show these two policies. The vestry was consideration placing these two policies on exhibit in a glass case in the church, to be seen not only by a large congregation of St. Philip's Church, but by the thousands of tourists who visit this old and historical church each year."

F. Dudley Hollick, who was the associate regional-manger of the insurance company, wrote to Ellison on August 16, 1954, with the good news that the executive department in New York made an exception "to the general rule and would allow these two policies to remain in force. In view of this, it will not be necessary for you to return the policies at the present time."

As it turned out, in November 1957 the vestry voted to cancel the $5,000 perpetual insurance policy on the organ and to increase the insurance on the building to $400,000.

✠ ✠ ✠

Malcolm D. Haven, senior warden in 1956, presented Ray Long of Thomas White and Associates who discussed his company's program of helping churches to raise their levels of giving. Bishop Carruthers had recommended the firm. Long said in some cases they had increased pledging by as much as 500% and as low as 78%. Because the vestry hired the company and borrowed the money from another account to pay the fee, they were anxious to have the 1957 pledges in as soon as possible. Pledges collected from 452 members totaled $62,126.84 out of $70,000 pledged for the year ending September 30. The average pledge was $137.52. The fee to Thomas White and Associates was $5,841.37.

The annual financial report for 1956 does not exist. In the October 1957 vestry minutes, J. Ross Hanahan, Jr. had no reply to his letter to Thomas White about re-canvassing the congregation. William B. Ellison reported that on the basis of anticipated income and expenditures, he forecast a net loss of $4,000. The vestry said that there would be sufficient carry-over from the 1956/57 funds to more than take care of the anticipated deficit. However, the 1957 parish report said, "The Canvass conducted under the Thomas White Plan, resulted in much greater giving and a larger budget."

In 1958, there was a question about members making contributions directly to the Women's Auxiliary, men's group, etc. and if that were a violation of the White Plan of one overall pledge. It was decided that was not a violation.

Pledges were in arrears by 15 % in October 1959 and in November after discussing the financial situation, consideration was given to leaving White and returning to the Every Man Canvass. In February 1960, Tom Myers explained that there was a deficit budget because the White Plan had not produced the expected income. A motion was passed that a letter be written to *The Living Church* protesting the figures being advertised by the White Company. The vestry was going out in teams of two to canvass members and that summer the church returned to the Every Man Canvass with John T. Welch as chairman. By December 1960, 463 pledges totaled $68,511.86 plus $500 designated for the church home.

PROPERTY & MAINTENANCE

The vestry approved an expenditure of $12.00 in 1943 so Miss Walsh could have a "stove" in her office. Mrs. Elizabeth O'Neill Verner was thanked for giving the church one of her etchings. S.F. Shackelford and Mayo Read were on the committee to raise funds for a suitable memorial tablet honoring Rev. Cary Beckwith. Colonel Alston Deas, who gave the church a copy of his book *The Early Iron Work of Charleston*, was in 1944 Chief of Training Literature and the Visual Aid Section of the Infantry School at Fort Benning, Georgia. W.H. Barnwell, vestry secretary, wrote a thank you letter to Lt. Colonel Louis Y. Dawson, Jr. for the gavel he made from wood from the steeple. Mrs. Charles S. Dwight in 1945 donated two cathedral chairs to the church.

Because Ben Scott Whaley in 1949 pointed out the danger of the old shells on the portico and in the vestibule, he called Colonel Paulsen from the Ordinance Depot who found the artillery shells dangerous. He took steps to render them safe but it was unknown how long the cannon balls had been in the church. Virtually every downtown house or building has had a cannon ball in it from the bombardment of Charleston during the War Between the States and/or from the Revolution.

Travers reported in June 1949 that the neighborhood parking limit had been set at two hours. Sunday parking problems often popped up in the vestry minutes and several letters of thanks were written to W.T. Smith, who owned a parts and service company located on the southwest corner of Cumberland and Church streets, for allowing St. Philippians to park on his property on Sundays.

In March 1950, Vestryman Dr. Richard W. Hanckel asked the church and grounds committee investigate the feasibility of lighting the steeple's cross and of installing a drinking fountain in the parish house yard. In the course of investigating the lighting of the steeple, Buster Huguenin and the steeplejack found major seepage, evidence of timber eating bugs, a cracked cornice, an opening in a window and the need to putty all of the steeple windows. Vestryman E. H. McIver took bids from two companies. The cost to repair was $467.

John Minott Rivers suggested in April 1950 that the chimes that were donated to the church by the late vestryman Ashmead F. Pringle Sr., who died in 1949, be recognized as a memorial to him. Ashmead F. Pringle Jr. and his family gave approval to erecting a small tablet on or near the organ.

There was a meeting in February 1952 of the building and grounds committee, the Sunday school, choir committees, the church home and the Women's Auxiliary to discuss the future needs of the various activities of the church. It had been twenty-five years since the parish house had been remodeled. By July, architect Henry B. Staats presented sketches of the parish house with the rector's office and the Sunday school at the east end of the building.

At a congregational meeting held on April 27, 1953, a motion passed that a building fund campaign of $60,000 be authorized to build a new parish house in the rear of the playground.

At the congregational meeting on May 7, 1954, a motion passed not to build a new building on the playground and the rector's office would remain in the parish office.

The cost of remodeling would be reduced to $50,000. Rooms on the ground floor were provided for choir robing, a choir rehearsal room, a modernized kindergarten and a store room. The second floor provided classrooms over the gymnasium. The Blanchard Construction Co. got the job. The vestry met on November 10, 1955, voting to accept the parish house from the contractor.

The vestry next established a committee to form plans so that members could furnish "memorial rooms" in the church school building. Helen Barkley and interior decorator Marguerite Sinkler Valk recommended draw curtains in conjunction with bamboo curtains donated by Mr. and Mrs. Heyward Furman. The curtains would cost about $272 and J.S. Stevens made a motion that Mrs. Barkley be given permission to try and use some of the old material. The vestry passed the motion.

Dr. George Orvin gave the tiles for the parish house floor in the vestibule, hall and the downstairs office. George, his wife Rosalie and their family still worship at St. Philip's in 2012.

In 1953, another discussion came up about hymnals. The Women's Auxiliary was pressing the church to adopt the so called new hymnal that had been out since 1940. The church was using the 1916 hymnal, Dick Reeves, who was chairman of the music committee, urged the vestry adopt the 1940 hymnal. Eight hundred copies were ordered.

GLEBE LAND

Back in 1945, the vestry voted to compare the rental property income with alternative sources of income.

A year later, I'On Rhett, Harold G. Dotterer and Stephen F Shackelford gave an opinion of the value of the remaining glebe land houses. Six Glebe Street, the most valuable property, was appraised at $14,500. Numbers 11, 14 and 16 Glebe Street were each valued at $7,500. Sixty-seven George Street which was in particularly bad condition was valued at $8,500. It was suggested that 67 George be sold at a price between $9,000 and $11,000 and that the money be used to repair the other houses. They were going to permit only St. Philippian realtors to list the house.

John Rivers, owner of WCSC radio and later television Channel 5, met in May 1947 with Dr. Edward W. Pratt the tenant at 6 Glebe Street. Pratt, who lived there with his wife Eunice and three children under sixteen, also had his medical office in the house. He had made considerable improvements to the house without having a lease. The vestry tentatively agreed to give Pratt a three-year lease, charge him $70.00 a month and the vestry would maintain the roof and the "guttery." In return, Pratt would have to tear down a wooden structure on the north side of the house and relocate the bathrooms in other parts of the house. He would also have to maintain the grounds.

In June 1947, the widow, Lola L. Green, who had lived at 14 Glebe Street for more than forty years, offered to pay $6,000 for the house. The vestry told her St. Philip's would only take $7,000 or more if they could get it. Green paid $7,000 cash for the house and she was still living there in 1951.

In April 1951, Dr. Pratt and his family were still living at 6 Glebe Street and he was again writing about the bad conditions of the house. The rent was increased from $70.00 a month to $100 and Pratt asked that some of the vestry come and see the house. Pratt wrote "the house is not in good repair. Plaster has fallen in the downstairs hall, kitchen and upper story bedroom." He said that since the rent has been raised, then the church could be expected to do some inside renovation. Pratt closed by saying that in the past five years "I have spent nearly as much in improvement of this property as I paid in rent. The paint job alone amounted to $985."

In June, there was a buyer willing to pay $15,000 for 6 Glebe Street. The vestry turned it down. In July, Rivers made a proposal to rent 6 Glebe Street to be used as a radio station with studios, offices and radio and television broadcasting. He requested a ten year lease with an annual payment of $4,200 for the first five years and $3,000 annually for the next five years. He wanted the right to renew the lease after the first ten year lease expired and he would pay an annual rent of $2,000. He said he might have to build a two story building for broadcasting, adjacent to the house of not less than 6,000 square feet. He would pay the church more money if that building were built.

Rivers had a few more requests such as putting a sound treatment on the ceilings "which would neither affect the appearance of the rooms nor extensively change the basement which has no architectural value." He also wanted to erect a television tower on the property. Rivers said he would have to secure permission from the Civil Aeronautics Administration and the zoning board before a tower could be erected and it might prove to be impractical.

Rivers ended up building his television studios and tower on the southwest corner of East Bay and Charlotte streets where there were many happy memories.

Kruse Muller of 20 Glebe Street wrote to Travers asking if he could purchase 6 Glebe Street. "I have noticed with regret the steady decline of your church property at 6 Glebe Street." He said he knew the church had a sentimental regard for number 6 but so did he. Both of his parents were born on Glebe Street and the house in which he then lived was acquired by his grandfather from St. Philip's. His object was to restore the house and use it as a home. The vestry took the house off the market and so advised Kruse Muller.

In October, there had been a small fire on the third floor of 6 Glebe Street and Vestryman J. Ross Hanahan reported a carpenter had repaired the damage.

Vestrymen William I. Holt and Dr. Richard W. Hanckel in January 1952 examined 6 Glebe Street and asked contractor Herbert A. DeCosta to draw up preliminary plans to convert the house into apartments or offices. There was no one more capable or sensitive to restoring historic homes than DeCosta who restored many historic homes including 66 Anson Street.

In 1953, Mrs. Pratt (There was no mention of Dr. Pratt.) agreed to pay $100 per month for the use of the first and second floors since repairs had been completed that included painting, rewiring, restoration of an abandoned bath room and installing sheetrock in the kitchen. F.J. Lilienthal took a five year lease for the ground floor for his dental laboratory at $55.00 per month. He would be responsible for the repairs and up-keep.

For the first time, it was decided the entire vestry did not have to approve small expenditures concerning glebe properties and the rectory. Randell C. Stoney, who collected the rent, was advised in 1955 the rent at 6 Glebe Street was in arrears. Holt reported the profit from 1949 through 1953 averaged $214.00 per year.

PEWS

A big change was coming to St. Philip's. On January 17, 1943, outgoing senior warden, John Laurens, gave his 1942 report at the congregational meeting. Laurens said, "I suggest the congregation seriously consider the question of eliminating pew rent and to have all pews declared free." J. Stanyarne Stevens, then senior warden, said, "Due credit should be given Mr. John Laurens for it was he who was brave enough to introduce the idea of free pews." Dr. Rivers also raised the question of doing away with pew rents. The vestry was to investigate.

And that is what the vestry began to do in January 1943 when Stevens and Laurens were requested to secure information from St. Michael's Church, Trinity Church in Columbia and Christ Church in Greenville concerning their experiences in discontinuing the system of rented pews. Dr. Albert R. Stuart, rector of St. Michael's, which had stopped renting pews in 1941, replied by March "that the freeing of the pews in St. Michael's had met with excellent results." There was no reply from the two other churches. At the June vestry meeting, pew rentals were discussed, "but the subject as a whole was reserved for future times." It was not until October that Stevens, Laurens and Coming Ball Gibbs were asked to prepare a letter to members of the church concerning the "freeing of the pews." At a congregational meeting on October 31, 1943, the vestry and members voted to end pew rents. In the vestry minutes, that was basically the end of that topic, but the *Charleston Evening Post* printed an article on December 17, 1943, that read:

250-YEAR-OLD CUSTOM OF RENTING PEWS
TO BE ABOLISHED AT ST. PHILIP'S JANUARY 1, 1944

"One of the last churches to maintain the old English pew rent system is St. Philip's. In October 1943, the vestry and congregation voted to discontinue the system on January 1, 1944. Although pew rentals brought income to the church, it was felt that system gave the false idea that members of the church had reserved seats and visitors were not universally welcome." The members did have reserved seats. Rev. Travers emphasized that visitors have always been welcome and that members of the armed forces are especially invited to all services. Notice they had stopped calling visitors "strangers."

Referring to the 18th century, the article said, "If visitors were in the city, they were somebody's guests, so they went to church with the family. Nobody was a stranger." The article concluded by exclaiming that this act would be the greatest change in recent times.

On January 1, 1944, all the pew numbers and name plates were removed from the doors with one exception. A pew on the front row in the south side balcony for some unknown reason has its name plate, "Pringle," intact in 2012. Someone suggested that, perhaps, Mr. Pringle volunteered to remove the name plates. Pringle descendants still sit in that pew even though they no longer rent it.

Rev. Ben W. Turnage, Canon Sam Cobb's assistant from 1977 to 1980, understood the Pringle pew name plate was kept for historical reasons.

Shortly after ending pew rentals, three teenage girls, Henrietta Lowndes née Morrison and two friends chose to sit in the Pringle pew that was empty. When Ernest Pringle arrived, he chased the girls out of the pew waving his leather hat, an event that may have been witnessed by Mary DeSaussure née Huger who sat with her parents just under the Pringle balcony pew.

Mrs. Lowndes said her mother, who had a difficult time adjusting to the new pew system, kept asking who all these strangers were sitting in the pews?

Stevens, the outgoing 1943 senior warden, commended the congregation in January 1944 saying, "Your vestry is greatly pleased over the freeing of the pews." He felt that this would do much for the "upbuilding of the church" and that it will tend to attract the stranger (a relapse here) because he will not feel as though he would be sitting in a reserved seat. He will feel welcome. "The freeing of the pews is the most outstanding accomplishment of the year."

In 1948, the church changed its by-laws simply stating, "All pews in the church shall be free." The next by-law revision was in 2011 and it restated, "All pews in the Church shall be free." This was done with a bit of tongue in cheek, but it does reiterate the fact even though "all pews are free" twenty-first century visitors are still intimidated about choosing a pew.

Travers was requested to put in a necessary notice in the weekly bulletin that was mailed in October 1954. Travers made a strong statement reminding the members of the parish that the pews were neither rented nor reserved. It was pointed out that on November 14, 1943, the congregation amended the by-laws and abolished pew rentals.

☩ ☩ ☩

Cornelius Huguenin in 1949 spoke to Julius Weil of Weils Mattress Factory at 28 Anson Street who said he would honor the price of $150 to recover fifteen pews but the pews would be stuffed with moss instead of cotton. He was told to proceed.

In January 1954, it was discovered that the steeple was once again in bad condition, rotting from dampness and an infestation of termites. The vestry voted to spend $1,000 on repairs. Gaillard reported that the General Woodworking Co. was making four cypress louvers for the steeple that would be treated with Wohman's Salts. In April, Gaillard reported the steeple had been treated for termites and the louvers had been finished but not yet installed. The total repair cost came to $667.

Because Gaillard also recommended that restrictions be placed on visits to the steeple, the vestry voted there would be no visits on Sundays and children would have to be accompanied by an adult.

C.B. Branan was fascinated in the 1950s while sitting with Mary Trott, his grandmother, looking up at all the countless cracks in the ceiling. His parents were married at St. Philip's in 1942 and Marshall Travers was his great uncle through Frances Dwight Trott.

In June 1954, the topic of air conditioning the church or any of its property came up for the first time. They wanted to cool the chancel and discussed air conditioning and an exhaust fan. The vestry authorized Travers to purchase three oscillating fans that were to be installed behind the choir stalls on both sides of the chancel. In 1956, air conditioning the church was discussed again. In 1958, Dr. Rivers proposed air conditioning the chapel. Dr. Anderson suggested it might be better to concentrate on air conditioning the church instead and they decided to obtain bids for both. The price to air condition the chapel was $1,600. It would be thirteen years before the church was air conditioned.

Senior Warden Malcolm Haven in February 1957 wanted to investigate the possibility of placing railings up to the chancel "for safety of the old and feeble." The vestry approved the railings and Carolina Iron and Fence installed them in March.

CHURCH HOME

Miss Nellie Hayne, who was appointed to the church home committee in 1943, was quickly moved up to vice-chairman with Miss Eugenia C. Frost as chairman. It was customary for the vestry to borrow money from the church home trust to pay other bills. The money was always repaid and interest was charged. In 1946, $1,081.81 was paid for wiring in the church home.

In May 1946, Mrs. Caroline E. Bevan was a widow and the matron of the church home. The matron, who was appointed by the rector and the advisory board, was provided with living quarters, heat, lights and a salary of $50.00 per month or as the board would agree. The matron would supervise the home, its cleaning and small repairs and she was expected to look after the residents when they were ill. She was expected to sleep on the premises but was free to pursue a normal life going out when necessary for business and pleasure and she would receive a paid two week vacation. She was not expected to run errands or do maid service for the ladies unless she so chose. After years of faithful service, she would be entitled at retirement to a permanent accommodation in the home unless she had become undesirable.

Mrs. Bevan had a large hospital bill. It was decided to postpone any decision regarding paying the bill until Coming Gibbs could be consulted about the Haig Trust paying medical bills for the ladies in the church home. It was not until December that Tom Myers and Mrs. Dockstader were authorized to release funds from the Haig Trust for needy ladies in the church home, including hospitalization and hospital bills. Gibbs suggested one way to use the money was to name one or two rooms after Mary Mahan Haig and only those rooms could be maintained by the Haig trust. In 1948, the Haig Trust paid Mrs. Bevan's paid $61.00 hospital bill.

No applicant would be admitted to the home unless she had been a member of St. Philip's for seven years and was not able to financially support herself elsewhere. Each resident must have her own gas meter and pay for electricity. Church home rules emphasized, "A spirit of love should be found here if anywhere - it was founded to help people and they in turn should want to help the individuals among whom they live. Any resident who continually fails to cooperate may be asked to leave."

In 1947, fire extinguishers were on each floor of the church home. Because the price of coal rose to $108 for the winter, Leo Hennessy was paid $75.00 to run the gas lines to each room, eliminating the need for coal.

The Haig financial report ending December 31, 1948, showed an income of $4,472.06. Expenses were $945.52. The cost of renovating and furnishing the Haig rooms was $477.69 and the rest of the expenses were spent paying the residents medical bills that ranged from $5.00 to $224.10. One gentleman, Mr. Williman, was a resident. Some of the other residents at this time were: Miss Helen Allston, Mrs. D.M. Dockstader,

Mrs. A.B. Eubank and Miss Marie Price. The deaconess, Miss Mary Trapier Gadsden, lived in a Haig room.

In 1906, Miss Gadsden had entered the missionary field by attending the New York Training School for Deaconesses in New York. She was then called in 1929 to be the deaconess-in-charge at the Church Home Orphanage in Puerto Rico where she stayed for many years as a missionary.

Senior Warden Carlton Davies was advised in March 1949 that the church home matron, Mrs. Dockstader, had asked the vestry to pay part of the home's utility bills. Mrs. Dockstader said she was paying the utility bills for the entire building from church home funds when the ground floor was used for offices, etc. She said the bills were as high as $30.00 a month and she did not know how she could keep paying that without cutting back on their limited funds. The request was deferred until the next meeting.

To defray the cost of installing "an electric elevator" in the church home, the vestry sold the church's series G bonds. A year later a "Dictograph Fire Detection System" was installed in the church home for $800.

Coming Ball Gibbs in 1952 wrote about the church home and its property that also included the adjacent Shell Shop. The residents lived in twelve rooms on the second and third floors that were usually full but at that time only nine rooms were occupied. The first floor was used entirely "for parish needs." On the Church Street side from north to south were the rector's office, his secretary's office, two robing rooms for the ladies in the choir and the library, also used for meetings and the choir warmed up on Sunday mornings. On the east side from north to south were the assistant rector's office, the organist's office, the mimeographing room, the robing room for the men of the choir and the committee room used for robing the children's choir. It was also used when cleaning silver, sorting magazines and clothes to be donated, preparing tea and food for the tea garden and much more. Under the steps there was a bathroom and a safe in which the silver was kept.

Gibbs wrote that the church home's trust fund amounted to $26,300 and all but $1,000 of that amount was invested in United States 2 ½% bonds. He felt they could safely liberalize investments. He complained that the church home paid the entire electric, gas and water bills including those for the first floor and the maid hired to clean the church home also cleaned the first floor. Gibbs said that fortunately, for the home, some of the ladies living there were able to make monthly contributions which they for obvious reasons did not want to call it "rent." During 1951, five of the ladies contributed a total of $740 to the home. Mr. and Mrs. William Hume paid $120 annually (as stated previously) for the use of the Shell Shop and the Women's Auxiliary gave $100 for a total income of $1,625 in 1951 on which they could barely provide.

Gibbs stated the church home had been misunderstood and considered as something separate and apart from St. Philip's parish for too long. "Since 1870, the home that has provided a service for a procession of needful ladies through the years has perhaps been quiet and not at all glamorous, but the service has been nonetheless important and valuable, and its proper and adequate continuance is just as much an obligation of St. Philip's Parish as any other obligation the Parish has."

The Haig Fund was used in 1953 to pay medical bills for some St. Philippians including Miss Martha Rivers $100, Patricia Dotterer $500, and William Stevens $250. The value of the securities of the fund was $58,814.60.

In 1954, the church hired Lloyd Mack to paint the church home green for a price of $1,070.14. Supervised by Carlton Davies, the vestry had the church home's roof painted for approximately $300. Gaillard was authorized to spend $150 to convert the church home's committee room into a sewing room.

A motion was passed at the January 1956 annual meeting permitting the vestry to run the church home. In February, the senior warden was to survey the entire situation of the church home and report back to the vestry as soon as possible.

In March, Coming Ball Gibbs proposed a committee of six. Travers, two vestrymen and three ladies, would oversee the church home's operations and report to the vestry. Gibbs also recommended new admission rules should be drawn up and that all church home funds be placed in the general fund handled by the church treasurer. Gibbs' recommendations were accepted.

THE RECTORY

In January 1943, Travers and Gibbs were authorized to look into the matter of renting out one or more rooms in the rectory. Remember, that the Travers family, while in Prescott, had to live in a house with two strange men.

Travers' daughter, Harriet Yarborough, remembers that two rooms on the third floor were rented. A Mr. Smith from New York hauled his piano up to his room on the third floor and a lady, who worked at the newspaper. A Mrs. T. did all the linens. It was a full house.

At the same time, Messrs. T. Allen Legare, DeWitt W. King and Clarence Schachte appraised the rectory for $18,000. At the March 1943 vestry meeting, it was decided to sell the rectory for $25,000 and it was not to be exclusively listed. In May 1944, the vestry received an offer on the rectory for $24,000. Not only did the Travers have to live with strangers, but it must have been very unsettling to know the house was on the market. After much discussion, the vestry decided not to sell the rectory.

The vestry on March 8, 1954, voted to pay all utilities up to $400 for Travers and up to $200 for Robey.

MUSIC & THE CHOIR

On June 27, 1949, the rector presented Cotesworth P. Means, who was in attendance at the vestry meeting, with a silver platter in grateful recognition of his twenty-six years of faithful service to the church. Means thanked the vestry and he reminisced speaking of his early experiences in All Saint's choir in Atlanta at age fifteen. After ten years as a professional in the quartette of St. Michael's in Charleston, the senior warden of St. Philip's asked him in 1923 to become the director of the St. Philip's choir. He paid high compliments to the organist, Dorothy Bollwinkle.

Means had several issues that he brought up with the vestry including the question should all choir members have to remain through the communion service. He suggested only a quartette was necessary for the final hymn. A lengthy discussion ensued. In July, the vestry said those choir members who did not want to stay through the communion service could leave through the side doors after the choir took communion.

Means hoped to hear from the vestry but advised them he would be on "the Island" during July. No one ever referred to "the Island" as Sullivans Island because there was only one island. That name "the Island" has been largely forgotten.

At the vestry meeting of May 7, 1951, it was announced that Means was resigning as choir director. He was asked to remain but wrote that he did not feel that he could do the church justice at that time.

Means said he had never taken an annual salary of more than $240 "if such was available." He confessed that he actually spent more than that amount every year for extra costs such as funeral flowers, wedding presents, special gifts, refreshments and prizes for the boys' choir. He said he treated it as salary to himself to be free to spend it as he saw fit.

The choir signed a petition urging Means to remain. The choir "felt it needed his high standards, mature guidance and superior knowledge of church music." Some of the signers were: Alice Gaillard Burkette, whose husband, "Burk," also had a beautiful voice, Franklin E. Robson, Jr., A. Franz Witte, Jr. and Mrs. Douglas S. Cone.

Miss Bollwinkle would continue as organist and take over the duties of choir director. Her salary was raised to $150 per month.

All choirs c. 1950

Four months later, it was announced that Means would return as choir director on September 1, 1951. In January 1952, Means was lobbying for a totally new building to house the choir but Mr. Staats, the architect, recommended the basement of the chapel be used for a choir room. In October, the vestry voted to spend $4,000 from the building fund to remodel the church home library for the choir's use although others would use the room.

In September 1952, Miss Dorothy Bollwinkle, who had been organist for twenty-nine years, wrote a nine page letter to the vestry with a litany of complaints. She played for all church services and in the Sunday school, for funerals and more recently the boys and the girls' choirs. She said organists in most churches are part time but at St. Philip's it was virtually full time.

Bollwinkle wrote Travers saying it would be better not to have the children's choir rehearse in the church home because of the noise and that it would be better for them to use the parish house. There were about sixty members in the children's choirs. She said, "As far as I can see, the Civilian Defense, the Speech School and Matty Matthews boxers (and I don't mean dogs) are all lined up for their winter activities and we are left out in the cold. It is alright to be civic-minded and Mr. Travers told me that I should live in the Dark Ages. His remarks may be funny, but it will be no laughing matter when on a Sunday morning the choirs do not perform."

She said it was an absolute necessity to hire a director of Christian education who would be given authority to train teachers. For each of the past six to eight years, Miss

Bollwinkle had paid $100 to $150 from her salary to attend a school of music for organists and choir directors. Miss Bollwinkle, who was the only woman on the provincial committee, was appointed by Bishop Carruthers to represent this diocese at a music conference at Sewanee. She asked Travers if the church would pay the $75.00 fee and he said he did not think the vestry would pay but Travers gave her $20.00 from his discretionary fund and the bishop gave her $50.00.

In San Francisco, three years earlier, the Episcopal national convention voted that employees of the churches were to receive social security. "Travers did nothing about this until it was almost too late." After battling for several months, Mrs. Dockstader, matron of the church home, and Miss Bollwinkle finally got it passed, but they lost the first six months.

After the vestry read Miss Bollwinkle's nine page letter, she received a raise in October 1952 to $1,200 per year and $300 per year each for the children's choirs for a total of $1,800. There were twelve paid singers including Mrs. I. Grier Linton, Means, who was a tenor, Richard J. Voigt, and Joseph R. Trott, Jr. The total amount paid to the choir librarian, Mrs. Edward F. Allston, for sheet music came to $1,525.17.

The boy's choir c. late 1940's.

The organ motor caught fire during the 11:15 a.m. service on October 18, 1953. The vestry agreed to pay up to $2,000 to replace the organ motor, to run new wiring from Philadelphia "Street" and replace the current fuse box with a modern breaker box.

By August 1, 1954, the boys' choir that Miss Bollwinkle[14] supervised had dissipated. The vestry voted to reduce her salary by $12.50 per month so someone else could be found to work with the boys' choir. The salary for the new person was to be $10.00 per week. Miss Bollwinkle wanted to discuss her salary with the music committee telling them she had no inkling that Robey was looking for someone new to work with the children's choirs. She added that only two weeks ago a large church approached her about a job and she did not even consider it.

On January 10, 1956, Means, again serving as choir director, gave his annual report stating "The past year was not outstanding in any particular way for the Church Choir." Of the $1,500 provided for the choir in 1955, $1,334.00 was paid to soloists and $76.47 for sheet music and supplies. That left $89.52 which Means would spend on furnishings for the choir rooms.

Means asked for more people to sing in the choir so they could make the 1956 choir the largest and finest in the history of St. Philip's. He also said, "While it might be true that not everyone who might like to sing is always acceptable, there is undoubtedly good choir material in the parish."

Means also reported that Miss Bollwinkle was making excellent progress with the children's choir with an average attendance at Saturday morning rehearsals of thirty-five. Miss Bollwinkle said that a spirit of great enthusiasm prevailed thanks to the valuable and effective assistance of Miss Mary Drake, Mrs. James Gibbs (Martha) and Mrs. Ray Herrin.

In September, Means wrote a glowing letter to the vestry thanking them for the great way the choir rooms looked. He was so pleased that he and Mrs. Means made a donation of $100 toward the parish house renovation fund.

THE CHURCHYARDS

In July 1943, the vestry hired George LaBruce at up to $15.00 to make a survey of the unoccupied spaces in the western churchyard. He did such a good job that the vestry sent him a letter of thanks and $50.00 for bringing the plat of the churchyard up to date. In February 1944, the vestry agreed to place flowers on the Kaufman graves on the dates specified by the Kaufman Trust Agreement at a cost not to exceed $20.00 annually. In 1954, the church purchased the flowers for the Kaufman grave from The Flower Garden for $6.02. At some point, the vestry disregarded that agreement.

---

14 Once again Miss Bollwinkle's name is spelled incorrectly in the vestry minutes.

In April, the cost of the burial lots was increased from $25.00 to $50.00 each.

Because the city health department sent a letter in 1945 about the increase of mosquitoes in the churchyards, Travers said he would co-operate in eliminating the pests. In 2012, the mosquitoes are still there, particularly in the western churchyard.

The vestry raised the price of burial plots to $75.00 each in 1948. Thomas E. Myers was to take care of "the cemetery business" and he would be paid a flat $200 per year. In September the vestry voted to only allow members of St. Philip's to be buried in its churchyard. Bentham Simons' request to buy burial plots was refused because he was not a member.

In November 1950, the churchyard committee headed by J. Ross Hanahan made a survey of tombstones and found twenty tombstones that needed repairs. Hanahan wrote, "In cases where vertical slabs have been broken or fallen over, it seems ... that the best method for permanent repair is to lay the slab in a horizontal position over the grave and, if broken, cement the pieces." He said the best way to gradually get the churchyard in order would be "for the vestry to appropriate a certain amount of money, from time to time, to be used for general repair work in the churchyard."

The vestry in February 1951 sold one burial lot to Mrs. E.E. Douglas and two lots each to Dr. Richard W. Hanckel and Dr. Rawling Pratt-Thomas. Mrs. Pratt-Thomas died in 2012 at 100.

TRAVELING TOMBSTONES

In 1939, the South Carolina Service Authority (Santee Cooper – pronounced "Cuper") began a project to flood large areas of the state by building dams that would result in the formation of two lakes, Moultrie and Marion. The purpose of all of this was to generate electricity. Many houses, buildings and cemeteries were covered with water and there was a large effort to reinteer as many bodies as possible. Some people requested that the bodies remain in the flooded ground and only the tombstones be moved. A slab of concrete was put over the gravesites of the bodies that were not being moved. The project was completed in 1941.

In 1951, Miss Anne Stevens Ravenel (1865 – 1954) wrote Travers explaining, "When the burial ground at our parish church, Trinity Church, Black Oak, was to be flooded by the waters of Lake Moultrie, the markers over the graves of my father, William F. Ravenel, my mother, Ellen M. Ravenel, my infant brother, Samuel DuBose Ravenel and my infant sister, Elizabeth Porcher Ravenel, were moved to the western churchyard at St. Philip's church." No remains were removed.

The traveling tombstones were relocated to St. Philip's by Miss Ravenel's brother, Theodore D. Ravenel, who died in Charleston in 1944, and is buried in the western churchyard.

Later, Miss Ravenel wanted to remove these markers from St. Philip's churchyard, and erect them in the new cemetery where her other family markers were moved. Tom Myers approved the request.

The "new cemetery" to which Miss Ravenel referred was a site owned by R. Dwight Porcher and his sister-in-law, Marguerite R. Porcher who was the mother of St. Philippian Margaret (Punky) Porcher. It is located on a county road between Bonneau and the former site of Black Oak Church where bodies from Pooshee Plantation, Black Oak Church and other plantations were reinterred. In 2012, the St. John's Hunting Club maintains the cemetery under the supervision of Park Dougherty.

Anne Ravenel (called Annie) ran a boarding house in Tryon, North Carolina, and later retired to Pinopolis.

St. Philip's 1953 audit showed there was a voluntary churchyard trust fund with a balance of $15,603.93. They planned to increase the principal and only use the interest to maintain the churchyards in perpetuity. That year $470.59 was spent.

In 1955, Mrs. Emily Ravenel Farrow received permission to plant some azaleas in the western churchyard.

Malcolm Haven reported to the vestry that the lot adjacent to the western churchyard was for sale for $10,000. It would accommodate 130 burial plots. That was the lot on the southwest corner of Church and Cumberland streets. It was purchased later.

RACE RELATIONS

A great majority of people living in 2012 have no idea about past race relations. Prior to 1865, blacks and whites worshipped together and in some churches there were more blacks than whites. It is a myth that the blacks at St. Philip's sat only in the balconies. Look at E.B. White's portrait that hangs in the narthex and you will see that blacks not only sat in the balconies but also in pews on the ground floor.

After 1865, blacks chose to worship in their own churches. It has been said that Sunday is the most segregated day of the week. Races were segregated in schools until September 1954 when the Supreme Court ruled segregation was unconstitutional. The army was desegregated by President Harry Truman in July 1948 and in 1950 the Supreme Court found that published policies of the railroads were in violation of the Interstate Commerce Act. For a while, trains originating in the north were integrated and trains originating in the South were segregated. The Charleston train station that was built in the 1950s has two separate waiting rooms – one for blacks and one for whites. In

November 1955, segregation ended on interstate buses and five years later segregation was ended in bus stations. None of these rulings or orders brought immediate change.

St. Mark's, a black church established in 1865 in Charleston, asked in 1875 to be admitted into union with the diocese and with all privileges of the convention. The request was denied but at the diocesan convention of 1889, it was voted to provide a separate organization for the "colored people" in the diocese. There would be a missionary district under the bishop to be composed of all congregations and missions of "colored persons" in the diocese. Its legislative body, called a "Convocation," would be composed of representatives elected by the respective congregations and missions with authority to elect its own officers. A great cause of friction was removed by establishing a convocation.

A resolution passed that any clergyman, who was entitled to membership at the 1889 convention, was entitled to membership in any diocesan convention. This enabled the Rev. J.H.M. Pollard, rector of St. Mark's, to attend any diocesan convention and not attend the convocation.

The Rev. John Johnson, former rector of St. Philip's, with the consent of the 1889 convention delegates, invited the 1890 diocesan convention to be held at St. Philip's. It was the centennial convention. Subsequently, certain members of St. Philip's objected to the convention being held at St. Philip's because a "colored man," Rev. Pollard, would be attending. A congregational meeting was held and a majority of those present agreed to have the convention at St. Philip's, but because many members of the congregation were disturbed and concerned, the bishop was asked to change the venue. Holy Communion church was chosen in its place.

As previously stated, Bishop William A. Guerry, between 1911 and 1914, wanted a suffragan bishop serving blacks in the diocese of South Carolina even though the entire diocese was agitated. This issue was one of the main reasons he was murdered in 1928.

St. Philip's revised its by-laws in April 1916 defining a member as a baptized, white person who was a member of the Protestant Episcopal Church in the United States.

The vestry in 1937 agreed to donate $100 to Archdeacon E.L. Baskerville "for work among the colored convocation of the diocese of South Carolina." His son, the Rev. Lewis A. Baskerville, was responsible for establishing Camp Baskerville near Pawley's Island. It opened in 1939 and the first group to visit was a group of Boy Scouts from Calvary Church in Charleston but the camp soon closed because of the threat of a polio outbreak. In 1941, the Rev. Stephen B. Mackey became director. In 1964, John Welch asked the vestry to approve giving a $100 grant to St. John's Mission to be used in sending several children to Camp Baskerville. The request was granted.

On January 19, 1948, the vestry read and discussed a letter from Mrs. Margaretta Pringle Childs, wife of St. Julian Childs of 73 King Street. She was "advocating representation of Negro Parishes at the Diocesan Convention." Her request was deferred until the next meeting when Bishop Carruthers was invited to attend.

Mrs. Childs sent an undated letter to the vestry concerning the right of "negro" parishes to be represented at the diocesan convention. She asked "the vestry to study the issue and that retired Bishop Thomas or Mr. Lumpkin or Mr. Thompson be asked to address the congregation to explain some aspects of our church since 1876 in its religious and ecclesiastical connotations, …" Mrs. Childs felt this issue was so big that it should not be sidetracked by the trivial matters such as shaking hands or sitting at a table with blacks.

The vestry vote came at their February 6, 1948, meeting after Bishop Carruthers led a discussion concerning the "Negro Parishes." The vestry would advise church members at the next congregational meeting that the parish delegation to the diocesan convention should be uninstructed on the question of "Negro Parishes" being represented. The motion was carried unanimously.

At the vestry meeting a motion was made to support a resolution, then before the diocesan convention, which provided limited legal "negro" representation at the diocesan convention. The motion was lost by a vote of five to four.

Ben Scott Whaley then moved to advise the congregation that the vestry was in favor of "limited legal negro representation at the diocesan convention provided that the representatives be clergy and lay men must have been a communicant of the diocese for at least five years. The motion was carried by a vote of five to four."

At the congregational meeting on February 8, the congregation validated the vestry's motion with a fifty-four to forty-six vote. Although the majority of those St. Philippians chose to permit black Episcopal churches to have limited representation at the diocesan convention, the motion was defeated at the 1948 and 1951 diocesan conventions. It was approved in 1953. St. Mark's was finally admitted as a parish and Calvary in Charleston and St. Paul's in Orangeburg were admitted as missions.

On December 5, 1955, a vestry committee was appointed to draft a letter to Bishop Carruthers questioning him on his views concerning segregation. The draft of the letter was presented to the vestry at a special meeting a week later. "A copy of the letter is attached to these minutes" (This letter has not been found). After considerable discussion, the vestry approved the draft of the letter and directed it be signed by the two wardens and mailed.

The vestry secretary on January 10, 1956, read Bishop Carruthers' reply to the vestry. The two wardens, Malcolm D. Haven and J. Ross Hanahan, Jr. wrote Bishop Carruthers on January 14 the following letter.

"Your letter was read to the vestry at their meeting on January 10th. Every member present was impressed with the full, clear, logical answers you gave to our questions. The vestry of St. Philip's wishes to express their appreciation to you for the time and effort that you have given this serious subject, and for your very fine presentation of your thoughts upon the grave situation which has risen throughout our Southern States. Your letter was an inspiration and help to all of us. We pray that our Heavenly Father will guide you and all those in authority in our Church and Government to a just, equitable and legal solution of this problem."

In 1956, a member of the church asked that no portion of his contribution be given to the national church. Haven was asked to write the member and explain the impracticbility of acceding to his request.

In April 1956, a committee of Haven and J. Ham Brooks was requested to look into the actions of the National Council of Churches. In May, Haven reported he had investigated but the report is not in the minutes.

The National Council of Churches (NCC) was founded in 1950 and it did not take long before the organization had riled up the ire of many white Southerners, primarily about race relations. The NCC claims that since its founding it has been the leader for ecumenical cooperation among Christians in the United States. The NCC's faith groups in 2011 are from a vast spectrum of Protestant, Anglican, Orthodox, Evangelical, historic African-American and Living Peace churches. They claim forty-five million persons in more than 100,000 local congregations are working with the NCC in communities across the nation.

The NCC's statement of faith: "The National Council of Churches is a community of Christian communions, which in response to the gospel as revealed in the Scriptures, do confess Jesus Christ, the incarnate Word of God, as Savior and Lord." This statement is accepted by all of the NCC's member communions (also called churches and conventions). Each member communion also has its own heritage, including teachings and practices that differ from those of other members.[15]

The NCC also networks with the many ecumenical and interfaith organizations established within the United States and abroad. And it promotes harmonious relations among Christians, Jews, Muslims, Buddhists, practitioners of Native American religions and many other faith groups in a society that is increasingly multireligious. The NCC has focused on building relationships between Christians and Muslims in the aftermath of September 11, 2001.

THE CLERGY RESIGN

Rev. Marshall E. Travers announced his resignation effective October 15, 1956. St. Philippian Catherine Jones in 2012 remembers Travers because he had a heart for

---

15 NCC information is from its website – www.nccusa.org

missions, he was leaving St. Philip's to start a mission church. Bishop Carruthers briefly attended the vestry meeting and spoke of the opportunities for expanding church work west of the Ashley River and the plans for its undertaking. Carruthers also spoke on the work Travers had accomplished at St. Philip's. Vestryman William Ellison suggested that St. Philip's help Travers new parish.

Carruthers suggested a committee seek the recommendations of leading Episcopal clergymen regarding a new rector. He suggested that careful consideration be given to the replies of the possible candidates and that inquiries for a new rector begin in the Southeast. Carruthers also suggested that laymen not be consulted until after the recommendations of responding clergymen were studied.

At the same meeting, Robey told the vestry he did not care to continue as an associate rector with a new rector. He felt there were only two choices. The vestry could choose Robey as the rector and find a new associate to serve under him or hire a new associate rector who would stay until the next rector arrived.

The vestry met again a week later and spent a considerable time discussing the problems raised by Travers' resignation. They decided to start a search for a new rector right away and they would ask Robey to remain in his present position with a pay increase of $50.00 per month until a new rector was found and approved by the bishop. The vestry told Robey of their decision.

As Travers received letters of welcome prior to his arrival, he also received letters regretting his departure from St. Philip's. The former rector of Grace Church, Rev. William Way, wrote that Travers was the most influential clergyman in the diocese of South Carolina. Dr. Josiah E. Smith of 60 Meeting Street, his wife, Nina, and their son, Alan, wrote that a spiritual life and their feelings for St. Philip's had been made more meaningful through Travers' kindness and advice. Smith continued saying that Travers gave his family a brighter and a happier place in life and that his guidance had been very dear to them.

R.M. (Red) Hitt Jr., editor of *The Charleston Evening Post,* wrote to Travers on

September 7, 1956.

"Dear Marshall,

Announcement of your decision to leave St. Philip's and pioneer in the wilderness west of the Ashley was received by me with mixed emotions. The prevailing emotion is one of deep regret.

"You were responsible for bringing me into the Episcopal Church at a time when I had all but abandoned churches, although I was brought up to attend church services not less than three times a week. Had it not been for you I probably would have turned out to be a heathen and would have missed the many happy and comforting experiences which have come my way through my association with you and St. Philip's.

"I wish for you and Mrs. Travers great success, happiness and satisfaction in your new undertaking. If ever I or my newspaper can be of service to you, just ring the bell.

Sincerely yours,
Red
R.M. Hitt Jr.
Editor"

J. Ross Hanahan, Jr. reported on the farewell reception arrangements for the Travers and that the receiving line would be composed of the members and spouses of the reception committee and the wardens and their wives. Travers was given a $750 honorarium upon his departure and permitted to live in the rectory until a new rector was elected. All rectory utilities would be paid by the vestry until January 1, 1957.

Robey was designated permanent vestry chairman. At the November vestry meeting, Robey reported that clergymen were upset because Travers was recruiting possible members for his new mission, but, even so, he thought Travers should be given a list of St. Philippian's who lived west of the Ashley. Robey's report and suggestions were accepted as information.

TRAVERS' CHURCH AND COMMUNITY ACTIVITIES

Travers served on the diocese's executive council, the Christian Social Relations and Mission Departments as chairman, the diocesan YPSL as executive secretary, the standing committee, Charleston Convocation delegate, general convention, provincial chairman, adult Christian education and president of the Charleston Ministerial Association, the Charleston Bible Society and Charleston Clericus.

He also served on the boards of the Crippled Children Society, Family Agency, Boy Scouts and the Muscular Dystrophy Association. Like Beckwith and Williams, Travers was the chaplain of the Washington Light Infantry. He was a member of the South Carolina Society and the Country Club.

TRAVERS AFTER ST. PHILIP'S

Travers new congregation first worshipped in a West Ashley theater. After building a new church at 95 Folly Road, Travers increased the membership from zero to 380 including forty-five St. Philippian families who transferred. A rectory was made available at 1 Albemarle Road in the Crescent and it was there that Travers died on Saturday March 2, 1963, at age fifty-eight.

The *News and Courier* wrote, "Marshall Travers possessed in large degree the attribute of charity of which St. Paul said comes first for any Christian. Though unassuming in manner, he had a strong character and strong purpose in life. Despite a serious continuing illness, he had a cheerful disposition through it all. Always faithful to his ministerial duties, he lived true to the best traditions of his faith." The congregation wrote about Travers, he was "… a man of unusual dedication and insight."

The funeral service was held at Travers' church, Holy Trinity, on Monday, March 4, 1963, with the Rt. Rev. Gray Temple and the Rev. A. Campbell Tucker, who was Travers' assistant at St. Philip's from 1947 to 1950, officiating. All the clergy of the diocese were in the procession. Connelly's announced the burial would be at St. Philip's.

Joseph H. Nixon, who was Holy Trinity's senior warden in 1963, announced the vestry named the educational building after "our late and beloved rector." Rev. Tucker filled in for Holy Trinity until the end of May when he and his wife returned to resume their summer duties at Shrine Mont Conference Center in Virginia. Nixon also announced the building fund totaled $48,000 and they expected to soon receive the final plans for their new church.

In 2012, the rector of Holy Trinity is David M. Dubay who was an associate rector at St. Philip's from 2005 to July 2008.

ROBEY DEPARTS AND THE SEARCH FOR A NEW RECTOR

On October 2, 1956, Robey discussed a plan with the vestry to catalogue its minutes and to set up permanent records. The vestry agreed and wanted the plan to begin with the 1948 minutes and to continue to the then present date. Mrs. Carl Millford, church secretary, agreed to catalogue the vestry meetings. God bless you Rev. Robey and Mrs. Millford. If not for you two, this book may not have been possible.

A petition signed by nearly 300 members was presented to the vestry on November 6, 1956, asking Robey to be the new rector. Senior Warden Haven was directed to acknowledge receipt of the petition and to assure the petitioners of the vestry's interest in obtaining the best man possible for the post. In December, seven members appeared at the vestry meeting to ask that Robey be called to be the next rector. Haven reported the search committee had narrowed its choice to one man.

Also in December, the vestry reimbursed Robey for the cost of redecorating his office.

On December 18, 1956, the vestry unanimously called the Rev. John Walter Tuton, rector of Trinity Church in Asheville to become rector of St. Philip's. Tuton turned down the call. He wrote that he took counsel with others and he had arrived at an irrevocable conclusion that he should not accept the call.

On December 26, 1956, Robey sent a letter of resignation to the vestry. He wrote, "I have been privileged to serve the parish of St. Philip's since March 1, 1953, and have been gratified by the success of my efforts, made possible by the loyal support of many of its members. However, by unanimous vote, you have called someone else to be the Rector of this parish. Therefore, I herewith submit my resignation to become effective March 1, 1957." The vestry responded they had taken his request under consideration.

In March, Robey also discussed with the vestry his need for ministerial assistance during the Easter season and he thought the decline of members taking communion was caused because there was only one minister. He also requested there be more parking and he wanted action to increase the size of the choir for Easter.

Robey did not leave on March 1, but sent another letter of resignation dated April 3, 1957, to take effect on May 3. He asked to stay in the rectory until May 15. Robey accepted the call of Bishop I. Louttit for service at St. Vincent's Protestant Episcopal Church in St. Petersburg, Florida. The vestry agreed to his request and gave him an honorarium of $1,000 as a farewell gift from the congregation. Remember, Travers' honorarium was $750. A farewell reception for the Robeys was arranged.

Haven replied to Robey on April 5, 1957. He wrote, "It is superfluous for me to mention the warm spot you hold in the hearts of all that have been in close contact with you here at St. Philip's. No one needs to tell you what you have done for many of us and even though you may read the words 'deep regret' with some degree of - should I say bitterness and possible cynicism (for which I could hardly blame you) – I'm confident in time you will realize they are sincerely meant. Our kindest and warmest regards follow you and Mrs. Robey to your new ministry."

In 1968, the vestry donated one burial lot to the Rev. Waddell Robey.

In 2011, Arthur M. Wilcox, who was a vestryman and vestry secretary in 1957, did not remember that there was any animosity toward Robey but he felt Robey was not chosen because of his older age. Beckwith was thirty-five when he came to St. Philip's, Williams was thirty-six or thirty-seven when he arrived and Clary was thirty-six. As previously stated, Robey was about the age of Travers.

Rev. Roderick J. Hobart, who was hired as interim rector during June and July 1957, suggested that proceeds from plate collections on communion Sundays be placed in the rector's discretionary fund and that the present discretionary fund be abolished. He also suggested that St. Philip's might contribute $10,000 to help establish a badly needed new mission at Surfside near Myrtle Beach. The vestry accepted his suggestion as information. The mission was established July 18, 1957, and was named The Resurrection at Surfside Beach. Hobart conducted a service there every third Sunday, sharing with two other clergymen. In 1962, Hobart lived in Conway.

At that time, Dr. Arthur L. Rivers, Dr. R. Maxwell Anderson, J. Heyward Furman, Jr. and Tom Myers went to Tarboro, North Carolina, "to look over The Rev. Mr. Clary." Myers moved that Clary be called at an annual salary of $7,200 instead of the previous offers of $8,000, an $800 automobile allowance and rectory privileges including utilities. The motion passed.

THE REV. SIDNEY GRAYSON CLARY

RECTOR

AUGUST 1, 1957 – AUGUST 31, 1964

On June 4, 1957, The Rev. S. Grayson Clary accepted the call to St. Philip's effective August 1. Clary attended his first vestry meeting on September 3 when he was elected chairman of the vestry.

Clary was born on October 16, 1921, in Disputanta,[16] Virginia, a small village of less than 400 people eight miles east of Petersburg where Beckwith was born. He received his A.B. from William and Mary College in 1943 and his B.D. degree from the Virginia Theological Seminary in 1949. He had married Olive Jean Beazley on August 3, 1946. They had two sons. He served churches in three small towns, Lawrenceville, Callaville and Alberta, Virginia, prior to serving as rector of Calvary Church in Tarboro, twenty miles east of Rocky Mount. Clary was thirty-six, the same age as Beckwith, when he began his rectorship, at St. Philip's.

Clary served under two bishops:

Bishop Thomas Neely Carruthers was born June 10, 1900, in Collierville, Tennessee. He received an AB degree from Sewanee in 1921, a MA degree from Princeton University in 1924 and received his BD from the School of Theology at Sewanee in 1925. He was ordained deacon in 1925 and ordained priest 1926. He married Ellen Douglas Everett of Columbia, Tennessee, in 1926 when he was the chaplain of the Columbia Institute

---

16 The *News and Courier* misspelled Disputanta leaving off the final "a."

and Junior College. Carruthers served as rector at churches in Houston and Nashville prior to being consecrated as bishop of the diocese of South Carolina at St. Philip's on May 4, 1944. He died on June 12, 1960, from a cerebral hemorrhage after a hike with young people at Camp St. Christopher.

In July 1960, the vestry invited the Bishop Carruthers Memorial Fund Committee to place a permanent memorial tablet in St. Philip's to honor him because of his numerous close connections with this parish. The memorial is on the north wall of the nave.

Bishop Gray Temple was born in Lewiston, Maine, on March 13, 1914. After graduating from Brown University in 1935, Temple graduated from the Virginia Theological Seminary in 1938 and was ordained deacon the same year. After being ordained priest in 1939, he married Maria Drane the next year. Temple then served as curate at the Calvary Church in Tarboro where Clary would serve about ten years later. Temple also served churches in Virginia and North Carolina and finally Trinity Church in Columbia. He was consecrated bishop of the diocese of South Carolina on January 11, 1961, in Charleston where Clary reported that "there was widespread participation in the consecration on the part of St. Philip's parishioners." He retired in 1982.

CHURCH SERVICES, MEMBERSHIP AND CLERGY

Clary inherited a congregation of 1,200 that Travers had built up from 726.

An early service conducted after Clary's arrival was attended by parents and their young people going off to school. A breakfast followed. The winter church schedule for services were 8:15 a.m. with communion every Sunday, the family service and church school at 9:30 a.m. and morning prayer and sermon at 11:15 a.m. Communion would be celebrated every third Sunday at the 9:30 a.m. service and communion every first Sunday at the 11:15 am service.

Clary stated in the 1957 parish report that his first five months had been a matter of getting to know the parishioners and learning the general operations of the parish. He praised the lay readers, Edward R. Ball, Malcolm D. Haven, H.S. (Dick) Reeves, Edward M. Walker and Arthur M. Wilcox, for their fine work.

During that time, Clary, who kept a very accurate record of his activities, reported in five months that he conducted 131 services plus baptisms, confirmations, marriages and burials. He also attended forty-eight parish meetings and held 100 personal conferences.

The *Parish Letter* was mailed to the congregation on a regular basis. In the eight page issue of July 28, 1959, Clary wrote he was very pleased that there was a marked number in those taking communion. Because there were 1,062 more communicants in the first six months of 1959 than there were in the first six months of 1958, Clary said this was an indication of the deepening spiritual life of the parish. There were also increases at each of the three Sunday services. Clary felt it was also significant that members maintained their pledges, indicating a growth of stewardship in the parish. He listed the fourteen parish births, thirty-four baptisms, fourteen deaths, nineteen received by transfer and fifteen transferred away. There were thirty-three received by confirmation. The three marriages were: Theodore Jervey Simons IV – Eleanor Frances Van Ness on December 27, 1958, Richard Edward Coen – Mary Vereen Huguenin on April 11, 1959 and Robert Charles Momeier – Elizabeth Howe Brown on May 2, 1959.

Although the vestry had promised to supply Clary with an assistant, he did not seem in a hurry find someone. He said he was negotiating with several people but it not until seven months later that an assistant was called.

REV. CHARLES LEONIDAS WIDNEY

ASSISTANT RECTOR

DECEMBER 1958 OR JANUARY 1959 - 1965

In late September, Clary suggested the Rev. Charles Leonidas Widney, assistant rector at Trinity Church in Columbus, Georgia, since 1952, would be suitable. Bishop Carruthers and a clergyman in the diocese of Atlanta had recommended Widney. The vestry authorized Clary to fly to Georgia to meet Widney and for Clary to issue a call if he felt right about him. The vestry approved. In October, Widney gave tentative acceptance and in November he gave final acceptance. He came to Charleston in late 1958 or early 1959.

Clary said canon law provides for the rector to call an assistant with consent of the vestry.

Widney, who was at least twenty years older than Clary, was a native of New Iberia, Louisiana. He attended high school in Chickasha, Oklahoma, and received his Bachelor of Arts degree in 1920 and his bachelor of divinity degree in 1922, both from the University of the South. His first eight years were spent in the diocese of Oklahoma and in 1930 he became rector of Otey Memorial Parish at Sewanee where he stayed for eleven years. For the next eleven years, Widney was rector of St. George's Church in Memphis and from there to Columbus arriving at St. Philip's seven years later.

Widney, who married Miss Bertha Clay Ragland of Shawnee, Oklahoma, had two children. The Widneys planned to retire in Charleston and Rev. and Mrs. Widney and their son were received by transfer to St. Philip's on November 21, 1958. In 1965, Charles L.

Widney Jr. was in Beirut, Lebanon, as a Near East representative for Chase Manhattan Bank in New York City and their daughter, Mrs. Jo Ann Booker, who in 2012 lives in Charleston, has four grandchildren.

Mrs. Booker said that her father loved to stay busy but he also loved his family vacations – usually traveling to Louisiana to visit relatives. In 2012, Mrs. Booker, remains faithful to St. Philip's and is a steadfast member of the altar guild.

REV. CLARY & DR. COVENTRY

One afternoon the Clarys were riding bicycles and found George and Rosalie Orvin at their home at 18 Meeting Street. The Orvins told them they had just returned from a year in England where Dr. Orvin had taken a year of graduate study in child psychiatry at the University of London at Maudsley Hospital. Clary said that a year in London sounded great and Orvin replied that perhaps he could do something for them.

Coincidentally, not only did the Orvins attend St. Marylebone (pronounced "Maribun") Church in London but they lived next door to its vicar Dr. Frank Coventry.

After Orvin returned home, he wrote to Coventry, about the idea of an exchange with Clary. In March 1962, the vestry approved the exchange between St. Philip's and St. Marylebone for a period of one year effective September 1, 1962. Both the Bishop of London and the Bishop of South Carolina approved the plan. In May, the vestry wrote a letter to welcome Dr. Frank Coventry who arrived on August 7, 1962.

Coventry was born in south London to a Methodist family. "While up at Emmanuel College, Cambridge, where he read English, he joined the Church of England, largely under the influence of C. S. Lewis." After he met his wife, Ursula, at Cambridge and married her in 1948, he taught school. The lack of spiritual values among the boys encouraged him to become a minister. Two years at the Lincoln Theological College led him to a curacy at All Saints' in Dulwich and later to St. Marylebone where he remained until 1973, apart from his one year in South Carolina. In 1973, he was made a Prebendary[17] of St. Paul's Cathedral."

In an article written by *Charleston Evening Post* reporter Charles Hunter, forty-nine year old Coventry said this was his first trip to America. He wanted to come here because it was very important "at the present time for the British and American people to become acquainted. If the people do get acquainted on the personal level, it will be easier for international understanding. I am here to learn about America and Americans." He arrived with his wife and two daughters, Catherine then age 12 and Sarah age 7.

---

17 A clergyman who receives a stipend from a cathedral or a subsistence allowance granted by the state.

Coventry attended his first vestry meeting on September 12, 1962, when he thanked the vestry for installing air conditioners in the rectory. A reception was held at St. Philip's after church to introduce the Coventrys.

John Wilson told Coventry that he needed to preach a Thanksgiving service. Coventry replied, "Not to a bunch of blasted non-conformists."

In January 1963, Coventry, who was an English Rotarian, addressed the Charleston Rotary Club. As far as he knew, Rotary was the only service club in England. He told of an English custom – no one smoked before the queen was honored with a toast.

Dr. Orvin admitted one day to Coventry that he was having a hard time with the British accent. Dr. Coventry replied that it was Dr. Orvin who had the accent and not he.

The Coventrys had trouble with insects and the heat but said Charleston had character and tradition and everyone knew the city's history. While helping with the "St. Philip's Town Tour," Catherine and Sarah discovered a bit of their homeland when entertaining Mary Pope Hutson, who was wearing her Charleston bonnet while sitting in her English pram. The event was featured in a picture in the *News and Courier* on March 14, 1963.

Meanwhile Clary was learning his way around. St. Marylebone Church is located on Marylebone Road diagonally across from Madame Tussaud's and one block south of Regent's Park. Shortly after the Clarys arrival, 150 people attended the annual service and garden party held by the Friends of St. Marylebone Parish Church. During the garden party, held in Regent's Park at The Holme,[18] the guests had the opportunity to meet the Clarys. Guests included the mayor and mayoress of Marylebone.

While Clary was in London in October 1962, the St. Philip's vestry discussed hiring a curate and a director of religious education. Clary wrote that he would prefer no one be hired until he returned although he warmly approved their interest in the youth. Senior Warden Richardson Hanckel reported that any contracts signed with clergy would expire prior to Clary's return and, in spite of Clary's letter, they wanted to proceed with their plan as soon as possible. Remember, Widney was still the assistant rector. By December, one curate declined the offer and none other had been found. The position of religious education remained empty as well.

Because several visitors had arrived too late for the services due to the time changes, signs were put up outside the church. Steps were to be taken to notify the hotels and motels.

Coventry and his family departed Charleston on August 31, 1963, to spend three days in New York prior to returning to London. He was interviewed by *News and Courier* reporter Louis J. Roempke about Coventry's feelings on his departure. "The

---

18   The Holme is a large building dating from 1818 located next to Queen Mary's garden.

lean minister" said he was particularly impressed with "the openness, spontaneous and forthrightness of the people here. You know it's quite a change from the typical English reserve." He thought he would be doing an ambassadorial job but quickly realized St. Philip's congregation was significantly English and Huguenot in its extraction. They liked fried chicken but not hominy grits. Coventry had been used to "milder politics but his children had learned that Kennedy was a bad thing."

Coventry was most impressed ecclesiastically with lay participation and the general activity of the congregation. He said, "Their attendance and interest in the Bible is more noticeable than in most parts of England."

On September 9, Clary expressed his appreciation to the vestry for his year in England. He said the exchange had provided a very valuable and meaningful year for him and his family.

Charleston Evening Post reporter Suzanne McIntosh interviewed Clary upon his return to Charleston – the article ran on September 11, 1963. He said, "I lived with the English people, was involved in their baptisms, marriages, births and deaths and I came to know some of them very well." Clary said that in England each parish has geographical boundaries and the church's membership consisted of everyone within those boundaries whether they were heathens, of other faiths or communicants of the Anglican Church. He would have to marry anyone who lived within the parish.

On April 13, 1964, Clary reported to the vestry he had visited the Virginia Theological Seminary and asked for recommendations from the dean and chaplain about possible candidates for a parish assistant for St. Philip's. Mr. Anthony Andreas from Youngstown, Ohio, who was recommended, would graduate from the seminary in May. The previous summer, Andreas had worked at St. Catherine's Church in Jacksonville and its rector described Andreas as a most capable seminarian. Clary invited Andreas to Charleston and to the April 28 vestry meeting.

There was a full discussion of Andreas' replies and the manner of handling himself. John Rivers said he disagreed with some of Andreas' statements but he would approve a call. Tony Harrigan, vestry secretary, said he could not support Andreas because he would not rule out street demonstrations as a possible part of his ministry. John Welch had called St. Paul University and was told of Andreas' superior academic ability while Rufus Barkley had a favorable report from Episcopal High School. Theodore Guerard regarded Andreas as responsible and level headed. Jack Todd would vote to call Andreas. Randell Stoney wanted to know whether inquiries had been made about other candidates and Clary said Andreas was the first man they had thoroughly considered. Everyone voted to call Andreas except one. The recommended salary would be $4,200 per year.

Bishop Temple gave his consent to call Andreas, but the bishop of Ohio informed Temple he would not release Andreas and he did not know on what basis his name could have been considered. The bishop said Andreas had been using calls from elsewhere to improve his position in his Ohio diocese. After the Ohio bishop called, Andreas phoned Clary and said he could not take the position. Clary withdrew his offer.

Harry D. and Catherine Jones, who were married by Clary, remembered he would send a "Happy Anniversary" card each year to all those who he had married.

THE YOUTH, MEN'S MINISTRIES, AND THE LADIES

In January 1958, the vestry adopted new rules for the use of the parish house:

use was restricted to church members, fee was $7.00 - $7.50 for the parish house and $2.50 for the sexton who would not clean up afterwards and no orchestra was permitted to play at parties other than square dances.

In 1958, the church school was having a good year with a staff of more than fifty and there was a weekly attendance of 250. That figure was 50% less than the previous years because forty-five St. Philippian families followed Travers to Holy Trinity west of the Ashley. In September, the YPSL divided into two groups, the juniors, age twelve to thirteen, and the seniors, ages fourteen and above. Alfred Pinckney was the president of the senior YPSL.

The two groups met together three times a year to discuss the conflicts of family living such as the telephone, car, clothes, radio, television, dating, allowances, school grades and more. After a thorough discussion, Clary very subtly asked, "Now, if the shoe were on the other foot, and all of you were parents who had teenage sons or daughters, how would you handle these conflicts?" After a little thought, the young people unanimously agreed they would do exactly as their parents were doing. Clary replied, "Well, you don't really have a problem do you? It is a matter of understanding."

The YPSL was looking forward to hosting the Youth Convention in February 1958 for the first time at St. Philip's. There would be 200 youths and advisors attending.

Louisa Rivers was president of the junior YPSL, Martha Allen, vice-president, Teddy Daniell, secretary and Cinda Waits (later married to Morris Cave), treasurer. Mrs. Elizabeth H. Daniell was the counselor.

Approximately seven boys served as crucifers, acolytes or flag bearers each Sunday directed by Craig M. Bennett Sr. as the master acolyte. At that time, twenty boys were trained or in training. Those boys participating were: Sam Allen III, Robert Ball Jr., Albert Bonnoitt Jr., Jim Boyette Jr., Ernest Childs, Teddy Daniell, Robert Foster, Lucas

Gaillard Jr., Charles Gibbs Jr., David Humphreys Jr., Dick McManus, Carl Millford Jr., Marvin Murdaugh Jr., Alfred Pinckney, Godfrey Pringle, Walter Pringle IV, Franklin Robson III, Baynard Seabrook, Richard Tassin, Legare Van Ness and Larry Walker.

The men's group was headed for the first half of the year by Ham Brooks and the second half by Edward Ball. They had a series of lunches, each with a speaker who touched on such topics as Psychiatry and Religion, Religion and Education, What is a Parish Life Conference? The Literary Importance of the Bible and many other topics.

The Woman's Auxiliary reported in 1957 an income of $3,917 and disbursements of $3,777.01. They made a profit $1,395.66 from the tea garden and a profit of $1,110 from the plantation tour. The report was submitted by Mrs. Marjere M. Uzzell (Mrs. T.M) whose husband taught Spanish at the High School of Charleston.

BISHOP CARRUTHERS' TRIP TO EUROPE

In July 1959, Bishop Carruthers' spoke to the St. Philip's ladies about his 1958 trip to the Lambeth conference in England. He said the conference's theme was reconciliation. He was taught that the elements of a Christian family were summed up by the following statements: worship God in church and in the home, forgive one another, share and be a good neighbor, be hospitable to a friend and a stranger. The bishop concluded his address saying, "God reigns, God calls, God sends. Every Christian has his part to play in this total picture."

This author was invited by Bishop Carruthers, his wife, Ellen Douglas and his son, Ewing, to join them on a part of their European trip. A highlight was attending the opening Lambeth service at Canterbury Cathedral with many trumpets that heralded the entering processional headed by the Archbishop of Canterbury. The bishops sat behind the choir. The conference is held every ten years, attended by Anglican bishops worldwide. English Bishops are lords as are the American bishops while in Britain.

Traveling together was interesting. En route to Oxford, there was a change of trains, with a ten minute connection in Sheffield, where we grabbed our seven suitcases and hauled them up many steps. Somehow we made the connection. Upon arriving at the hotel in Oxford, Ellen Douglas decided to lecture Ewing and this author on the evils of liquor and before we knew it she was standing on a suitcase in the lobby lecturing to anyone who would listen.

The four of us went to the Vaudeville Theatre on The Strand to see a funny musical called *Salad Days* that had a long run in London. The music made you tap your toes and my favorite memory of Bishop Carruthers was seeing him laughing and doing a jig of sorts as he exited the theatre.

Bishop Carruthers was a wonderful person as was his wife. In 1957, she held weekly Bible studies for teenagers at the bishop's residence at 132 South Battery. She had a party at their house for the 1957 High School of Charleston graduates and needless to say, there was no alcohol.

In December, the Women's Auxiliary made a formal request to hire a cook or chef to oversee meal preparations for occasions such as the Men's Club. In February 1950, Mrs. Francis S. Minott (Myrtle deLeisseline),[19] who was widowed and had moved into the church home, was hired as "Parish House Hostess." She resigned in 1962.

Also under the direction of Mrs. Minott, the "Sewing Group" met each Wednesday morning at the church to "make aprons, stuffed toys and other items of fancy work." A photograph of the "Sewing Group" appeared in the *News and Courier* on October 30, 1960, to promote St. Philip's upcoming annual food sale. Those pictured were: Mrs. Thomas P. Stoney, Mrs. L.L. Oliveros, Mrs. M.A. Bolt, Miss Pauline Dill, Miss May Martin and Mrs. Minott.

Eleven years later, when Sam Cobb was rector, the "Sewing Group" was still meeting on Wednesday mornings after the communion service. Members were anxious to have new sewers (Cobbism: "not sewers") with young eyes to give them a boost. Cobb said this was a grand group of ladies who have been meeting nigh these many years and who have provided many lovely and useful articles for the fall bazaar.

In 1961, a Sunday was set aside for students. At the 11:15 a.m. service Miss Mary Minott Burgess, the granddaughter of Mrs. F.S. Minott, sang *The Omnipotence* by Schubert. She later became a noted opera singer.

The church school reported in October it was using all available space plus some other space in the church home. The vestry decided to place vinyl tile at a cost of $132 on the floor of the Boy Scouts' room and let that be used for the church school overflow. Dr. Edward S. Izard and Howard Yates were the new cub masters.

A motion made by the vestry in March 1962 forbade the serving of alcoholic beverages in the parish library as was a rule already in place in the parish house.

Mary Lilly Bennett wrote an article for the *News and Courier* about the church house tours.

"Down the street they come – singing, whistling and shouting – no Pied Piper needed. Across the bricks, the flagstones and into the waiting houses ... (the children) prove that Bermuda shorts, and blue jeans do mix with Queen Anne and the Chippendale influence – that 'high-tops' and loafers are serenely at home on polished pine. They are Twentieth Century youngsters – yo-yoing, passing Scout tests, dressing for Sunday

---

19 Mrs. Minott's name was misspelled in the 1961 Charleston City Directory as Minnot.

school and hanging from tree limbs." Pictures featured Charlotte McCrady rearranging the furniture at 35 Church Street and Park Dougherty picking a flower for Sally Wilson at 90 Church Street. Alida, Llewellyn and Frances Sinkler were playing with dolls at 39 Church Street. Tickets were sold at the Fort Sumter and Francis Marion hotels.

In 1970, the plantation tour had a net profit of $2,913.33. In 1972, the plantation tour was sold out after selling the allotted 300 tickets at $7.00 each. Pat Wardlaw and Dottie Kerrison were in charge of the 1984 tour. The 1986 plantation tour encompassed Edisto Island. Co-chairs for the tour were Anne Craver and Nancy Wallace with Vicki Causey as ticket chair. The 1989 tour featured Wadmalaw Island.

The parish picnic was held at Coburg Dairy on June 16, 1962, thanks to the Hanckel family. In July, John Wilson reported that negotiations were in progress towards getting the new tennis nets installed and the courts painted. The tennis courts were south of the parish house. Mrs. G.C.A. Salvo (May) was approached about becoming the new "Parish House Hostess." The salary would range from $80.00 to $100 per month. The Episcopal Young Churchmen were meeting successfully in October.

In November 1962, there was a proposal for incorporating the Sunday school budget into the church budget because it would allow closer supervision from the vestry. The church school committee basically said no. Instead, the committee would furnish the vestry with a proposed 1963 church school budget and a monthly statement of church school receipts and expenses.

The vestry decided that all disbursements for the Sunday school of more than $1.00 must be approved by the school's superintendent and the church school treasurer could only pay the bills that were so approved. It was also required that a written outline of a proposed Sunday school program for the coming year including courses, teachers, etc. be turned into the vestry no later than May 1963. The superintendent later reported the curriculum had been settled and the staff had been fairly well filled out. He asked that the vestry try to find a replacement for him by the end of the next school year.

Mrs. Rufus Barkley Jr. (Nella) "President of the Women of St. Philip's" reported the women had set aside $1,500 to be used for youth work. She suggested that Sewanee be included in the vestry's church budget.

In December 1963, Mrs. George Orvin (Rosalie) agreed to supervise the "Junior Episcopal Young Churchmen." She continued the post through 1965.

In May 1964, Clary brought up the subject of a new Sunday school superintendent and had spoken with Arthur Wilcox about taking the position. Wilcox said he would consider taking the post if he were asked but only if the manner of operation be thoroughly revised. He termed the Sunday school a disgrace to the parish, lacking discipline, interest and achievement on the part of the children. Wilcox proposed removal of children who were unruly, suggested examinations for promotion from grade to grade, teacher training and a formal operation of the Sunday school as a school in the strict sense. He said that under such a system the Sunday school might be small in numbers, but that it would be meaningful. The curriculum would be designed to prepare youngsters for confirmation.

Wilson agreed with Wilcox's main points of criticism but Dr. Rivers questioned if enough teachers could be found and he predicted families would leave St. Philip's because of such a rigorous system. Clary replied that the parish must realize that Christianity has a discipline. Dr. Anderson did not know if the disciplinary system was the answer.

The vestry passed Tony Harrigan's motion confirming the authority of the Sunday school superintendent to remove any child who seriously disturbed the classroom. Clary said he believed that the parish could develop a plan for the Sunday school that would involve the factors of discipline, training and parental assistance.

The vestry was deeply concerned. Wilcox agreed to work with the Sunday school for the year ahead.

The Sunday school dilemma was resolved and the situation had been improved. It was reported in October 1965 that 250 children were attending Sunday school and that attendance was eighty-five per cent. The vestry approved the purchase of a blackboard for $42.00, lockers for $268 and a desk for $50.00.

THEOLOGY, EVANGELISM AND MISSIONS

In June 1958 Clary sent a contribution to Rev. Marshall Travers from St. Philip's Easter collection for his Holy Trinity mission. In December the church made a donation to the mission in Johnsonville.

Bishop Carruthers, in May 1959, sent a thank you letter to St. Philip's for its $749.43 Easter offering to the St. Andrews Mission. The 1960 offering of $906.50 was given St. Luke's Mission in Latta and for missionary purposes.

At the vestry meeting of January 9, 1961, Clary reported in general terms about possible opportunities for mission work in the community. **A mission fund of $2,000 was established** (bold letters by author). Other than payments to the diocese and cash collections from the plates, this was the first time that a budget had been established for missions.

THE MOLLEGEN AFFAIR

Clary and the vestry unanimously voted to extend an invitation to Dr. Albert T. Mollegen to give a series of lectures about Christianity and communism at St. Philip's on February 5 and 6, 1962. The vestry paid his expenses and an honorarium.

There were letters to the editor concerning Mollegen's lectures. C.C. Star from Quakertown, Bucks, Pennsylvania, wrote … "the Rev. Grayson Clary should hang his head in shame" for inviting Mollegen to St. Philip's. Star continued, "I'm not an Episcopalian but I do consider myself a Christian with principles. My husband and I refuse to sell any of our land which borders an Episcopal Church because it is part of the National Council of Churches and sponsors such ministers as Dr. Albert T. Mollegen." L.E. Williams of Sullivans Island wrote a lengthy letter blasting Mollegen and whoever invited him to St. Philip's. Marguerite S. Hale of James Island wrote "It appears to me that Dr. Mollegen was interested in everything but his Father's business."

Mollegen was professor of New Testament language and literature at Virginia Theological Seminary. Remember Clary graduated from that seminary in 1949 and he surely must have known of Mollegen and may have even taken a course from him.

Mollegen had been scheduled to speak at Clemson College during Religious Emphasis Week but his engagement was canceled. The president of Clemson, Dr. R.C. Edwards, and Mollegen said the cancellation was by "mutual consent." Edwards announced that a group of people in the Charleston area had raised questions about Mollegen's activities. The only name that was actually made public was Virginia B. Gourdin, who had been elected to the General Assembly in 1958 as the first female legislator from Charleston County. She was the fifth female to be elected to the general assembly. Miss Gourdin said the main concern of the group was not to block Dr. Mollegen from speaking but to determine whether he had ever issued a retraction of his activities in the 1930s and 1940s. She died in 2009 at age 88 and is buried at the French Huguenot Church in Charleston.

During the 1950s and 1960s, Americans feared that communists would destroy the United States with Russian missiles aimed at America and vice-versa. It was a frightening time. School children were told to prepare against a Russian nuclear attack by sitting under his or her school desk. Panicked people dug bomb shelters in back yards. Senator Joseph McCarthy was always on the lookout for communists.

Mollegen belonged to communist organizations and participated in other suspect groups. He was not at all surprised that these groups would be on the House Un-American Activities Committee and said that he had resigned from all of them. But from articles in the *News and Courier*, it would seem Mollegen had little recollection about his previous activities.

During one of Mollegen's lectures he spoke about the National Council of Churches being primarily non-political. A lady in the audience asked him why he had signed a petition concerning communists being members of the American Civil Liberties Union (ACLU). Mollegen replied "I have no recollection of it. If it happened before 1930, it was defensible but wrong. If it happened after 1939, it was wrong. And I don't think I did it." The communist newspaper, *The Daily Worker*, reported on March 13, 1940, that Mollegen was one of seventeen signers of an open letter condemning the ACLU's executive board for barring communists from being office holders and members of its national committee.

Mollegen said, "Remember there were no people who worked harder for civil liberties than the communists between the years of 1925 and 1939. They held everything else in abeyance." He did say, "I believe the days of communism are numbered."

People wanted to know if Mollegen had changed his ways. J. Douglas Donahue, state news editor of the *News & Courier,* asked Mollegen, "Do you agree with a widely known fellow clergyman that the virgin birth of Jesus Christ is not necessarily true?"

Mollegen replied, "I served on the drafting committee for the Episcopal Bishop's pastoral letter of November 1960 which affirms our church's commitment to the Apostles' and Nicene creeds. I am in total agreement with the document as our bishops finalized it."

The 1960 pastoral letter said a good bit about the creeds. "Our church is irrevocably committed to the historic Creeds and regards the Nicene Creed as it was affirmed at the Council of Chalcedon in A.D. 451, as an indispensable norm for the Christian faith … It is one of the tragedies in Christian history that large sections of Christendom have abandoned the Creeds partially because they did not hear what they were really saying. Our Church has not done that, principally because it is unafraid of truth, come whence it may. That God's truth will not contradict itself is self-evident. The Anglican acceptance of that principle permits us to hold to the great Creeds as religious and theological dogmatic statements <u>without denying or dominating new ways of finding truth on other than religious and theological levels</u>" (author's note – John 14:6).

Other comments included, "Both the Bible and Creeds must be constantly interpreted in terms of the language and thought forms of successive times. This living interpretation is a necessary although a dangerous work. It is a dangerous work because the rephrasing of the Gospel may bring the restatement under the power of the culture in which it is rephrased. Contemporary interpreters are in danger of becoming heretics even as champions of orthodoxy are in danger of becoming unintelligible. From this dilemma, spring some of the tensions and the controversies in the Church."

Clary said to Mollegen "We are grateful to you for stretching our minds. As our spirits grow, may we learn to examine new ideas as we live under our living God." A total of 1,200 people attended the lectures.

In October 1962, Vestryman John T. Welch told Coventry of the great interest and pleasure with which his sermons and fall Bible talks were being received by St. Philippians. Another series of Coventry's Sunday Bible studies were taught from January through

March 31, 1963. The theme – covenants – began with the covenant of the promise to Abraham and ended with the new covenant of Christ. In 2012, Mary DeSaussure remembered how much she loved Coventry's sermons.

Clary told the vestry that he was going to continue his policy of offering sermons, talks and any other opportunities presented to help the congregation grow in its concept of the church and the nature of worship.

Plans were made for a teaching mission, open to the public, in early May 1964 to be given by Rev. Edward Nason West, Canon of the Cathedral of St. John Divine in New York City. The committee making the arrangements was headed by J. Ham Brooks.

Canon West, while teaching at St. Philip's, said he would emphasize the need for greater understanding among Christians of various denominations. He said there were more than 250 different religious bodies in this nation, and many of their members think of the church as an organization or building. They don't realize they are the church. West added that "The church is one because God is one. Go anywhere in the world and the church's oneness is the same. The unity of the church lies in the spirit of God." He continued "the real sin against the Holy Ghost is the failure to recognize Him and where he is working."

Clary advised the vestry that Cadwallader Jones wished to give a number of Bibles to the church. The offer was accepted with thanks.

BISHOP JOHN SPONG

In July 1964, the vestry decided to bring the Reverend John Spong to St. Philip's for a teaching mission and they wanted to include St. Michael's. Spong was the rector of the Calvary Church in Tarboro where he in 1957 had succeeded Clary as rector. Remember, Bishop Gray Temple was also rector of that church in the late 1940s.

Spong was born in Charlotte on June 6, 1931. He was a Phi Beta Kappa graduate the University of North Carolina at Chapel Hill and he received his Master of Divinity degree from the Episcopal Theological Seminary in Alexandria. He served churches in North Carolina and Virginia from 1955 to 1976 when he became the bishop of the diocese of Newark from which he retired in 2000.

Spong had a life changing experience after reading a book published in 1963 by the Anglican Bishop of Woolwich, John A.T. Robinson. The book, *Honest to God,* aroused a storm of controversy by stating, among other things, "Secular Man needs a secular theology." Robinson had already achieved notoriety for his defense of the book *Lady Chatterly's Lover*. In his final interview, C.S. Lewis commented on the book saying "I prefer being honest to being *Honest to God.*"

Even though Robinson created a controversy, no other bishop could ignite the flames of indignation and outrage than Spong did. Spong wrote many books beginning in 1973 – one was called *Can a Bishop Be Wrong?* Later ten (orthodox) writers and scholars challenged Spong about his book. Some who challenged Spong were Bishop C. FitzSimons Allison, retired bishop of the diocese of South Carolina, Bishop James M. Stanton of the diocese of Dallas and Peter C. Moore former dean of the Trinity School for Ministry. In 2012, Moore is associated with St. Michael's.

Spong rejected the historical truth of some doctrines such as the Virgin birth and resurrection of Jesus. There was strong criticism from the Archbishop of Canterbury.

Some said that Spong was the legacy of James Pike who was the flamboyant bishop of the diocese of California who was charged with heresy in 1961. Pike died in an Israeli desert in 1969.

Allison said that Spong had a real knack for appealing to the spirit of this age, but Spong "had denied the basic Christian beliefs he vowed to uphold as a bishop." Allison added, "If Spong were truly honest, he would resign as bishop. It is not only a question of theology; it's a question of honor."

FINANCES AND THE VESTRY

Three new faces on the 1957 vestry were Dr. R. Maxwell (Mac) Anderson, F. Bartow Culp and J. Ham Brooks.

In March 1957, the vestry contacted E. Milby Burton, who was the director of the Charleston Museum, to examine old records of the church to see what should be preserved and at what cost. Burton took an inventory and recommended many of the books needed repairing. Some needed laminating such as the 1832 – 1839 burial records and others needed binding such as the 1760 Book of Common Prayer. In the latter book, all references to the king of England were scratched out after the American Revolution. The South Carolina Archives offered to laminate at half price since there were no state records for much of that period. It is not clear that any action was taken.

Arthur Wilcox in June 1963 agreed to meet with Milby Burton concerning the church's historical records. After Welch read a letter to the vestry in February 1964 drawing attention to the poor condition of the parish registers, the matter was briefly discussed. Wilcox was asked to look into the possibility of laminating the books. At the same time, Miss Anna Wells Rutledge suggested forming a historical committee to bring the parish records up to date and Clary suggested to the vestry that a history of the parish be written.

Returning to 1952 when church treasurer William S. Stevens resigned his position on December 31, Joseph A. Bell became his successor in 1953. E. Roy Daniell, who was a descendent of Gov. Robert Daniell, was a new member of St. Philip's. In 1955 he asked to be the church's auditor. He got the job and Daniell recommended that the church treasurer, Bell, be furnished with his own adding machine and a place to work.

In January 1957, Joseph A. Bell was reelected treasurer and Theodore J. Simmons, III, would be his assistant until September 30. It got very confusing after that. Bell was asked to resign by May 1 and Simmons would become treasurer. In September, Bell was reinstated as treasurer. In October that reinstatement was rescinded but there was no resignation from Bell. Then it was suggested Simmons become treasurer and Bell his assistant. That was reaffirmed in January 1959.

Joseph A. Bell was a wonderful, fun loving gentleman. He would spend time at the Carolina Yacht Club where he loved to greet everyone as they entered to remind them that he was the oldest member of the club. Bell also reminded members that as the oldest member he was given the privilege of kissing all the ladies. Bell was last listed in the Yacht Club's 1968 – 1969 membership book.

Mrs. Burgh Smith (Billie D.), who lived at 1329 South Edgewater Dr., applied for the job of church secretary but the vestry attempted to hold the position in abeyance pending the arrival of the new rector. Finally, they decided in 1962 to hire Mrs. Smith prior to Clary's arrival.

In January 1958, J. Ross Hanahan was elected senior warden and Dr. Arthur L. Rivers was elected junior warden. In February the vestry rented two parking places for the rector and the church secretary for $5.00 per month each.

Clary reported in June that Miss Mary S. Fludd left eight acres and a residence in Summerville to be equally divided between St. Philip's and St. Paul's. The property had been appraised at $12,000. In October, St. Philip's received a list of bids received in response to the advertisement with a high bid at $16,750 and a low bid $5,050. The vestry rejected all offers and asked the executor to sell the property by private sale.

In February 1959, Ed Ball reported that since the Fludd property had sold for $25,000, St. Philip's would receive $10,000 but the estate's lawyer was withholding $2,500 to pay for St. Philip's share of the expenses. The vestry protested the attorney charging the church fees.

In 1960, Coming Ball Gibbs recommended paying the estate lawyer's fee of $300 to bring the matter to a conclusion but he recommended that a discreet inquiry be made whether or not interest had been earned on the principal.

Dr. Francis Bonneau Johnson in February 1959 left a bequest of $1,000 to St. Philip's. In October, Mrs. Susan J. Slade left a bequest of $92.17 and there was also a bequest by the late Miss Eugenia Calhoun Frost of $10,000. Miss Frost loved the chapel that was rebuilt in the memory of her parents and the vestry agreed to use the $10,000 for chapel maintenance.

In June 1959, after some discussion the vestry agreed to give a $100 contribution to help build an atomic reactor at St. Paul's University in Japan.

St. Paul's University, also known as Rikkyo University, was founded in 1874 in Tokyo by Bishop Channing Moore Williams who had been an early missionary in Japan. St. Paul's, the largest Anglican university in Japan, maintains close ties with the Episcopal Church and the Anglican Church of England to this day.

The university chapel is among nine chapels and thirty-three churches that make up the Tokyo diocese of the Anglican – Episcopal churches. These Episcopalians value a balance between the Bible, tradition and reason and the university chapels strive to provide education based on the spirit of Christianity.

There is a large research institute at St. Paul's University called the Education for Sustainable Development Research Center (ESD) that includes the Institute for Atomic Energy.

Clary in February 1959 read a breakdown of St. Philip's pledging:

0 to $1.00 198 members, $1.01 - $2.00 106 members, $2.01 - $3.00 42 members, $3.01 - $5.00 58 members, $5.01 - $10.00 34 members and $10.01 or more, 15 members

Out of 684 possible pledges, 453 pledged and 231 did not.

In May 1959 Roy Daniell resigned as St. Philip's auditor and was replaced by George McKnight.

In 1960, new to the vestry were Francis S. Dougherty, who took over as secretary from Craig M. Bennett Sr., Charles H. Gibbs and F. Mitchell Johnson. Tom Myers was elected senior warden and Cadwallader Jones, junior warden.

The new members of the vestry in 1961 were H.D. (Jack) Todd, John T. Welch and Thomas P. White. Cadwallader Jones was senior warden, Richardson M. Hanckel junior warden and Francis S. Dougherty remained secretary.

The vestry approved the 1961 budget at $86,380. Welch drafted a letter to solicit pledges from new parishioners and a note was placed in the Sunday bulletin requesting those who were leaving for the summer to pre-pay their pledges prior to leaving. John

Hyde was the new chairman of the Every Man Canvass and Rufus Barkley was vice chairman.

In February 1962, the vestry granted permission to the "Historic Activities Committee" of the Colonial Dames to copy certain church records, providing the records would be handled carefully and that all work would be done in the church office. Three copies of the published records were to be given to the church.

James Hamilton, the sexton, left his job and Prince Moseley was hired as sexton on January 16. 1963. C.A. Salvo (Clifton) was authorized to supervise the sexton's work and to see that an appropriate notice would be placed in the bulletin. In April, the vestry wrote Salvo a letter of thanks for the work he was doing supervising the sexton.

At the January 1963 vestry meeting, Charles H. Gibbs was elected senior warden and John T. Welch Jr. was elected junior warden. Francis Dougherty remained secretary.

In January 1964, having in hand pledges totaling $85,143, Welch proposed a budget of $95,000. The deficit would be publicized asking the congregation to make up the difference. John T. Welch became senior warden and Theodore (Teddy) B. Guerard became junior warden. Anthony Harrigan was secretary.

The real estate insurance was adjusted. The church building was valued between $500,000 and $600,000. The church home was valued at $80,000, the rectory at $50,000 and the tea garden at $4,200.

In April 1963, a building fund began with $1,700. In July 1964, J. Ross Hanahan Jr. donated fifty shares of cement stock that was sold for $1,137.18 to be placed in the building fund.

PROPERTY AND MAINTENANCE

In June 1957, Bartow Culp reported chunks of cement have fallen from the steeple and that a leak had developed in the roof near the organ console. In November, Carlton Davies, who made a report concerning necessary repair work on the steeple, received a bid of $3,800 that was accepted from the Ev-Air-Tight Co. of Philadelphia.

Hand railings were installed in the sacristy in 1958.

Davies was re-elected to the permanent property committee for a three year term ending in 1962. Gibbs asked that a letter be written to Davies thanking him for his many years of service to the church.

Maintenance was a challenge in 1959. In February, plaster fell just above the organ console, in June termites were found in the chapel and the steeple needed more work. Termites in the chapel returned in 1962.

Hurricane Gracie entered into St. Helena's Sound near Beaufort before noon on Tuesday, September 29, 1959, with winds at 140 miles per hour. The Beaufort area took the worst of it but Gracie headed north and there was at least five million dollars of damage in Charleston.

Because a large number of trees were felled by the hurricane, cleaning the churchyards proceeded slowly. Sonny Hanckel gave the church his chain saw and a man to cut up some of the larger limbs. Senior Warden DeRosset Myers reported most of the hurricane damage was to the roofs, including the copper sheathing near the top of the steeple. All the roofs were to be inspected. Contractor C.W. Blanchard estimated repairs would cost $3,500 not including any work on the roofs or steeple. Myers expected insurance to cover the damage.

The vestry offered the use of the parish house to St. Michael's during their period of reconstruction caused by the hurricane.

The idea of installing a sprinkler or fire alarm system in the church came up in January 1960. To protect the church, the vestry hired a watchman named Donaghue at $60.00 per week to be on duty from dusk to dawn. After much discussion, the Grinnell Company got the job and began installation of the sprinkler system on July 5, 1960. The night watchman continued his rounds but in September he resigned. The vestry suggested, with reference to the parochial report to the diocese, that Donaghue's salary "be given special treatment so as not to raise our Diocesan Apportionment."

In November, the sprinkler system was fully activated and the work on the alarm system was to be finished a few days later.

The vestry in May accepted a gift from Mrs. J. Stanyarne Stevens of two matching tables to be used to hold alms basins.

A new altar rail, given by an anonymous donor, was installed in May. It was decided to leave the poor box unlocked considering the regularity of its being broken into. Clifton Orvin was authorized to go ahead with the minor repairs to the pews, organ paneling, chapel side door, window cords, etc. Nat Ball pointed out damage to the plaster occurring above the altar and paint peeling in the vestibule. The pew latches were in a state of poor repair and it was suggested the ladies could finance an overhaul of the pews over a period of time.

W. T. Smith in February 1965 sold the southwest corner of Church and Cumberland streets to St. Philip's to be used as a parking lot for $37,500. The lot remains a valuable asset in 2012.

GLEBE LAND

Randell Stoney reported to the vestry in November 1956 that 6 Glebe Street was once again in poor condition. A lengthy discussion was about to begin whether to repair or sell it. In January 1957, Stoney reported because the church could not afford to repair the house, he would see if the College of Charleston would be interested in purchasing the house. In February, Stoney reported that F. J. Lilienthal made a $15,000 offer for 6 Glebe Street. Tom Myers heard some criticism from members about selling the house and he suggested prior to selling the house that the vestry obtain figures that showed beyond a doubt the infeasibility of keeping it. Stoney did get an estimate on repairing 6 Glebe from Herbert A. DeCosta showing it would cost $20,000 maximum and $16,000 minimum.

In January 1958, J. Ross Hanahan said the committee on the Glebe Street house believed it best to sell the house.

Dr. Anderson, Coming Ball Gibbs and Randell C. Stoney submitted their minority report. "The undersigned wish to submit an additional report in regards to the disposition of the Glebe House. It is our feeling that St. Philip's Church has too great an intimate historic connection with this valuable piece of architecture to lose control of or jeopardize its preservation. We therefore recommend that the gradual restoration of the property be undertaken as a project of the Church as part of its civic contribution to the community."

In February 1958, the College of Charleston indicated an interest in purchasing 6 Glebe Street. In March, Lilienthal wanted to purchase the house and restore it. The vestry continued to discuss the issue.

In the spring of 1958, Dr. Anderson's mother-in-law, Margaret S. Middleton wrote that an earlier rectory, or parsonage-house as it was called, became too confined causing the assembly to pass an act in 1770 that a new rectory should be built. The house, later known at 6 Glebe Street, was on a four acre lot that would allow proper out-houses, and room for a garden, orchard and pasturage. Mrs. Middleton wrote the house consisted of three substantial floors and an attic. The four rooms on each floor were bisected by a wide hall. The cypress paneling and wainscoting were "satisfying." Winding steps led to the attic.

Rev. Robert Smith, who became rector of St. Philip's in 1756, lived in the "new" rectory. Afterwards, he became the first bishop of the diocese of South Carolina. Miss Ellen Frost Parker said the last minister to live at the rectory was the Rev. Thomas Frost who died in 1804 – three years after Smith's death. The house was rented after 1804.

The vestry opened 6 Glebe Street the second Sunday after Easter so that members of the church could view the house. Fifty-seven adults toured the premises.

The zoning board in 1958 agreed to let the church turn 6 Glebe's lawn into a parking lot that would hold sixteen cars wrapped around the house. In 1959, the president of the Preservation Society, John Muller, thought the society should take over the house. Charles L. Tice was interested in renting the house for two years at $50.00 per month and he would make repairs. Citizens & Southern Bank was considering renting the entire parking area. Grace Church used 6 Glebe Street while Meadowcroft Hall was being built. The Junior League wanted to turn the house into a senior center.

Groups were still vying in 1961 for the use of 6 Glebe Street. Vestryman F. Mitchell Johnson, who was a trustee of the college, said in January the college was ready to purchase the house for $15,000 and they would lease the house for ten years at $1.00 a year to the King's Daughters. The glebe house committee recommended St. Philip's lease it to the King's Daughters but they declined and pointed out there were a great number of broken windows. T.C. Edwards suggested re-glazing the windows and then tacking hardware cloth over them. The vestry agreed to the use of the hardware cloth but not the glazing.

On September 11, 1961, Vestryman Charles Gibbs reported that a contract for the sale of 6 Glebe Street to the College of Charleston for $17,000 had been successfully negotiated and signed. An initial payment of $850 was paid and the balance was to be paid on or before December 31, 1961. The money was placed in the glebe fund.

The purchase of 6 Glebe Street was made possible by donations from descendants of Bishop Smith who not only lived in the house but was instrumental in starting "The College." William Mason Smith, William Mason Smith, Jr. and J.J. Pringle Smith each donated $5,000. The house was restored and in 2012 it remains the home of the president of the College of Charleston.

CHURCH HOME

In November 1956, Mrs. D. M. Dockstader resigned as matron of the church home. The vestry accepted her resignation with regret and said she could keep her quarters rent free as long as her doctor considered her in sufficiently good health. Miss Virginia T. Price was appointed matron with free quarters, a monthly salary of $75.00 and was authorized to sign checks on the church home's petty cash fund. In March 1958, Miss Price had her salary increased to $90.00 per month.

Clary reported in November 1957 that a bequest of $200 for the church home was made from the estate of Jane Couturier Thomas.

Miss Price wrote in the 1957 parish report that the "big news" at the church home was that the second and third floor halls, two bath rooms, guest rooms and the television room were painted during the past summer. The halls were painted blue and the rooms were painted pink making everything look clean and fresh.

There was sad news because Mrs. Dean Dockstader, former matron, died in April 1957 after a long illness and Miss Martha Rivers died in the fall or early winter of 1957 after a long illness. Mrs. Bagwell, who had been there less than two years, went to Germany to visit her daughter and son-in-law who was in the United States diplomatic corp. She had a heart attack in Germany and did not return to Charleston. Miss Mary Beckwith filled one of the empty rooms, but there were still three vacancies. In December 1958, Dr. Alice Gregg moved into the home.

The vestry replaced an ancient oil stove at the foot of the stairs with a gas forced air furnace at a cost of $500. A fire escape was also installed for $1,400.

In 1959, the alcove on the second floor and two other rooms were refurnished, two more bathrooms were added and the fire alarm system was in working order. Dr. Gregg moved out, Mrs. Burt moved into the home and Mrs. S.A. Taylor left the home to move into the Church Home for Women on Bee Street.

Mrs. William Stoney retired from the church home committee and she was replaced by Mrs. Emily Whaley. In 1964, Mrs. Dwight Gadsden and Mr. B. Owen Geer were again appointed to the church home committee.

MUSIC AND THE CHOIR

Vestryman Thomas P. White in September 1956 reported that some of the organ mechanism had been damaged by water and that extensive repairs were recommended. On April 2, 1957, Bartow Culp reported the organ manufacturer advised that the condition of the console was such that it could not be economically repaired. A new console would cost approximately $5,000. The vestry authorized $4,972 for a new console and voted the money should come from the maintenance reserve fund.

In June 1957, the vestry authorized a brass plaque dedicated to Cotesworth P. Means, choir director, to be placed on the new organ console. Means reported in January 1958 that he had begun a male chorus that would sing once a month as an integral part of the choir. Twenty-five men were participating.

There were always complaints about the lack of parking near St. Philip's. In February 1958, Dr. Anderson reported that Means complained that there was insufficient parking because cub scouts met on Thursday, the same night as the choir. In November, Clary read a letter from Means condemning the cub scouts for meeting on the same night. The reply from Clary and the senior warden, J. Ross Hanahan, said the vestry deplored the tone of his letter and that the parish house should not be reserved for the exclusive use of the choir on practice nights.

The battle continued into December when Means sent a voluminous letter of reply to the vestry. Clary and Hanahan replied again. Means' long letter was not kept in the vestry minutes.

At the vestry meeting of October 12, 1959, Means' letter of resignation (again) was read. A letter was drafted expressing the gratitude of the vestry and the parish for his many years of service in the church. Letters of disapproval, including one from choir member Richard J. Voigt, and two others protested Means' departure. Voigt wrote, "It is not for us to know the reasons why Mr. Means decided at this time to tender his resignation. Vestryman Myers was asked to talk to these three people. The music committee and the rector were directed to find a suitable replacement.

Cotesworth P. Means, a former South Carolina state senator and an amateur boxer, was first mentioned as being in the choir, as was previously written, on March 12, 1924, when he was hired as a tenor. He remained with the choir for thirty-five years.

Miss Dorothy Bollwinkle, who also first joined the choir in 1924, accepted the position as organist-choir director with a one year contract that could be canceled by either party with ninety days-notice. Her salary was $3,000 per year.

In March 1961, Miss Bollwinkle said she would not be able to attend a music conference at Myrtle Beach April 22 and 23 because there was no one to sit with her mother. The vestry decided to not only pay for her expenses but to also pay for a sitter for her mother. It was also suggested that the chairman of the music committee should go as well.

A music festival for junior choirs from Charleston was held at St. Philip's in May 1962. Not only was Miss Bollwinkle urged to attend a church music conference of choir masters that was held at Sewanee in July, Clary also asked the music committee to pass on his compliments to her and the choir on the Palm Sunday and Easter music.

The year 1963 marked the fortieth anniversary of the performance *The Crucifixion* being performed at St. Philip's on Good Friday. "A timely and significant feature of this fortieth anniversary is the presence of Dr. Frank Coventry, rector of St. Marylebone's Church in London." Sir John Stainer, English organist, teacher and composer, wrote *The Crucifixion* in 1887 for St. Marlebone's and it has been performed there every Lenten season.

The 1963 performance was in memory of St. Philip's former rector, Marshall Travers, who died March 2, 1963. Miss Bollwinkle was the organists and choir director.

Means had another blow out in May 1963 making accusations about Clary in a letter including exhibits A through E. The vestry sent the letter back to him. Senior Warden

Charles Gibbs said there was nothing he could add to the situation except to hope Means would continue coming to St. Philip's. Clary was kept informed in London.

THE CHURCHYARDS

Members of the congregation who owned lots in the western churchyard asked permission to plant a screen of trees against the west fence. In February, Loutrel Briggs, who was the premiere landscape architect in Charleston and beyond, agreed to make recommendations concerning the erection of a new fence in the western churchyard. The plan was deferred until the 1961 budget was completed. Briggs' gardens were cherished but, unfortunately, many of them have been lost.

The Calhoun Insurance Co., which also abutted the western churchyard and the Congregational Church were willing to participate in building the wall project. By October 1962, the churchyard wall was completed at a cost of $2,013. The sexton was instructed to lock the churchyard each evening.

In October 1959, the sale of one burial space each was made to the estate of Miss Melanie Ball and Mr. David D.S. Cameron, who in 1962 donated $25.00 towards the building of the fence in the western churchyard. Four spaces to Dr. and Mrs. Robert M. Anderson were also approved.

In 1960, more than sixty-nine burial plots were sold at the new increased price of $100 per lot. Some of those who purchased lots that year were Mr. and Mrs. E.L. Jagar, Mr. and Mrs. William McG. Morrison, Jr., Mr. and Mrs. Carlton Davies, Mr. and Mrs. Cadwallader Jones and Miss Washington Green Pringle.

The vestry in February 1961 approved selling one undersized churchyard lot to Tom Bass, Jr. for $25.00. In November, the vestry agreed that the Alston family could disinterre the body of the late Edward Alston but the vestry required the widow to put it in writing and that the family pay all expenses. They also had to leave the lot in satisfactory condition. In January 1962, Vestry Secretary Francis S. Dougherty wrote in the minutes that a motion was passed authorizing the purchase by Mr. and Mrs. Francis S. Dougherty of the churchyard lots formally owned by Mr. and Mrs. Edward F. Alston.

In June 1963, Craig Bennett reported that the work of re-copying and verifying the churchyard records had been completed. The vestry sent a letter of thanks to Bennett and Mrs. H.D. Todd (particularly Mrs. Todd) for their time consuming and meticulous work. Not only did Bennett present plats of the churchyards that showed there were approximately 135 platted lots that were empty but he also presented two individually framed plats of the two churchyards. They were to hang on the church office walls.

RACE RELATIONS

In November 1957, the vestry approved the senior warden denying the use of the parish house auditorium for a non-segregated meeting.

As previously written, Rev. Charles L. Widney arrived from Columbus, Georgia, at St. Philip's in late 1958 or early 1959 as the assistant rector.

In May 1957, Widney, along with seventy-nine Georgia ministers from Atlanta and other areas, signed a Manifesto on Racial Belief. It stated, "We do believe that all Americans, whether white or black, have a right to the full privileges of first class citizenship. There were six statements:

1. As Americans and Christians, we have an obligation to obey the law.
2. Freedom of speech must at all costs be preserved.
3. The public school system must not be destroyed.
4. Hatred and scorn for those of another race, or for those who hold a position different from our own, can never be justified.
5. Communication between responsible leaders of the races must be maintained.
6. Our difficulties cannot be solved in our own strength or in human wisdom ... it is necessary we pray earnestly and consistently that God will give us wisdom."

In 2012, this manifesto sounds tame, but in 1957 it was a bombshell. As you read on you will find that Widney and Clary had similar beliefs about integration.

In April 1958 the vestry instructed St. Philip's diocesan delegates to support the delegates of St. Andrews who wanted to have the convention go on record supporting a resolution: "Resolved that this vestry go on record as disagreeing with the policies of the National Council of Churches on racial integration and political action." At the diocesan convention, the resolution passed unanimously.

On September 9, 1960, the vestry passed a motion six to five, "to meet at the church entrances any Negro or Negroes, who may appear with the apparent intention of attending one of the regular worship services at St. Philip's and to politely, but firmly refuse them admission, but to suggest that they attend one of the several available Negro churches; it not being, however, the intention of this motion to exclude Negroes such as family servants and friends from attending such services as weddings, confirmation, funerals, etc. in which they may have a personal interest. The Rector asked to be recorded as being opposed to this motion"

The next day, Clary stated to the vestry, that "he was diametrically opposed to the action taken at the Vestry meeting held, Friday, September 9. 1960, to refuse admittance of Negroes to worship service in St. Philip's" and if he were to remain as rector, he would seek through sermons, talks and any other opportunity which presented itself, to help the congregation grow in concept of the church and the nature of worship." This being so, Mr. Clary asked the vestry to decide if they were willing for him to remain as rector.

Following discussion of this question, a resolution was passed by a unanimous vote as follows:

"The Vestry, acknowledging that the Rector disagrees with the action taken at the September 9 meeting, hereby recognizes the Rector's right to express himself accordingly and to preach the Gospel as he believes in it. Furthermore, the Vestry reaffirms its entire confidence in the Rector as the religious leader of this Parish."

Another downtown non-Episcopal church had cards printed to hand out to any blacks who might try to enter that church. The cards explained why they could not enter.

In October, the vestry raised a question "as to whether it was wise to conduct the Every Man Canvass in view of the substantial undercurrent of feeling at this time concerning the church's affiliation with the NCC." It was suggested "it might be more practical from the standpoint of finances to carry over this year's pledges and only contact new members and selected older members."

It was reported in December that a number of persons, due to their concern about the NCC, had written letters declining to pledge for the coming year, or reducing their pledge, or expressing their dissatisfaction. A motion passed stating, "that a person who had normally pledged in the past, but had not pledged for 1962, should be re-contacted. Should such person continue to decline to pledge, he should be asked to write a letter to the vestry."

On behalf of Mr. Hagood, president of the "Men of St. Philip's," an invitation had been extended to Dr. Miller of the NCC to speak before the men. Miller was fully booked but suggested the names of three other men.

In January 1963, the senior warden was instructed by the vestry to remind the new vestrymen of the resolution passed by a former vestry that "colored people" could not enter St. Philip's. One vestry member said he doubted that a resolution made by a former vestry could bind a succeeding vestry, "but that resolution notwithstanding, he would be guided in his actions by his own conscience."

On February 11, 1963, the vestry unanimously passed the following resolution:

"WHEREAS certain unknown groups are encouraging attendance at our services, who are hostile to our way of life, and content to disrupt the worship which the congregation of St. Philip's Church have had for centuries enjoyed.

"NOW THEREFORE BE it resolved that and Declared that it is the policy of this vestry that all those who earnestly desire to worship with us shall be welcomed, but that no persons shall be admitted to St. Philip's Church who has come to mock and undermine the established communion among us and to destroy the traditional harmony of our services and

"BE IT FURTHER RESOLVED that if any Negroes be admitted, they shall be requested to use the North Balcony."

A special meeting of the vestry was called on August 27, 1963 to pass a resolution stating that St. Philip's disagreed with certain political and social policies and undertakings of National Council of the Episcopal Church. Because of that, the vestry resolved that consideration be given to the withdrawal of financial support to the national church by reducing or eliminating the diocesan apportionment. The senior warden would appoint a committee to recommend what amount of money was to be withheld. This issue was to be discussed by the vestry between September 9 and September 20. September 9 was eight days after Clary returned from England.

The vestry met on September 30 and prepared a resolution to present to the congregation on Wednesday, October 16 at 7:30 pm with approximately 325 members attending in the parish house. The meeting opened by singing *The Church's One Foundation* and followed by prayer from Clary.

The beginning of the resolution was the same as that was read on August 27 stating their displeasure with the National Council of the Episcopal Church. The details were then presented. In preparing the 1964 budget, one-third of the diocesan apportionment would be withdrawn and that the bishop and the diocesan executive council be requested to withhold an equal amount from the general church quota. Further, the bishop would be requested to advise the presiding bishop of this action. The money that would be set aside would be reserved for use outside of St. Philip's parish.

After some procedural issues were discussed, the resolution was then discussed and debated with twenty-three who rose to speak pro or con. Mrs. Cornelia D. Tucker made a motion that was seconded and passed that the resolution be put to a vote.

One hundred and fifty two voted in favor and 127 were against. Only one vestryman voted against. The resolution was thus adopted. In December, a letter was received from Presiding Bishop Lichtenberger responding to a letter sent by the vestry.

One of the many parishioners, who loved Frank Coventry, sent him a letter about a month after the October 16th congregational meeting with details. He wrote, "You have heard about our congregational meeting, I gather. I honestly didn't find it too 'fierce,' though there was a great deal of feeling before and after the meeting. Mr. Clary was quite fair in conducting the meeting, (some people don't agree with me there), but he did everything possible to keep the question from coming to a vote at all. He prolonged the meeting, (I feel deliberately, though – again – some people don't agree with me).

We stayed from 7:30 p.m. to 11:30 p.m. although some people stayed until the last vote was tallied which was after midnight.

"While some members were against giving any money to the national church, others felt donations designated through the national church for missions should be continued. Those who were against giving money ignored that.

"Those against the resolution repeatedly said we received twice as much back from the national church as was given from St. Philip's. Those for the motion pointed out St. Philip's received just slightly more than was given to the national church 'and it all goes to colored schools.'"

Clary spoke at the very end and he dwelt on the emotions a great deal. After he finished 'it was the Good Guys against the Bad Guys. Those who didn't want to withhold were the Christians – us other sinners could vote to withhold if we wanted to." The writer of this letter wanted to say that it seemed the national church was acting in an un-Christian manner."

Clary upset the vestry saying their discussions were strictly political and they were accused of having said "so let's leave God out of this discussion." The vestry denied that.

Two weeks later at the Every Man Canvass supper, Clary got up and said that the parish had voted to withhold all money from missions and he felt St. Philippian's were too insulated and selfish. He said the mission of the church was to spread the Gospel, and "we had not voted to do that." The letter writer stood up and disagreed with Clary. The next day the letter writer had a long conference with Clary and felt for the first time there was an understanding of him. Apparently, he had not thought out his talk and he was misunderstood, at least that was what he said. Clary said he was just warning the parish not to become too self-centered. He even went so far as to say that the church should stay out of politics. The writer said later, "Glory halleluiah … That's real progress …"

The letter writer closed by saying that missions were terribly important, but the state of the Sunday school was so fouled up that it would a great place to begin supporting missions.

Just after the January 1964 congregational meeting, a St. Philippian expressed hope that the actions taken about the diocesan apportionment and the Episcopal Church's participation in the NCC would remain a fixed policy for a year and that no further controversy would ensure. At the February vestry meeting, there was long discussion whether or not the national church would remain affiliated with the NCC and perhaps that should be studied before implementing the wishes of the congregation. Senior Warden John Welch proposed a three man committee be appointed to implement the vote of the congregation that requested the national church withdraw from the NCC. The vestry agreed.

A resolution was approved stating that St. Philip's ties with the NCC must be terminated in the interest of Christian unity and fellowship. Also delegates to the next general convention were to vote to dissolve all ties between the diocese of South Carolina, the national church and the NCC. The NCC was accused of espousing controversial undertakings of questionable Christian character that had created discord and disunity among the members of this diocese.

THE REVEREND SIDNEY GRAYSON CLARY RESIGNS

June 30, 1964

Gentlemen:

"It has been my privilege to serve as the Rector of this Parish for seven years. We have shared some difficult times together, but the years have been interesting ones and I hope that each of us has grown in his relationship with God and through Him with one another.

I am herewith submitting my resignation as Rector of this parish to become effective August 31, 1964. I am accepting a call to the Diocese of Minnesota.

Best wishes to you.   Faithfully yours,
S. Grayson Clary

The same day, the vestry voted to accept the resignation with regret and at the July 13 vestry meeting a search committee was formed.

LIFE AFTER ST. PHILIP'S

Clary, who may have felt relief upon his departure, felt strongly that blacks should be able to worship in St. Philip's along with the congregation. He could not change the church and Clary could neither stop the resolutions about keeping back apportionments nor the demands there would be no association with the NCC.

One parishioner said that Clary's wife, Jean, had positive feelings for integration even stronger than her husband.

Clary found his perfect church in St. John the Evangelist in St. Paul, Minnesota, where he was rector from 1964 – 1986. An article from the August 10, 1969, issue of *The Living Church* told about Clary and his new church. "A church that radiates helpful goodwill not among it parishioners alone, but to everyone of whatever faith, race or color … Clary and the Rev. David Benson established a reading room. Many children, including whites, Indians, Mexicans and increasingly blacks, came to read books and they were taught reading skills." The Boy Scout troop was not only multiracial but also some were from broken homes. A new neighborhood activity was in the realm of music headed by Mrs. Henry (Shirley) Kartarik who had a youth choir of sixty and an adult choir of twenty. Clary's church of 800 was growing. He had also become a civic leader.

In April 2011, this author had a phone conversation with Jean Clary. The Clary's live in Chapel Hill, North Carolina, and Gray, as Jean calls him, is in a "special unit." Jean said St. Philip's was a lovely church. They loved living in the rectory and that they had many friends and many enemies. Jean added that he told the vestry that if they excluded any blacks from entering St. Philip's, that would be his last day at the church. But the vestry never actually forbade anyone to enter and the blacks respected Clary. Blacks never attempted to disrupt a service at St. Philip's. Jean said, "It was a difficult time for Gray but he felt he was part of a change."

Canon Sam Cobb, who would follow Clary as the next rector of St. Philip's, met a lady in Cody, Wyoming, who said her great-grandfather was John Johnson the civil war rector of St. Philip's. Cobb, who replied he was the civil rights rector, and continued that he had been congratulated on the way he had handled the race issue. But said Cobb, it was not he who handled it but it was Gray Clary who handled the race issue at a very difficult time.

REV. CHARLES L. WIDNEY

INTERIM

SEPTEMBER 1, 1964 – JUNE 1, 1965

CHURCH SERVICES, MEMBERSHIP AND CLERGY

Widney remained priest-in-charge. Bishop R.E. Gribbin would often fill in as a supply minister as long as his pension permitted. Sosnowski said when Gribbin was preparing communion on the altar he would repeat random verses of scripture out loud. He also would pop in the church offices to visit but he never stayed longer than ten minutes.

In January 1965, Rufus Barkley, who was junior warden, expressed the vestry's appreciation for the help Widney gave the parish.

THE YOUTH, THE MEN, AND THE LADIES

In September 1964, Rufus Barkley, reporting on the Sunday school, said that Mrs. Lawrence (Rhett) Barrett née Stevens was employed to work with the school for approximately twenty hours a week. Rhett Barrett would work at St. Philip's for twenty-five years as office manager.

Rhett Stevens was born and raised in Bennettsville where she went to high school followed by Lander College in Greenwood. During World War II she worked with the Sixth Naval District which had taken over the Fort Sumter Hotel. After the war, she worked in Columbia at the Loyalty Insurance Co. where she met Larry. They were married in 1948, moved to Charleston and joined St. Philip's. Rhett Barrett said in 2011 that after they had worshipped at St. Philip's for a second time someone asked her to chair the tea garden. She said that she had no idea what that was, but she learned quickly and was successful. She got to know many St. Philippian's.

One day, while picking up her child from Mrs. Dotterer's kindergarten, located in the parish house, Dotterer asked Barrett if she could type a school schedule. Because Barrett went over to the church office, borrowed a typewriter to type the schedule, the secretary took notice of Barrett's typing and asked her to come and help in the office. Barrett was hired full time in 1969. Cobb would later describe her as his right hand and John Wilson, a former senior warden, said she ran the church and held everything together. Even though she moved to North Carolina, she drove from there once a month to worship at St. Philip's. Barrett, who now lives in Mt. Pleasant, still faithfully attends St. Philip's in 2012.

Mrs. Dotterer's nephew, Gillie Dotterer said, "Aunt Sue, as she was called, not only called a spade a spade but would call a spade a shovel."

At Barkley's recommendation, $500 was allotted for new Sunday school furniture, especially the playground swings, because of certain safety measures needed to be updated. In February 1965, Barkley said it was necessary to call the police to the church playground because bricks had been thrown at the sexton.

THEOLOGY, EVANGELISM AND MISSIONS

Jack Todd in October 1964 said the finance committee recommended the following disbursements: $200 to Rev. Thomas S. Tisdale for mission works in the Charleston hospitals; $1,000 for a new roof to St. Andrews Mission, "a Negro congregation" on the Summerville highway; $150 to the youth center on Chapel Street and $500 to St. Johns mission in Charleston. The Rev. Henry Grant, who sent a thank you letter to St. Philip's, was also the minister at St. Stephens Episcopal Church at 67 Anson Street.

The Christmas offering went to Camp St. Christopher and Camp Baskerville. In February 1965, the vestry discussed future financial parish support for seminaries at Sewanee and Alexandria, Virginia. One member was going to lower his pledge amount so he could donate to the Virginia Theological Seminary. Many others were becoming disillusioned with the increasing non-orthodox "theology" being taught at some seminaries.

In January 1965, Senior Warden John Welch suggested giving $850 to missions in Dillon and Latta and $1,050 to St. Matthew's Lutheran Church in Charleston that recently had suffered in a disastrous fire on January 13, 1965. The fire began in the early evening and grew out of control because an incandescent light fixture that overheated while the interior was being painted. Many of St. Matthew's interior decorations were saved such as the pews that St. Philip's allowed to be stored in their new property at Church and Cumberland streets.

Canon Sam Cobb was in Charleston the night St. Matthew's burned trying to decide whether or not he should come to Charleston. He said it was a terrible and dramatic night with the burning steeple that could be seen all over the city.

FINANCES AND VESTRY

The finance committee, consisting of Rufus Barkley, Dr. Rivers, Welch and H.D. Todd submitted a letter in July 1964 to the vestry. They stated members of the finance committee had been disturbed for some years by the disproportionately large percent of the church's pledge income being subscribed to the diocesan apportionment budget.

As a matter of sound fiscal policy, the committee suggested that twenty percent of the estimated pledge be subscribed to the diocesan apportionment budget with, of course, no change in giving to the church's diocesan assessment. On this basis, the proposed 1965 budget would be $101,230.

Welch reviewed the apportionment figures in the diocese, noting that many parishes had limited the apportionment. He wanted the vestry to advise the parish that spending was more than it was taking in and that it was necessary to balance the parish budget.

On September 14, 1964, the vestry decided to hire Charles R. Lewis, a former Southern Railroad employee with good recommendations, as sexton. He was paid $1,800 annually, (just under $40.00 per week), plus all utilities and received a paid two week vacation and a half day off once a week.

In January 1965, Theodore Guerard was elected senior warden, Anthony Harrigan was senior warden and continued as secretary. A new face to the vestry was Herbert R. Stender, Jr.

In April, John Wilson gave a report on St. Philip's various funds. He said the Frost Fund was unrestricted and the interest from the Fludd Funds was unrestricted. Wilson made a correction in May that the Fludd Funds income was to be used solely for the maintenance of church buildings. He added there were four church home funds that should be combined into one fund.

GLEBE LAND

Senior Warden Teddy Guerard in February 1965 raised the question of selling the remaining Glebe Street property. No one objected to considering the idea. In April the vestry agreed to sell providing the church received $11,000 net. It would first be offered to the tenant and second to the College of Charleston.

CHURCH HOME

A $240 buzzer and microphone were installed at the entrance of the church home for safety reasons.

In February 1965, Teddy Guerard reported to the vestry that Miss Virginia Livingston Hunt expressed the wish to give $20,000 to St. Philip's Church Home as a memorial to Miss Cornelia Cress, a native of Charleston who died in 1933. In April, 130 shares of Eastman Kodak valued at $19,860 were received from Miss Hunt.

In April 1965, the ladies on the church home committee were unanimous in asserting Miss Price, as head of the church home, was not performing her duties satisfactorily and they recommended she be replaced. The vestry asked Randell Stoney and Guerard to find a replacement. Miss Price could keep her room until June 1. In May, the vestry would look for ways of giving Miss Price financial aid and she was notified of her replacement.

THE CHURCHYARDS

In November 1964, the vestry rejected the request of Rev. William P. Rhett, United States Army, for the purchase of two burial spaces in the churchyard. Bill Rhett said he had been called to both St. Philip's and St. Michael's and he chose St. Michael's because he knew he would be there only a year before he entered the chaplaincy. That caused St. Philip's to reject his request.

Later, Rhett was able to purchase two lots in the St. Philip's churchyard where he placed two tombstones that started to sink. Rhett was told they could be propped up

with cement but he said no that he wanted dirt. The next time the funeral director had a funeral he took the overflow dirt from a Methodist Church funeral and hauled it to St. Philip's. The Methodist dirt was put in place to prop up the tombstones but after a while the tombstones started to sink again. A friend said, "You should not have gotten Methodist dirt. You need Episcopal dirt." At the next St. Philip's funeral, the overflow dirt was removed from a burial plot and taken to the Rhetts burial site. Time will tell.

The vestry at its May 10, 1965, meeting authorized a suitable token of esteem to be given to Widney for his services to St. Philip's for six and a half years. Widney said he would continue to conduct services when and where called upon. Widney retired on

June 1, 1965, the same day Cobb arrived in Charleston. Widney died before October 11, 1965, when Mrs. Bertha Widney, his widow, purchased two burial lots.

Catherine Jones said in 2011 that Widney had leukemia but very few people knew it. He worked almost to the end of his life. One hot day, Widney collapsed during the service and that tragedy made the vestry think it was time to air-condition the church. Jones said he was a blessed man.

In November 1965, the finance committee recommended selling the eighty shares of Cleveland Cliffs Iron Co. given by Mrs. Charles Dwight with the proceeds going to the churchyard fund.

In March 1966, the vestry decided that a number of Quaker tombstones that were being removed from their King Street site could be placed on the north wall of St. Philip's churchyard.

In 1965, Charleston County had purchased property on King Street just south of Queen Street from the Society of Friends in Philadelphia. Previously, there had been three meeting houses, the last burned in 1861.

The site was maintained as a burial ground and in the middle of it there was an old house. Architect Albert Simons said, "Although the house has received no repairs for many years, it is apparently structurally sound and the interior is Greek revival in character, simple but good for the period." The house was torn down.

Because the parking garage was going to be built on the back part of that site, the Quaker bodies would be reinterred to the front part of the lot. Although early Quakers did not use tombstones, by the nineteenth century there were a few.

In 1974, the county was ready to double the size of the parking garage so the bodies that had been moved in 1965 now would be moved again along with other bodies. They were moved to Meeting Street next to courthouse in the small park that has a monument to Mendel Rivers.

In 2011, the rector of St. Philip's, J. Haden McCormick, and this author, armed with a list of those who had been interred in the Quaker burial ground, searched the St. Philip's churchyards for Quaker tombstones. None was found.

In 2002, county council voted funds for a nice marker with the names of the fifty-two Quakers. Finally, in 2010 it came to pass and the marker was placed in the Barrett Larimore Park.

There is also a marker on King Street that hangs on the Gothic cast iron fence in front of the parking garage. It tells us about Mary Fisher Bayly Crosse, a Quaker in Charles

Town by the early 1680s who walked alone through Turkey in 1660 to preach the Gospel to Sultan Mahomet IV. He listened politely but he was not converted. He offered Mary an escort to the sea, but she walked back alone trusting in God and made it safely back to England. How do we share our faith?

RACE RELATIONS

The dioceses of South Carolina and Upper South Carolina were the only dioceses of Episcopal Churchwomen that had separate chapters for "Negroes and whites." Mrs. Leroy Ragin of Pinewood was the chair of the black chapter and Mrs. T. Elliot of Orangeburg was the chair of the white chapter

During this time, a bi-racial committee was formed to consider the church work of the "white and Negro" women of the diocese. The committee grew out of the concern expressed by Bishop Temple at the May convention of the Episcopal churchwomen that the church work among the "Negro" women was declining. The blacks felt, Temple said, that the diocese was not interested in them. He suggested a committee that would be a sounding board seeking a common ground to overcome the racial barrier but the committee had no authority to act. Several women were appointed to the committee including Mrs. Stephen B. Mackey from Charleston.

Cobb and members of the vestry, who attended the 1966 diocesan convention, gave reports. Arthur Wilcox said the reasons given for closing the Bee Street Home for elderly women were cited as financial losses and fire hazards. He continued stating assertions on these points were challenged and disproved. The fire chief said the home was not a fire hazard. It was learned that the upper diocese only contributed $1,300 per year to its support. Wilcox said Bishop Temple had been quoted at a meeting of the women of the diocese as saying the issue in the proposed closing was racial, not financial. Wilcox added that seemed to be another irritating case of misrepresentation. Rev. Albrecht, who had attended the women's meeting, said the bishop specifically mentioned that five year's work on the home had gone down the drain, but did not mention the race issue.

Apparently, the diocese integrated Camp St. Christopher in 1966. Wilcox said the camp was already feeling the effect of integration with prospective enrollment being very low.

THE SEARCH COMMITTEES

Dr. Orvin said Dr. Frank Coventry, who was so popular that many St. Philippians wanted to call him as the rector when Clary departed.

Dr. Coventry returned to England in August 1963 and he was approached as early as November 1963 about returning to Charleston. Also a St. Philippian parishioner was asked to pass on an unofficial request to see if Coventry would consider returning to serve as the minister of the French Huguenot Church. For many years The Huguenot church had only one service each year and their members joked they attended services every time the doors were opened. By 1963, they wanted to re-open the church on a full time basis.

At this point, the Huguenot board of directors was established and there was money in the bank but there had been no public announcement. Coventry did not accept their offer.

In July 1964, the vestry called Frank Coventry to be rector of St. Philip's. By September 10, Coventry had declined the offer because his mother and Ursula's mother were elderly. He felt because of that he could not move his family from England.

Sam and Nancy Cobb returned from England in March 1977. Cobb said in *The Spire* "that one of the most enjoyable parts of the trip was seeing and being with the Coventrys. Frank, Ursula, Sarah and Katherine send their love to their St. Philippian friends ... Their home in London is a mecca for many in this congregation who travel to London just as it was for the Cobbs."

Coventry died in England in 1994 at age eighty-one.

In October 1964, the search committee reported that an extensive investigation was being made of clergymen under consideration. The vestry decided that Rufus Barkley, Teddy Guerard, and Dr. Mac Anderson, should visit some of those being considered.

That same month a call was issued to Rev. W. Moultrie Moore Jr. Rector of St. Martin's church in Charlotte.

A month earlier, St. Philippian Jim Flint and his son attended Sunday services at St. Martin in the Fields in Atlanta. Cobb said that a minister could scope out those people sitting in the nave who are there to check on a possible candidate to serve another church. Cobb spotted Flint as such a person and at the coffee afterwards he introduced himself to Flint who said they were in town to see a Braves game. Cobb thought the man was lying and he kept pushing Flint until he admitted St. Philip's in Charleston needed a rector.

The next Sunday Guerard visited St. Martin in the Fields and he was right to the point. He said to Cobb "I'm Teddy Guerard from Charleston and we're looking for a new rector at St. Philip's." They had a good conversation but Cobb said he was not looking for a new parish. St. Philip's forgot about Cobb until December when Anderson, Guerard and Welch reported on a visit they had with Canon Cobb who said he was happy where he was and they would have to make him even happier if he were to move. John Wilson made a motion on December 9, 1964, that a call be made to Cobb. The motion passed unanimously.

Nancy said she would not move to Charleston and her husband replied he would go by himself. Nancy then said she would go with him. Cobb visited Charleston in December while the search committee continued checking other possible candidates. John and Julia Welch picked up the Cobbs and took them to the Fort Sumter Hotel. Cobb said it was terrible to see that huge house, the rectory, when he knew they would not come.

Hearing that, the vestry also offered alternative choices for living arrangements. The vestry also agreed to let Cobb, with the approval of the vestry, hire church staff.

In mid-January 1965, Cobb returned to Charleston alone just to wander the streets incognito. Cobb was walking down Church Street near the rectory when Elizabeth O'Neil Verner, who was sitting in front of the Heyward-Washington House, turned to Cobb as he walked by and she asked him "to come to her." She said, "I have a realization that you are a knight-in-shining armor that is coming to St. Philip's." Cobb was flabbergasted, a rare happening. Mrs. Verner and Cobb became fast friends.

At the same time, the senior warden offered Cobb an annual salary of $10,500, use of the rectory including utilities, an automobile in the range of $2,500 to $3,000 and $600 for their son's education at a local preparatory school. In addition, the vestry would pay moving expenses, contribute to his pension fund and repaint and redecorate the rectory as necessary. It was also proposed that new rugs and drapes be purchased for two rectory rooms. The vestry approved the entire package. In April 1965, the vestry accepted the low bid of $2,644.26 for a Ford for Cobb from Paul Motor Co. Car payments would be made. In 1967, the wardens were authorized to trade in Cobb's car for a new one if they deemed it appropriate.

THE REVEREND CANON SAMUEL THOMPSON COBB

RECTOR

JUNE 1, 1965 – MAY 31, 1982

Samuel Thompson Cobb (Sam), who was born in Lake Butler, Florida, on May 14, 1916, the son of Jesse Daniel Cobb and Ethel Thompson Cobb, had one sister and two brothers. He began playing the piano at age six. The family moved to Jacksonville where he began to work at age fourteen. After graduating from high school in Jacksonville, he joined the Texaco Oil Co. At the outbreak of World War II, he joined the army and in 1943 he was assigned to Miami Beach and stayed there until his discharge in 1946. He spent his time playing the organ for the Episcopal and Catholic chaplains. Cobb, as he put it, was the only Brahms man on the beach.

After the war, Cobb returned to Texaco for a short time but then enrolled at Emory University in Atlanta. He graduated in 1949 with a bachelor of arts and entered the Methodist Candler School of Theology from which he received his divinity degree in 1951. Episcopal Bishop Gribbin ordained Cobb as a priest on May 1, 1952.

Cobb said in a 1978 interview with the *News and Courier* that religion had always been an important part of his life even though his parents seldom attended church. "My mother had respect for it and I guess my father did but they were never involved in church work. I guess you could say they thought church was a good thing. But when you walked in to the house, it was not obvious that we were walking into an atmosphere that was greatly different from the outside."

Cobb continued, "I did not have a dramatic born-again religious conversion. I've never had a St. Paul on the road to Damascus experience ... My conversion process was a slow steady one that culminated with my Army experience." Cobb often referred to his experience as a slow drip, drip process.

Nancy Caroline Gaillard was born on April 27, 1927. In 1949, Cobb was invited to Nancy's debut and they were married three years later on September 26, 1952, when he was thirty-six and Nancy was twenty-four. They had one son, Samuel Gaillard Cobb, who was born June 30, 1955 and confirmed at St. Philip's on January 14, 1968. Gilly, as he was called then, and his wife Barbara had Cobb's three grandchildren: Alicia, Jesse Daniel, named after his great-grandfather, and Maile Elizabeth.

Shortly after being ordained, he was assigned to the Holy Innocents Protestant Episcopal Church located in a mill town in Atlanta. Cobb said, "It was in Atlanta he began his climb and without knowing it he moved into the right part of town and they just started to be invited to things. How? This sounds trite and a little egotistical, but just by being my charming self."

Cobb became a canon when he served at St. Philip's Cathedral in Atlanta from 1952 to 1959. He then served at St. Martin in the Fields in Atlanta from 1959 to 1965 when he came to St. Philip's.

CHURCH SERVICES, MEMBERSHIP AND CLERGY

Cobb attended his first vestry meeting on June 7, 1965, when William Barnwell III "of this parish" made known to the vestry his desire to become a candidate for Holy Orders. Church regulations required that he receive approval from the vestry of his parish. The vestry gave unanimous approval and in 1967 sent him a $100 ordination present.

REV. FLEETWOOD J. ALBRECHT

ASSISTANT RECTOR

FEBRUARY 1, 1966 – OCTOBER 31, 1968

The vestry called the Rev. Fleetwood J. (Pete) Albrecht on January 17, 1966, as assistant rector and he began work at St. Philip's on February 1. They offered him a housing allowance of up to $180 per month because the vestry no longer rented 67 South Battery. They lived at 15 Formosa Drive. Albrecht participated in his first St. Phillip's vestry meeting on February 21, 1966.

Albrecht was born on February 7, 1924, in Hardeeville, son of Fleetwood James Parrish Albrecht and Helen Augusta Walker Albrecht. After attending the College of Charleston where he joined ATO, he graduated from Louisiana State University and worked several years as a forester with the International Paper Co. in South Carolina. He lived many years on Sullivans Island while in the forest products industry. During World War II, he served in the India/China/Burma theatre as a communications officer. In 1952, he married Ellen Jones at the First Baptist Church in Doerun, Georgia. Always active in his church, he felt God call him to the ministry. He began seminary when Ellen was seven months pregnant with their third child. Albrecht graduated from the Virginia Theological Seminary in 1961 and was ordained as a priest in 1962. Before coming to St. Philip's, he served at St. Matthews Church in St. Matthews, at Eutawville and at St. Thomas in North Charleston. During his time at St. Philip's, from 1966 to 1968, Albrecht's wife said "he had a wonderful relationship with the sexton, Charles Lewis, and he always considered him a friend."

Cobb announced in 1968 that Albrecht would leave St. Philip's on October 31. In appreciation of his services, a farewell reception was held. Dr. Izard and the church gave the Albrechts $375 and Mrs. Verner's "picture" of St. Philip's.

He went from St. Philip's to St. Thaddeus' Church in Aiken. Later the Albrechts moved to Mt. Pleasant where they returned to their home church, Holy Cross on Sullivans Island.

In January 1973, Cobb welcomed back his old friend, Pete, who returned seven years after his departure from St. Philip's. Cobb said "Pete was still amongst our favorite people." His subject was "Light" as revealed in the New Testament.

Albrecht died from Alzheimer's in Mt. Pleasant on July 17, 2006. Ellen said their son, Charles, who lives in Mt. Pleasant, was a God send in helping to take care of his father in his later days. Albrecht, who is buried in the Mt. Pleasant Memorial Gardens, was survived by his wife and two daughters, two sons and seven grandchildren. Ellen said in 2011 that she was still feisty and playing cards.

On May 9, 1966, Cobb told the vestry that he had been a participant in a Roman Catholic wedding ceremony in Charleston. He had been permitted to say such prayers as he chose with the understanding that he would not repeat the vows. Cobb commented that he had been treated with great cordiality by the officiating Roman Catholic priest, Rev. J. Lawrence McLaughlin. Anthony (Tony) Harrigan noted this must have been a first.

Harrigan was correct. According to the bride, Miss Frederica Elizabeth Bremer and her husband, James Heyward Harvey, Jr., this was the first time in South Carolina that a non-Catholic Christian minister was allowed to participate in a Roman Catholic marriage service. The wedding was at St. Mary's on Hasell Street on May 7, 1966. The Harveys honeymooned in Nassau. Betsy and Heyward in 2012 are faithful worshippers at St. Philip's.

REVEREND FREDERICK S. SOSNOWSKI

ASSISTANT RECTOR

NOVEMBER 1968 – JANUARY 20, 1975

At the same time Albrecht left, Cobb said he had spoken to the Reverend Frederick S. Sosnowski who was very interested in the position of assistant rector. Sosnowski did take the job and he arrived at St. Philip's in November 1968 where he remained until January 20, 1975.

Fred Sosnowski, who was born in Charleston September 1, 1925, lived with his family on Wadmalaw Island during his early youth. He graduated from John's Island High School in 1942. During Sosnowski's first semester at Clemson, illness forced him to leave, later enrolling at the University of South Carolina where he majored in American history. He graduated in 1951.

Sosnowski enrolled in the Virginia Theological Seminary in 1952 because he said, "that if the Gospel is that important then I need to do something about it." While he was in the seminary, he married Mackie Ramsay in San Marcos, Texas, in 1954. He was ordained a deacon in 1955 at St. John's on Johns Island

Sosnowski became assistant rector at Trinity Church in Columbia and chaplain to Episcopalians at the University of South Carolina. He was ordained a priest in 1956 at Trinity in Columbia where he remained until he became rector of St. Matthews Episcopal Church in Henderson, Texas, from 1957 to 1959. At this point, Sosnowski decided the ministry was not the right thing for him. Even though his parishioners wanted him to stay, he left the ministry for nine years.

When he returned to the ministry in 1968, his first call was from St. Philip's.

In 2011, Sosnowski said he did not consider himself a colorful person. It would seem that because Canon Cobb was definitely a colorful person, the two complimented each other very well

Sosnowski said he and Cobb took turns twice a week visiting sick St. Philippian's who were mainly at Roper Hospital. Sosnowski said people would get angry if they were not visited, but often they did not realize they had to notify the clergy. To keep people from becoming angry, clergy in those days could and did check the hospital register to see which St. Philippian's were in the hospital.

There were also home visits and weddings. Sosnowski, who said the music would overwhelm him, would start the matrimonial service and then Cobb would finish. While at St. Philip's, he trained in counseling because he felt would also help him in later life.

Sosnowski said the church at that time had a membership of 1,800 but only one third were active. One Easter, he and Cobb gave communion to 800 people during three services.

When he left St. Philip's in 1975, Sosnowski served as rector of St. Jude's in Walterboro and said the church looked like a postcard. From 1975 to 1994, Sosnowski was the director of the Pastoral Counseling Center in North Charleston.

From 1985 to 1995, Sosnowski was at St. James on James Island in a part time position and then he briefly served as a counselor at St. John's.

In 1982, Sosnowski obtained a house his great-great-grandfather built in 1835 in Rockville where he and his wife, Polly, still live in 2011. Also this year, his son Jamie will be entering Trinity School for Ministry and will take his wife with him.

Cobb, who entered the hospital on June 29, 1969, for surgery, recovered and he received a $150 gift from the vestry toward his family vacation on the west coast.

In October 1970, Cobb announced the bishop had named him dean of the Charleston deanery and he asked for prayer support as he left for Houston to attend the general convention. There was no money for delegate expenses other than Cobb. Because the general convention was going to vote on female ordination, Gene Geer raised the question about putting off the everyman canvass until after the Houston convention ended. The vestry decided the campaign would proceed. The vote to ordain females passed by the laity but was narrowly defeated by clerical delegates.

REVEREND RALPH MILLEDGE BYRD JR.

ASSISTANT RECTOR

AUGUST 1, 1971 - 1974

In April, Mary Lilly Bennett reported there was a search for a third clergyman for St. Philip's. Cobb reported the next month that he had lunch with the Rev. Ralph Byrd and he would not be available until August 1 due to prior commitments. Even so, the vestry extended a call. Byrd accepted the call in June and in September 1971, Byrd was welcomed at the vestry meeting. The senior warden reported that with three clergymen more calls would be made. Cobb said he wanted to reach as many parishioners as possible and not just those in need.

Rev. Ralph Milledge Byrd Jr., who was born in Charleston on May 28, 1938, the son of Col. and Mrs. Ralph Milledge Byrd, grew up in faculty housing on the campus of the Citadel where his father was dean of the college. After graduating from the Citadel in 1960 (Company T), he attended the Virginia Theological Seminary. Byrd was ordained as a deacon by Bishop Temple at Grace Church in 1963 and ordained as priest by Bishop Temple in 1964 at St. Andrew's in Mt. Pleasant.

Byrd worked at Grace with the youth until 1971 when he came to St. Philip's. He married Miss Elizabeth (Bett) Ravenel Boykin, the daughter of Mr. and Mrs. Lemuel Whitaker Boykin III of Yonges Island, on June 24, 1972, at St. Philip's. Cobb and Bishop Temple officiated. After graduating from the College of Charleston, Bett taught at the Goose Creek Elementary School.

St. Philippian James Rembert in 2011 said Byrd was fun to be around.

Byrd's grandfather, William Porter Cart, mentioned earlier, was a St. Philippian and his wife a St. Michaelite. They compromised and moved to Grace where they sat in pew fourteen for many years.

Byrd said looking back that his three years at St. Philip's were the happiest in his ministry and he thought the world of Cobb who hired him to work with the youth. Cobb told him what he needed to do and Cobb left him alone. While Byrd was at St. Philip's, EYC attendance peaked at 300, one of the largest EYC's in the country. "Charlie" Lewis, the sexton, would fix hors d'oeuvres for the youth rather than the usual chips. It was his treat.

During a wedding, Lewis, turned and said, "Mr. Byrd you see that woman in the back? She's a bridal consultant and we don't allow bridal consultants." He marched back there and told the woman this church has only one bridal consultant and "he is me." Byrd said Lewis was the best bridal consultant he had ever seen.

One day Rev. Ben Turnage saw Lewis shaking like a leaf. When asked what was wrong, Lewis said he had seen a ghost. Turnage assured him it was a nice ghost.

After leaving St. Philip's, Byrd went to Christ Church in Savannah where he remained until 1978 when he joined the staff of the diocese of North Carolina in Raleigh. In 1981, he took a position at St. Martin's Episcopal School in Metairie, Louisiana, where Byrd said in June 2011 that his title at the school was "The Dean of Christian Life." He asked what that title meant and the school admitted they had just made it up. Byrd was later the school's interim headmaster until 1989 when he became rector at St. Augustine's Episcopal Church in Metairie.

He retired in 2000 remaining in Metairie where his house flooded in the 2005 Hurricane Katrina. But fortunately he was covered by insurance and he rebuilt the house. After Katrina, his bishop urged him to take St, Mark's, a small church in Harvey, Louisiana, on the "west bank" of the Mississippi River. When he arrived he said he saw the ugliest church he had ever seen – it only had a back door because they saw no need for a front door. Byrd led the way in upgrading the building that included adding a front door. Byrd in 2011 was still working at St. Mark's and he loved his parishioners. In his "retirement," he belonged to a group of retired Episcopal priests called the "Watering Hall" and he had his daily subscription to the *Post and Courier* mailed to his home. He read it avidly. "The day he left St. Philip's he was almost in tears and he always missed St. Philip's and Charleston."

Byrd died Sunday, June 3, 2012, in the East Jefferson General Hospital in Metairie. There was a memorial service on June 9 at St. Augustine's church in Metairie and a memorial on June 16 at Grace Church in Charleston where he was placed in its columbarium. Surviving are his wife, two daughters, Elizabeth Brignac and Caroline Christman, his mother, Elise Robertson, his brother, Arthur Jenkins and sister, Joye Trott. There are three grandchildren: Joseph and Charles Brignac and Catherine Christman.

Byrd was "an accomplished musician and had a lifelong love of the theater. He was devoted to God, his family and his friends and he loved to tell a good story and share in laughter. Although he knew the location of the true Holy City (Charleston), he loved New Orleans in all its character, beauty, rich history and irreverence."

In February 1973, the usher's schedule was complete through the next February. Five men would usher each Sunday except during the summer when only four were needed. Vestryman Christopher C. Pearce asked that ushers not seat anyone during prayers and Vestryman Francis (Frank) C. Rogers suggested that an asterisk be placed on the bulletin to denote times when late comers could be seated. Cobb said he would try Rogers' suggestion. Vestryman David H. Maybank reported in June that the head usher system was working well.

There were several christenings listed in *The Spire* on May 6, 1973:

1. Roderick Reynolds Guerry and Caroline Gooding McIntosh Guerry, children of Roderick LeRoy Guerry and Marilyn Stalvey Guerry, March 25.
2. John Palmer Gailllard IV, son of John Palmer Gaillard and Henrietta Freeman Gailllard, March 24.
3. Robert Chance Algar, son of John Philip Algar and Joan Hitt Algar, April 14.
4. Gardner Brockway Miller, Jr., son of Gardner Brockway Miller and Nancy Hitt Miller, April 14.
5. Catherine Phillips Ydel, daughter of Wilhelm Christopher Ydel and Bayless Ydel, April 22.

A Cobbism: An anonymous lady complained, among other items, that the rector was in church collarless. Cobb was on vacation and he came to church as a worshipper and not as a participant in the service. He added that as a matter of history, the collar was a very recent clerical adornment and nowhere in rubric or canon law is the clergyman required to wear a collar, especially when he was on vacation. The only rubrical admonition is that he be decently habited – in fact, he felt he was more than decently habited. He felt that he "was at least a semi-example of sartorial elegance as he attended church that Sunday in a new suit and tie from Jack Krawcheck's half price July sale." Cobb begged the lady to talk to him or one of the other clergy or the wardens, Peter Read and Alfred Pinckney who, Cobb said, were not only competent, but they are good "Churchmen." He asked her to talk to someone and "do not tote your ire about with you. It gets mighty heavy."

The Spire in January 1973 listed the confirmation class that was the largest in recent history. Some in the class included: Vereen H. Coen, Anne Harleston Furman, Benjamin Gerard Hartzog, Mary Ravenel Harrigan, Nancy Llewellyn King, Ford Menefee, Steven Moultrie Ball, Eleanor Hope Geer, Elizabeth Flagg Pulkinen, William Barnwell Vaughan, George Edward Wilson and Rebecca Manigault Gilbreath. The next issue had a correction. It should have been printed as Rebecca Motte Gilbreth.

Mr. and Mrs. Henry Scott Sr. moved to Charleston at 34 Smith Street. He was a concert pianist. *The Spire* in September 1973 thanked Scott, "our talented communicant who gave our Church School children such pleasure on this past Sunday with his magic and piano playing." Henry would later play for the Charleston Symphony.

Henry and Mary Belle Scott introduced their son, the Rev. Henry Lawrence Scott Jr. (Renny) to Charleston. *The Spire* on December 16, 1973, reported that Renny would talk to the Wednesday study and prayer group on December 26 and again

On January 3, 1974. He was serving as chaplain at the University of Massachusetts. *The Spire* noted his parents made a grand contribution to the parish and also in the life of our town. Renny's arrival as rector of St. Philip's was ten years in the future.

On January 20, 1975, the rector read Sosnowski's letter of resignation to the vestry followed on January 30 with a letter he wrote to Senior Warden William Barnwell:

"Dear Bill,

Please extend to the Vestry my heartfelt thanks for the most generous gift. I appreciate your thoughtfulness, and shall use the check for something … or maybe several things … which I need, and which will surely remind me of my association with all of you and with St. Philip's church.

The past six years has been a time of interesting work, new friendships and much personal satisfaction. For all of this and for a chance to work in God's field at this church, I am truly grateful.

My very best wishes to you all.
Fred Sosnowski"

REVEREND HENRY NUTT PARSLEY, JR.

ASSISTANT RECTOR

April 25, 1975 – JULY 1, 1977

On April 25, 1975, Cobb announced that he and the vestry had hired The Rev. Henry Nutt Parsley, Jr. as the new assistant rector. Parsley attended his first vestry meeting on May 19. The vestry approved his salary of $8,500 per year plus a utility allowance of $900 per month, auto allowance of $1,400 per year, hospitalization insurance of $420 per year and a rent allowance of $300 per month.

Parsley would leave St. Philip's July 1, 1977.

Parsley, who was born in 1948 in Memphis, later attended Porter-Gaud School in Charleston. His wife's name is Becky. He served parishes in South and North Carolina. After St. Philip's, he went to All Saints in Florence from where he sent a thank you letter to St. Philip's for the generous check and "most attractive" lamps. He was then rector of Christ Church in Charlotte. He was elected bishop-coadjutor in 1996 and the tenth bishop of the diocese of Alabama in 1999, with his seat at the Cathedral Church of the Advent in Birmingham. Parsley is also the chancellor of the University of the South at Sewanee.

At the general convention held in Columbus, Ohio, in 2006, Parsley, who ran for the office of presiding bishop, came in second with Katherine Jefferts Schori winning. Parsley resigned as bishop in 2011.

Ten members of the vestry testified in a letter dated January 19, 1976, to Bishop Temple that Donald Alston Fishburne was sober, honest and "godly" ... and that he possessed such qualifications as fit him to be admitted a Postulant for Holy Orders. Fishburne, who was born in Charleston August 1, 1951, the son of St. Philippians Mr. and Mrs. Henry Fishburne and the grandson of Mrs. John Sosnowski, was ordained to the diaconate by Bishop Temple at St. Philip's. His first church was St. Mathias in Summerton. In 2002, he was at St. Michael and All Angels Church in Sanibel, Florida.

At the 1976 diocesan convention, Rev. Henry Parsley was elected to the Porter Gaud board of trustees. Senior Warden DeRossett Myers opened up a discussion about having more St. Philippian's elected or appointed to diocesan positions. Cobb reminded the vestry that he was a member of the diocesan board of trustees, Mary Trott was active on the provincial and national level and Helen Barkley was a delegate to the general convention that was held in Minneapolis September 11 – 23. Three large issues were brought up at that convention: women could be ordained although it was not compulsory, the choice being left to the discretion of each bishop; the homosexual issue that resulted in a task force being formed to report on the ordination of homosexuals and the *Book of Common Prayer* (BCP) issue. The majority of the laypersons voted to either retain the 1928 BCP or send the draft proposal back to the liturgical committee.

It would be difficult say which of the three issues would raise the most ire. Cobb said in December 1976 that he would not use the new BCP until the bishop's pastoral letter was published.

Helen Barkley gave a report on the general convention in the October 10, 1976, issue of *The Spire*. Cobb wrote the following:

"**THE ADULT FORUM** will pit **TIME MAGAZINE AGAINST MRS. MATTHEW (HELEN) BARKLEY.** Well, not exactly, but the Forum on Sunday will give you a chance to hear Mrs. Barkley, who was a delegate to the Convention. Barkley said, 'It was an incredible Convention and **TIME** with its usual pithe and flairs. America's Episcopal Church has long managed to be all things to all men – and women, internally it has accommodated its various factions with a reasonable degree of harmony. Externally, it has functioned as an ecumenical bridge between Protestantism and Catholicism because it contains elements of each. Those days may be over. LISTEN AND DISCUSS!"

Dr. James Ravenel in October 1976 requested more hymnals to be placed in the pews. It has always been a mystery and always will be a mystery as to where the hymnals go.

Baptisms included in 1976 were:

1. Braxton Stuart Tucker son, of Joseph Frederick Tucker III and Helen Claiborne Cabell Tucker

2. Helen Henagan Kerr, daughter of John Jennings Kerr and Caroline Marshall Hanahan Kerr
3. James Morris Ravenel Jr., son of James Morris Ravenel and Elizabeth Ross Barkley Ravenel
4. Katherine Bissell Phillipps, daughter of William Hall Phillipps and Claudia Bennett Anderson Phillipps.
5. Francis Cordes Ford IV, son of Francis Cordes Ford, III, and Frances Henderson Ford
6. Sarah Gabrielle Moise, daughter of Benjamin McCutchen Moise and Dorothy Anne Miller Moise
7. Sarah LaVonne Phillips, daughter of Ted Ashton Phillips and Sarah LaVonne Nalley Phillips.

DeRosset Myers in January 1977 asked Cobb if there was a need to approve a chalice bearer – he would support it. The subject came up again in February when Cobb described the general duties of a chalice bearer and told the vestry the bishop said they had complete authority to approve a chalice bearer.

On Sunday January 30, 1977, Rev. Robert Oliveros would "take over from Cobb and Parsley. Oliveros has been kind in helping us on previous occasions … We think everyone knows that Oliveros is a product of this parish and the son of our esteemed communicant, Mr. Lovell Oliveros." Cobb and Parsley were absent on January 30 because they took 104 parishioners to Kanuga where they had a great time in the snow. There were no casualties.

In February, Cobb announced that Renny Scott would be at St. James on James Island for two days in March. Cobb said Scott was "a most engaging speaker and person." In March, Cobb told the vestry that during his trip abroad the assistant bishop of London invited him to participate in a service.

North Moore invited new vestry members to see the procedures of ushering. Dr. Ravenel complained that ushers and Charles Lewis sometimes engaged in loud conversations in the narthex and ushers who did not show up would be dropped. In September, Moore had straightened up the ushers and he reported that everything was running smoothly. Franklin Robson said there should be female ushers. Cobb replied there was no prohibition as to this but the last time there were three ladies on the vestry, they vehemently did not want to serve. Moore said he would be glad to put them on the usher list if they volunteered and Robson said all members of the congregation should bear this responsibility. Ben Hagood thought this would be "an opportunity" for ladies to serve. Mary Trott suggested taking it up at a fall "Women of the Church" meeting.

Parsley reported in April 1977 his trip in to the College of Preachers was very helpful. He was taught the length of the sermon was not important anymore but quality was. A devoted member of the church strongly disagrees saying, "Lengthy sermons can be deadly."

REVEREND BENJAMIN WHITFIELD TURNAGE

ASSISTANT RECTOR

SEPTEMBER 1, 1977 – MAY 25, 1980

Cobb called Rev. Benjamin Whitfield Turnage as the new assistant rector who settled into 77 Tradd Street as he began his duties on September 1, 1977. He appeared on September 26, 1977, to attend his first vestry meeting.

Ben, was born in Charleston on May 19, 1945, the son of Benjamin O. Turnage, Jr. and Adelaide O'Neill Turnage, who met on Sullivans Island and were married in 1938. While his father was serving in the Pacific Theater during World War II, his mother, Ben and brother lived with her parents.

After attending many schools, he graduated from high school in Rome in 1965. He entered the Citadel in the fall of that year but by January 1967 Turnage had decided that was not his calling. After his mother died, he moved to Fort Sheridan, Illinois, to live with his father. His father, who then retired in 1968, returned to Charleston, subsequently married Fronnie Baker Allen. They lived in the Country Club and were very active at Grace Church.

Turnage married Charlotte Best in 1968 and graduated from Baptist College in 1971. From 1968 to 1971 Turnage attended St. Philip's and taught Sunday school. He spoke to Bishop Temple about attending seminary but was advised to get an advanced degree on which he could fall back because many did not make it through seminary. He then went to Clemson University and he graduated in 1973 with a Master's Degree with the emphasis in entomology and experimental statistics.

After Turnage graduated from the Virginia Theological Seminary in May 1976 with a Master in Divinity, he was ordained deacon by Bishop Temple in June at the Church of the Redeemer in Orangeburg. He went to St. Luke's on Hilton Head for fifteen months where he started the church's first EYC. He was ordained priest by Bishop Temple in January 1977 at St. Luke's Church.

From there the Turnages went to St. Philip's, where they became good friends with the Cobbs and Bill and Dottie Rhett. Remember, Cobb went to the Methodist Candler School of Theology. Turnage always called St. Philip's "The High Methodist Opera House" because of where Cobb went to seminary and the music was so beautiful as was his particular liturgical style.

When Cobb announced his retirement in 1980, Turnage left St. Philip's. Cobb wrote, "We hate to see them go but we are thankful for the tremendous contribution they have made to St. Philip's life and we are happy to send a missionary from this parish to the diocese of Atlanta." They left on May 25, 1980, and Turnage took up his duties as the rector of the Epiphany Church in Atlanta in June. He divorced in 1981. In 1984, he married Melissa and resigned his position. He was accepted as assistant rector of Christ Church in Macon and remained there until 1984 when he became rector of Trinity Episcopal Church in Long Green, Maryland, where he remained for sixteen years before retiring on January 1, 2005.

In 2012, Ben and Melissa live in Birmingham and have two daughters, Jennifer age twenty-seven and Alexandra age twenty-five. Melissa had two sons from a previous marriage. Adam White was killed on September 11, 2001 in the World Trade Center and Winston M. White is a vice-president of William M. Bird in Georgia where he heads the logistics division.

The new Book of Common Prayer (BCP) became official in the Episcopal Church in 1979. North Moore asked about its availability. Parsley said that St. Philip's was the last church in Charleston to try the new book although Mary Trott said the new book had received a good reception at Grace Church. Also, the Society of the Preservation of the 1928 BCP had been disbanded. Cobb asked the vestry to stick together on the use of the new book despite personal feelings but he "reflected" that for devotional purposes the 1928 BCP should be left in the pews.

Cobb gave Turnage the job of leading a service using the new BCP for the first time. While Turnage was in the pulpit, Ernest Pringle, who was in the balcony on eye level, did not look pleased with Turnage. After the service, Pringle closely approached Turnage and said, "Sonny, you're not running me off with the new service." Turnage said. "I'm glad" and after that they became friends. Turnage remembers that Pringle always rode his bicycle wearing white gloves regardless of the temperature.

Turnage admitted, "I know exactly why Sam had me celebrate communion from the 'new' prayer book. I would deflect any anger away from him and I was willing to do that because the assistant can always say, the rector made me do it. In spite of what some people thought of Sam, he was a good man."

1977 baptisms included:

1. Anne Simons Middleton daughter of Philip Alston Middleton and Judith Hanckel Middleton
2. Eugenia Tapscott Leath daughter of William Jefferson Leath Jr. and Suzanne Barnwell Leath.
3. James Moultrie Townsend III, son of James Moultrie Townsend Jr. and Lucretia Gibbs Townsend.
4. Amy Lee Ruddy daughter of Frank William Ruddy and Barbara Anne Smith Burnet Ruddy.

1978 baptisms included:

1. Jeanne Hyde Bucknam daughter of Joseph Porter Bucknam and Jane Hyde Smith Bucknam.
2. Edward Frost Lowndes III, son of Edward Frost Lowndes II and Marie Thomas Lowndes.
3. Henrietta Porcher Ravenel daughter of Daniel and Kathleen Johnson Hall Ravenel.
4. Helen Barkley Ravenel daughter of James Morris and Elizabeth Ross Barkley Ravenel.

New members in 1978 included:

1. Rev. and Mrs. John Q. Crumbly (Neda)
2. Mrs. M.D. Molton (Dot)
3. Mrs. Douglas G. Norvell (Virginia)
4. Mr. and Mrs. William McIntosh III (Suzanne)
5. Mr. and Mrs. Charles W. Knowlton (Debby)
6. Mr. and Mrs. Louis Palles (Kristen)
7. Lt. Col. and Mrs. John O'Neil Turnage (Anna Lyle)

In February 1980, Cobb announced that he would retire as of May 31, 1982, because he felt the parish should have time to consider and pray over the selection of his successor. He added that "Have no fears that I will not be a lame duck rector. My adrenalin flows too freely, my love of the Lord's work is too intense, my love of St. Philip's too overflowing, to allow me to rest on my laurels I may have stored up. I simply plan to make the next two years the best of my ministry. Many thanks for your love."

New communicants in 1980 were: Gary Michael Billingsley, Benita Baker Brooks, Eric Allen Brooks, Anne Cogswell Burris, Robert Spann Cathcart IV, William Pettigrew Clare, Caroline Heyward Evans, David Andrew Forsythe, Elizabeth Garden Frampton, Dorothy Lee Gibbs, Walker Pearce Maybank, Sarah LaVonne Phillips, Thomas Bacot Pritchard, Jo Heather Pryor, Vida Barnwell Robertson, and Jane Whitlock Webber.

REVEREND BRUCE WHITMORE

ASSISTANT RECTOR

SEPTEMBER 15, 1980 – JULY 27, 1982

Cobb announced in *The Spire* on August 17, 1980, that Bruce Whitmore, who was from Minnesota had just graduated from the seminary at Sewanee and on September 13, he was ordained to the diaconate in the diocese of Minnesota. Cobb went to Minneapolis to be one of the presenters and he asked St. Philippian's to pray for Bruce at his ordination and to remember his wife, Sandy, who could be overlooked on this sort of occasion. Cobb also hoped to meet his predecessor, Rev. Grayson Clary. In Charleston, the Whitmores were waiting for the renovations of Dan Ravenel's back apartment to be completed before they moved in at 68 Broad Street. Cobb said they were a very attractive couple. Whitmore began work on September 15 with the agreement that he would leave St. Philip's in 1982 when Cobb retired. Whitmore left to serve in Bogalusa, Louisiana.

THE RT. REV. CHRISTOPHER FITZSIMONS ALLISON

In the year 1980, Bishop Allison brought forth the beginnings of a momentous theological change in the diocese of South Carolina. His focus was to preach the Word of God.

Allison, who is called Fitz, was born March 5, 1927, in Columbia and graduated from Columbia High School. He completed three semesters at the University of South Carolina before he was eighteen and entered the army in 1945. The war ended while he was in training but he spent eighteen months in Italy where he attained the rank of first sergeant. Allison returned to Columbia, spent one semester at the University and then enrolled at the University of the South (Sewanee), graduating with a B.A. degree in 1949.

In June 1950, Allison married Martha Allston Parker from Georgetown at Prince George Church. They have four children and in 2011 ten grandchildren.

Allison, who attended Virginia Theological Seminary (VTS) from 1949 to 1952, was ordained deacon in 1952 and a priest in 1953.

From 1952 to 1954, Allison was the assistant minister at Trinity Cathedral in Columbia and chaplain at the University of South Carolina. From 1954 to 1956, he studied at Christ Church, Oxford, and was awarded his doctoral degree. For eleven years after Oxford, he taught in the theological school at Sewanee and in 1967 he became a professor at VTS remaining there until 1975.

By 1975, Allison had become frustrated by low academic standards, the inflation of grades and the unfaithful influence on the seminary by the "God is Dead" movement. He perceived that with this gradual accommodation to the unbelieving culture, the students were not being adequately trained for Christian ministry. He served for sixteen years on the General Board of Examining Chaplains where the results of the examinations showed an astonishing lack of essential knowledge on the part of seminary graduates.

Allison said that "he spoke at colleges, clergy conferences, etc. and was criticized by colleagues because he spoke an orthodox theology."

Because Allison moved from VTS to become rector of Grace Church in New York City in 1975, average Sunday attendance quadrupled during his five years there. While in New York, Allison was an adjunct professor of homiletics at the General Theological Seminary.

He helped found Trinity School for Ministry in 1976 at Ambridge, Pennsylvania, that is now a thriving evangelical seminary with 900 teachers and students. The Rt. Rev. Mark Lawrence, bishop of the diocese of South Carolina in 2012, was one of its early graduates.

A special diocesan convention was held on Saturday May 17, 1980, to elect a bishop coadjutor. Whoever was elected would succeed Bishop Temple when he retired. Dr. Jim Forrester from Georgetown nominated Allison. Former St. Philip's rector Grayson Clary had also been nominated, along with others. Delegates to the special convention were: Tom Myers, Dr. James Glenn, Alfred Pinckney and Helen Barkley.

Allison was elected and by June 8, 1980, accepted the position. He was consecrated on Saturday, September 25 at the Gaillard Auditorium. Bishop Temple retired and Allison was installed as the twelfth bishop of the diocese on January 2, 1982, at the Cathedral of St. Luke and St. Paul. Presiding Bishop John M. Allin was the "installer" and Bishop Temple preached.

As bishop, Allison had to look after 26,000 Episcopalians in seventy-nine congregations, attend the meetings of twelve boards and work twelve to fourteen hours a day.

Allison said that "the experience of teaching in three seminaries and attending meetings of the house of bishops and the general convention convinced him that the church's direction was toward serious destruction. Its doctrine and teaching were on a collision course with classical Christianity and the false teaching was in dire need of correction. There are very few scholars in the house of bishops and the increasing administrative duties of a sitting bishop virtually excluded any time for needed sound scholarship. The best illustration of the self-destructive drift of the church is the fact that in its self-proclaimed 'Decade of Evangelism' the church lost 400,000 members."

In January 2011, this author asked Allison how he changed the course of this diocese to bring in more orthodox preaching and teaching. He said first he brought in Scottish Bishop Stephen Neill, (1900 – 1984), an internationally famous Anglican missionary and scholar, for two months to preach and teach scripture in parish churches and missions. He also brought in faculty from the Trinity School for Ministry to preach in churches and to teach during clergy conferences. Englishmen John Stott and Michael Green, solid Christian teachers and scholars, also brought their teaching to the diocese. Allison said, "The laity welcomed the speakers. Most of the clergy found it enlightening, an encouraging supplement and as a corrective to their seminary education."

Stott died July 27, 2011 in Surrey at age 90. His obituary said, "He was a giant of the evangelical world - perhaps the most influential evangelist of whom most people have never heard."

This author asked Allison how he guided Gospel based ministers into the diocese of South Carolina. Allison said it was not easy. "I would guide search committees to consider those ministers who graduated from Trinity or were otherwise orthodox but it was hard and I made some mistakes." He added that the Cursillo ministry already existed in the diocese and he gave it full approval. He asked John Caldwell, one of the nine founding members of the Kairos Prison Ministry, to bring Kairos to the diocese. Those two endeavors made incomparable contributions to the spiritual life of the diocese.

Allison retired as bishop in 1990 and when asked why he retired so soon, he said, "The reason for my early retirement was, and has been, to devote myself to writing, teaching, speaking, publishing and debating in an attempt to turn the Episcopal Church's teaching towards a more classical Christianity. And I shall continue to do so. We can plant and water but only God gives us the increase,"

In 1994, Allison published *The Cruelty of Heresy*, a book designed to show the crucial pastoral importance of the creeds that were being denied by Episcopal leadership. Other books written by Allison were *Fear, Love and Worship – Guilt, Anger and God* and *The Rise of Moralism,* all of which are in print. His most recent book, *Trust in an Age of Arrogance*, was published in 2009.

Allison is the co-founder and newly retired chairman, of "Mere Anglicanism," a yearly conference in Charleston of Christian scholars, now an official endeavor of the diocese with Bishop Michael Nazir-Ali as its patron.

Allison continues to lecture and teach and in 2011 Fitz and Martha are happily living in Georgetown on property that has been in Martha's family since 1822.

Allison's love of Christ shines through to others. All you have to do to feel his warmth and love is to shake his hand. His Christian love will surely shine on generations to come.

Baptisms in November 1980:

1. Richard Smith Whaley Stoney Jr. son of Richard Smith Whaley Stoney and Maureen Olivette Smith Stoney
2. Mary Randolph Cutler daughter of Richard Mortimer Cutler Jr. and Mary Randolph deSaussure Cutler
3. Katherine Alexander Maybank daughter of David Huguenin Maybank and Ann English Maybank

In May 1981, Cobb wrote in *The Spire*, "This Easter was surely the most thrilling at St. Philip's for many a year." The attendance was approximately 1,400 for all services, including the thirty-five "adventuresome" members who showed up for the 5:00 a.m. service much to Rev. Whitmore's joy. Cobb said that he had reserved his energy for the later services. Former assistant rector of St. Philip's, Rev. Fleetwood Albrecht, assisted in the Easter services.

Prior to World War II, St. Philip's had a few ties with Japan. In 1981, former senior warden Otis Conklin taped a service and sent it to his daughter Rhett Bird and her husband David who were at Misowe Air Force Base in Japan. The Rev. Sato, rector of St. Luke's Episcopal Church, who also held services at Misowe on a regular schedule, took the tape and translated it into Japanese. If you have loved ones far away, why not send a CD or two of some of our minister's sermons.

In June 1981, "The Reverend Brook Myers, son of St. Philippian DeRossett Myers, preached a fine sermon that was splendidly delivered." Former rector of St. Philip's,

Grayson Clary, along with his wife, Jean, and their two sons, who were spending time at the beach, were in church. They were welcomed back.

THE YOUTH, THE MEN AND THE LADIES

In June 1968, the plans for the Sunday school were going smoothly and Julius Guerard, the new Sunday school superintendent, was most enthusiastic. In October, Sosnowski reported all Christian education classes were functioning normally and a teacher's program was conducted each Sunday for four weeks. Enrollment again reached 300. The pre-school was growing and E.K. Pritchard and Mayo Read conducted a small assembly in the chapel that the children enjoyed. After this "little church service," the children would go to their separate classes. The tenth grade through twelfth graders met in the library for discussions groups under the direction of Mrs. Dorothy Anderson, Mrs. Elizabeth Ball and John Wilson.

John Wilson declared in 2011 that Dot Anderson is a saint and he enjoyed teaching with her. He would teach, as he was taught by a former teacher, standing up in in the middle of the room because it kept the children attentive. He said he was very happy to see how well his students grew up, in particular Randell Stoney among others.

Mrs. Albrecht was given permission to use the parish house during inclement weather for the Hope School, an organization for mentally challenged children.

On February 17, 1969, the vestry sent a letter of thanks to Edgar R. Robertson of 21 Longitude Lane for the "magnificent job he had done for many years as head of the ushers."

In 1970, Dr. George Orvin taught the twelfth graders. Julian J. Walker Jr. was the superintendent of the church school and Ted Simons IV was his assistant. Mary Lilly Bennett was chairman of the Christian education committee. Many lay people as well as the clergy were asking, "What is the real purpose of our Church School?" One Director of Christian Education (DCE) answered, "The purpose of Christian Education in Trinity Church is to encourage a deeper relationship with God in order to be a Christian in the world. This does not in any way mean that we do not teach factual knowledge ... We do teach facts, but our primary focus is building relationships with God."

In 1970, Mary P. Herrin reported on the altar guild's activities in the past year. They prepared more than 100 communions, changed the hangings for all seasons, polished silver, helped at baptisms, weddings and funerals. Herrin reported the flowers were always lovely and the linens fresh and clean. This could not have been done without so many helpers.

The Rt. Rev. and Rt. Hon. Robert Wright Stopford, Lord Bishop of London, was in Charleston to celebrate its tercentennial and to participate in a communion service at

St. Philip's. The church's altar guild along with members of altar guilds from other Episcopal Churches prepared communion for 3,000 people and it was served with very little confusion. Herrin said Cobb worked very diligently on that occasion and she thought he should take most of the credit. Herrin added that Julia Pritchard picked her up whenever she failed.

In March 1970, the vestry discussed the playground and its problem with "wrong users." It was decided to make minimum repairs to the basketball and tennis nets and they would consider fixing the tennis courts. Dr. William Cain said the short courts had adversely affected his tennis game. In April 1971, John Wilson pointed out that the concrete was in extremely poor shape and asphalt seemed to be best but there was no practical way to get an asphalt machine into the parish house yard. The vestry decided the courts would not be resurfaced or rebuilt.

In October, Gene Geer submitted a request from the Junior League of Charleston to use the church nursery during the week for their members who did not have servants and therefore had difficulty in fulfilling their community service commitments. By January 1971, the nursery was operating three days a week under the chapel. Nancy (Sister) Linton Rowe (now Buchanan) sent a letter of thanks to the rector.

In February 1972, Cobb organized a committee called the "Men's Special Project," chaired by Gene Geer, to reconstitute the men as one of the motivational forces in parish life. Committee members included Frank Ford Jr., John Settle, David H. Maybank, Dick Coen, Horry Kerrison and Jenkins (Jenks) Gibbs.

A Cobbism: "LADIES ARE SEEING RED." Our girls preparing for the 1973 Town House Candlelight and Supper Tour approached the Mills Hyatt House asking for permission to sell tour tickets from the hotel. When they were told they could not sell their tickets from the hotel, the ladies reminded the personnel that St. Michael's sold their tickets there. They were told the rules had been changed, but St. Michael's had made their request so long ago they had been grandfathered. No one else could sell tour tickets.

The ladies in charge of selling the tickets to the St. Philip's tour asked Canon Cobb to talk with the hotel's manager. Although he tried first to reach this gentleman over the telephone, he was unable to penetrate the "secretarial" curtain." He then made two trips in person to the hotel in order that he might talk personally and reasonably with the manager. The first visit was in a coat, shirt and tie – all to no avail. Canon Cobb was told the manager was busy and was not even asked if he cared to sit and wait or if he would like to make an appointment. He was "treated like a ball-bearing salesman from Butte." He went again, this time armed with the accoutrements of the faith – collar, rabat and preaching suit. Again, he was not accorded the courtesy of seat, voice or vote. On the second visit, Canon Cobb mentioned the fact that St. Michael's being the only organization allowed ticket selling privileges was not quite kosher. That evening the *Charleston Evening Post* carried a picture and a story on the College of Charleston tour – and yes, you are right, carrying the information that tickets would be available at the Mills Hyatt Hotel. Canon Cobb and the girls managing the tour felt they were dealt with in a very cavalier manner.

The concern of our girls working on the tour really was not how their rector was treated – their concern was that St. Philip's was discriminated against. The concern of Canon Cobb was that in a city where "we all try to work together for the common good, a notable organization, the Mills Hyatt House, was losing the valued goodwill of a number of the hardest working and most valuable citizens in the community. This article has been not to do violence to anyone, but simply to answer the many questions that have been asked about this affair during the past ten days or so."

Cobb said in July that "since an article that publicized all the complaints about the Mills House was published in the March issue of *The Spire*, it was only fair to announce that Cobb received communications from the manager and he had received a very fine personal letter from Richard Jenrette and all was well. Cobb said, "The best part of an argument is to end it. Thus it good to announce in bold type THAT THE MILLS HYATT HOUSE AND ST. PHILIP'S CHURCH ARE IN LOVE AND CHARITY EACH WITH THE OTHER, it is our feeling that no one won or loss – it is just good to luxuriate in the feeling we are good friends again." The article never said if the girls got to sell the tickets at the Mills Hyatt Hotel.

The dinner tour was held on March 24 and for $9.50 one could visit "seven prominent houses and gracious gardens within two blocks" Shrimp creole was served in the garden and around the pool at Mr. and Mrs. John Welch's house.

A Cobbism: "Mrs. Raymond (Lenore) Kessler was the hardworking and talented chairman – (excuse me – chairwoman). This was Jean Cabell's second year as ticket chairman, (author - Cobb slipped up there.) Charlotte McCrady was in charge of 'talking people into letting us use their home.' Jo Ann Booker gathered a bevy of beauties who served dinner to the guests. Mary Bennett and Libby Guerard did an almost flamboyant job with publicity. Ann Lesesne was so talented she could make kitchen arrangements look glamorous. And those Huguenot Tortes! – they were made by Alice Patrick's mother, Mrs. Thomas Lemacks (Candy). A group of the most handsome gentlemen in Charleston served as hosts."

In April 1973, Frank Rogers announced that Eugene (Gene) Lesesne would replace him as the new Sunday school superintendent.

Byrd reported in May that planning for next year's work in the church school was underway. "An evaluation of this year's work showed that many new techniques were tried and that generally it had been a good year." Catherine Jones taught grades one through three, Johnson Bissell, Jr. took grades four through six and Fran Read had the pre-school classes. Forty people had agreed to teach the next school year.

Byrd reported on the plans for the production of the opera *Noye's Fludde* (*Noah's Flood*) that was put to music in 1957 by Benjamin Britten based on a play from the Chester Mystery Circle.[20] Britten requested that *Fludde* be performed in churches or large halls – not in a theater – and that the cast should be made up primarily of amateurs. It was to be performed March 31 to April 4, 1974, with performers from the St. Philip's and St. Michael's EYC. The problem was there were no electrical outlets in the balcony of St. Philip's and flood lights were required. The vestry authorized spending no more than $450 to install the plugs.

The vestry minutes did not divulge that Byrd asked the vestry to loan the necessary $10,000 needed to perform the opera. The vestry agreed. Julian Wiles, an Episcopalian from St. Matthews, directed the opera and there was a cast of about 100. Certain special musical instruments were made at St. Philip's. The ark was built in front of the nave by the choir pews and around the pulpit where some of the singers were. During the entrance procession, Cobb, the clergy and choir had to walk up the ark's gangplank, through the ark and down the gangplank on the other side. Cobb ensconced himself on the ark in his giraffe costume. Byrd was the voice of God.

An admission was charged and the $10,000 was returned to the vestry in spite of the fact that a window washer stole some of the proceeds from the opera.

In June 1974, Mrs. Emily Ravenel Farrow donated an air conditioning unit for the nursery. Emily died in 2011. Mrs. Mary Trott requested permission for Chi Omega Sorority to use the tea garden or the parish house for a function. The vestry agreed.

In October, 133 attended the "Young Churchmen" headed by Jack Hitt. This number leveled off to about 100 including fifteen in the junior high group.

As early as March 21, the diocesan bicentennial celebration that was to be held at Middleton Gardens on May Day was being promoted in *The Spire*. Cobb said St. Philip's was allotted 400 tickets "but so far we have not had to call out the gendarmes to handle lines waiting for tickets." There were to be bagpipers, choirs and bands. May 1 was washed out so the alternate date was May 15 which also was "W E T". Cobb wrote, "The St. Philip's Banner stood staunchly amid our undaunted band of pilgrims under the imperfect shelter of an oak tree. Our historical display, expertly engineered by Bartow Culp and Anna Rutledge was a find success. Some said Episcopalians were finally being baptized – by immersion." Nine hundred attended.

Kitty Holt was president of the "Women of St. Philip's" in 1976.

Those confirmed in May 1977 included: Joseph Douglas Balentine, Thomas Ogier Barnes, Robert Hasselle Bowles Jr., Russell Bogert Guerard, Ann Hollister Hamilton, Edward Carwile LeRoy, Garnette DeFord Hughes LeRoy, Arvid Reenstjerne Lesemann

---

20 The Chester Mystery Plays is a cycle of mystery plays dating back to the 15th century.

III, Edward Owsley Marshall, Ian Yandell Marshall, Thomas Plumblee Morrison, John Preston Reed, Thamar Pringle Sistarer, Mary Virginia Tezza, Harriet Hayne Vaughn and Judy Catherine Warren.

A member of the church in 1977 requested to use the tea room and the parish house for two weeks in April and two weeks during Spoleto to serve food. The church would share in the profits. There was a long discussion.

Cobb said that even though this parishioner had been very accommodating to the church in the past, he would have some concern about the possible confusion commercial use would cause with a new sexton and his duties. Dr. Ravenel requested a vote of the vestry on commercial use of the tea garden during Spoleto.

Philip Middleton said such use could have an adverse result on the tax exempt status of church property while Henry Scott pointed out there had been some resistance to such commercial use at past vestry meetings. Ravenel made a motion, seconded by Scott that would deny commercial use of church property. North Moore concurred with Ben Hagood that if a public service was needed then the church should provide it and not an entrepreneur.

The request for commercial use at St. Philip's was defeated eight to two. But the vestry did approve ladies of the church using the tea garden from May 25 to June 5 to serve snacks with all of the financial profit benefiting the church.

In 1977, Mary Trott continued as a member of the diocesan council but "the most wonderfully startling news for us at St. Philip's is that Helen Barkley became the first lady member of the diocese's standing committee." Monti Jones headed up the fall bazaar, Florrie Fair was chairman of the Christian education committee and Winnie Wilson was the Christian education consultant. Mrs. John Jagar (Marge) headed the altar guild.

Two new pre-school coordinators, Jane Cox and Mary Anne Hanckel, took over in September 1978. Winfield Sapp and E.K. (Boopa) Pritchard acted as superintendents.

Cobb wrote in 1978 in *The Spire* "SUCH WAS THE ENTHUSIASM SURROUNDING THE APPEARANCE OF Dot Anderson and LaVonne Phillips at the last of our adult forums that popular demand has catapulted these notable girls back into the limelight. They will teach an overview of the Old Testament."

In another of his 1978 *Spire* writings Cobb said the steeple climb for the confirmation class was a success except only boys showed up with the exception of Mary Ann Stender Bagwell who "came all the way from Clemson to climb the steeple. I believe she really came because it was Mother's Day."

Cobb had a part time job. His son, Gilly, had a newspaper route delivering the *News and Courier* to 174 customers but when he became incapacitated for several weeks by torn ligaments, Cobb volunteered to substitute for him. Many communicants were on his route and no one complained about Cobb's service. Cobb received a "bale of letters" from many places after news accounts of "the priestly newspaper carrier" were published.

The vestry suggested the hours that the church was open to "tourists" should be limited. In May 1979 *The Spire* was calling for volunteers to share the beauty of the church and provide a place for visitors to pray and for meditation, primarily on the weekends. Craig Bennett was in charge of the "Inn Keepers Guild." In October volunteers were still being sought.

Cobb had been *The Spire's* editor since his arrival at St. Philip's in 1965. Although he had enjoyed it immensely, he was turning over the editorship to Miss Chardon Harrigan. New Year's 1980 found Cobb once again as editor of *The Spire*. Harrigan became Mrs. Jenks. Only Cobb, Jenks and Mary Lilly Bennett had been editor. Cobb's pleading for a replacement met "a glacial response."

As part of the Lenten program, Mrs. Newton Gordon Cosby, who spoke at a luncheon and the following evening, was considered an outstanding Bible teacher. Her husband was the pastor of The Church of Our Savior, a non-denominational church in Washington, D.C. The church had only folding chairs and never more than 200 members. To retain membership, each person had to reapply each year and if that was not done, the membership automatically lapsed. To advance from apprentice membership to full membership, one had to take a course called "The School of Christian Living" for one night each week for two years. The church mission was faith based service and was so successful that thousands of people in need have been served by hundreds of organizations started by members of the church. Rev. Cosby preached his last sermon in 2009 at age ninety-one.

The first function of the rejuvenated young adult's club was an oyster roast at "Hewitt's Folly" on "the island." The Monday morning Bible class was held in the home of Mrs. William C. (Kitsy) Westmoreland at 107 Tradd Street. The Wednesday evening Bible study group began in April 1979 at the home of Col. and Mrs. John Burrows at 70 King Street.

The 1979 new youth communicants were; Donald Jay Davis, Elizabeth Floyd Gay, Stephanie Benedict Gay, Augusta Porcher Hipp, David Michael Holton, Julia deWolf Pinckney, Frances Campbell Read, Robert Alfred Richards and Thomas Pinckney Rutledge Rivers Jr.

In May 1981, Cobb wrote that the Sunday school had gone from one curriculum to another, mostly in an honest effort to find something that suits everyone. That did not work because such a lesson plan does not exist. The cry was "Bible, Bible and more Bible and even more Bible" and they agreed Whitmore's curriculum was thoroughly grounded in Scripture. They were going to ask parents to read the Bible stories to their children at home and at church school and to discuss what these verses meant to those living at the time of Christ and what they mean to those today. They believed a division of responsibility between story and meaning would have very real possibilities. Ron Plunkett was church school director.

In October 1981, the Bible verses assigned to be read at home were interestingly from Leviticus 19 verses 1 – 4, 9 – 18 and 33 – 37. The main theme of this chapter is "God Commands Holiness." Many people have forgotten verse 18, "but you shall love your neighbor as yourself. I am the Lord." Many associate loving your neighbor only within the New Testament.

Early in 1981, the first two sessions of the Sunday morning Bible class were led by Nan Morrison whose subject was *Themes from the Bible*. "Nan, a professor at the College of Charleston, already has a splendid reputation as a speaker and teacher within the parish." In 2011, her interesting book, *A History of the College of Charleston 1936 – 2008*, was published.

Mrs. Ashmead (Drexel) Pringle III was president of the Women of St. Philip's in 1981 and had selected the Oak Home as the project for the women. Donations of $500 each were made to Hospice, the Battered Women's Shelter and to Bishop Allison's discretionary fund. A donation of $1,000 was given to the organ fund in honor of Canon Cobb.

Mrs. Josephine Hutcheson, then of 56 Society Street, was a strong supporter of the cub scouts and wanted to organize a new pack at St. Philip's. In 1981, St. Philip's was the sponsor of Troop 50 and Hutcheson wanted to organize two dens. Den One would meet at the Marian Hanckel Kindergarten and Den Two would meet at St. Philip's every Tuesday at 3:00 pm with Hutcheson as den master. Three years later, under her maiden name, Josephine Humphreys completed her first book *Dreams of Sleep* and went on to write more books including *Rich in Love* in 1987. It was made into a 1993 film.

Alfred Pinckney in 1982 reported on the efforts of a sub-committee headed by Mrs. J. Moultrie (Boo) Townsend Jr. to establish a vacation Bible school and Ivan V. (Andy) Anderson agreed to head the adult forum.

THEOLOGY, EVANGELISM AND MISSIONS

In February 1967, Dr. Harry Gregorie inquired regarding the chartable functions of the parish, suggesting these projects could be brought into better focus.

Jennie Rose Porcher reported that clothing was being distributed to needy people. Among organizations that benefited from the activities were the Cancer Society and

York Orphanage. Porcher said many people helped and that the congregation had been very generous.

Cobb, in May 1970, asked the vestry to contribute $1,000 to Father Grant's operation Compenso at Camp Baskerville on Pawley's Island. The money would permit some low income children to enjoy a residential summer program.

In June 1970, Tom Myers presented plans to renovate and enlarge St. John's mission. St. Philip's was asked to contribute. The cost was $100,000 and would be funded by a private foundation and the United States Department of Health and Welfare. The next month the vestry pledged $5,000, contingent upon the success of the center's campaign to raise the $100,000. In 1972, St. John's asked for the $5,000 and the money was sent. A letter of thanks was received from E.K. Pritchard, Jr.

In April 1973, Peter Read thanked those who had worked on the "Candlelight Supper" that brought in a net profit of $3,500. Read also announced the 1973 plantation tour was a tremendous success. Mary Bennett asked if the profit from one of the three fund raisers could be allocated for use outside the parish.

In 1973, Spong's name popped up again. Cobb reported in *The Spire* that "our good friend," The Reverend John (Jack) Spong would be speaking at St. Michael's Parish House at 8 p.m. To encourage St. Philippian's to attend, Cobb wrote in *The Spire*, "Come and renew our friendship with one of our favorite people." Spong also spoke to a women's group.

Sosnowski said that the theology of St. Philip's was orthodox with Christ as the center and the foundation. Why then would Cobb, invite Spong, who has been one of the most radical and controversial bishops in the Episcopal Church, to speak to St. Philippian's? One source said that Cobb was a great pastoral minister to many but Cobb's long suit was not discerning doctrinal distinctions. Sosnowski later said he did not hear anything that was that radical. Another source said that in 1973 Spong was not as radical as he was later. Rev. Ralph Byrd said one of the beauties of the Episcopal Church is that there are many voices in the church and Cobb wanted to expose his parishioners to different viewpoints. Some of his parishioners liked that and many were furious.

In a phone conversation in 2011 with the Rev. Ben W. Turnage, who was Cobb's assistant for three years, was asked about the eclecticism of the speakers, teachers and preachers Cobb brought to St. Philip's. Turnage agreed "it was a mixed bag. Cobb liked to expose people to all situations and he would say anyone is welcome to the Lord's house. He would rather err to the side of Grace and he was a very spiritual man."

Spong issued his "Twelve Theses" during the time of the 1988 Lambeth Conference. The presiding bishop, Frank Griswold, only complained about Spong introducing his theses at that time because Griswold knew it would cause further irritation with the African and Asian bishops.

The first two of the twelve theses read, "Theism, as a way of defining God, is dead so most theological God-talk is today meaningless. A new way to speak of God must be found … And it becomes nonsensical to seek to understand Jesus as the incarnation of the theistic deity. So the Christology of the ages is bankrupt." And they go downhill from there. Spong does have a following.

Tapes of talks by the Rev. Everett (Terry) L. Fullam were played four Mondays in February and March 1975 in the "Tea Garden." It has been said that Fullam was the best stand up Bible teacher anywhere. At this time, Renny Scott was the assistant rector at Fullam's church and, perhaps, it was Scott who sent the tapes to Helen Barkley.

In 1975, three Bible studies were using commentaries by Scottish Presbyterian minister and author William Barclay (1907 – 1978). His son, Ronnie, continues the program now called the New Daily Study Bible Series and remains a best seller.

In 1977, Barclay wrote *A Spiritual Autobiography* in which he shared his personal views that included:

1. Skepticism concerning the Trinity. For example, nowhere does the New Testament identify Jesus with God. Perhaps, Barclay overlooked the following three Bible verses:

    Mt. 3:17 John baptizes Jesus – "And suddenly a voice came from heaven, saying, This is my beloved Son, in whom I am well pleased,"

    Mt. 17:5 The Transfiguration - God said, "This is My beloved Son, in whom I am well pleased. Hear Him."

    Jn 14: 8 – 10 Philip asked Jesus to show them the Father … Jesus replied, "Have I been with you so long, and yet you have not known me, Philip? He who has seen Me has seen the Father; so how can you say, 'Show us the Father?' Do you not believe that I am in the Father, and the Father in Me …"

2. Barclay believed in universal salvation. He wrote, "I am a convinced universalist. I believe that in the end all men will be gathered into the love of God."

    By now Barclay has found out if he was correct.

In May, the Christian education committee wanted to broaden its base and they tried to do that first by all being evangelists in our own church.

On page two of the March 7, 1976, issue of *The Spire,* the headline read:

"NEXT WEEK IS RENNY SCOTT WEEK"

Scott was speaking at several churches in the diocese. Thursday was Scott's day at St. Philip's. In the morning he would be in the "Tea Garden House" for various small groups and then at 7:30 p.m. after cake and coffee he would speak to the parish family. Cobb wrote, "This would be a fine opportunity to hear one of the grand young men of the church."

A young teenage St. Philippian named Hayden McIntosh (later Geer) was losing her faith so she made an appointment with Cobb to discuss that with him. He said faith is questioning and it is normal to do that, but it is also believing while questioning. He said that people have an innate recognition of their creator when they use His name to curse others. His answers boosted her faith. Years later in 2002 when McIntosh was battling an illness, she was able to call Cobb to thank him for restoring her faith so she could ask for God's strength.

McIntosh took piano lessons from Cobb as did many others. One day at Cobb's house, she was scratching her arm and Cobb told her to stop scratching or she would get impetigo. McIntosh said she lied to Cobb and told him she already had it. There were no lessons that day and Cobb sat on the far side of the room from McIntosh.

Dot Anderson introduced a discussion of the charismatic movement that began around 1960. No decision was reached as to the involvement of the vestry. The name charismatic was coined by an American Lutheran minister, Harald Bredesen, in 1962 to describe what was happening in mainline protestant denominations. Charismatic is an umbrella term used to describe the belief that the gift of the Holy Spirit, as described in the New Testament, is available to contemporary Christians.

Rev. Dennis Bennett, rector of St. Mark's Episcopal Church in Van Nuys, California, announced in 1960 that he had received the outpouring of the Holy Spirit. He became a leader of the Episcopal charismatic movement and began a renewal movement with tens of thousands of worldwide Anglicans and within the Roman Catholic and Orthodox churches.

J. Haden McCormick, rector of St. Philip's, preached about Pentecost on Sunday June 12, 2011, asking that we all pray for an outpouring of the Holy Spirit. Dot Anderson was there to hear the sermon.

It was Anderson who reported that the office of refugee resettlement at the Episcopal Church center in New York had issued a call for sponsors for 15,000 Indochinese refugees who the United States government agreed to admit into this country. A sponsor must provide temporary shelter, help find a job and assistance with learning

English. Cobb formed a committee that included John Wilson who felt that that Vietnamese Chi Diep, who was a professor at the College of Charleston, would be happy to assist. Two years later in 1980, Diep was "praised for his tireless efforts that provided vital assistance in the settlement of numerous refugees in our area."

Anderson expressed great concern about the World Council of Churches because of its grant of $85,000 to Robert G. Mugabe for his Zimbabwe Patriotic Front in Africa that consisted of "the most merciless and bloody handed of the black guerrilla terrorists." The black majority overthrew the white minority and many considered him a hero. In 2009, Mugabe was listed as the sixth most ruthless dictator. Zimbabwe was formerly called Southern Rhodesia.

Cobb was asked to meet with the bishop because of the great concern about Mugabe. In April 1979, the vestry unanimously passed a resolution that the national church should withdraw from the World Council of Churches and a copy was sent to the diocese. Notice of this was put in *The Spire* so the congregation could be advised.

Cobb wrote in *The Spire* in September 1978 about Christian education. "Christian education means to be educated in Christ. This is done in various ways, all of them making legitimate contributions to being educated in Christ. We learn through facing the Lord Jesus Christ privately in our Bible readings and in our devotions. We are educated in Christ by our public witness to Him in the corporate worship of the parish – in praise, thanksgiving, the receiving of the Sacraments and the hearing of His word. We are educated in Christ seeking to know Him through study groups and through the history and traditions of the Church and service to Him. All of this adds up to a commitment to our Jesus Christ as Lord and Saviour."

In a newspaper article, Cobb said "he had some slight feeling that God and Charleston are synonymous, but I don't think it exists to the extent that it augers of spiritual ill health." He continued "some of us tend to be a wee bit pious and ingrown about our faith. There is a need to be constantly reminded that we are all sinners … I came as chief of a band of sinners."

John Wilson attended the 1979 general convention in Denver. One resolution that was passed stated, "All real and personal property held for or by the benefit of any parish, mission or congregation is held in trust for this church and diocese thereof in which such parish, mission or congregation is located." At the time, some Episcopalians may have missed the significance of this resolution. It provided a large road block for those churches that, later, would choose to leave the Episcopal Church.

Spaniard Eduardo Bonnin Aguilo (1917-2008), who founded The Cursillo in Christianity in Majorca in 1944, saw it spread in the Roman Catholic Church. "The whole essence of Cursillo is simply to help the person, not only to live the Good News, but to become the Good News …" Cursillo took hold in the Episcopal Church in the mid 1970's and, as Bishop Allison said, the first Cursillo in South Carolina was held at Camp St. Christopher in 1978. In 1980, Cobb was going to attend Cursillo because no one could attend unless his or her rector had previously attended.

LaVonne Phillips was the speaker for the adult forum in May 1980. Cobb wrote, "She will meander through the Gospel of John in several novel and fascinating ways." Cobb wrote for *The Spire's* September 28, 1980, issue, "AT TIMES EPISCOPALIANS ARE ACCUSED OF NOT CARING ABOUT STUDYING THE BIBLE. Certainly the accusation has some validity. Here at St. Philip's we attempt to give everyone who wishes it a chance to indulge in Bible study." Cobb said that there were Bible studies on Monday morning, Tuesday evening, Wednesday after communion and Friday morning. Cobb and Rev. Whitmore were available to start other Bible studies.

Cobb wrote from another source in 1980 regarding the church attendance of parents and its effect on the children in the family. If both mom and dad attend regularly, 72% of children remain faithful. If only dad attends regularly, 55% remain faithful. If only mom attends regularly, 6% remain faithful and if neither attends regularly, 6% remain faithful.

The article continued, "We have often heard 'I don't want to force my child to go to church. If I do, he or she may resent it and not have anything to do with church

later. HUMBUG." Cobb called this is an excuse, an escape from responsibility. No good parent, he said, lets his child choose his or her dentist, doctor, school and many other things and still many parents balk at the most important thing in life and beyond life.

In February 1981, Bishop Allison led a discussion of his book *Fear, Love and Worship*. Cobb said that although St. Philippian's were not enthused about attending evening functions at the church, seventy people showed up to hear Allison.

Becky Gregorie, daughter of Harry and Jane Gregorie, was in Port au Prince, Haiti, from January to June 1981 working at St. Trinite Schools. Becky reported that although the poverty is unbelievable, it does not seem to affect the warmth and friendliness of the people. She added that they overcome their poverty with their character.

Gregorie attended the MUSC Medical School in 1981 where she met David Baird who she married in 1987. Becky, who specializes in Ob-GYn and David, a general surgeon, live in on a farm in Ravenel in 2012 where David raises grass fed beef cattle. They have four children: Wills, Janie, Rebecca and Henry. In 2004, the Bairds went on a family mission to Romania.

The vestry in April 1982 commended the Episcopal Church Women of St. Philip's. Through their diligent and committed efforts, they raised approximately $18,000 which they donated to community charities.

FINANCES AND VESTRY

In December 1965, Wilson, speaking for the finance committee, reported that for the first time the parish budget would be based on actual pledges in hand. St. Philip's accepted an apportionment from the diocese of $17,629. There was an understanding that if the parish budget of $91,000 was not reached, then the parish would adjust the apportionment figure accordingly in the last three months of 1966. A 1965 budget of $108,830 was approved.

In January 1966, those new to the vestry were: Richard E. Coen, Dr. Harry B. Gregorie Jr. and Ben A. Hagood.

When J.H. Brooks moved from Charleston in February, a replacement needed to be elected. Cobb received word from Bishop Temple that the way St. Philip's elected its wardens was not consistent with the rest of the diocese. The by-laws committee and Cobb would confer with the bishop and in the meantime F. Bartow Culp was elected to replace Brooks.

Later, Cobb informed the vestry that he should not be chairman of the parish council when vestrymen were being nominated. The vestry agreed and said the senior warden would serve as chairman.

In December, Tony Harrigan moved that the church give as much to the diocese in 1967 as was given in 1966. The 1966 apportionment was paid in full. In February 1967, the vestry made a pledge of $22,000 to the diocese with the usual adjustment provisos and that would include a review in November 1967.

At the same meeting, Cobb reported that enough money had been donated to laminate old church records.

Newly elected vestrymen in 1967 were: B. Owen Geer Jr., I. Mayo Read, Jr. and Robert M. Hitt. Dr. Maxwell (Mac) Anderson was elected senior warden and Richard (Dick) Coen was junior warden. Ben Hagood and Frank Ford would head the canvass again.

Tom Myers reported in June that pledges were being paid more promptly in 1967 than ever before. For the first time, the vestry approved the purchase of liability insurance for approximately $350.

It was decided on May 13, 1968, that there would be a unified church budget including the budget of the women and that women would have representation on the finance committee. Red Hitt said the vestry should look with favor on this idea and plans should be made for the consolidation. Less than a month later Hitt died suddenly during a civic meeting. On June 10, the vestry expressed its deep sorrow over the passing of its fellow member, Robert M. Hitt, Jr.

The women voted in September to merge their treasury with that of the church to facilitate the handling of money and also to better coordinate their charity programs. Culp moved the vestry accept their offer and work out details for placing women on the finance committee.

John C. Wilson, Jr. and Frank C. Ford, Jr. were in charge of the 1968 "Every Member Canvass."

LADIES ON THE VESTRY

In May 1967, Cobb said it was necessary to conform with a recent diocesan decision that St. Philip's by-laws should be amended to allow women to serve on the vestry.

The issue did not come up until the November 1968 congregational meeting. Cobb reported "And while on the subject of change, amongst the most delightful full-of-possibilities happenings in the history of St. Philip's parish which eventuated in a parish meeting this past November – the word vestryman was eliminated from the St. Philip's lexicon. I want to congratulate both the men and the women for a charming bit of foolhardiness - the women for wanting to serve on the vestry and the men for wanting them."

In 1968 no lady ran for the vestry but in 1969 Mrs. Helen Barkley did run for the vestry. She was not elected. In 1970, no lady ran. Mrs. Mary Lilly Bennett ran in 1971 to become the first lady elected to St. Philip's vestry.

"Mrs. Bennett suggested that in order to maintain the dignity of the services that women on the vestry not be requested to serve in capacities traditionally and more appropriately masculine such as ushering."

With Mary Bennett elected to the vestry in 1971, Mrs. Mary Louis Webb was elected in 1972 and Mrs. Wilmot Gibbs in 1973. There were three ladies on the vestry.

A Cobbism: Canon Cobb was asked about fifty times, "How do feel about having three girls on the Vestry? The answer was GREAT. He said he would be somewhat stunned if the situation ever turned out to be 'Sam Cobb and his all-girl orchestra,' but felt it was a privilege to work with those the congregation elects."

In 1974, Mary Lilly Bennett and Mary Louis Webb went off the vestry. Helen Barkley, the fourth lady elected to the vestry, served that year with Wilmot Gibbs. In 1975, Barkley served on the vestry with her son-in-law, Dr. James M. Ravenel.

The first nine ladies elected to the vestry were: Mary Lilly Bennett 1971, Mary Louis Webb 1972, Mrs. Wilmot Gibbs 1973, Mrs. Helen Barkley 1975, Mrs. Joseph T. Trott

(Mary) 1977, Mrs. Dot Anderson 1978, Mrs. E.C.M. Waller (Adelaide) 1979, Mrs. Mary Lilly Bennett 1980 and Mrs. James Glenn (Lucy) 1981.

Cobb had been geared up since his arrival to commemorate Charleston's tercentennial in 1970. DeRosset Myers was named chairman of this committee. When Charleston began its planning it was called "The Tricentennial," then someone, perhaps Frank Gilbreth alias Lord Ashley Cooper, found out there was no such word as "tricentennial." In September 1968, acting secretary Mayo Read was the first to use the correct word, tercentennial. Another secretary and we are back to "Tri-centennial."

Anna Rutledge and Cobb had a long discussion about tercentennial publishing activities. A Cobbism: Canon Cobb admitted his "inability to gather together the strands after his talk with Miss Rutledge." It was suggested that the senior and junior wardens join Cobb in another talk with Miss Rutledge in hopes that three heads would be better than one."

The South Carolina General Assembly passed a law in 1706 that a register must be kept in each Church of England parish. However, St. Philip's did not begin its As of February 28, 2013, there were thirty four PEC congregations joining in with the January 4 lawsuit. An additional thirteen congregations decided to stay withPEC and are considering their own participation in joining the litigation at a later time. As of March 3, 2013, TEC has nine parishes and seven missions staying. Sadly, the charming church St. James in McClellanville chose TEC. Five missions and two parishes are undecided. PEC has forty seven parishes and churches which is 80% of the 30,000 members of this diocese.

registers until 1720 with a few entries from 1719. The original St. Philip's registers still exist. The 18th century registers were originally printed in two volumes. In 1904 A.S. Salley Jr. edited the *Register of St. Philip's Parish 1720 – 1758* that was printed by Walker, Evans and Cogswell Co. in Charleston. In 1927 D.E. Huger Smith and Salley edited the *Register of St. Philip's Parish 1754 – 1810* that was published by the South Carolina Society of Colonial Dames and printed in Charleston. Because both volumes were long out of print, in March 1969, the University of South Carolina Press agreed to publish the church registers. In 1973, The Colonial Dames printed the *Register of St. Philip's Church 1810 – 1822*, edited by Elise Pinckney.

George C. Rogers Jr. (1922 – 1997) historian, history professor and later dean of the University of South Carolina history department, wrote a forward to the first register which read "This is a wise decision for these volumes are valuable to both genealogist and historian." Rogers pointed out that Edward McCrady had written a short history of St. Philip's in 1897 and that a new history of St. Philip's was needed to place beside George W. Williams' history of St. Michael's.

In 1972, the church received $400 in royalties from the University of South Carolina Press for the reprinting of the Smith and Salley church registers.

In September 1968, Cobb announced a $10,000 bequest from the estate of Mrs. Aida Trapier who died in Washington, D.C. March 3, 1968. In April 1969, $1,000 was received from the estate of Louisa Waring. The detailed financial report of June 1969 was delayed because the CPA was having difficulty with computers.

In 1969, Ben Hagood was elected senior warden and Ford was junior warden. New faces to the vestry in 1970 were Lovell Lott Oliveros and Dr. William Cain. Arthur M. Wilcox returned. Cobb congratulated John Welch in 1970 for a good job as chairman of the finance committee and for his ability to enhance the rector's knowledge of finances and budgets. Cobb was given permission to write personal letters to members who had not fully paid their 1970 pledges and he received about $1,000. The final amount pledged was $117,686.80.

Christopher C. Pearce and Peter Read were in charge of the 1972 Every Man Canvass. Mrs. Blackman was the church secretary. A new face on the vestry was C.B. Branan who was a crucifer at St. Philip's as a child.

Eighteen year olds were allowed to vote when the twenty-sixth amendment was ratified on July 1, 1971. The congregation followed through and at the 1972 annual meeting they voted to change the by-laws to allow all communicants from eighteen years and older to vote. In February 1973, Cobb asked that the by-laws be reviewed.

In 1973, Peter Read was senior warden and Alfred Pinckney junior warden. Read asked the vestry to become enthusiastically involved in church activities.

Ted Simmons III resigned as church treasurer in January 1973. John Wilson announced pledges that had been collected totaled $127,513 which was short of the goal of $132,425.70.

Peter Read requested special recognition for Mrs. Alfred G. Pinckney (Julianna) for her work writing the church's checks.

In December, Mrs. Dwight Gadsden bequeathed $5,000 to St. Philip's and $2,000 to the churchyard.

Cobb was always happy to support the Every Man Canvass albeit somewhat differently. In the November 4, 1973, issue of *The Spire* he wrote "We are a fortunate people. God has not asked that we give up any felicities (listed below) – only that we be thankful for them. One of the ways we can express our thank-fullness is to share our resources sufficiently that our parish can maintain itself without having to use so much of its time and its emotion on being concerned with just getting by.

"If we are to make this budget, it will mean we must count on increased pledging from parish members." Cobb said that even with newcomers, the major portion of this increase would come from all of us – your rector included. He added that he tithed although some said he did not tithe because his was "after taxes."

Cobb asked if St. Philippians were thankful for some of these felicities: cruises, automobiles, bourbon and water, movies, bicycling, shrimp and hominy, rum and coke, swimming pools, trips to Europe, cocktail parties, shrimp and beer, beauty parlors, bank accounts, ocean racing, air conditioning, *News and Courier*, snappy clothes, mountains, gardens, servants, martinis, sail boating, beautiful old houses, oyster roasts, red rice, preaching and dinner on the grounds at Punkin Hill, wigs, health club, riding, vacations, books, private schools, *Evening Post*, water skiing, fine furniture and Scotch & soda. Loyalty Sunday would be November 18.

In 1974, Alfred G. Pinckney was senior warden and Dr. William H. Barnwell II, was junior warden. Thomas E. Myers was the new treasurer. Tom's brother, DeRosset Myers, was the secretary. Frank Rogers and Col. Gene Foxworth headed the Every Member Canvass. Foxworth was president of the Charleston Kiwanis Club. An admiral had been president before him and a general after him. Later, someone asked how did a colonel get to be president? Foxy replied, "Because I was a Marine."

Two new members on the vestry were R. Edward L. Holt and W.B. Chisolm Leonard.

Sexton Charles Lewis moved into the parish house while repairs were being made to his home provided by the church. Lewis and Cobb had very similar voices. A matron member of the church called Lewis at the church and when the phone lines were connected she said, "Charles, what is that s.o.b. Sam Cobb doing to you now?" After a pause, the voice said, "This is Canon Cobb." The matron quickly hung up.

There was a comment from a member of the vestry, "that Sam Cobb was hired as our rector to run the spiritual end of the church as well as the business end. Therefore, the vestry should not have to be involved in so many of the details of the church."

In 1975, Dr. William Barnwell was senior warden and Frank Rogers, junior warden. Otis Conklin headed the Every Member Canvass. New faces on the vestry were Philip A. Middleton, secretary, Henry L. Scott (Renny Scott's father), Dr. James (Jamie) Ravenel and Francis (Fran) S. Dougherty.

DeRosset Myers asked why the pledges were running behind. Tom Myers stated that custom had shown that those who did not pay for the previous year were probably not going to pay the current year. There was a balance of $20,154 remaining from the recent sale of the former Hayne house at 26 New Street. Anticipated receipts were $172,000.

In May 1975, Cobb chastised the vestry for not attending all the meetings. The May meeting had been scheduled for the twelfth, but it had to be canceled because of a lack of a quorum and the meeting was rescheduled for the nineteenth. Four members were absent on the nineteenth – Rogers, Foxworth, Gibbs and Tom Myers, treasurer.

In 1976, DeRosset Myers was the new senior warden and Ed Holt, junior warden. New members on the vestry were Mrs. Joseph Trott (Mary), Ben Hagood Sr., John Kerr and Otis Conklin.

A Cobbism: (swiped from elsewhere), "The Rector of a parish, (not St. Philip's), was called by the I.R.S. about a $1,500 contribution claimed by a parishioner. 'Did he give that amount?' asked the investigator. The Rector hesitated, then replied, 'I'd rather not say just now, but if you'll call back tomorrow, I'm sure the answer will be yes."

In November 1976, sexton Charles Lewis' resignation was pending because he would lose his railroad pension and his social security if he kept working. Lewis said he would stay on a little longer, receiving no salary if given a place to live.

The 1977 senior warden was Otis Conklin and junior warden was Eugene Foxworth. Franklin Robson was a good secretary and Mary Trott was the lone female on the vestry. New members were Robert Richards, John Welch, and J. North Moore.

The senior warden wanted the vestry to pursue three items: the organ, the Cumberland Street property and the church home building and its use. Henry Scott reported the endowment fund was now more than $300,000.

The new sexton, Lornet (Leonard) Taylor, started on March 1, 1977. He would not need living quarters as he was a minister in a local church and lived in Charleston with his family. Charles Lewis would remain as St. Philip's sexton emeritus.

Dr. Ravenel brought up the unusual removal of Rector Stuart Matthews from Grace Church. Cobb said national church rules were in existence at that time and suggested the St. Philip's by-laws should be clear on this point. Grace's previous rector, Ralph Meadowcroft, served Grace from 1946 to 1972 and was dearly loved by its congregation. Any dissenters had long since left the church when Matthews came to Grace in 1973 as rector.

As time went by, small secret groups increased in size planning when and how to fire Matthews. The day after the new vestry took over in 1976, they fired Matthews without any warning. Matthews, in a shaky voice, read the letter requesting his resignation letter be read out loud to the congregation. Matthews was visibly stunned. The Rev. Benjamin Smith became the rector that same year.

In 1978, John Welch was senior warden and Robert Richards was junior warden. New vestry members were Dot Anderson and Col. John (Jake) Burrows. By January, $171,000 in pledges had been received, $1,000 short of the goal. In October, Henry Scott was unanimously elected to perform as the investment counselor for all St. Philip's trust funds.

Dr. James A.L. Glenn was senior warden in 1979 and Dr. William B. Ellison was junior warden. Arthur M. Wilcox was secretary. Vestry members elected were J. Palmer Gaillard Jr., Dr. Harry B. Gregorie Jr., Mrs. E.C.M. (Adelaide) Waller and Arthur M. Wilcox. Glenn welcomed Mrs. A. M. (Katharine) Wilcox who attended a vestry meeting as president of the women of St. Philip's. Man and wife attended the vestry together for at least one meeting.

The 1979 budget of $212,530 was the first budget of more than $200,000. Cobb wrote, "This budget reflects not only inflation but increase in the activity and responsibility. Tom Morrison accepted the job as head of the Every Member Visitation for the next year.

The vestry in 1979 voted unanimously to pay the $35.00 per month medical insurance premiums for the sexton, Leonard Taylor. Cobb's salary was increased to $23,849 and Byrd's salary was increased to $11,024 yearly plus $160 for utilities, $382 rent allowance and an automobile allowance of $225 monthly.

The vestry in January 1980 was out to save money. They were experimenting with the heating system in the church and the chapel and discovered one half of the heaters in the church were usually sufficient for complete comfort. Members were urged to dress warmly. In September, a call went out looking for members to join a "Do it yourself group." Members were asked to replace broken windows, do woodworking, upholstery, painting, etc. "Putting these talents to work for St. Philip's would be a tremendous expense saver and would give you satisfaction. Call Craig Bennett."

Those elected to the vestry in 1980 were Dr. William Barnwell, Mary Lilly Bennett, Alfred Pinckney, N. Winfield Sapp and Dr. Daniel Ravenel. Arthur M. Wilcox was elected senior warden and J. Palmer Gaillard, Jr. was elected junior warden. Tom Myers was treasurer and Sapp was secretary. In 1980 vestryman Col. John Burrows was congratulated on his recent appointment to the Citadel Athletic Hall of Fame.

Elected to the 1981 vestry were: Mrs. James (Lucy) Glenn, R.E.L. Holt, Alfred Pinckney and Dr. H. Clay Robertson, III. J. Palmer Gaillard Jr. was senior warden and N. Winfield Sapp, junior warden. Lucy Glenn was secretary.

The congregation approved a 1981 budget of $232,100.

Sexton Charles Lewis in July 1981 decided to fully retire, citing reasons of loneliness living alone in the vast parish hall and that he really was not feeling up to par. He asked to stay on until he found a place where he could have his dog, Beauty. Lewis had been sexton for seventeen years and had been a part of St. Philip's longer than any person then presently on the staff. Charles did not want to be forgotten and he was still catering his private parties. He moved to 38-D Ashley Hall Plantation Road on Highway 61. Lewis died in 1989.

The "new" sexton, Leonard Taylor, had been hired on March 1, 1977, but few parishioners knew him because he had only recently started working on Sundays. Leonard "was anxious to please." In September, the vestry agreed to Cobb's wish that Taylor's salary be increased to $160 per week since he was then working full time.

The owners of 158 Church Street, located on the northeast corner of Cumberland and Church streets, had been trying to obtain a beer and wine license for their restaurant, McCabe's, but had been unsuccessful primarily because of St. Philip's objections. The church had appealed the matter to the circuit court which upheld the granting of the license. The church then appealed to the South Carolina Supreme Court.

There had been three fires at McCabe's and the owners wanted to demolish the building and build a "similar structure." St. Philip's opposed that because the current building was valuable to the ambiance of the neighborhood. It was built in the late 1860s as a grocery store, saloon and residence. The members of the Board of Architectural Review (BAR) toured the building and denied the demolition. The South Carolina Supreme Court denied St. Philip's appeal and by May 1982, the restaurant had its beer and wine license.

In 1982, Winfield Sapp was senior warden and Dr. H. Clay Robertson III was junior warden. Charles V. Boykin was a new member on the vestry.

PROPERTY & MAINTENANCE

George Hamrick, realtor, said the empty lot on the northwest corner of Cumberland and Church streets could be rented for $200 to $250 per month. No action was taken. Regarding purchasing the W.T. Smith property (southwest corner of Cumberland and Church streets), John Rivers in January 1965 moved that $17,500 be taken from the glebe land fund and the remaining $16,500 borrowed from one or two banks, paying it back within five to seven years.

Once again, the air conditioning issue came up in September 1965. On motion of John Rivers, the vestry would investigate the cost for the church and installing an improved heating system. Shortly afterwards, the vestry decided to obtain an engineering report prior to asking for bids. It was not until November 1966 that the air conditioning committee, consisting of Cobb, Dr. Anderson and Barkley, reported that Cummings and McCrady had been hired to proceed with the engineering and specifications for the heating and air conditioning system for the church.

Looking north at St. Philips c. 1970

Charles Bessinger was W.L Hilton's only employee who would climb up a high, very heavy wooden ladder that took four men to carry and rise, to change portico and other high lights at St. Philip's. He was able to take his family, including a young son, Chuck, to the top of the steeple in 2011 and Chuck said he has never forgotten that day and the wonderful view. The family now owns Bessinger Electric Co.

St. Philip's lore of some years later states that Caroline Bardon received a marriage proposal in the steeple. She accepted.

In June 1966, the vestry borrowed up to $120,000 for ten years for land purchase, repairs and improvements to church property and consolidation of debts. Of this sum, $45,000 would be used to pay for the W.T. Smith property, approximately $40,000 for air conditioning and $14,000 to repay a then current debt.

Ben Hagood reported L.G. Ferguson would charge $4,500 to refinish the pews downstairs and upstairs and the same amount to paint them. The vestry requested assistance from Miss Sue Tarpley Sanders for advice of colors for possible painting. Advice was also sought from landscape architect Loutrel Briggs, concerning an overall landscaping plan for the churchyards.

W. Daniel (Dan) Beaman, later the church's architect, moved from Greenville to Charleston and was searching for a church. As he visited St. Philip's, he wondered why the first two pews on the opposite sides of the center aisle had their doors painted white while all the other pew doors were natural. Cobb happened in and Beaman asked about the painted doors and if they were for "important people?" Cobb said no they had been painted as a test to decide if all the pew doors should be painted white. Beaman said, "but these four pews must have been painted five years ago. How long does it take to make a decision?" Cobb replied, "Son, you obviously must not be from Charleston."

In February 1967, Junior Warden Richard (Dick) Coen, who reported that the church property was generally in good condition, suggested developing an inventory of church property.

In March 1967, Coen reported that Cummings and McCrady had drawn up final plans and specifications for the air conditioning system to be installed in the church. In June, Coen reported the several firms that were bidding on the air conditioning project asked for more time to turn in the bids because they were bidding on several government projects. Cummings and McCrady's plan that was approved in August included the vestibule (narthex) and balconies. An all-weather hot-cold water system that would replace the radiators was incorporated that would be completely concealed except for the fan coil. The total cost would be $73,163.

In October 1967, the property committee reported the air conditioning was proceeding as planned. In March 1968, Senior Warden Coen reported the new heating system in the church was operating successfully and the testing of the cooling system would begin in a few weeks.

Mrs. Read Graves asked the vestry if they would give two or three radiators that were being removed from the church to the Old Slave Mart Museum. The vestry tentatively agreed to the request.

In March 1970, it was decided to scrape down the church's front doors to the bare wood and add only a sealer and no color. Visitors from around the world have admired the beautiful doors.

The vestry decided in October 1970 to hire Homer Peeler, a cabinet maker who worked for the Charleston Museum, to repair the pews in the northeast section to find out the cost of repairing all the pews. When the selected pews had been completed in May 1971, Peeler said it would take $8,000 to complete the remainder. In October, Geer suggested a strong effort should be made soon to complete the refinishing.

Thirty-five pews in the center section in 1972 were to be repaired although the vestry had only $600. The vestry had to ask parishioners for $2,900. In April, Peter Read said "Albert Simons chose a bone white color to paint the pews" and Cobb said there was $2,500 to $3,000 in the pew fund plus a $3,000 anonymous gift so they could start a new section. In September, Read said Peeler worked hard to improve the condition of the pews. A motion passed that enough money be taken from the pew funds to repair the locks on the pews.

Painting the pews began in January 1973. L.G. Ferguson would scrape, paint and touch up those pews that had been repaired for $3,850. In March, work was progressing and Ferguson was thought to be doing a splendid job.

Cobb pointed out in March that after the second church burned in 1835, the present church was built over that rubble. He added that the crawl space was cluttered "to say the least." One might say that since much of the second church is under the third church then it could be said that parts of St. Philip's church are older than St. Michael's. St. Philippians, well into the 19th century, called St. Michael's the "new church."

In December, Mrs. Dwight Gadsden bequeathed $5,000 to St. Philip's and $2,000 to the churchyard.

Cobb asked the vestry to visit Dick Reeves in the Ashley House.

The vestry in May 1972 wanted to illuminate the steeple and $500 had been left for that purpose. Three lights were required for complete illumination at a cost of $2,310. The vestry appropriated enough to install one light and asked for donations in *The Spire*. In June, Cobb said an anonymous donor promised funds for the north light on the steeple and it had been installed.

In September, the vestry was going to get a quote to air condition the parish house.

St. Philip's was moving on up to modern technology in April 1973 when Cobb requested an electric typewriter and a new addressograph machine, together costing $2,000.

In June, Charleston Day School, which had moved into 51 State Street on the southwest corner of State and Cumberland streets in 1973, asked the church for the use of St. Philip's playground during the week. The wardens would talk with the school headmaster Edgar (Ned) S. Jaycocks. In September, there were no arrangements made but

Cobb had the vestry send a plant to the school upon their opening in the new location. St. Philippian Brendan O'Shea is the headmaster in 2012 and his wife, Roberta, has been on the St. Philip's vestry.

In November 1973, Frank Rogers suggested the finance and property committees look again into the possibility of renting parking spaces in the lot on the southwest corner of Cumberland and Church streets. In January 1974, Peter Read and Wilmot Gibbs moved that a reasonable number of parking places be put aside for member parking, but not so many to prevent the use of renting to the business community. The motion carried.

Francis Dougherty in March 1975 reported that there were complaints about visitors who went into the church smoking and left the butts on the floor. Charles Lewis was having trouble getting the cigarette butts cleared out of the main aisle. It was generally agreed that this was a rarity and at this time the church should remain open for visitors.

At the vestry meeting of April 21, 1975, Frank Rogers said there was some evidence of earthquake damage in the "sanctuary" because a large fault had appeared in the arch over the choir stall. Rogers added the claim with the insurance company would be settled as soon as possible and that "During repairs, the 'sanctuary' might have to be closed." By June, the exterior earthquake damage was seventy percent completed and the church accepted a settlement of $13,300.

Not only was there an earthquake in April 1975, moderately strong shocks had occurred near Charleston in 1952, 1959, 1960 and 1967. Earthquake shocks have occurred since.

Bill Ellison, junior warden, announced in February 1979 that the roofs of the parish house, chapel, church home, office and tea garden all needed repairs. E.R. Hasell not only won the bid at $5,950 but was asked to do other work and to inspect the roofs twice a year.

The Montessori School received permission from the vestry to continue to occupy space in the parish house. Robert Richards reported that the parking lot and the Philadelphia Alley house generated $9,630 yearly although taxes did have to be paid on the house. In March 1982, Vestryman Charles Boykin recognized the invaluable contribution Craig Bennett made to the property committee.

GLEBE LAND

In June 1965, Randell Stoney said a new higher figure was expected to be offered for three houses on Glebe Street property. In July, the vestry accepted $9,500 and debated how much of this money should go toward debt and how much for operating funds.

The 267 year old tradition of Glebe land had ended.

THE CHURCH HOME

In March 1967, the vestry discussed church home operating problems. Harrigan suggested that admissions should be halted until the church home committee considered the situation. But by June, the problems were solved because two new members moved in: Mrs. F.J. Seabrook and Miss Dorothy Bollwinkle. Resident Mrs. Rife was asked to cease her china repair business.

By May 1968, architect Read Barnes proceeded with his preliminary work on a rendering for the church home building, but there was some question about how the trust funds could be used. In December, the plans were changed and the entire church home building would be renovated for $47,000.

In 1968, John Rivers donated a television set to the home. Two new church home board members were Mrs. J.A. (Alice) Burkette, née Gaillard and Mrs. E.E. Beatty (Agnes). Ruth Davis moved into room 38. The board members decorated a beautiful Christmas tree with lovely gifts under it and a box of oranges and grapefruit was sent to the home at Easter.

In January 1969, Bartow Culp reported that a sherry party was planned for the church home ladies in the near future. Mr. Reed from Columbia left $5,000 to the church home. A member of the congregation said, "That would pay for a lot of sherry."

Cobb in May 1970 was bothered by the complaints made to the church staff by the residents of the church home. The vestry wrote a letter to the home's director, Mrs. Minott, notifying her that complaints were to be addressed to Bartow Culp the head of the church home committee and not the clergy or staff.

In August 1970, Mr. and Mrs. B. Owen Geer, Jr. donated a "lovely" color television set to the home. "All the ladies were enjoying it very much."

Early in the year, the hot water heater gave out and it was replaced "by a nice new electric one." There were always stopped up pipes and the thirty year toilet on the third floor was replaced. Plaster fell and old blinds were replaced. In October, a duct was installed on the first floor of the church home for $50.00 to keep heat from being wasted on the third floor. The bathroom on the first floor was remodeled by Johnny Lilienthal's Crest Construction Co. for $680 – the low bid.

In February 1972, the property and church home committees were directed to initiate a study offering choices about the future of the home: maintain it somewhat as is, modernize it, or relocate the tenants from the home. Cobb asked that the study be conducted with care and caution. In March, Peter Read said the committees decided not to modernize but to keep the ladies as comfortable and happy as possible citing various repairs that had been made. In May, the second floor walls and ceilings were repaired and painted. The vestry toured the church home.

An applicant in February 1973 was turned down because she was not a communicant even though the home was equipped to take eleven occupants and only six resided there. Another plumbing incident in the church home had damaged the ceiling in the church office. In 1974, Mrs. Minott was in the hospital and Mrs. Crumbly was the acting supervisor.

In April 1975, the vestry discussed the possibility of again renovating the church home. Cobb said the home was an anachronism and it was less than half full and that he was constantly plagued with many small problems and details. There were certain deed restrictions on the home which would have to be worked out before any meaningful discussion on renovation could be held.

The parish had an outstanding debt of approximately $74,000 and no one wanted to see it go higher. Rogers said it could cost as much as $250,000 to make all necessary renovations on all of the church property and that financial situation was a stumbling block for the renovation of the church home.

Tom Myers in December reported there was no restriction as to sex or race of anyone living in the home. The entire third floor of the church home was empty and it was suggested Lewis could live there and only minor changes would be needed. Cobb tried to discuss the matter with Mrs. Minott, church home director, but she was bitterly opposed. Nearly all the vestry received calls from the four residents of the home imploring Lewis not be permitted to live on the third floor. Their reasons were many and varied: the women were not always fully clothed, Lewis had a dog and there was concern about the number of guests Lewis had, particularly at late hours. Cobb and the wardens met with two of the ladies and they remained strongly opposed. Cobb decided it would be impossible to let Lewis live on the third floor.

By then Lewis was living on the second floor of the parish house where some changes were made to accommodate him. Cobb said that when people asked where Charles Lewis was going to live, he told them that several years ago the vestry built a lovely apartment in the parish house – an apartment of which Lewis was so proud that he would be happy to show it off to anyone who was interested. "Charles turned out to be a great interior decorator."

On Monday evening February 21, 1977, Tom Myers, who had just left the vestry meeting, returned and announced the church home was on fire. The meeting was adjourned for forty-five minutes. After that time, the meeting resumed and carried on with their business. Cobb thanked the vestry for its assistance during the fire which did considerable damage to the church home and some damage to the downstairs church office. There was no write up in the newspaper.

This incident led to the vestry to re-think the future of the church home. They inquired if the home was still useful and asked for a report in six months.

Otis Conklin in October shared with the vestry the architect's plans for converting the church home into apartments. Cobb said this plan would not violate the trust as its purpose was to furnish a home away from home. In November, senior warden Foxworth said the feeling of the church home board and committee was that the building should not remain the same.

Conklin advised it would cost $250,000 to renovate the church home into apartments. He was going to look into converting the building into offices.

Myrtle Minott died in 1978.

Bill Ellison in September 1979 reported that one company said the best use of the church home building would be commercial office space with perhaps a "shoppe" on the first floor because office space costs less to create and there are tax incentives. However, Sparkman said that the execution of these plans were by no means certain for various reasons.

By June 1980, the church home committee asked for a feasibility study that cost $4,880.00

It is not clear when the ladies were moved from the church home and whether or not they were re-located. On January 7, 1981, a report was given stating the building had been vacant too long to qualify for its former multiple unit use. That would mean it closed in the beginning of 1980 or sometime in 1979.

Cummings and McCrady researched the building that they thought was built in the early 1800's although that may or may not be correct. They thought the last third of the building, ending at Queen Street, was not original. They reported that there was a good chance the foundation was settling on the interior walls and to prevent that they needed to maintain two parallel walls down the middle of the building and to remove most of the interior partitions trying to keep the loading on the foundations the same. He said as long as the loads were vertical, no great trouble would be anticipated.

In March 1981, Dot Anderson reported the final recommendation of the committee was the building should be firmly boarded up and maintained as is. "Perhaps some use could be found for the building in the future." The church home committee was asked to further investigate. As we know, the building became the ministries hall.

THE RECTORY

In May 1969, the vestry purchased a plaque from Historic Charleston Foundation to be placed on the rectory.

In 1971, the stucco fell from the second story of the rectory and Johnny Lillenthal was to give a bid. The bricks on the side of the driveway needed to be moved to accommodate modern cars. Mrs. Dwight Gadsden left a bequest to replace the fallen plaster.

Arthur Wilcox and Lovell Oliveros in January 1973 moved to investigate the possibility of selling the rectory. A special rectory committee was formed that included the wardens, Ed Ball, John Welch, Mrs. Craig Bennett, Mrs. Theodore Guerard, and Mrs. Samuel T. Cobb. The decision was finally made in September that the rectory would not be sold.

Buist Rivers commented on a pre-dawn fire at 90 Church Street next to the rectory. Cobb reported the fire, "thereby enabling firemen to rescue the lone occupant, Lucas Simons."

A Cobbism: In the fall of 1973, "Our sister parish and mellow competitor" (St. Michael's) asked Canon and Mrs. Cobb if the rectory could be used for their Christmas Candlelight Tour of Homes. They happily said "YES!" This caused some comment in the community from St. Michaelites and St. Philippians. The St. Michaelites asked the Cobbs, "Did Mrs. B. H. Rutledge Moore (Elfrida or Frida as she is called) really ask if the house could be used?" Then they wanted to know if asking for the rectory "was nervy." The Cobbs did not think either St. Michael's or Frida were nervy and they were "looking forward to cooperating with our friends across from the post office." Cobb did not even think we should ask for a percentage. St. Philippian's were just as intrigued and asked "what could St. Michaelites let us use?" Cobb suggested that on certain festive occasions, St. Michael's could allow us to use their bells. What think ye of this St. Michaelites? Remember, St. Philip's had no bells at that time.

In April 1981, Ashton Phillips, who was the owner of Carolina Eastern, Inc., made another generous offer to the church. Ashton and his wife, LaVonne, were restoring 41 State Street and they wanted Sam and Nancy Cobb to live there until the Cobbs died. The only thing the church had to pay was the monthly rent of $650 for five years and after that it was rent free. Phillips, in return, would make contributions of 130% of the rent. The Cobbs were to maintain the house, pay all utility bills, insurance, etc. and Phillips would pay the property taxes. The vestry accepted his kind offer and the Cobbs moved in January 4, 1982.

In February 1982, a month after the Cobbs left the rectory it was rented for $725 a month for eight months with the tenant having the right to sublease the rear house "as is."

MUSIC, THE CHOIR & BELLS

In February 1966, Cobb and Dr. Harry B. Gregorie, Jr. were appointed to the music committee with Cobb as chairman. By December 1967, the vestry noted that Cobb was completely in charge of the church's music.

After forty-four years of service in the choir, Dorothy Bollwinkle resigned effective June 1, 1968. The vestry sent a letter notifying her of monthly $100 life retirement payments, subject to yearly vestry approval, and she was also given a severance payment of $1,000.

Several inquiries had been made concerning the choirmaster and organist job. The vestry decided to invite John Sanders of Alexandria, Virginia, to St. Philip's so the vestry could meet with him about the job. In September, Cobb reported that he had been hired and the choir was very pleased with his talents. Sanders seemed very happy.

In April 1969, the rector commended Sanders, the choir and guest singers for the splendid rendering of "The Crucifixion." There was a discussion about paying the children's choir and it was decided each should receive 50 cents per week if they attended choir practice and sang at the 9:30 a.m. service.

Gene Geer reported there was interest in hanging bells once again in the steeple but Cobb said it could not be a budget item. Mrs. Virginia Neyle made a $500 donation for the bells. Other interested parties were Charles Duell, Frances Palmer, Dr. Maxwell Anderson, Dr. Edward Izard and his wife, Anne Kirk Izard.

After John Sanders resigned as organist in September 1972, Cobb and Byrd interviewed applicants for the position. Listening to one applicant, who played terribly, Cobb turned to Byrd and said, "I have to hire this person even though the music is awful." Byrd asked why and Cobb replied, "I gotta be nice." Byrd said the applicant lasted two days.

The choir director was replaced by Miss Nana Eubanks of Pageland. Byrd said she was great.

Cobb announced in February 1973 the junior choir was working on a cantata, "*100% Chance of Rain,*" possibly by Walter S. Hartley. Cobb was very pleased with Miss Eubanks and an anthem sung from the rear balcony had been particularly effective. In April, Miss Eubanks made a case for a new organ and in June the vestry paid a $95.00 registration fee for her to attend a conference.

A vestry committee asked the bell committee to write a letter to the congregation stating the bell drive was not an official fund raising function because it would affect other giving in the church.

Options for purchasing bells included: buying from an old English church, paying $22,000 for a chime of eleven bells or a peal of three or four bells that cost less.

It was announced in *The Spire* on June 29, 1973, that Miss Eubanks made a difficult decision to leave St. Philip's. She had graduated from Eastman School of Music at the University of Rochester the past June and it was her strong wish to teach in a college situation and an opportunity opened up in Alabama with a considerable increase in salary. Cobb said, "Nana had done great, even unbelievable things. Not only that, but by her charm of person and personality she endeared herself to our congregation. Everyone loved her cheerful fullness."

In October, Miss Eubanks donated $500 to the organ fund.

In September 1973, the new choir director was Dr. William (Bill) Oplinger of the College of Charleston and the organist was Mrs. Roderick Guerry. Cobb said dividing up the two jobs would cost about $300 more than last year.

Sue Guerry née Stalvey had Charleston relatives including her mother who later moved to Savannah. She graduated from the University of North Carolina at Chapel Hill and went on to have a Bachelors of Music Degree and a Masters in Music from Chapel Hill. Sue was Phi Beta Kappa and a member of the Order of the Grail Valkyries that was given to those few "who made significant contributions to our university's climate through excellence in scholarship, dynamic leadership and innovative service."

Sue married Roderick (Roddy) Guerry from Savannah at St. Patrick's Catholic Church in Beaufort on September 16, 1959. Roddy is of Huguenot descent and a cousin of Bishop William Alexander Guerry and other ancestors who worshipped at St. Philip's. Roddy, a doctor who worked at the Medical University of South Carolina, also taught Sunday school at St. Philip's in "Learning Center number one." Roderick Leroy Guerry transferred into St. Philip's by March 1973. In October, Dr. and Mrs. Guerry were welcomed into the fellowship of St. Philip's.

In December 1973, they decided to return to Savannah. Sue in 2011 said she loved working at St. Philip's because Cobb was so supportive of the music but the organ "was difficult to play."

THE BELLS

The bells were a big event in 1976. On June 28, it was simply reported, "The Bells have been installed. John McCrady certified his inspection of the steeple and declared that all was safe. The bells will ring on July 4." There would have been no bells without, as Cobb put it, the "determined ladies" who he diplomatically listed in alphabetical order: Mrs. Witsel (Virginia) Neyle, Mrs. George (Frances) Palmer, Mrs. Edward (Julia) Pritchard and Mrs. Sinkler (Marguerite) Valk. Cobb wrote, "They took up where the Confederacy left off and we will forever be grateful. God bless you determined ladies."

During "The War," Confederate authorities requested St. Philip's eleven bells be removed and taken to the ordnance department in Augusta so they could be melted to make cannons.

The Confederate government agreed to replace the bells when the war ended but with the loss of the Southern cause all hope of their restoration expired, if the "determined ladies" did not replace eleven bells as promised by the Confederacy, they did replace four of them.

The bells were cast at the Van Bergen Foundries in Annecy, France, twenty miles south of Geneva.

Six hundred St. Philippian's and friends participated in a 10:00 a.m. dedication service on Sunday, July 4. Mrs. Neyle composed a hymn that was performed during the introit. The logistics included the congregation following the crucifer, acolytes, choir and clergy out of the church into the churchyard while the choir remained on the south portico as the congregation filled the churchyard. Excerpts from 19th century vestry minutes were read and there was a prayer of dedication. Each of the four "determined ladies" would set one bell in motion. "With the pealing of the bells, the blessings and shouts of 'thanks be to God' the service ended with magnificent and holy cacophony.[21]" Donations for the bells were still needed.

THE NEW ORGAN

The search for a new organist was on in January 1974. The senior warden said that the financial problems had hopefully cleared up and a new organ should be considered but a different report was made in March 1975. There was no money to repair the organ and no plans to raise money for a new organ. There was $3,000 on hand for the organ. Mrs. Barr D. Yonker (Sarah), the new organist, was asked about repairing the organ. She said, "The present organ was built in 1921, that it is fifty-four years old and therefore consists of fifty-four tired old parts. Repairs would be temporary and there would be recurring expenses." Yonker added that she could only play on one-half or two thirds of the organ and never knew in advance whether the key that she struck would ultimately result in a musical note. Remember, the previous organist, Sue Guerry, said it was tough to play the organ. The committee added it would take approximately two years for the organ to be rebuilt and installed.

Yonker, in a letter to the vestry, said they had an excellent man, Vernon Thrift, from Winston-Salem, who could maintain the organ. She said that only about half of the organ pipes were useable and on Maundy Thursday she found the rear trumpet pipes sounding eighteen notes without her assistance. Thrift came to take care of everything. Yonker also recommended the valuable, historical organ located in the chapel should be restored for the bi-centennial.

In March 1976, Casavant Freres' bid was $128,000 including the antiphonal organ in the rear of the church. In November, the committee recommended purchasing the new organ even though the organ fund only had a balance of $16,500 including a $1,000 donation in memory of Martha Benson Gibbs. Martha's husband was former vestryman

---

21 Cacophony is defined as a "harsh and discordant sound." Is that what Cobb meant?

James (Jim) Gendron Gibbs. The vestry signed the contract with Casavant Freres in December 1977. Dougherty, who did a great job raising the money, was appointed chairman of the organ fund drive.

An anonymous benefactress restored the 1839 Appleton organ that was placed in the chapel. It sounded officially for the first time on Friday April 18 when a concert was held there.

Senior Warden John Welch in May 1978 announced $100,000 had been pledged toward the $130,000 needed to pay for the organ and he stated he was calling a halt for further solicitations at that time. Cobb was not available to make the trip to Montreal so he sent Mrs. Yonkers to insure the organ was in good shape prior to it being shipped on November 6, 1978. Most of all, Yonkers was entranced with the beauty, its versatility, quality of workmanship and tonal resources of the new organ. The organ was setup in a great three-story barn like structure. Casavant did not go to a stockpile of pipes but instead each pipe was made especially for "our organ." Work had been going on at St. Philip's for a week preparing the chamber for the organ and it was expected the new organ would be played for the first time on December 24, 1978. There were kinks that had to be worked out, but many members and visitors were astounded at the beauty and majesty of the instrument.

In the May 28, 1978, issue of *The Spire* Cobb put in an article "A Tribute to Francis Dougherty and to Our Congregation, The Drive is Practically Over. Few people have worked harder in the interests of St. Philip's these last several months than the chair of the organ fundraiser. What he has done is quite remarkable but then we had a remarkable congregation with which to work. One St. Philippian family donated $20,000." Cobb had his seven feet five inch Yamaha grand moved into the church where he would give an all Chopin recital fund raiser for the organ.

Some parishioners would donate one pipe at $50.00 and others gave a rank of pipes that cost $2,800. Some paid immediately and others paid over a period of years. Cobb donated $500 for ten pipes to be paid over a three year period.

On Sunday January 21, 1979, the new organ was dedicated to the Glory of God, in thankfulness for those who were so generous to make it possible and in loving memory of those honored by gifts to the organ fund. The sermon in song was – Cantata No. 106 *God's time is the Best Time* by J.S. Bach.

Easter in 1979 was filled with joy by large enthusiastic congregations at both services. The choir sang beautifully and the tambourine in the anthem "added another and unusual touch of joy to the service."

The old organ was sold to St. Barnabas Episcopal Church in Bay Village, Ohio, for $2,500 plus shipping charges.

In February 1980, Fran Dougherty advised the vestry that all pledges made to the organ fund were paid and that had brought in $135,000, leaving a shortfall of approximately $24,000. Dougherty presented a plan to raise from $4,000 to $5,000 by working with artist James D. Polzois to sell 200 copies at $27.50 each, of his water color of the choir entering the front door in the rain with umbrellas. Polzois, who was the substitute organist at St. Philip's on numerous occasions, had his studio at 24 State Street. In November, a $10,000 anonymous donation to the organ fund was given. The donation and the prints virtually ended the organ deficit.

W. Benjamin (Ben) Hutto, coordinator of Piccolo Spoleto Organ Recitals, was denied a request by the rector for Spoleto to have a midnight duo-organ in St. Philip's on Friday, June 5, 1981. Cobb explained that the vestry had decided it would be unwise to have this function in view of recent grave robberies. He graciously offered a morning slot on June 5 but that was not feasible. Hutto was disappointed but he moved the function to the Cathedral of St. Luke and St. Paul.

THE CHURCHYARDS

THE SMITH SISTERS

The vestry approved the sale in September 1965 of three burial lots, one each to Miss Julia Mayrant Rees (1894 – 1975), Miss Edith Kinloch Smith (1890 – 1981), and Miss Charlotte Haskell Smith, (1893 – 1975) who lived at 8 St. Michael's Alley.

Julia, a cousin of Edith and Charlotte, made Charleston benne wafers and she also taught Sunday school at St. Philip's. Edith and Charlotte's parents were Algernon Sydney Smith and Annie Hayden Smith. Edith was a legal secretary for fifty-two years at Mitchell and Horlbeck. Charlotte, who graduated from the George Peabody College with a B.S., taught at the High School of Charleston in the home economics department where a lot of cinnamon toast was made. Catherine Jones, who was taught by Charlotte, said in 2011 that to this day whenever she smells cinnamon toast she thinks of Miss Smith who retired in 1957. The ladies purchased a dilapidated house from Miss Susan Pringle Frost and restored it.

Sam and Nancy Cobb were invited to 8 St. Michael's for mint juleps. After returning home, the Cobb's son, Gillie, asked how the drinks were to which Cobb replied that "the first drink was delicious and the second drink was unnecessary." The ladies had a tradition that on New Year's Eve each would climb up on a chair and at midnight each would jump off her chair into the New Year. They were known as the Alley Cats.

In February 1966, the South Carolina Daughters of American Colonists sought permission to erect a marker where the two signers of the Declaration of Independence were buried at St. Philip's. "It was decided to ask for further information." That was a good move because only one of the four South Carolinians, who signed the Declaration of Independence, was buried at St. Philip's. That was Edward Rutledge. The other signers were: Thomas Lynch, Jr., who was lost at sea, Arthur Middleton, who was buried at Middleton Place, and Thomas Heyward, Jr., who was buried in his family cemetery at Old House near White Hall. Charles Pinckney, who signed The Constitution, is buried at St. Philip's and Charles Cotesworth Pinckney and John Rutledge, both of whom signed The Constitution, are buried at St. Michael's. In 1967, the vestry did give approval to the South Carolina Society of the Daughters of American Colonists to place a marker on the churchyard wall to honor Edward Rutledge and Charles Pinckney.

In 1966, Craig Bennett was chairman of the churchyard committee.

In February 1967, Junior Warden Dick Coen stated that it was distressing that St. Philip's was supposed to be a landmark of the city yet the churchyards were in poor condition and he recommended professional help to improve their overall appearances. Quick action was taken and the vestry hired M. William (Billy) Hills, who had Three Oaks Nursery on Johns Island, to do the landscaping and maintenance. The vestry authorized up to $800 for repairing churchyard tombstones and Loutrel Briggs began work on plans for a walkway and a wall.

Coen reminisced in 2011 that there were many opinions about changing the dirt walkway in the western churchyard. After a rain, the water would flow into low places and holes in the walkway that made it particularly difficult during a funeral when pallbearers were carrying a coffin.

The vestry in December paid $1,526 to Arthur R. Michael to construct a flagstone walkway. Instead a brick walkway was built. Coen said Michael was an outstanding mason. Shortly afterwards, Dorothy Legge attended a funeral in the western churchyard for the first time and she exclaimed, "My heavens, it looks as though you built I-26 right through the churchyard," or words to that affect.

By October 1967, the repair of the tombstones and other work was proceeding. In December, at Coen's urging, the vestry spent $294 for planting trees in the churchyard. He remembers planting a magnolia tree and a dogwood tree in the eastern churchyard just next to the steps leading into the narthex from the south. It has always been the first dogwood in the city to bloom and Magnus Monsen would walk by every year to announce it was once again the first to bloom. Mrs. Nellie Sinkler Taylor and her husband, Colonel Roger Taylor, are buried next to the dogwood tree and some people call it "Miss Nellie's dogwood tree." The large crabapple tree in the front of the western churchyard was moved by Coen from the back when it was only eighteen inches high.

In 1968, Miss Alicia Rhett purchased one burial lot. Although there was an article in the newspaper about Rhett's performance as India Wilkes in Gone with the Wind, she never liked talking about it.

"JALAN SAMA TUAN ALLAH"

Two burial lots, numbers 4189 and 4189a, were sold to J. Blake Middleton. The inscription on Mrs. Middleton's (Totsy) tombstone reads: "Jalan Sama Tuan Allah," Malay for "Walk with God." Their daughter, Lane Middleton, explained that after they were married in 1926, her parents had moved to Sumatra with the Socony Vacuum Oil Company, where they lived until 1930. Totsy eventually decided to have her tombstone memorialize their wonderful days in the Dutch East Indies.

The Middletons returned to Charleston and Blake offered to purchase the magnificent Nathaniel Russell House for his wife. She declined because there were not enough closets. Then in 1960, Blake secretly purchased 42 Society Street that was included in the Historic Charleston's Ansonborough renovation. Totsy was a stalwart preservationist and was happy to be a "pioneer in Ansonborough."

A large, orange and white stray tom cat that would be named Jackson wandered onto the Middleton's property and settled in. When it became apparent the cat had no intention of leaving, Totsy took the cat to be neutered. About a week after he returned home, he showed up on their doorstep wearing a collar. No one ever knew who put the collar on Jackson or whose cat Totsy had had spayed.

Jackson had a strange habit of crossing a wall and then climbing up a neighbor's fire ladder that was perpendicular with the wall until he reached the rooftop over the second floor piazza. Jackson would then howl until someone went to the third floor and opened a window. He was photographed in the Middleton's dining room, in *Charleston Home & Gardens*, published by the Preservation Society of Charleston.

In April 1970, the vestry decided they would investigate the subsoil of the lot on the southwest corner of Church and Cumberland streets to see if old foundations would prevent the lot being added as an extension of the western churchyard. By January 1971, foundations under the lot on the southwest corner of Church and Cumberland streets had been removed but other foundations and an old oil tank were still underground. It would cost $3,000 to remove these items.

In September 1972, Ashmead Pringle purchased four burial lots.

There was no explanation, but in January 1973, Cobb found 100 lots in the churchyard. In May, Joseph H. McGee, Jr. (Peter) wanted to have the brick walk way continued through the western churchyard to the back gate as a memorial to his mother. The walk way was not extended. The vestry sold four burial lots to Mrs. Andrew S. Drury in the eastern churchyard. The vestry said because the lots were between the fence and the walkway leading to the church's south door only flat stones could be placed there. In 2010, the original stones were replaced with larger stones.

Burial lots were sold in 1974 to Teddy Guerard, Mrs. Lawrence (Rhett) Barrett, I. Mayo Read, Jr., George Stevens, Mattie Matthews (the boxing instructor), Dr. Robert S. Cathcart and Dr. George Orvin.

The vestry allowed the Greek Orthodox congregation to place a commemorative stone on the grave of Mrs. Maria Gracia Dura Bin Trumbull, the first Greek woman to settle in America. She was the daughter of a Greek merchant from Smyrna in Asia Minor. She married Scottish physician Dr. Andrew Trumbull, who brought 1,500 settlers from Mediterranean islands and Smyrna, and then started a new colony on June 26, 1786 in Florida called New Smyrna. These were the first Greek Orthodox worshippers in North America. Among the settlers were Ignacio Ortegas and his wife, who came as indentured servants, were the direct ancestors of the Rev. J. Haden McCormick who became rector of St. Philip's in 2000.

By 1777, the colony basically failed and Dr. Trumbull, his wife and their children moved to Charleston. Her husband, who died first, has in his honor, the largest monument in the churchyards. Maria Gracia Turnbull died in Charleston on August 2, 1798, at age sixty-two. She was buried next to Trumbull's huge memorial under a flat tombstone that was replaced in 1974 by the Order of Ahepa.

In May 1975, burial lots were sold to Mr. and Mrs. Henry L. Scott and Dr. and Mrs. James Glenn.

Do you remember Ray Stevens' song *The Streaker*? In October 1977, Cobb spent some of his time trying to catch a streaker who "haunted" the churchyards for two years. The phantom-like male reportedly appeared in the altogether near the churchyard gates and then dashed away. The sudden appearances of the man in his undressed state sent unsuspecting tourists scurrying and frightened several groups of young children. Church officials and neighbors were not amused. Another sighting and search by Cobb, along with police officers, netted only a neatly arranged pile of women's clothes that caused the police to speculate the man either left or entered the area dressed as a woman. The high point of streaking was in 1974 when thousands of "streaks" took place around the world.

The vestry accepted C.B. Branan's proposal to maintain the churchyard grounds. Dr. Glenn in 1978 presented the pros and cons of attempting to cut down or salvage the

"Darlington Oak" from which a branch had fallen during a storm and damaged one of the churchyard walls. Van's Tree Service charged $1,500 to plant a live oak where the Darlington formerly stood.

In 1976, the vestry approved the sale of two burial lots to Merritt Tovey.

Washington Green Pringle, called Tassie by her friends, died February 14, 1978. Her parents, George Trenholm Pringle (1857-1933) and Washington Colclough Green, (1861-1938), were married in Sumter on March 31, 1880.[22]

There were five children: George Trenholm Pringle, Benjamin Garden Pringle, Washington Green Pringle, Lucy Green Pringle and Robert Alexander Pringle. Tassie's father was associated with Pringle Brothers, wholesale dry good merchants.[23]

Tassie taught at Craft School, a 19th century three-story masonry building on Legare Street, and lived with her family around the corner from the school at 27 New Street. Henry Hutson said he, and possibly others, would call Miss Pringle "Washie" behind her back. She was teaching at Craft in 1938 and remained there until 1958 when she literally crossed the street from Craft to teach at the Catholic Cathedral Grammar School. At the same time she moved to Savannah Highway where she was to live in her retirement.

A statute was placed in Washington Park by her friends in memory of Marguerite Sinkler Valk, who died on February 5, 1979.

By August 1979, a moratorium was placed on requests for burial lots until it could be verified just how many lots were available. In September, Palmer Gaillard reported there were no more burial lots in the churchyards and that Mr. and Mrs. C. C. Pearce and Mr. and Mrs. Nat Cabell would receive letters declining their requests for burial lots.

The Congregational Church requested the gates be reopened between their church and St. Philip's western churchyard as it had been in the past. The gates were previously closed because of derelicts drinking, loafing and sleeping in the churchyards but the vestry decided with the help of the police, they would try opening it again.

Two former vestrymen died in 1981 – F. Bartow Culp and Theodore Jervey Simmons, III. Somehow in 1981 five burial lots remained.

After much discussion over a long period of time, St. Philippian's voted down a proposal at the 1982 congregational committee to expand the western churchyard. The vestry's offer was to allow burial of cremated ashes with a memorial plaque placed on the walls of the churchyard.

---

22 SCHS *Magazine* Vol. 47 p. 232
23 Ibid.

RACE RELATIONS

In October 1969, a member of the vestry suggested that St. Philip's should begin impeachment proceedings against the Presiding Bishop John Hines. It was pointed out that under the church canons only the house of bishops could impeach a bishop. Another suggestion made was that St. Philip's withhold any financial support to the national church. These suggestions were received as information.

With only one dissenter, a resolution was passed that the only money that would go to the national church would be from individuals who specifically requested their money go to there. The vestry commended the bishop and South Carolina delegates who attended the 1969 general convention for the stand they took and the votes which they cast.

The cause of all of these suggestions and resolutions by the vestry was a very contentious 1969 general convention that was held in South Bend, Indiana, from August 31 to September 5. Church officials realized, "The general convention was an unusual event in the church's history and spotlighted the church at a time of extreme turmoil, division and dramatic confrontation with the past."

"In 1967, the presiding bishop and others took an eye-opening tour of Harlem with African-American activists. Following the tour, presiding bishop John Hines in 1967 pushed through a 'Special Program' called the GCSP that was intended to respond to the poverty and injustice of the American ghetto. The executive council redirected the church's funds to community organizations and grassroots efforts aimed at the urban underclass throughout the United States. The GCSP represented an enormous break with the status quo and past leaders – black and white."

Hines opening speech called for a renewed commitment to social justice and a willingness to listen to the differing opinions within the church. Confrontation, however, erupted when members of the Union of Black Clergy and Laymen (UBCL) wrestled the microphone from an authorized speaker at the first session of the convention and introduced Muhammed Kenyatta, a member of the BEDC who demanded that the issues of racism and reparations be heard. Ultimately the Convention voted to raise an additional $200,000 for development in African-American communities.

One source said Hines was an extremely nice man but that did not deter many people from sending him hate mail.

In 1973, the GCSP no longer existed as a separate agency of the national church and no funds were specifically committed to its programs. "Anything that would be done in ministry for the poor and the oppressed, the ethnic minorities and the powerless would be done through normal church agencies and departments which have traditionally done this ministry for us." The GCSP stirred up a storm.

Remember the times. The Watts race riots were in 1965 in Los Angeles. There were at least three race riots in 1967: Newark and Plainfield, New Jersey, and Detroit. Martin Luther King, Jr. was shot in 1968 and in 1969 it was very tense in Charleston during the Medical University strike. The National Guard enforced Charleston's curfew.

Cobb said that during the Medical University strike, African-Americans did go to St. Philip's and they were treated very cordially and warmly. "The parishioners, under that kind of pressure, acted like aristocrats in the best sense of the word." Cobb added, "He was confident his parish will change as society and the church itself changes. But, he remarked St. Philip's will move at its own pace … We're not a stodgy, aristocratic parish. We're warm, loving human beings."

During this time, there was a rumor that the African-Americans were going to have more sit ins in many of the downtown churches. Cobb announced that all were welcome in St. Philip's. The sit in consisted of two young African-American girls who happened to sit next to the member who wanted to impeach the presiding bishop. He was quite rattled as were some others.

In March 1973, Cobb said that several black children from St. Mark's were attending St. Philip's EYC.

The by-laws were amended in 1979 to better define membership in the church: "Every baptized person whose name shall appear on the official parish register of members of St. Philip's by virtue of confirmation, reception, transfer by letter from another congregation or by statement of faith in writing accepted (after consultation by a member of St. Philip's clergy), is hereby declared to be a member of the congregation. Minor children of members are also declared to be members."

There was no mention of race as there had been in the past. A parishioner said that Cobb would not have come to Charleston unless there was an agreement that all would be welcome at St. Philip's regardless of race.

Cobb in 1982 was quoted, "The racial tensions that had plagued the diocese and the national church were receding and Episcopalians were mellowing in their attitudes. It made life easier for us all."

SAM COBB'S DEPARTURE

Cobb was not present at the May 10, 1982, vestry meeting. The only motion was to give Cobb a full month's salary as a retirement bonus and an unencumbered title to a 1981 Datsun station wagon which the church had provided him. With two vestrymen absent, the motion passed.

Cobb's last vestry meeting was on May 24, 1982. In June, Tom Myers reported more than $10,400 had been donated for the Cobbs of which $2,168 was used to pay for the farewell reception held at 65 South Battery, the home of Dr. and Mrs. Robert Bowles. The remaining amount of $8,450 was given to the Cobbs. Winfield Sapp complimented the parish's generosity and he acknowledged a letter from Cobb thanking the vestry for making his last months happy and smooth. Cobb will reappear.

REV. CANON KNUD A. LARSEN III

INTERIM

JUNE 1, 1982 – SEPTEMBER 9, 1983

Larsen was born in Chicago on August 14, 1908, where he was raised by his widowed mother with his two siblings. He graduated from the University of Illinois and then attended McCormick Theological Seminary (Presbyterian) where during his second year he married Mary Hamlin McDonald, a Congregationalist, on July 28, 1936, in Elgin, Illinois. Mary was born on July 29, 1908, and she chose the wedding date for the 28th so they would be the same age when they were married. Mary joined her husband in becoming a Presbyterian.

His first church was a small town in southern Illinois with a congregation of coal miners who taught him to tithe. The miners were paid $18.00 per week and each Sunday they would put $1.80 in the plate so Larsen, who made $15.00 per week, put $1.50 in the plate each Sunday.

They left Illinois and went to Brick Presbyterian Church in New York, he as an assistant minister. At the same time he began working on a graduate degree in New York City at the Union Theological Seminary that was founded in 1836 by Presbyterians, later multi-denominational.

The Larsens decided to join the Episcopal Church. He said, "It was without too much trouble because he had five years of experience in the ministry and a bishop taught him how to administer communion in the Episcopal Church. Liturgically it was quite different but the theology was almost the same." After serving two churches in New

Jersey from 1945 to 1951, he was called as rector at Grace Church in Rutherford, New Jersey. Later he worked for the national church's youth department in New York City for five years.

Larsen had a great deal of pain in his leg and the doctors told him it was a malignant cancer. They decided to move to "a more moderate climate" but before they moved the doctors decided the pain was actually caused by a series of crushed discs. He had corrective surgery that took away his pain. Having been cured, they decided to continue with their plans to move to Leesburg, Florida, where he served as rector in a small Episcopal Church for eighteen years. They remained because of the challenge of building up this church to be one of the state's strongest congregations and because the congregation would not let them go. When it was time to retire, the Larsens decided a complete divorce from the church was the best move. Larsen said, "If a minister does a good job, his congregation would not relate to him but to the Lord."

They retired to Charleston in 1973 because they knew a few people here and their oldest son, Daniel, was at the Citadel. They joined St. Michael's where the rector, Edwin C. Coleman, put him to work. They bought a big house on Rutledge Avenue and much later they moved to Bedon's Alley before moving to Bishop Gadsden. He served in many churches in the diocese of South Carolina except St. Michael's.

Looking back, Larsen said they had experienced life's lows. "The bottom of their life fell through when their third child was born a mongoloid (now called Down Syndrome) and he had to take Mary home from the hospital without a baby."

Mary died February 23, 2002. Father Kal, as he was affectionately known, died March 18, 2006. Their three children are: Colonel Daniel M. Larsen, Mary Jordan and Peter Larsen who in 2011 is the rector of St. John's Episcopal Church in Southampton, New York. Peter's first wife "deserted our marriage in 1983." Peter and Nancy (his second wife), who was a high school chemistry teacher, have been happily married for twenty-five years and raised three children. At Mary's death, there were eight grandchildren and nine great-grandchildren.

CHURCH SERVICES, MEMBERSHIP AND CLERGY

Larsen jumped right into the thick of things and attended the June 15, 1982, vestry meeting.

At the same meeting, Larsen inquired about the many weddings that were being scheduled for people with little or no connections with St. Philip's. He felt they not only consumed much of the clergy's time but they cost the church money. The vestry's general consensus was weddings in the church for non-members were inappropriate. Because some concern was expressed about the definition of "member in good standing," the secretary was instructed to contact the diocese for a definition. The definition given was that at least one member of the party must attend church regularly and financially support the church. Other rules included giving at least thirty-days notice of the event and that the couple must be counseled by the rector at least three times.

Larsen did not mince any words. As soon as July, he pointed out in *The Spire* that numerous repairs were needed to the property. The parish hall was infested with termites, the church parapet was falling but being repaired, the roof leaked in some places, the church home building needed restoration and a new Xerox machine was necessary for the office. Larsen said he used to visit Episcopal churches all over the country for the presiding bishop and he had never seen a church that did not own one piece of vestments. He said the list would grow "as to the needs." The 1983 budget included $500 for vestments. Larsen also inquired about the 1,361 communicants on the parish list and wanted to know where they all were because only two or three hundred were showing up each week. He wanted to find out who belonged to St. Philip's. He made it clear that more St. Philippian's should give money and those who were giving should give more. Larsen described himself as a "trouble shooter."

Larsen almost got shot in his foot. Cobb was furious and he demanded Senior Warden Winfield Sapp to get an apology from Larsen. Larsen said that he didn't do anything wrong. Sapp worried about it, but did not know what to do. Searching for a solution, Sapp call Bishop Allison who told him it was not his job to mediate and that he would take care of it. Three years later, Cobb apologized to Sapp.

In September 1982, Larsen reinstated three Sunday morning services: 7:30 a.m. communion and sermon, 9:00 a.m. families and 11:00 a.m. morning prayer, second and fourth Sundays. The 7:30 service proved popular with attendance between eleven and forty worshipers.

Ushers were chastised for not turning in attendance records at the 7:30 a.m. service. It was decided that better supervision was needed.

In January 1983, a survey of St. Philip's parish was conducted by the Rev. Sidney Holt. The report began, "St. Philip's is a conservative congregation strongly worship oriented, quite self-centered and a badly divided congregation." The vestry strongly felt the congregation was not badly divided, but believed, that as a result of the exposure to a heavy measure of the less conservative forms of worship during the past year, a substantial portion of the more liturgically conservative element of the congregation has been stirred by a fear that permanent, radical change was being forced on them. This exposure must be credited to Larsen.

Rev. Holt did see a "brighter side." First, St. Philip's found among its people a surprising number who responded well to change and innovation and the congregation is finding new and unexpected life. Secondly, the congregation had developed a measure of openness and honesty about itself which permits true self-evaluation. The vast majority of the people, though angry and frustrated, are looking for a reasonable accommodation of their needs and not a surrender to their views. Holt said, "There is a middle ground on which the bulk of the congregation can meet and reunite."

At the same time a church census was taken by age with 610 people responding: ages 18-35 14.5%, 36-55 38.5%, 56-75 36% and older than 75, 11%.

In May 1983, the vestry passed a motion. "In our desire that every assurance and support be accorded to the new Rector of St. Philip's Church, we should like to establish the policy that no official ecclesiastical offices are to be performed at St. Philip's by the previous Rector or interim Rector. This policy can be changed at the discretion of the new Rector, but our recommendation is that the policy be in effect for at least one year after the arrival of the new Rector."

THE YOUTH, LAYMEN AND THE LADIES

Larsen's request to help work with Polish refugees was turned over to the ECW. He also discussed the need for a place to conduct training sessions for those released from mental hospitals. The vestry approved the use of the parish house for that purpose.

Mrs. Charles Boykin asked for help in selling chances for a rug and doll house at the bazaar. Former mayor and St. Philippian, J. Palmer Gaillard, always made beautiful doll houses that he donated to the bazaar.

In December 1982, Alfred Pinckney introduced Mrs. W. C. (Dorothy) Carter III to the vestry to review a letter she had sent to each of the members requesting the position of director of Christian Education, (DCE). By March, she had been hired, coming in with a great enthusiasm. Her reports to the vestry were usually four pages long. Dorothy Carter's husband, Dr. William C. Carter, III, would be elected to the vestry in 1984.

Bill Ellison was in charge of the new "Intergenerational Activities." He reported much success and response in setting up committees to: visit the sick - five volunteers, visit the elderly and shut-ins - twelve people, new members - five people, to volunteer in the church office, six people and to plan interfamily activities - five people.

Jimmy Hagood led a Bible study on the Gospel of Mark on Sunday evenings at Beckie Gregorie's house. Eight people attended the first session. Andy Anderson sent out a questionnaire on adult education programs finding the two most popular topics were how faith and Christianity impact life today and Bible studies. Studies on social and historical faith were the least desired.

In March 1983, a resolution was passed to establish the St. Philip's Historical Society. Its purposes and functions would include researching the history of the parish, collecting data and artifacts, arranging for writing and publishing of appriopiate pamphlets, etc.

W. Morton Pine was the chairman of the historic society. Dr. Lyon Tyler, who came with a $2,000 grant, was already assembling materials and documents. There were more than eighty volunteers. Tyler, who was president of the Full Gospel Business Men's Fellowship, had Scott talk there in April 1984. The flyer said, "Renny Scott is the exciting new rector of St. Philip's … who is packing them in at staid old St. Philip's. Church attendance increased forty percent in the first three weeks." Tyler left many records of Scott's rectorship in the St. Philip's archives and

he planned to write a history of St. Philip's. But, instead, he inherited land in Tennessee and moved there where he still lives in 2011.

Lyon Tyler is the grandson of John Tyler, born in 1792 in Virginia, who served as president of the United States from 1841 – 1845. Prior to the War Between the States, Tyler failed to reach a compromise between north and south. He then worked to create the Confederacy and he died in 1862 as a member of the Confederate House of Representatives.

THEOLOGY, EVANGELISM AND MISSIONS

Lucy Glenn in December 1982 reported the outreach committee was composed of Boopa Pritchard, Mayo Read, William Helms, Mrs. Eugene Foxworth, Mrs. Henry Scott and Dr. Harry Gregorie. The committee recommended that 5% of the Every Member Canvass go to outreach in 1983 with the recommendation that it be increased 1% a year moving toward a tithe. The committee recommended that the 1983 percentage go to the following: 30%: to the Charles Webb Rehabilitation Center, 30% to York Home, 30% to the Soup Kitchen and 10% to the Pastoral Counseling Service.

In January 1983, the vestry adopted a resolution about the spending of the $71,500 accumulated interest of the Haig Fund as of December 31, 1981. The Ladies Benevolent Society would receive a minimum of $10,000 and the rest of money would first be spent on needy St. Philippians. Any balance would be disbursed by the vestry at the end of the year.

FINANCES AND VESTRY

In June 1982, Winfield Sapp broached the idea to the vestry about hiring a business manager and Mayo Read was to present a proposed job description the next month.

In July, Sapp reported St. Philip's was a residuary beneficiary of the estate of Mrs. Frances H. Dill Rhett and upon the death of her sister, Miss Charlotte Dill, the church would receive more than $300,000. The trust required the income would first be used for the upkeep of the Rhett and Aiken monuments and tombstones and second for the maintenance of the church buildings.

Mary Bennett recommended brief biographies of vestry nominees should be sent out in advance of the annual meeting so that nominees could be introduced at that meeting. Both suggestions were received positively.

Because Tom Myers reported the sexton, Leonard Taylor, had no pension, the vestry agreed to fund such a pension through the Church Life Insurance. The mayor made a request of all local churches to make payments to the city to help pay for the services they receive from the city. The church's finance committee recommended that $3,000 be considered for next year's budget.

In 1983, Dr. Clay Robertson, III, was senior warden and Alfred G. Pinckney was junior warden. Barbara Claypoole was the vestry secretary. The 1983 budget was $303,500.

MARY LILLY BENNETT

Mary Read Lilly was the daughter of Dr. Edward Guerrant Lilly, later to be the minister at First (Scots) Presbyterian Church in Charleston, and Elisabeth Read Frazer. Mary Lilly attended Ashley Hall, the College of Charleston where she was a Tri-Delt and Mary Baldwin College. She wanted to take graduate courses at the University of North Carolina at Chapel Hill but the admission administrator told her there was no room. As she was leaving, the administrator said the only Lilly he knew was Henry Lilly who was the head of the English department at Davidson College. When Mary told the administrator that was her uncle, he said, "Oh, come on in we'll make room for you."

While Mary was in graduate school for one year studying creative writing, she became an honors student, a member of the president's forum, editor of the literary magazine and was named in 1947 – 1948 *Who's Who in American Colleges and Universities*.

After graduating, Mary worked as a reporter for *The Charleston Evening Post* in the 1940s and 1950s. She married Craig Miller Bennett, Sr., in 1952. Her husband was a staunch member of St. Philip's as he remains in 2012 but Mary did not leave the Presbyterian Church until her father was called to a church in Hartsville.

When Mary did join the Episcopal Church and St. Philip's, she protested about being listed as confirmed because, to her, it inferred she had not previously been a Christian. So, the rector wrote that she "had been added to the rolls." As written elsewhere in this book, it is easy to see that Mary was a great blessing to St. Philip's. As previously written, she was a lay reader and in 1971 she was the first lady to be elected to the vestry. She was re-elected to the vestry in 1980.

Mary was also active as president of Charleston Junior League, a member of Colonial Dames and the Poetry Society.

Mary died at home at 31 Meeting Street on July 9, 1983, and a commemorative service was held at St. Philip's on Wednesday, July 13. Those living survivors in 2012 are her widower, Craig M. Bennett Sr. and their family: son Craig M. Bennett Jr., faithful to the choir, his wife Sandra and their children – Sallie, Katherine, John and Craig III, who is active in leading the Alpha course at St. Philip's and son Edward G Bennett, his wife Adelaida and their children Edward G., Jr., Eliza and Pilar.

PROPERTY AND MAINTENANCE

Because of the repair work that was done on the steeple between April 1 – 12, 1982, three people, including Dr. Jim Stallworth, called Charles Boykin asking the vestry to reimburse the cost of having their cars towed due to the use of a crane. The vestry agreed. In October 1984, several parishioners received parking tickets on Sunday mornings. It was reported the police officer writing the tickets "was sorry" that he had to take this action, but the improperly parked automobiles on Cumberland Street created a substantial hazard in the event of fire.

In June, the vestry agreed the Huguenot Church, as they requested, could have the use of the tea garden for their Sunday school on a temporary basis until September. In January 1984, the Huguenot Church asked to use the library and sewing room for their Sunday school. At the next meeting, a motion was passed to ask Charles Boykin for estimates to renovate those two rooms plus the hall and bathroom. The vestry approved the Huguenot Church's rent free use until March 31, 1985. It could be extended by mutual agreement.

St. Philip's waterproofed the second floor porch on the south end of the building in order to prevent further leaks in the sewing room and the library. St. Philip's gave the Huguenot Church $2,000 so they could renovate the two rooms. The Huguenots did the work to restore the two rooms by painting and repairing the small "water closet/toilet" off the entrance hall and to have liability insurance. A notice in The Spire in 1984: "<u>VESTRY MEETING</u> - Tuesday, September 4, 5:30 P.M. in the Huguenot Room."

In July 1985, the Huguenot Church asked St. Philip's to be allowed to use several rooms in the parish house for their Sunday school. Boopa Pritchard understood the Huguenot Church had also made a similar request to Charleston Day School. John Kerr made a motion that the vestry respectfully decline the Huguenot Church's request. The motion was unanimously approved. In 1987, the Huguenot Church requested the use of St. Philip's parish offices so people in wedding parties could change clothes. That was denied. In 1990, deRosset Myers, a member of the Huguenot Society's board and property committee, said the Huguenot Church and the Huguenot Society were desperately looking for space to house their offices jointly in that neighborhood. Myers said he thought the first two floors for the former church home would provide ample room for them and they would purchase or lease the building. Myers said plans called for the St. Philip's staff to move to the new parish house.

In May 1992, George Greene reported he had received a communication from the Huguenot Church concerning some arrangement for the use of St. Philip's office building. The general consensus of the vestry was that the church would not divest itself of any property but the feeling was the vestry should hear any proposal they might make.

In June 25, 1982, vestry secretary Tom Myers wrote a letter James T. Kearney who was the general manager of the Spoleto Festival USA. He stated:

"I am writing to call attention to some problems that came up during the practice session of the Westminister Choir in St. Philip's Church on June 4. Food was brought into the Church and refuse was left behind, *including chicken wings resting on the organ* (Italics per author). In addition to this, the air conditioning was not functioning properly, and there were several rude and peremptory complaints as to why it wasn't working and when it would be repaired."

A reply from Mr. Kearney is not noted in the vestry minutes.

In the summer of 1982, Philip Simmons was given the job to replace parts of an iron fence and to secure the loose iron rail inside the church at the west end of the choir stalls. No estimate was given but he was told this work was very necessary and to "do the job."

Philip Simmons, who was born June 9, 1912, on Daniel Island, spent seventy-seven years as a blacksmith. He began with horse shoes but by the time he retired seventy-seven years later his craft was considered an art form. His work is seen throughout Charleston, the Lowcountry, in the Smithsonian, the South Carolina State Museum and in Paris and China. He received many awards. He did most of his work on Blake Street in his blacksmith shop next to his house. It is now open for visitors. Simmons died at Bishop Gadsden on June 22, 2009, at age ninety-seven. The day of his funeral the public was asked to place a white piece of cloth on any of Simmon's works, primarily gates and fences.

THE CHURCH HOME

Helen Geer, who was organizing the 1982 bazaar, asked the vestry about including some of the church home's surplus furniture in a silent auction. The vestry agreed as long as Boykin and Myers determined which items could be sold.

THE RECTORY

In October 1982, Boykin mentioned the numerous and significant maintenance problems of the rectory. Larsen indicated that most priests prefer to own their own houses in order to have something when they retire. This discussion would lead to another long and drawn out discussion about selling the rectory. In July 1983, Teddy Guerard said his committee was unanimous in agreeing to sell the rectory but a report was due in September.

THE CHURCHYARDS

In April 1982, Larsen reported the theft of plants from the churchyard. A question was also asked about hanging paintings that were for sale from the churchyard fence particularly on Good Friday. A solution was not reached.

In May 1983, the vestry agreed to give a burial plot to Larsen even though he was a member of St. Michael's. The rule was, "The vestry may provide, if available, a lot to the Bishop of this Diocese, his wife, and to a former clergyman of St. Philip's, and his wife."

After Larsen left St. Philip's, a live oak tree was placed in the northeast corner of the western churchyard as a memorial in thanksgiving to Father Kal. The tree is large and strong in 2012 as pointed out by C.B. Branan who planted the tree.

THE CALLING COMMITTEE

In February 1983, the vestry met with Bishop Allison for two hours about calling a new rector. The vestry gave complete discretion to the search committee but they were asked to prune the then sixty-one clergy on the calling list to approximately fifteen by March 15. Tom Myers compiled a very thorough pamphlet called *In Search of a Rector.*[24]

The search committee members were: Ed Holt, chairman, Helen Barkley, Dr. William Barnwell, II, Craig M. Bennett, Tom Myers, Alfred Pinckney, Peter Read, Dr. Clay Robertson III, Winfield Sapp, Mrs. Adelaide Waller and Arthur M. Wilcox.

By March 16, the list had been cut to twenty prospects.

Twelve visits were made in the southeast to hear prospects. Rev. Rick Belser, later rector of St. Michael's, was interviewed at Trinity on Edisto Island and Rev. Hill Riddle in Roanoke. Later Riddle, who would become rector of Trinity in New Orleans, was a very brave man. Even though Riddle condemned Mardi Gras balls during a sermon,

---

24 There is a copy of this pamphlet in the archives in Larsen's folder in the rector's box

no member of his congregation walked out. Four prospective candidates came to St. Philip's.

The committee felt that Rev. Henry Scott's qualifications set him above the other candidates and they would not make a second recommendation.

Helen Barkley, (with Adelaide Waller agreeing), wrote, "I have known Renny Scott for approximately nine years and believe him to be one of the most spiritual persons I have ever known. He is absolutely sound theologically and is better versed in the Bible than anyone I know. To my knowledge, he has preached in several churches in our Diocese. He is an outstanding preacher, who preaches entirely from the Bible without notes. I believe Renny Scott is completely trustworthy and that he will abide by congregation's will in the manner of conducting services." Helen felt that if Scott were to leave in five to ten years he would leave behind a church filled with active, working Christians, young and old, and that St. Philip's would be the foremost church in the diocese.

Craig Bennett, Sr. said, "There will be changes, however. Each of us will feel these changes and we will all be far better Christians as a result." Bennett asked Scott why he would come to St. Philip's. He replied that he felt a personal call and also his church in Virginia was so large he was unable to be a pastoral minister. He wanted to return to being a pastoral minister and felt that there would be a greater possibility to do that at St. Philip's with its more cohesive congregation.

There were trepidations. Some said the church needed a "safe, low key minister." Others responded that there had been "safe ministers" for more than twenty years and the congregation was dwindling. They wanted someone who was magnetic and outgoing and was "in touch with the Lord." Many felt this was the chance of a lifetime." There was a concern that Scott would speak in tongues but after speaking with Bishop Allison, Clay Robertson had no reservations about that at all. See First Corinthians chapter fourteen.

Four members of the search committee were so afraid of Scott, that they had rump meetings at the Carolina Yacht Club. In the end, only one member voted against Scott.

Arthur Wilcox wrote on June 8, 1983, responding to the search committee's request to have a unanimous vote, "I have declined to make it unanimous and I owe an explanation." Wilcox said, "Scott was charming, articulate and a charismatic personal style which had impressed every member of the search committee except me as readily adaptable to St. Philip's. In my opinion, Renny will not so much seek to adapt himself to St. Philip's as he will try to persuade St. Philip's to adapt to him … If he is successful, St. Philip's risks becoming a church that is a distorted reflection of the Renny Scott personality, divided between those who accept speaking in tongues and other manifestations of religious fervor as part of our worship and those who do not. At best, that will be an uneasy relationship. At worst, it will create further divisions."

Another concern Wilcox had was that Scott would be at St. Philip's five to ten years and then would leave the church with a huge void. The response to that was there was agreement he would not be here forever but he would leave behind a strong and large group of dedicated Christians and that St. Philip's would certainly be far better for it. Wilcox hoped the vestry would continue to search for a new rector

"who could better handle our diverse, opinionated congregation."

The vestry, after listening to many viewpoints, made some conclusions: Scott wanted to get back a more traditional ministry, he was deeply in touch with the Lord, he delivered superb sermons and he had good pastoral capabilities. He and his wife, Margaret, were from refined, genteel backgrounds that socially would fit in well at St. Philip's. Another plus was that Scott's parents moved to Charleston several years earlier and his father served on St. Philip's vestry.

A motion was made on June 14, 1983, to unanimously support the call for Rev. Henry (Renny) Scott, Jr., to be rector of St. Philip's. However, the vote was not unanimous. Wilcox had not changed his mind since writing his letter of June 8 and he did not vote for Scott. Clay Robertson said he would make the call and he would advise the vestry when he received an answer. Scott accepted the call by June 17.

Scott, and his family, would arrive in Charleston around August 25, 1983. On September 9, Scott and Bob Oliveros, who officiated at Larsen's last service at St. Philip's at 7:30 a.m., said "The organ swelled and rolled and we were all in Heaven," A tremendous breakfast followed and a "thoughtful" gift was given to Larsen. Scott left after the breakfast to participate in a two day vestry retreat at Camp St. Christopher. He returned to Charleston on September 10, the day the he officially began work. He preached his first sermon the next day. Sunday school began September 18 and his first vestry meeting was September 19.

THE REVEREND HENRY LAWRENCE SCOTT, JR.

RECTOR

SEPTEMBER 10, 1983 – MAY 18, 1986

Scott,[25] nicknamed Renny, was born April 3, 1945, in New York City. Shortly afterwards, his parents, Henry Lawrence Scott, Sr. and his wife, Mary Bell Scott, moved to Tivoli, New York, because of the conditions brought on by World War II. Scott said there were two Episcopal churches in Tivoli, a small village of 800 people – an elegant brick church for the rich and a small wooden church for the poor.

Scott, who was a good student, loved attending St. Paul's School in Concord, New Hampshire, from 1959 to 1961 where he was a class officer, captain of the cross country team even breaking some records in track. He traces his own search for God to his school days at St. Paul's. Scott said, "something was missing" and he was looking for something he could not put into words but somehow he felt he needed to head to the South. When he was a junior at age seventeen, he ran away from the school with no plan but he persuaded a girl in New York City to drive him to Sweet Briar College in Virginia. The female students hid him in a dormitory for five days and finally persuaded him to go home. His parents wanted him to go back to St. Paul's and the school wanted him to return. He finished the year there but he finished his senior year at Rhinebeck High School, graduating in 1963.

From Rhinebeck he entered Yale University in 1963, graduating in 1967 with a major in political science. At Yale he was one year ahead of George W. Bush and one year behind Senator John F. Kerry. George Pataki, former three term governor of New York,

---

25 Renny Scott gave his biographical information to this author in 2011.

was his roommate. Scott and Kerry represented Yale in a trans-Atlantic cable debate with Cambridge University in England.

Scott grew up thinking he was headed into law and politics. He studied the encyclopedia from cover to cover researching every great leader from generals to kings to presidents. Years later, in a Bible study in an Episcopal church in Rhode Island, where he was working during the summer, he became fascinated with Jesus as a man long before he knew He was God. Scott said, "He was unlike any great man he had ever studied." At the end of the summer, he knew he wanted to commit his life to Christ, but he did not know how. He had heard Billy Graham on television and discovered he was doing a crusade in Pittsburg. Scott got on a plane to be there where at Graham's invitation he went forward on September 3, 1968, and committed his life to Christ.

As a lifelong Episcopalian, he did not realize of the possibility of a lay ministry, so he assumed that those who wanted to serve God became priests. Scott went to Harvard Divinity School on a Rockefeller Fellowship and from there he went to the Episcopal Theology Seminary in Cambridge, Massachusetts, from which he graduated in 1971. He was ordained a priest on September 12, 1971, at St. Andrew's Episcopal Church in Long Meadow, Massachusetts where he served as an assistant rector. Scott stayed there one and a half years and then, at the bishop's request, became chaplain to the University of Massachusetts for two years.

Scott married Margaret Carr Howell of Atlanta in her parent's home on July 17, 1976. They have four children: David Howell Scott, senior manager at Ernst and Young in Atlanta; Mary Bell Scott, English teacher at Christian Heritage School in Dalton; Frances DeJongh Scott, who in 2011 just received her master's in social science in education from the University of Georgia, and Henry Scott III, who is an accountant with Ernst and Young in Atlanta.

Scott was invited to speak at "Jesus 78 and 79" in Orlando as the token Episcopal priest. While thirty thousand young people came both years, he was given a "small group" where he had a tent that sat two thousand. This was the height of what sociologists called "The Jesus Movement in America."

Scott, in his ministry, traveled to twenty-four countries on five continents. In 1968, he did mission work outside of Bogota, Columbia. In 1974, he was a delegate to the first World Conference on the Holy Spirit held in Jerusalem. In 1975, Scott traveled behind the Iron Curtain including East Germany, Czechoslovakia, Hungary and Romania where he smuggled Bibles and worked with underground churches. Scott said those people realized there was no hope in the communist system and he learned what it cost to be a Christian in such circumstances. In 1976, Scott went on a World Vision trip to Kenya, the Sudan and Tanzania where "Bishop Alfred Stanway built the fastest growing Anglican diocese anywhere in the world and established a new congregation every week for twenty years." In 1981, Scott was invited by President Milton Obote to lead team Uganda where they built a conference center on Lake Victoria and taught the Bible to Uganda youth leaders.

From 1974 - 1977, Scott served as associate rector of St. Paul's Episcopal Church in Darien, Connecticut with the rector, Rev. Terry Fullam. The presiding bishop described Fullam as "the best stand up Bible teacher in the Episcopal church." One thousand clergy with members of their congregations came to St. Paul's to discover what God was doing. In a 1978 issue *The Episcopalian* reported that Fullam said, "I want to call off the Every Man Canvass. No one should ever be embarrassed into contributing." Initially business men reacted negatively but the pledge cards were returned without names.

One week later Fullam made many in the church gasp when he preached, "God does not want your money unless you are willing to commit your lives to Him. You cannot bribe God nor tip Him; He does not want conscience money. In Isaiah we read 'Bring me no more vain offerings.' Even though there were no fundraising events, the average family weekly contribution at St. Paul's had risen fourfold since 1972."

Bob Slosser, senior editor of the Washington desk of the *New York Times*, wrote a booked entitled *Miracle in Darien* describing the church.

Scott was called from St. Paul's to serve as the first full time rector of the Church of the Apostle's in Fairfax, Virginia, and served there from 1977 - 1983. When Scott arrived, the fifty members of the church, who met in a school cafeteria, had an annual budget of $30,000. When he left, the church had a congregation of eighteen hundred and a weekly budget of $30,000.

"The churches in Darien and Fairfax were two of the fastest growing churches in the Episcopal Church at that time."

CHURCH SERVICES, MEMBERSHIP & CLERGY

Sam Cobb said in 1986 that the membership of St. Philip's was 1,200 and that Scott added another 600 to the rolls. Lynda (Frenchie) Richards in 2011 said they saw the Wednesday afternoon service grow from five people to 350 during Scott's rectorship.

In 1983, there were fourteen children confirmed: Charlotte Guy Anderson, Tamara Michelle Duncan, James Allen Lester Glenn, Jr., Thomas Lynch Hassell, Peter Maybank, Martha Izard Middleton, Thomas Plumbee Morrison, Jr., Susan Elizabeth Orvin, Alfred Palmer Owings, Jr., Caroline Pinckney Rivers, Carolina Liles Robson, Lewis Hughes Simmons, III, Linda Ann Simmons and Caroline Heyward Simons. There were fifty-two adults confirmed including William David Hewitt, Rebecca Warren Hewitt, Rees Moyler Johnston, Thomas William Johnston, Jr., Alfred Palmer Owings, Sr., Donald Tropp Rutledge and William and Carolyn Warlick. Six were received from the Roman Catholic Church.

REV. TERRELL LYLE GLENN, JR.

ASSISTANT RECTOR

June 1, 1984 – MAY 31, 1987

INTERIM

JUNE 1, 1987 – OCTOBER 3, 1987

ASSISTANT RECTOR

OCTOBER 4, 1987 - 1990

Scott had been looking for an assistant since he arrived at St. Philip's. Finally on April 2, 1984, Scott introduced the Rev. Terrell Lyles Glenn, Jr., to the vestry as a prospective assistant rector. Glenn had preached at St. Philip's the day before.

Scott sent out a letter to the congregation saying that Terrell Glenn had accepted a call as assistant minister and would begin the first week of June. Glenn, age twenty-five and single, had a deep commitment to the faith that was nurtured at Trinity Cathedral in Columbia where he grew up. His father, Terrell Glenn Sr., was a trial lawyer with the McNair Firm in Columbia and his was mother was Louise Owens also from Columbia.

Glenn graduated from St. Andrews School in Delaware, received a Bachelor of Arts Degree from the University of South Carolina and his Master of Divinity Degree from the Virginia Theological Seminary in Alexandria, Virginia. He was an outstanding student at VTS and was elected president of his class. Glenn, an ordained deacon, was ordained a priest on May 12, 1984.

He was currently serving as assistant to the vicar at the Episcopal Church of the Ridge which consisted of four missions: St. Paul's in Batesburg, Grace Church at Ridge Spring, Our Saviour in Trenton and Trinity Church in Edgefield. He and the vicar alternated services on a weekly basis.

Scott wrote, "Terrell has distinguished himself in his gift of teaching, pastoral abilities and as an outstanding youth ministry. Terrell feels particularly called to minister to junior and senior high students. Since there is a strongly felt need here at St. Philip's to develop a ministry for our young people, God's call on Terrell's life to serve in this way is a great gift to our Parish Family."

Glenn married Teresa deBorde from Columbia in 1988 and they have three children: Terrell III, Ellison and Cecilia.

Glenn left St. Philip's in 1990 and served at St. Andrew's Church in Mt. Pleasant, and then started the Church of the Apostles in Raleigh which grew from only the Glenn family to a staff of seven and an attendance of 375. In 2000, he was called as rector of All Saint's Church in Pawley's Island which had engaged in a lengthy, but successful, legal battle to withdraw from the diocese of South Carolina. The church joined the Anglican Mission in the Americas (AMIA). Glenn and two other ministers were elected on September 4, 2007, under the jurisdiction of Rwandan Archbishop Emmanuel Kolini as missionary bishops to the United States. In February 2011, Glenn resigned as rector of All Saint's to focus solely on overseeing the fifty-four congregations that made up the Apostles Mission Network. In 2012, he lives in Charlotte.

There have been at least six clergy at St. Philip's who became bishops. The first three were bishops of the diocese of South Carolina: Rt. Rev. Robert Smith 1791 – 1801, Rt. Rev. Christopher Gadsden 1840 – 1852 and Rt. Rev. William Bell White Howe 1871 – 1894. The fourth was Rt. Reverend Henry Parsley who became bishop coadjutor in 1996 and the tenth bishop of the diocese of Alabama in 1999. He retired in 2011. Rt. Rev. Terrell Glenn, Jr. and the Rt. Rev. Thomas Johnston were ordained in the AMIA Church.

Before Glenn arrived in Charleston in 1984, he advised the vestry he would like to live in the Philadelphia Alley house, formerly church rental property. It was pointed out that no work had been done on the house in eight years and the renovation would cost $5,098. Although termites had been found in some of the windows, Glenn had moved in by June 4, 1984.

In July 1984, lifelong member of St. Philip's, Mrs. R.T. (Louise) Perry of 30 New Street wrote to the vestry concerning the idea of having three services on Sunday. She thought it was a wonderful idea and hoped the time would come when the many members who loved guitar music and communion on Wednesday afternoon would also have guitar music at one of the three Sunday services. "Why shouldn't St. Philip's at least give it a try? Come on – let us take a leap of faith." She had spoken with many people of different age groups and found many felt as she did. In August, the vestry voted not to initiate a third Sunday service at that time because of a lack of unanimity.

At the same time, Dr. William Carter suggested establishing an internship at St. Philip's for communicants who were considering entering the ministry. The internship would be mutually beneficial as it would allow a person to observe the everyday life of a parish rector while providing a full time lay minister under the supervision and guidance of the rector. A donor, who gave $18,000 to the youth ministry, gave his endorsement and approval of such an internship under Glenn with special emphasis on assisting Glenn in the area of youth ministry. Scott stated that Christopher Mercer Huff had recently indicated a desire to enter the ministry and both Scott and Glenn thought Huff to be a worthy candidate.

By October, the Wednesday afternoon service had outgrown the parish house so Scott and Glenn changed the venue to the church.

The vestry had a very lengthy discussion about the sound system used by the music leaders at the Wednesday afternoon service. Glenn knew that the musicians wanted nothing but quality and if the sound system were not needed, it would not be used.

In November, Mrs. Barbara Claypoole reported she had received complaints that the lead male singer's microphone was too loud. Glenn said they were already working on a solution.

By November 1984, the two Sunday services were "overcrowded." There was a movement to add a third Sunday service as soon as possible. Scott said that adding a service at that time would wreck-havoc with the Sunday school system and suggested the third service not be added until September 1985.

On one Sunday, Scott preached that one of many who did so much and were never recognized was Frances Waring Voigt. He called her a saint from the pulpit and everyone at St. Philip's regularly called her St. Frances. Mrs. Voigt, among other things, headed the altar guild at Christmas and Easter. Her husband was Richard J. Voigt who had sung in the St. Philip's choir.

On November 15, 1984, Herbert Stender wrote a letter to senior warden Dr. Maxwell Anderson saying how much he and his wife, Molly, enjoyed the Wednesday afternoon service. Stender added, "I know that I am not speaking for just Molly and myself, because this was the topic of conversation among the congregation. Everyone was simply delighted."

He closed, "I cannot help but comment on the new life which abounds everywhere in St. Philip's. We are all so grateful for having both Renny and Terrell lead us in our walk with Christ. For this we thank God, and we must also not forget the vestry for the very important part they played in bringing this about.

In His Name,
Herbert"

Mrs. Robert (Barbara B.) Pringle of 166 Wentworth Street was not enamored with Scott. She was baptized and "Came to the Lord" in a small church in Tennessee.

She and her husband moved to Charleston and had been members of the church for thirty-nine years. A survey was taken of what kind of worship service the congregation desired and, according to Pringle, the answer was conservative. She said "Scott is not a conservative but more like a Fundamentalist Baptist. I am not the only person this upsets."

At the December 17, 1984, vestry meeting Dr. William Carter gave a rousing speech extolling the new-found freedom and joy that he and his wife, Dorothy, had experienced by sitting in the balcony on Sunday mornings. He admitted it was tempered somewhat by a noticeable gap between the rear of the balcony and the wall. Charlie Boykin said the gap had been there for years and had been checked out by engineers who stated that it was not a structural defect, but the gap expanded and contracted as the weather changed. No further action was suggested.

In January 1985, Scott advised the vestry that he was making a "minor" change in the service format by dropping the New Testament lesson. "This was in keeping with the order of worship in the Book of Common Prayer."

In 2011, John Kerr said his former mother-in-law, Alida Hanahan, loved Scott. She got the vestry to give her $500 so she could properly decorate Scott's second floor office. Later, when Mrs. Hanahan and the others were unloading the new furnishings, the police gave her a ticket for parking illegally.

One St. Philippian, who had five generations of her mother's family buried in the churchyard, had attended St. Philip's for ten years. In January, she sent a two page letter to the vestry and to Scott in which she had nothing good to say about Scott.

She wrote that for many years she had taken pleasure in the dignity, beauty and comfortableness she had found at St. Philip's that was now unfortunately filled with a state of emotional intensity which she found distressing. She was sorry to see the charismatic

Christian or Christian renewal come to St. Philip's. She intensely disliked Scott starting the service by shouting "Good Morning" with the congregation responding. She thought his services were more like entertainment than a worship service to God. She found the tenor of his sermons insidious. "They were filled with talk of miracles, some of which caused her to doubt."

Perhaps the final straw for her was when Scott invited Evangelist Lee Buck to speak. She thought Buck was more suited to a fundamentalist church and that his sermon was poor. After sitting through "that poor piece of oratory," she transferred to St. Michael's and remains a member there in 2012.

"Buck had been a senior executive in the insurance business for many years before coming under the ministry of the evangelical, charismatic preacher Terry Fullam in Connecticut where Buck received the fullness of the of the Holy Spirit and began his own ministry of evangelism."

Buck, who at age eighty-three died in Atlanta in 2006, "was probably the Episcopal Church's best known lay evangelist for many years before leaving The Episcopal Church and joining a parish under another ecclesiastical authority. He could no longer abide the Episcopal Church's apostasies."

In 1994, *Post and Courier* reporter Steve Mullins wrote a long article about the split in churches between the "frozen-chosen traditionalists" and the "elitist Bible beaters." Some used the terms "moss-back blue-bloods" and "new super Christians."

Bishop Allison said that some aspects of the charismatic movement "gave rise to condescending, and that's just plain sin." Allison said on the other hand the renewal movement's interactive worship services have merits. He added that when he was a rector in New York there was faithful lady, a member for twenty-three years, who collapsed in church and an ambulance was called. The only person she knew in the whole church was the receptionist. That, he said, is what can come of zero interaction in an extremely traditional prayer-book church. Allison said that he saw charismatic clergy go over his head to become bishops because, "they, of course, have a straight line to God's unlisted number. Episcopalians are very leery about that." The reporter added, "Church-goers on each side of the divide are as blunt as the bishop, but less willing to have their names published."

The Rev. Charles H. Murphy, III, rector of All Saint's at Pawley's Island said, "his church has been here since the Revolutionary War, so we have our pedigree. But quiet, anonymous, invisible Christians are not what the New Testament is about."

The article, continued, "Rev. Scott was arguably the most charismatic and most controversial clergyman in decades." It was reported that Scott brought people into the church that did not regularly attend church or were from other denominations.

Terrell Glenn said about St. Philip's in 1994, "God is in the process of forging a new identity out of that conflict. It could emerge as an extraordinarily strong and vibrant parish."

In March 1985, Dr. Bill Carter proposed inserting the collect, readings and the Psalms into the church bulletin on the appriopriate Sundays. He wanted to try it for one church season. The motion passed unamiously.

In April 1965, at the request of Betsy Tezza and John Kerr, the vestry agreed to budget $5,000 per year for Chris Huff while he was in seminary. At the same time, Scott advised the vestry he would like to keep his pastoral roll for another year because he felt it had been invaluable in enabling him to get to know parishioners he would not have otherwise known.

In 1985, twenty-six children and seventy-eight adults were confirmed and five people were received from the Roman Catholic Church. Some of those confirmed were: Emily Ballentine, Marianne Gaillard Clare, Richard White Hanckel, Collier Helms, Capers Owings, Alonzo Anderson Burris III, Grace Kelley Creel, Tracy Crisp Graudin, Steven Douglas Graudin, Joan Marie Hagan, Gerald Lee McCord, Carol McCord and Gordon Reames Payne.

Grace Creel "had a disastrous marriage." After obtaining a divorce, she moved west of the Ashley. She had been "unchurched," but wanted to find a church so she started visiting churches and faithfully reading each of the Sunday write-ups on the different denominations. None of the churches was quite right for her and then one Sunday she saw a write up about St. Philip's. After reading the article, "for the first time and the only time in her life she knew God was giving her instructions. He told her to go to St. Philip's." Creel moaned and said but "I never go anyplace alone and would the 'South of Broad' ladies accept her?" In spite of that, she obeyed and joined St. Philip's. Creel said the worship was very charismatic but she was comfortable with that and God used Scott to open her ears and eyes. Her story of doing much of God's work behind the scenes at St. Philip's continues in 2012 and surely longer.

In July 1983, Rev. Coleman wrote a welcome to Scott in St. Michael's *The Word*. "Renny Scott brings the best of what we expect in our Church's ordained leadership. But things will not significantly differ unless that leadership is joyfully received with all its challenges. The day of lay passivity (in all the church) is over! The New Testament knows only Disciples, Followers and Servants. Everyone has his/her cross to carry daily as witness to the Risen Crucified One."

By December 2, 1985, St. Michael's had called Rev. Richard I.H. (Rick) Belser as its new rector and Scott felt it was appropriate for St. Philip's vestry to welcome Belser as rector and to offer him our prayers and best wishes on his endeavor. Scott would draft the letter.

Scott at the vestry meeting on May 5, 1986, thirteen days prior to his resignation sermon, distributed a document entitled "A Brief Vision for St. Philip's because he felt the vestry needed to know what "we were about and where we are going."

THE YOUTH, LAYMEN, AND THE LADIES

It was reported in 1983 that there had been a precipitant drop in Sunday school attendance. In 1970, registration had been 300 with an attendance of 190 but since then registration had declined to about seventy and was often less than forty.

In September 1983, Alfred Pinckney reported Mrs. Dorothy Carter had resigned and Maria Hanahan, the daughter of Bill and Jane Hanahan, would take over as interim teacher until June 1984. This was not the first time Maria had taught Sunday school. She was to be assisted by Mrs. Nancy Price for six months.

When Scott thanked Hanahan and Price for their work during the past year, he said "our hearts go with Maria. She had done a remarkable job those last six months and those who had worked closely with her will miss her terribly." Hanahan and Price were each given a Thompson Chain-Reference Bible. Barbara Claypoole and Dorothy Carter were in charge of the Sunday school for the upcoming year.

They also received Bibles at the end of their term in May 1985.

The 1983 bazaar netted a profit of $8,502.11.

In late 1983, Scott asked Price to complete a two part evaluation of the Christian education program and of the "Director of Christian education." He asked Price to concentrate on assessing each of the segments of Christian education currently in place as well as the potential for each of them. Carter was also to be evaluated. Price did a very thorough job turning in a seventeen page report.[26] Carter received rave reviews from all who were involved in the evaluation but sometimes was spread too thin because she had to carry so much responsibility.

In August 1984, Mayo Read presented a lease agreement between the church and Charleston Day School for the use of the playground. The vestry approved. Remember, the church rejected a similar request from Charleston Day in 1973.

Dr. Carter was also in charge of lay readers and he was co-chair of Adult Education with Ed Holt. Becky Riggs distributed a list of goals for St. Philip's for 1985/1986. They wanted to establish a Bible study for women, put together a pictorial directory, establish a new-comers club and continue the compassion

---

26 The entire report may be found in the St. Philip's archives in *Vestry Minutes of St. Philip's 1980 – 1984* p. 277 - 295.

ministry. In March 1985, Martha Elizabeth Vetter was hired by the vestry as the new Director of Christian Education.

In October 1985, Scott introduced Dot Anderson, who was the new president of the ECW. She would serve as an ex-officio member of the vestry for the coming year.

THEOLOGY, EVANGELISM & MISSIONS

In 1984, The Bishop Gadsden retirement home received $15,000 and the vestry recorded a non-binding hope that a total of $45,000 would be given over the next two years.

The Boy Scout Troop sponsored by St. Philip's had received no money in years and were desperate for basic camping gear and other essentials. The committee gave $1,500 to Boy Scouts Troop number fifty.

At Scott's first vestry meeting, John Kerr announced he had begun to form a ministry to tape Scott's sermons. In October, Mary Anne Hanckel and Alfred Pinckney would tape sermons and take them to shut-ins and the sick. The vestry agreed to fund the cost of the tape ministry but a donor gave $4,350 toward that mission.

A nice notice was placed in *The Spire* in 1984, "In the Name of Christ we bid you welcome to this Church. May those who sorrow find comfort; the weary, rest; the troubled, peace; the happy, joy; the stranger, friends; and to all, the sense of God's Presence in His Holy Place. You will find a small, white visitors card in the pew."

In March 1984, an initial statement of purpose of the mission/ministry committee was made. Some of the ideas included: a need to know what was actually going on in the particular agencies or organizations to which the church gave money. It was recommended that there should be actual hands-on involvement by a member of the m/m committee and/or congregation in each such organization and worthy groups should be sought out rather than responding.

In May 1984, Eleanor Simons was the contact person for those interested in participating in a new prayer circle. The prayer chain is operating in 2012.

James Hagood, II, reported his parish committee was planning to print a brochure that would explain to visitors and newcomers what St. Philip's had to offer in the way of work, worship and fellowship within the parish.

In December 1984, a motion passed unanimously to donate $10,000 to Hospice and a motion passed six to four to give $4,000 to the United Way. The money came from the Haig Fund and both donations had stipulations that the money go toward the medical needs of the indigent. Teddy Guerard said the church would get more satisfaction if they could deal directly with needy individuals. Everyone agreed with him, but no one could identify needy individuals.

Dr. Bill Carter asked the vestry to donate $2,000 to the St. Andrew's Clinic that served the truly indigent and even though drugs were donated by various companies, there still remained a shortage. After a lengthy discussion, the vestry decided they could approve the donation without sending it to the administers of the Haig Fund.

At the same time, Mayo Read reported thirty people signed up as volunteers, as did

another ten after the Sunday adult forum, to keep the Interfaith Crisis Ministry homeless shelter open during part of the winter. St. Philippians' would be there on December 31, January 2, 1985, and the last week of March.

The mission committee in January 1985 recommended spending $29,850 during the first half of the year. There were no donations to Sewanee or Virginia Theological Seminary but in 1984 there was a $2,000 donation to the Trinity School for Ministry in Ambridge, Pennsylvania. In 1985, the donation to Trinity was increased to $3,000.

THE CHARLESTON FLIGHT OF MERCY

In February 1985, Scott reported to the vestry on the progress known as The Charleston Flight of Mercy. Its members were mainly St. Philippians who had organized a fund raising effort to charter a cargo plane filled with food, blankets and medicine for starving Africans. The vestry said it was necessary to elect a treasurer for the organization and that only the treasurer and one other designated person would be allowed to sign checks. Tom Myers was elected treasurer and he and Rhett Barrett were authorized to sign checks.

"The Charleston Flight of Mercy was an impossible dream born in the heart of one man of God, who was Renny Scott, in response to the famine and mass starving in Africa." The goal was to raise $250,000. The day after this dream was first uttered publicly from the pulpit of St. Philip's, fifteen or twenty interested people met to form the Flight of Mercy committee. The committee chairs were Louisa Hawkins, Joanne Ellison and Son Trask who did a tremendous amount of work to make this happen. "The only thing these people had in common was their commitment to Jesus." They started with bumper stickers and the word spread quickly and the response was overwhelming. Contributions, large and small, poured in. Wash ladies would come in with their one dollar bills. Volunteers manned phones, stuffed envelopes, gave talks, etc. "The Flight of Mercy became a community effort crossing all barriers of race, religion and economic status."

Though the goal was $250,000, it was necessary to have $100,000 in hand before the Easter flight could take off. Amazingly, the goal of $100,000 was in in hand three weeks before the Easter departure and two weeks before Easter almost $200,000 had been raised. The plane left at 7:30 a.m. following an Easter service at the new terminal. The flight carried thirty-one metric tons of high calorie oatmeal, three tons or 100,000 rehydration tablets and one ton of medical supplies and blankets. There were five passengers on the plane: Thomas E. Myers, Jr., Dr. Thomas Kirkland, Frank C. Smith, Harry Clark, Mrs. William W. (Cam) Elliott and Paul Samuels who was from World Vision. All had helped to organize the flight. As previously written, Scott had worked with World Vision in 1976.

Harry Clark, a successful business man, "met Christ" about a year and a half before he took the flight. Christ made tremendous differences in his life. Clark said, "Because of the trip, I met some people and I felt a real calling from the Lord to go and do something. It's easy to say I believe in something and I'd like to help, but I'm busy right now. It's hard to help the person next to you or the person down the street but the Lord decided I should go to Africa." In 1986, Clark was headed back to Africa to work in Kenya with World Vision. The organization is still going strong in 2012.

The Charleston team spent three nights in Ethiopia and two at a World Vision feeding camp in Ajibar, 150 miles north of Addis Ababa, where 40,000 people were being fed. One of those days freezing rain fell over the country and several deaths were reported due to those conditions. The team had to fly home commercially.

The Easter flight was the only flight that was made but another shipment of supplies was sent by sea to Chad. Louisa Hawkins said in 2011, "it was a miracle."

In November 1985, Scott distributed a resolution passed at the recent diocesan convention regarding the sanctity of human life. He further advised that Canon Howe would speak on the subject on Sunday, November 10. Since the 1973 Roe vs. Wade Supreme Court decision, "courts have repeatedly thwarted efforts to enact even the most modest pro-life reforms." In 2011, Representative Ron Paul is sponsoring the Sanctity of Life Act of 2011, (H.R. 1096). On the other side, there is the Religious Coalition for Reproduction Choice, (RCRC). Its website reports, "The Episcopal Church is the only whole Christian denomination that holds a membership in the RCRC."

In December 1985, Edward and Adelaida Bennett and their family traveled to Ibague, Colombia, where Adelaida's family lives, with $1,500 donated from members of St. Philip's, St. Mary's and others. The Bennetts arrived just six weeks after a volcano destroyed the town of Armero located near Ibague. With part of the money, they were able to purchase shoes, socks, underwear and personal hygiene items. On December 23 they found sixteen new patients in the hospital and they returned the next day with packages for all sixteen. Edward and his cousin, Carlos Villa, spent $400 to put two badly needed carpenters and two shoe repairmen in business. The Bennetts were thanked. "We at St. Philip's should be thankful for the way God provided Adelaida and Edward to be our ambassadors to Colombia and the way a small amount of money was used to meet so many needs." In September 1986, the missions/ministries committee sent $1,000 to the Second Presbyterian Church in Ibague.

Betsy Tezza at the February 17, 1986, vestry meeting reported that a young couple, who were St. Philippians, had their first baby who had to be delivered by caesarian section. They had no insurance and no funds with which to pay the hospital bill. She wondered if the bill could be paid from the Haig Fund. It was approved but Dr. James M. Ravenel and Dr. Harry Gregorie would see if the hospital would be willing to absorb the fees. Dr. Ravenel was successful in getting the hospital to forego its charges and the obstetrician donated his services.

In March, Glenn distributed a brochure to the vestry from World Servants and explained he would be taking a group of approximately twenty young people to the Dominican Republic from June 16 to 30. The cost was $1,145 per person including travel, housing and meals. They were to build a church and also help install a water system. The "Mission and Ministry Committee" voted to provide $5,000 and Parker Coleman made a tape of religious songs hoping to raise $2,000 for the cause. Glenn asked the vestry to pray for the financial needs of these young people. Prior to the group's departure, Dr. Harry Gregorie showed slides of his previous work in the Dominican Republic. Anne Pinckney, a member of the team, told the congregation, "I feel that God has called me to go to the Dominican Republic to build a church ... to tell others about God and His love ... and to help me appreciate the things I have which I often take for granted."

FINANCES & THE VESTRY

In 1983, Mrs. Wilmot Gibbs bequeathed $500 with no restrictions to the church. George Buist bequeathed $2,000 to the churchyard fund and Nick Zervos wanted to donate $500 in honor of Larsen's work at St. Philip's. The vestry decided to use that $500 to purchase some significant plantings for the churchyard.

Scott did not waste any time. By October 1983, he had proposed the development of a faith budget for 1984. The total budget was $500,000 - $300,000 from pledges and $200,000 from the faith component.

There were only four parts to the budget:

1. Giving included a $50,000 tithe to the diocese that was a 15% increase from the previous year. Offerings to other ministries would receive $50,000. Scott said he would present God's challenge of a Biblical tithe, but would not badger our people with endless requests throughout the year. Another $50,000 went to ministries giving direct assistance to the needy such as the soup kitchen, etc.

2. Equipping the staff had a budget of $150,000
3. Enabling also had a budget of $150,000 for support ministries, facilities and utilities and basic maintenance. Another $50.000 was marked for major maintenance.
4. A contingency fund of $50,000 was to be used for the repayment of all outstanding debts with the remainder going to the restoration fund.

In January 1984, the vestry established nine standing committees chaired by nine vestry members. The committees were: worship, Christian education, parish services, outreach, churchyard, finance, property and ushers. There were to be no more than four committee reports per meeting and the twice monthly vestry meetings should not last longer than one hour and a half.

The faith budget was set at $430,000. As of September 30, 1984, receipts were $452,353.26 plus there had been a balance of $38,988.32 as of December 31, 1983, for a total of $491,341.58.

In March, Scott announced the two wardens would have lunch with Scott on Tuesdays and anyone who wanted to bring up an issue could join them. The tradition continues in 2012. Haden McCormick has breakfast with the wardens every Tuesday morning at the Harbor Club.

John J. Kerr was a vestry secretary with a sense of humor. He wanted to settle the issue of how to correctly write that the vestry met twice a month. He used a dictionary.

"bi-month-ly – 1. Occurring once every two months. 2. Occurring twice a month; semimonthly. – n. A bimonthly publication. – adv. 1. Once in two months. 2. Twice a month. bimonthly, biweekly: These words are ambiguous, since they can mean either once every two months (or weeks), or twice a month (or week). The ambiguity can be avoided by using semimonthly (or semiweekly) when the latter meaning is intended." The word "bimonthly" was chosen.

Teddy Guerard, a delegate to the diocesan convention, reported that Dr. H. Clay Robertson, III, a fellow delegate to the diocesan convention, was elected to the diocesan council.

The budget for 1985 was established at $600,000 up from the1984 budget of $430,000. By January 1985, 355 pledge cards had been turned in for a total of $449,638.48. The proposed 1986 budget was $700,000. Scott said this figure was 32% over projected 1985 collections of $530,000 which, in turn, was 23% over 1984 collections.

At the same time, the restoration fund was initially provided with $41,724.06. In January, Scott presented to the vestry seven needs and to raise funds he suggested the name "St. Philip's 100th Anniversary Restoration Fund." Scott said that the title "100th

Anniversary" came to him as he was kneeling in the sanctuary and noticed a memorial above the shelf which holds the bread and wine to be consecrated for the Eucharist. In reading the plaque, he found that it was a memorial to the mercies received in the earthquake of 1886. In November 1985, there was $302,000 in the restoration fund.

Dr. Anderson stated that this was his last vestry meeting. He said this had been the best vestry on which he had served because of the work of its members. He praised all for their attendance.

In March 1985, Scott advised the vestry that Elizabeth Mackell left St. Philip's 10% of her one million dollar will to St. Philip's with no restrictions. Betsy Tezza moved the money be put in the restoration fund. The vestry agreed.

In August, Eleanor Simmons resigned her position as church receptionists. Rhett Barrett looked for a replacement.

Scott wrote that one of Jesus' favorite subjects was giving. Of the thirty-eight parables that He told, sixteen were about giving. "Why? Because Jesus knew that givers are winners, takers are losers." He said, "Where your treasure is, there your heart will be also." He knew that our hearts would flow where our gifts go.

He talked about his family and how he was teaching his children to tithe, and how it took three years for him to learn to tithe. Scott continued, "God says put me to the test, see if I will not open the windows of heaven and pour down blessings upon you. There is no question that He means financial blessings. But His blessings aren't restricted just to the financial ones. I pray this way to God: Lord, don't limit the blessings of my life to finances. Bless my marriage, bless my children, and help me to be a blessing. These are the far more important, far more significant blessings that God wants to shower upon His children who place their faith in Him."

In January 1986, Frank Rogers thanked those who would be leaving the vestry after three years of service. Those were: Barbara Claypoole, Teddy Guerard and Ricky Hanckel.

In February 1986, Scott passed on an idea from Jim Donald at Kanuga to establish prayer partners among the vestry members who would pray for each other during Lent and that they would get to know each other better. A drawing was held and the following were selected as prayer partners: Terrell Glenn and Betsy Tezza, James Ravenel and Kitty Holt, Renny Scott and E. K. Wallace, T.W. Johnston and Robert Richards, Boopa Pritchard and Bill Barnwell, Andy Anderson and Jimmy Hagood and Harry Gregorie and John Kerr. No one had a title on this list.

Also in February, John Kerr was chosen the new senior warden and the vote between Robert Richards and Jimmy Hagood for junior warden was a tie. Richards won.

In February, Scott once again suggested the vestry consider putting together a 150th anniversary to raise the necessary two million dollars to restore the church.

In response to a newspaper advertisement, twenty-two people sent resumes applying for the job of St. Philip's business manager including Edward Vincent. Robert Richards voted the position be given to Vincent at a salary of $28,000 to $30,000, an IRA of $2,000, health insurance coverage and the use of a Toyota station wagon. A motion passed unanimously to hire Vincent.

In March, Scott asked the vestry to consider doing away with special offerings during the year and that responses to special requests be made from the outreach budget. The one exception would be the United Thank Offering.

PROPERTY & MAINTENANCE

In September 1983, Herbert Stender donated the landscaping of the parking lot. In November, the vestry discussed having a handicap ramp built to the south middle door but instead purchased a portable ramp which no one seemed to know it existed, particularly non-members. Five years later a permanent ramp was built for approximately $7,000. It remains there in 2012.

Church and nursery attendance increased so much between March 1983 and March 1984 that everyone was caught off guard. Fortunately, a property evaluation was taken at that time and found a mess in the nursery. There was poor lighting, the room was always damp and musty, there was no ventilation and there were three, workers, one age twelve, for thirty-five infants. South Carolina law required one adult for every six infants. In addition, infants and toddlers were in the same room, there was a high germ rate and outdoor stairs that were hazardous in the rain. The nursery was immediately moved.

In September 1984, Elizabeth L. (Betty) Hanahan, owner of a real estate and insurance company of the same name, wrote to the vestry, "I want to thank you very much for letting me handle the rental of 27 Cumberland Street for many years. It is also a pleasure to work with Rhett Barrett and anything I had to know she found out in a hurry. I am glad Mr. Glenn took the house and I hope he will be there for many years." Betty is buried at Old St. Andrew's and she left her famous butterscotch squares receipt to a St. Philippian couple.

At the same time, DeRosset Myers was monitoring the legal aspects of the will of Mrs. Frances H. Dill Rhett who left a one million dollar estate to be shared by St. Philip's, the Ladies Benevolent Society and the Charleston Museum.

On June 3, 1985, John Kerr received a report from John McCrady and Dan Beaman of Cummings & McCrady:

1. "The church was built with its foundations in a strata of clay. We know this because McCrady had Soil Consultants run tests around the church. This clay is compressing under the weight of the construction, and has been for many years. The sanctuary which is newer, and the tower, which was built later than the nave, are both settling at a different rate than the nave which is the oldest part of the church. Apparently, the nave was constructed after the fire on the original foundations."
2. "At the present time, the newer sanctuary is settling faster than the nave or tower and this settlement is causing the cracks. The area under the altar is sinking faster and is pulling everything around it down with it. The east wall of the nave is being pulled outward by the movement of the sanctuary."
3. "We recommend that you rope off the eastern most portion of the balconies until we could investigate the structure further,"
4. "We advised you that we would try to find a contractor who could open up the balcony floor to allow us to check the condition of the floor beams in the wall."
5. "At the present time, we do not believe that this settlement has caused any serious problems. We have not been in the attic, however. The building will continue to settle. At some unknown future date it may become a problem. For now, we can only recommend that the vestry continue to watch for additional movement. Also, in the future, new exterior cracks should be investigated before they are restuccoed.

In July 1985, the church had completed a set of St. Philip's records from 1720 – 1914 on microfilm that had been presented to the church. The vestry thanked Mort Pine and all the others who helped in this project.

In September, Molly Stender expressed a desire to replace coverings for all of the old kneeling benches. The vestry was happy to accept her offer.

Charlie Boykin served as business manager from February 1986 to May 1986 and was replaced by the Rev. John Ball. The church would pay his moving expenses from Barnwell. Ball grew up in Summerville, attended the University of the South where he received a degree in chemistry. In 1955, he returned to Sewanee after deciding to enter the ministry. Ball served at Christ Church in Denmark, St. Alban's in Blackville, St. Ann's in Atlanta, St. Mark's in San Antonio and then he returned to Blackville and Denmark. He also served at the Church of the Holy Apostles in Barnwell. Ball's two brothers, Ed and Frank, are St. Philippians and his wife Nell née Ingle is from Charleston. Ball began work on June 16, 1986.

THE RECTORY

In June 1984, Scott purchased a house and moved out of the rectory that caused a resurrection of the many St. Philippian's who wanted to sell the rectory. In September, Richard W. Hanckel III, appraiser at Hanckel and House advised the church it was his opinion the house was worth $350,000. Hanckel did not want his work to be considered a conflict of interest due to his affiliation with the church. Later, Hanckel advised the church the rectory could be rented within a range of $700 to $1200 per month and the rear apartment, with some repairs, from $200 to $400 per month.

At a special vestry meeting on October 29, 1984, the future of the rectory was discussed. While the majority of the vestry was sentimental about keeping the rectory, they realized the only thing to do was to sell and use the money to meet some of St. Philip's pressing needs. A straw vote was taken with ten wanting to sell and four in favor of keeping it. No decision was made. By January, the decision was made to rent the rectory to protect it from vandalism, the elements, etc.

In July, a Mr. C and his family wrote a letter to the vestry stating they wanted to live in the rectory. They understood that if and when a new pastor came they would have to move "but hopefully that would not happen for many years." They volunteered to replant the garden, upgrade the dependency and they would be happy to store the few items remaining in the house. There was considerable work that was needed in order to prepare the house and the C family was willing to take on the responsibility so that St. Philip's would not have to do anything but turn over the keys and collect the $8,000 annual rent. He closed his letter, "we pray for a favorable reply. Thank you."

Mr. C leased the rectory for one year for $8,000 "as is" from June 14, 1985, to June 14, 1986, and in August he also leased the dependency. A mature dog was permitted to be in the house.

By May 12, 1986, the vestry had given Mr. C notice the lease would not be renewed because Glenn wanted to move into the rectory. Mr. C made several phone calls to Boopa Pritchard asking for an additional ninety days before termination of the lease but the request was turned down. Mr. C rented the dependency to a Mr. Ducklow without receiving specific permission from the vestry. That violated the lease. The tenant, having no idea the lease had been terminated, was distraught.

The parting was not pleasant. Rhett Barrett advised the vestry the rectory and its yard would have to be de-fleaed and, in addition, the house needed a thorough cleaning. Pritchard wrote the vestry that they would let Mr. C know how much, if any, of the $600 deposit would be returned to him.

MUSIC & THE CHOIR

The vestry in October 1983 ordered nine adult black duraloom cassocks and six adult cottas with traditional round yokes from "c.m. almy & son, inc." in Rye, New York, for $854.50 including a 5% quantity discount.

In October 1985, Sarah Yonker asked for a raise. The vestry decided to raise both her salary and Bill Oplinger's salary to $650 per month because they had only small raises in the past.

Charlie Boykin wrote to the vestry that his wife, Vivien, who had spent her life in the musical world, wanted to donate a baby grand piano that would be placed in the chapel. The vestry thanked her for her gift.

In January 1986, Scott presented a copy of the new 1982 hymnal to Yonker and he discussed the changes that had been made. He felt the church should start using the new hymnals. Kitty Holt suggested waiting until we had a new music director

before a final decision would be made (Was it Kitty Holt who saved the 1940 hymnals that are still in use in St. Philip's in 2012?).

THE CHURCHYARDS

In February 1984, Craig Bennett requested permission to have the names and dates of his parents engraved in two floor tiles in the north aisle just forward of the cross aisle. Finally, in August, after much prayer and discussion, Bennett's request was turned down. The vestry had discussed the question of memorials in the church at several meetings over the last few months.

The vestry voted unanimously that no memorial would be permanently affixed to the interior or exterior of the church building or chapel. The vestry, however, could make an exception and approve a memorial to:

1. a rector of St. Philip's Church
2. a bishop of the diocese of South Carolina
3. communicants who died in a war

FRIDAY, MAY 16 & SATURDAY, MAY 17, 1986

Scott called Mary Perry and Tracy Graudin, both of whom worked for the church, to his office on Friday afternoon and told them he would resign on Sunday. The Graudins had planned to take a trip that weekend but changed their minds.

Scott gathered together with the vestry on Saturday afternoon and told them he would resign from the pulpit the next day. The vestry replied that if he did decide to stay they needed to know his problem and if he did leave they did not need to know.

SUNDAY, MAY 18, 1986

This was the date of Scott's resignation sermon that was turned into a circus by the worldwide news. In fairness, the complete transcript of the sermon herein is copied from *The Evening Post* printed on Wednesday, May 21, 1986, (as received from St. Philip's), without any comments or changes, except for the first ten paragraphs in which he talks about the two ways of teaching. One way is teaching by example and the other way is teaching by contrast. Scott also said that he had a great conviction that there would be a great future to this church as parishioners learn to lean on Jesus Christ.

THE SERMON

"And this morning I want to share a message that hopefully will teach by contrast. In James, Chapter 3, the first verse says this; 'Don't many of you desire to be teachers, my brethren because you do not know that we who teach will be judged with a stricter standard?'

"And then in first Timothy 3 where Paul was writing to the young man Timothy, whom he had laid hands on as a sort of father in the faith, he said this to Timothy: a spiritual leader must be above reproach. That's the first thing he said and then he gave a whole bunch of other criteria. Then the last thing he wrote was this: Moreover they must be well thought of by outsiders, lest they fall in reproach and the snare of the devil.

"And I have wrestled with those scriptures and we have an illustration on the global scene today in the presidential election in Austria with Waldheim, where an incident in his past, forty years ago, compromised his present effectiveness. Now what's true in the political world is 10 times more true in the kingdom of God.

"Back in 1967, I was a senior in College - a happy-go-lucky, free, wild character. And I met a girl who was graduating from Vassar college, and we dated a bit and she told me something I had not – I was about a year away from meeting Jesus Christ – and she told me she was a witch.

"Now, I was a sophisticated New Yorker who had an Ivy League education, and you know that was for Halloween and sort of ridiculous and a joke and I knew nothing about the occult or demonic activity.

"I just thought it was unreal – knew nothing about the Holy Spirit's activity. And she said she put a curse on my life and I just thought it was a joke. But for fourteen years issuing from that relationship a pattern of bondage developed in my life and I remember crying out to God for freedom.

"And nothing I did could set me free. And I remember one day just being at the end of my rope and I said, 'Lord, is the only way to keep from dragging your name through the mud to end it all?'

"I heard this very distinct voice that I believe was God. He said, 'Well, Renny, that certainly would keep me from changing you.'

"And I thought to myself you mean you will change me one day? And then I heard this voice say this: 'Yes, but not in time to save your pride.'

"Little did I know what that meant at that time. You know, pride is just being afraid to be known for who you are. Well, years went by and still I struggled. And then one day a lady was interceding for me at the Key Bridge Marriott Hotel in Washington, D.C.

"And the Holy Spirit fell on her and she just began to pray and was broken and didn't know why, but was praying for me. And we discovered all this after the fact through her prayer journal and through our experience.

"Margaret and I were driving many miles away back from the sixth anniversary of our wedding and the Holy Spirit spoke to me simultaneously as that woman prayed for her pastor who happened to be me. And this is the scripture God brought to my mind with sudden clarity. Proverbs 28 verse 14 says this: 'He who conceals his transgressions will not prosper, but he who confesses and forsakes them will obtain mercy.' And I knew in that moment the path I needed to walk.

"And so that next Saturday morning, Margaret and I called together seven senior wardens with whom I'd walked and did walk very closely for six years at the Church of the Apostles. Every man was older than I was. They were wiser than I was, and we gathered together on a Saturday morning in our home and I shared my whole sad story of bondage and they were wonderful.

"And I offered to resign at that point, and then I made a fatal mistake that many people make when they are trying to discern what God wants them to do. They look at the logistics. And I thought to myself 'yikes, I've resigned. How do I make a living? How do I support my family? What will I do? What are ministers good for but to minister?'

"And as I looked at that and then I looked at these seven men and they with great compassion and great grace prayed with me and assured me of their prayerful support and assured me the effectiveness of my ministry. They said continue on.

"And we went through a year of inner healing and prayer, and God freed me in a way I never dreamed possible. I know what it is to be in bondage, and I know what it is to be in freedom.

"But you know, that morning I became a Jonah. You know the story of Jonah. He heard clearly what's God's will for his life but he lacked the courage to do it. And it says that Jonah fled to Tarsus, and you know the rest of the story. And I was led to Charleston.

"Jonah was swallowed by a big fish, I was swallowed by a big church.

"And from the belly of the whale, Jonah prayed to his Lord and God heard him. And from the altar of St. Philip's, I prayed and the Lord heard me. And this was my prayer, 'We do not presume to come to this thy table, O merciful Lord, trusting in our own righteousness, but in Thy manifold and great mercies. We're not worthy so much as to gather up the crumbs under Thy table, but Thy property is always to have mercy.'

"Well, we prayed that and during that year that I was going through inner healing and that sort of thing, I went with other people back to everyone I knew who had been offended or hurt by my sin and there was reconciliation and forgiveness.

"But just recently one of those individuals has issued a malpractice suit against Bishop Lee in Virginia and Bishop Allison here in South Carolina for allowing someone like me to be in the ministry.

"And so, you know, the same thing happened to Jonah as he was on that ship knowing what God wanted. A storm came up. And Jonah said that the only way to deal with the storm is to throw me overboard, and everybody said we can't do that. In great compassion and human decency, they said we won't do that.

"But Jonah knew what God had spoken to him before and then he was thrown overboard, swallowed by a whale, and spit up on the shore.

"Then God just said to Jonah, will you now do what I asked you to do? And Jonah did?

"Well, similarly in the midst of this storm, God is allowing me to be spit up on the shore and God just meets me there and says: 'Now will you do what I asked you to do?'

"I've got basically two choices that are beautifully illustrated in the Old Testament. One, there are two kings that sinned while they were in leadership. One was King Saul and one was King David. When Samuel the prophet confronted Saul with his sin, Saul said honor me before the people. And Samuel agreed to do that, but Saul became a shell of a man and then he became possessed by demons and ultimately he ended in suicide.

"On the other hand, King David, when the prophet Nathan confronted him with his sin, he said: 'against thee and thee only have I sinned. Create in me a clean heart, O' God, and put a new and bright spirit within me and cast me not away from thy presence and take not thy Holy Spirit from me.'

"David's way is the only way. Judgment begins with the household of God. I've decided to walk on the path that God gave me to walk on four years ago. And a month ago I wrote a letter to the Bishop – actually hand-delivered it – and offered my resignation.

"And Bishop Allison, although he was the object of a suit and in jeopardy, with great compassion and great sensitivity to me, said: 'Renny, don't do anything hastily. Would you go to Dr. _____[27] for me and just make sure we're not over reacting.

"You say, well, Renny what possible redemptive thing is in all this? What is the good news in the midst of a situation like this? Well, I think back on that bishop of mine who said don't smoke and don't drink, who is now with the Lord in Heaven. Didn't have a judgmental bone in his body. Filled with compassion, but he knew that sins had consequences and he was just sharing that with the people he loved and his priest.

"And I guess Paul would say it this way: Be not deceived, God is not mocked. We reap what we sow. If we sow to the flesh, then from the flesh we'll reap corruption. If we sow to the Spirit, from the Spirit we'll reap eternal life.

"If there are those of you that are thinking 'Well, how does this apply to me?' Hear this good news: there's no condemnation for those who are in Christ Jesus. For hear the promise of the gospel, anyone be in Christ, he's a new creation, the old is passed away. Behold, the new has come but don't make a mistake: sin does have consequences. God forgives. God restores. God makes new. But there comes with each sin a future limitation on our effectiveness and fruitfulness in the service of God.

"For me, that limitation is on my spiritual role in leadership, not my relationship with God, not my relationship with my friends, not my relationship with my family but it means that I should be removed from leadership. You know the flesh cries out: no it's too painful, I can't face it. But the good news is this that when Jonah obeyed although there was significant loss, God restored his usefulness. And when David repented, although there was significant and grievous loss, he had paid the price all his life. God called him a man after his own heart.

"Let's pray: Father in Heaven, we're so grateful to you that you've that laid a foundation in this church, that you've been at work here long years before we ever came, and will be at work long after we go. We thank you that the foundation is laid

in Christ Jesus. And Lord we pray that you will teach us to walk in the light as he is in the light. That we might have fellowship with one another and know that the blood of Jesus Christ cleanses us from all sins in Jesus' name. Amen"

Scott left the church through the back door with John Kerr escorting him to his car. Glenn walked out on the main aisle sobbing.

Both the *Atlanta Constitution* and the *News and Courier* reported in June that law suits had not been filed.

---

[27] The doctor's name was not in the sermon.

AFTERMATH

Because a regular vestry meeting was scheduled, coincidentally, the day after the resignation sermon, the vestry could react immediately. Kerr and Glenn discussed Scott's resignation and asked that all the vestry be supportive of Scott and his decision. Kerr advised that he, Glenn and Robert Richards had discussed severance pay and benefits for Scott. Kerr moved and the vestry unanimously agreed to continue his current compensation package through the end of 1986 or until such time as he obtained suitable full-time employment.

Glenn announced the Wednesday afternoon service would continue, all other planned activities would move forward and it was still his intention to proceed with the June trip to the Dominican Republic. Glenn also advised the vestry to think about a replacement and added that if anyone's spiritual discipline included fasting, it would appropriate in this situation. Kerr already had a list of three possible interims given him by Bishop Allison, who had been out of town the weekend of the resignation. The bishop advised he was available to meet with the vestry as a whole or individually.

Bishop Allison was quoted in the *Post and Courier* as saying he did not think Scott should have resigned and that he regretted using the word "witch." Scott was quoted, "Saying as far as the witch controversy goes, he calls it all an unfortunate misstatement blown out of proportion by the press." He said he had "used the story about the curse often at St. Philip's, but it was misconstrued when he put it in the context of his resignation sermon. I used the wrong set of words, and the press had a field day with it."

Glenn and Kerr felt the vestry should do something to express its appreciation for Scott's outstanding ministry.

Frenchie Richards said in 2011 that all of a sudden Glenn, who was twenty-six and at his first church, was running the church with the vestry. Frenchie said she thought God gave Glenn, who was gathering experience, a gift of wisdom and he pulled it all together.

On Tuesday May 20, John Kerr had a letter mailed to the congregation:

"Dear Members of St. Philip's:

On Sunday, May 18th, 1986, The Rev. Henry L. Scott, Jr. resigned from the office of Rector of this parish and from active ministry in general. While this announcement has been a severe blow and great disappointment to us all, it is nevertheless clear to your Vestry that Renny has made a prayerfully studied decision as he indicated in his resignation. Renny now is responding obediently to something God not only told him to do four years ago, but again has called him to do in recent weeks. A tape of the resignation sermon is available in the church office upon request. The integrity, grace and courage with which Renny and Margaret are facing the ramifications of their decision is inspiring. We pledge to them our constant prayers and unyielding support.

"The Vestry's immediate response to the news of Renny's departure was prayer. We seek first and foremost to have the mind of Christ for the future of St. Philip's and that shall come as we turn our hearts and minds and wills toward our Saviour. As a result, we anticipate God's guidance in the selection of an interim rector and in the eventual call of a new rector for this parish. The Vestry has also been in constant communications with Rt. Rev. C. FitzSimons Allison, Bishop of the Diocese of South Carolina. He will be with us this Sunday for confirmation.

"As for the future of St. Philip's Church, we have complete confidence in the goodness of our Heavenly Father. God has promised in His word that 'He who began a good work in you will carry it on to completion until the day of Christ Jesus, (Philippians 1:6). Our Lord Jesus has begun a tremendous work in the parish family of St. Philip's. All of us are being encouraged and nurtured in our relationships with God and each other in ways never before thought possible. This shall not change. Renny is a dear man of God and served this parish faithfully for more than two and a half years. One of the greatest gifts that he gave to us was a vision for what we could become through faith in Christ. Your vestry is committed to the pursuit of this vision and will obediently follow God's will as he reveals it to us. We bid your prayers for the important decisions that have to be made and we joyfully anticipate the manifold blessings that shall come from God's gracious hand.

Faithfully (signed by the vestry)

John J. Kerr, senior warden, Robert A. Richards, junior warden, Andy Anderson, Jr., Dr. Harry B. Gregorie, Jr., Kitty Holt, Edward K. Pritchard, Jr., Betsy Tezza, Dr. William H. Barnwell, Jr., James M. Hagood, II, Thomas Johnston and Dr. E.K. Wallace, Jr."

Glenn preached in early June delivering "a moving sermon about emotional suffering." He asked for prayers for Scott and his family. Another Sunday, The Rev. Rick Belser from St. Michael's gave a sermon at St. Philip's giving encouragement and healing.

Gary Beson, a member of St. Paul's Summerville, "was challenged by the preaching of Renny Scott in 1984, where he gave his life to Jesus Christ in the pews of St. Philip's." He has been heavily involved in work at St. Paul's including renewal conferences at Kanuga with the help of his wife, Sue. Rhett Barrett, who ran St. Philip's for many years, admitted she never had much interest in religion until God used Renny to open her ears.

Joanne Ellison was quoted in the *Atlanta Constitution*, "His insight and compassion were tremendous. He was very gifted. He had a way of starting an idea and seeing it unfold. He was a light in the darkness. When he left, a part of me died." Another parishioner, who admired Scott said, "But I can tell you one thing, to me, Renny Scott was and always will be one helluva Christian."

LIFE AFTER ST. PHILIP'S

After the resignation, Scott and his family moved to Atlanta with little money, no job and no idea what to do next. He prayed and finally he felt God's answer and that was to go and minister to the homeless. Six months after arriving in Atlanta, Scott joined a group of Christians called the Family Consultation Service (FCS) who had devoted their lives to working with the poor since 1978.

The organization had built forty homes and a twenty unit apartments for moderate income residents. Then came Glencastle, a former debtor's prison built in 1897 that was given to FCS when an Atlanta businessman, Tom Cousins, purchased the prison for $210,000. Scott was chosen as director by November 1987. Three million dollars was raised to turn the prison into sixty-eight efficiency apartments that would rent for about $200 a month. Five architectural firms donated their services. The project was a success.

The Scotts joined the Church of the Apostles in Atlanta that had thirty-seven members and met in a private school chapel. Since then the church has grown to 150 – 200 members and Scott teaches Sunday school and confirmation class but does not preach from the pulpit. Scott has returned to Charleston on several occasions.

In June 1990, Scott sent out a letter that he was resigning from FCS to become headmaster of a small Christian secondary school – grades eight through twelve – in Atlanta. The Mount Vernon Christian Academy is flourishing in 2012. As previously, written, Renny and Margaret now live in Dalton, Georgia.

RT. REV. MOULTRIE MOORE

INTERIM

May 19, 1986 – September 1986

CHURCH SEERVICES, MEMBERS & CLERGY

At the May 19, 1986, vestry meeting, John Kerr was given three possible candidates for an interim minister by Bishop Allison. The vestry voted to call Bishop Moultrie Moore as the "interim-interim" minister until Canon Peter Gillingham arrived from England in October.

Bishop Moore was born in Mt. Pleasant, attended Porter Military Academy and was a graduate of the College of Charleston. He received his Masters in Divinity from the General Theological Seminary in New York City. Moore was ordained priest in 1940 by Bishop Thomas and served churches in Kingstree, Andrews and St. Stephens. In 1942, he moved to the diocese of North Carolina where in 1967 he was elected suffragan bishop of that diocese. He was elected Bishop of the Diocese of Easton, Maryland, in 1975. Moore and his wife, Florence Muirhead Porcher, returned to Mt. Pleasant in 1982 to an active retirement, allowing him to serve at St. Michael's and Holy Communion prior to coming to St. Philip's. He attended his first vestry meeting at St. Philip's on July 7, 1986.

CANON PETER GILLINGHAM

INTERIM

OCTOBER 10, 1986 – MAY 31, 1987

At the July 7 vestry meeting, Kerr asked members to start thinking about furnishing a carriage house for the Gillinghams because he preferred to be away from the church. They rented 2-A Ladson Street from Dr. Tommy Kirkland and his wife, Trish. Kitty Holt was in charge for arranging furniture and furnishings and church business manager, Rev. John Ball, suggested that the church "pound" the Gillinghams explaining "pounding" meant the house would be stocked with food, flowers, etc. prior to their arrival. The vestry thought that was an excellent idea. The Gillinghams moved into their apartment by October 9, 1986, just after vestryman Tommy Johnston and his family had moved out.

There was a write up in the July 1986 *Spire* about the Gillinghams: During his forty-five year career, Canon Gillingham had lived in splendor and in slums. After attending Oxford University in Oriel College from 1932 – 1935, he had been a parish priest, a naval chaplain, a chaplain to two private schools and domestic chaplain to His Majesty King George VI and Queen Elizabeth II. After his retirement in 1982, he served four parishes in South Africa and then came to South Carolina to serve as an interim rector at St. John's on Johns Island where they fell in love with the area. The son and grandson of clergymen, he also has a son carrying on the family tradition. Gillingham died on April 9, 1996, at age eighty-one.

Both Robert Richards and long-time Beaufortonian resident, Sally Pringle, remember everyone liking Gillingham. Pringle remembers he and his wife, Diana, spent time in Beaufort where they would rent an apartment very near St. Helena's church.

Kerr welcomed Gillingham to the vestry at his first meeting on October 20, 1986, where he thanked the vestry for "providing so nicely for the creature comforts." In November, Gillingham advised the vestry they had a ticket to return on April 7, 1987, but if they had a new rector before that date, they could move to their "house" in Beaufort. If there were no rector by April 7, he could only stay as late as May 30. Gillingham did require three Sundays off in January. Andy Anderson very seriously doubted there would be new rector by April 7.

In November 1986, Rev. Fred Sosnowski, former assistant rector, approached Gillingham about working for St. Philip's two Monday's a month. Both Gillingham and Glenn agreed that Sosnowski could be very useful with visitations, performing marriages and marriage counseling and handling counseling in general. The vestry hired Sosnowski.

Tommy Johnston commended Terrell Glenn and Tim Surratt on the outstanding job they had done with the church's youth. At the next vestry meeting, Glenn requested the vestry change Surratt's designation from interim to youth minister.

Gillingham advised the vestry that 1987 would be the 150th anniversary of the construction of the present church. He suggested activities to celebrate this anniversary and he and Glenn began working on ideas. Gillingham was correct that the church was rebuilding in 1837, but the construction was not completed until 1838 and then without the steeple.

Plans for the jubilee celebration included activities from May 1987 to May 1988. The planning committee included: Gillingham, Glenn, Boopa Pritchard, Alfred Pinckney, Jim Hagood, Joanne Ellison and Nick Zervos.

As previously written, Gillingham did depart on May 31 and the vestry made Glenn interim rector until the next rector arrived.

THE YOUTH, MEN'S MINISTRY & THE LADIES

The 1986 bazaar was held on Saturday, November 9 with Mary Cutler in charge of the raffle tickets, Florence Anderson headed the cleanup and Terrell Glenn was in charge of the carnival. Rhett Barrett and Jane Burnet were taking in clothes and Dottie Kerrison and Pat Wardlaw were in charge of the luncheon. Kim Baldwin was chair of the bazaar that netted $8,839.15.

Conversational dinners were returning in the fall of 1986. "Call Tracy Graudin at the office."

Charles L. Allen of 327 Pelican Place in Mt. Pleasant wrote a letter to the vestry in late winter 1987. "On a recent Sunday, Lee (his son) climbed into the van and told me that he had had a very good time in Sunday school. His other son, Matt, sung songs at home that he learned in Sunday school. Both boys show only slightly restrained eagerness in getting ready for church." He said "there may have been some controversy but Martha Vetter's approach is reaching receptive chords in my boys' hearts. I applaud you for your support of Martha."

Vetter planned to leave at the end of June with no reason given and Suzanne McCall was hired temporarily from June through August. Vetter was honored on Teacher's Day May 6, 1987, and was given a bonus check for $2,000.

THEOLOGY, EVANGELISM & MISSIONS

Gillingham, at his first vestry meeting, mentioned one of his aims would be to make the narthex more welcoming and he wanted more communicants to keep the church doors open. He wanted to post sermon topics and provide a tract rack. It saddened Gillingham to see the church doors locked at times in the morning and afternoons when so many people were reduced to wandering through the churchyard. He was reminded of our Lord's word, "Why seek the living among the dead." A new St. Philippian, Budd Franklin Smith, volunteered to organize those who opened the church.

Bill Elmore's new intra-communication committee had its first meeting in March 1987. The thrust of the committee was to have fourteen vestry and committee members call on St. Philippians in their homes. Each "caller" would visit four homes. The purpose of these visits was threefold: 1) to let parishioners know that the members of the vestry and the committee, as representatives of the parish, are interested in, and have a loving concern for <u>all</u>, 2) to <u>listen</u> to whatever the parishioners may want to express – whether complaints, suggestions, concerns, etc. and 3) to attempt to answer responsibly any questions that may be asked.

FINANCES & THE VESTRY

Boopa Pritchard, vestry secretary, took some heat. In August 1986, Dot Anderson asked the minutes to show she attended 95% of the meetings and one of the few times she did miss was reflected in the July 21 minutes. Tommy Johnston complained because most of the time his name was spelled "Johnson."

Also in August, Ball stated that the diocese only covered Scott's personal health insurance through July. The committee authorized Ball to pay his premium through the end of the years if the diocese would not pay.

In 1987, John Kerr, Andy Anderson and Jimmy Hagood were leaving the vestry. They were thanked for their diligent and outstanding service.

The proposed budget for 1987 was $698,660. As of February, $534,969.95 had been raised from 398 pledges. There was $391,969.95 in the restoration fund. The Haig Fund had a balance of $133,553.88 and was to be used for medical expenses of any needy person in Charleston as the trustees should approve. The principal could not be distributed.

Mrs. Dorothy Dickinson was the sexton's assistant and Donna Hickman was the parish receptionist. Dorothy said working at St. Philip's was a highlight in her life.

In September 1987, DeRosset Myers announced the Dill estate had been settled and St. Philip's would receive 4/18th of the settlement. The amount received in 1989 was $175,082.20. In 1991, residual funds of $34,000 were received from the same estate. Additionally there was one third interest in two residential lots in North Carolina as part of the same estate. Later in 1991, an additional $22,222 was received from the Dill estate.

Pauline Dill, who was St. Philippian Lavinia Thaxton's Godmother, lived to be 100.

At the same time, Glenn spoke to the vestry about its work during the past several months and urged that they not be discouraged at the imperfections in their working together. He suggested that they were not to concentrate on the "trees" that we lose sight of the "forest." He pointed out a number of factors which should cause rejoicing and urged they move forward in unity and a spirit of mutual support and cooperation. Following Glenn's remarks, the vestry further discussed ways in which they could jointly carry out their responsibilities.

PROPERTY AND MAINTENANCE

In March 1987, Boykin reported that for some time there had been concern about the overcrowded conditions of the sacristy. It was estimated that to correct the situation it would cost between $100,000 and $150,000. An interested benefactor would pay the cost of drawings and estimates.

Alfred Pinckney suggested renting the two parking lots and estimated the income could be $1,000 a month. Ball had received one bid of $728,000 for repairing the steeple.

THE RECTORY

In September 1986, Frank Brumley, who owned the Charleston Day School building, wanted to swap it for the rectory, the church home/office building, the tea garden, guaranteed parking spaces and $500,000. There were other considerations. After Brumley left, there was a lively discussion. The vestry had just recently decided to rent the rectory rather than sell it and then Brumley forced the issue again.

It was decided to call a congregational meeting to discuss Brumley's proposal. But on September 15 Pritchard suggested that if the rectory was not used in the swap, it could be sold and proceeds divided between the restoration fund and a fund to help future rectors in acquiring appropriate housing. The vote was delayed until October 6 when it was defeated six to five. Kerr and Richards asked the minutes show they were in favor of selling the rectory. Four days later, Kerr sent a letter to the congregation stating the thirteen room house with 5,047 square feet was appraised at $510,000. House renovations would cost $100,000 and another $50,000 was needed for the dependency. Work on the church/home office would cost $434,000.

Even though a large portion of the living room ceiling had fallen exposing the fireplace above, Gillingham said it was preferable for the rector to live downtown. He wanted to talk to the congregation.

In March 1987, there was a brief discussion of the ultimate disposition of the rectory. Richards said the vestry should let the property committee look into that issue. The vestry hired Alice Patrick to take an inventory of the furniture, etc. in the rectory and to appraise the more valuable pieces.

THE SEARCH COMMITTEE

The church began its search for a new rector in July 1986. Andy Anderson was named chairman of the committee and it was decided to have three members from the vestry, one from each "class." Kerr was responding to letters from members who had concerns about the selection of a new rector. By December, twenty of the forty-seven names of possible candidates had been qualified. By February, there was a "High List" of nine possible candidates. James E. Hampson at Christ Church in Huntington Valley, Pennsylvania, was on that list.

Before March 2, the search committee members were announced: Andy Anderson, chair, Dot Anderson, Helen Barkley, Joanna Drake, Palmer Gaillard, Jane Gregorie, George Greene, Ben Hagood, Ed Holt, Frank Rogers, Molly Stender and Dr. E.K. Wallace, vestry liaison.

Vestry secretary, William B. Elmore, a retired lawyer who had moved to Charleston, wrote a letter to the vestry with suggestions about how to choose a new rector. He found good material in a book called *Holiness* by J. C. Ryle, who was appointed in 1880 as the first bishop of Liverpool.

Elmore said look for soundness of doctrine in preaching rather than simply the ability to stir the emotions and impress listeners with cleverness. He added that throughout all Christians sin's roots remain alive in the bottom of our hearts even though "checked" by God's grace. "There are no 'super-Christians' – there are at best only slightly, redeemed souls. He wanted a rector "who understood there was no quick fix – that we do not through some single life changing experience overcome sin once and for all, but that, empowered by God's grace, we are called to continue throughout our lives the daily struggle with the sin which doth so easily beset us, (Hebrews 12:1)."

In April, the search committee's budget was increased from $5,000 to $12,000.

In June 1987, Andy Anderson contacted some additional people in regard to Hampson: Bishop Alden Hathaway of the diocese of Pittsburg 1981 – 1997 and the Rev. Peter Moore, former dean of the Trinity School for Ministry (and in 2012 associated with St. Michael's). They were good friends of Hampson. Hathaway was one of those to whom Anderson spoke. Anderson also spoke to members and clergy in two of his former churches.

Four clergymen came to Charleston and after the interviews a cocktail party was given for them, the search committee, the vestry and their spouses. After the last of these interviews, the vestry convened on three separate days and at the last meeting the vestry enthusiastically endorsed Hampson. On June 4, 1987, the vestry unanimously voted to call Hampson,

Hampson replied in a letter of July 8, 1987, to Robert Richards the senior warden: "After much prayer, conversations with my family, and consultations with a few Christian friends, we decided to accept your call to come as 'the next permanent Rector of St. Philip's Church.' First we were surprised by the call, then sobered, and now finally excited and enthusiastic. May God's hand be upon this new ministry and may His Spirit preside over the deliberations and actions!" He would arrive in the second half of September and would make October 4, 1987 his first Sunday at St. Philip's.

REV. JAMES EUGENE HAMPSON, JR.

RECTOR

OCTOBER 4, 1987 – SEPTEMBER 1, 1999

Hampson, who was born in Shreveport, Louisiana, on February 2, 1937, graduated in 1959 from the University of Oklahoma where he met Sarah Elizabeth Oden, his wife to be. He received his Bachelor of Divinity from the Episcopal Theological School in Cambridge, Massachusetts, in 1962. Hampson was involved in a range of ministries: as a co-founder of SAMS-USA (South American Missionary Society), as an original and a still active trustee of the Trinity School for Ministry and as a trustee of FOCUS, an organization committed to Christian leadership in private schools.

The initiative for Hampson to help found SAMS-USA came from the opportunity in 1974 to know and work with English Bishop Stephen Neill who was a staunch supporter of private mission societies providing overseas ministry. As previously written, Bishop Neill was in Charleston in 1983.

Hampson, who was the rector of "lively and growing parishes in Massachusetts and Pennsylvania," was rector from 1977 to 1987 of St. John's in Huntington Valley, Pennsylvania, a parish of more than 800 communicants.

There are three Hampson children. When Hampson came to Charleston in 1987, Anne, 22, was a graduate of Converse College's school of music, James, 20, was a student at Sewanee and Mary, 18, was entering Washington and Lee.

A reporter asked him about his ministry and Hampson replied, "I don't know of any shortcuts in the ministry; all I know is the Gospel, prayer and hard work."

Hampson served under three bishops: The Rt. Rev. Christopher FitzSimons Allison, who retired in 1990, and the Rt. Reverend Edward L. Salmon, Jr. who was consecrated on February 24, 1990 as the thirteenth bishop of the diocese of South Carolina. Bishop William J. Skilton was the suffragan bishop of the diocese of South Carolina from 1996 to 2006.

Salmon was born in Natchez, Mississippi, on January 30, 1934. He graduated from Suwanee in 1956 and the Virginia Theological Seminary in 1960. He was ordained priest in 1961 in the diocese of Arkansas where he served. Later he had churches in Missouri. He married Louise Hack in 1972 and there were two children, Catherine and Edward L III. Salmon participated in many organizations such as chairman of the board of SPEAK which publishes the *Anglican Digest* and he was chairman of the board of Nashotah House Seminary at Nashotah, Wisconsin. In 2012, Salmon was dean of Nashotah House.

Salmon has been described as deliberate, contemplative, conciliatory and having a good sense of humor, He is a skilled carpenter, has remodeled old houses and is an expert bridge player. Salmon preaches the Word of God.

CHURCH SERVICES, MEMBERSHIP & CLERGY

On October 7, 1987, the vestry absolved Glenn of a $3,100 debt he owed to St. Philip's and the senior warden wrote him a letter. "We can never thank you enough for your leadership and wisdom shown during the difficult period St. Philip's has had. The fact that we have arrived at this 'new beginning' intact spiritually, financially and numerically is largely due to you and on behalf of the vestry and congregation I thank you from the bottom of my heart." The vestry looked forward to working with Glenn for a "very long season." It was signed by Senior Warden Robert Richards. Glenn, who lived in Mt. Pleasant, would remain at St. Philip's another three years.

Hampson wanted to meet parishioners so a series of intimate gatherings in member's homes were held. Some of the members who participated were John and Joan Algar, Bobby and Mimi Cathcart, Ed and Kitty Holt, George and Molly Greene, Bill and Suzanne McIntosh, Frank and Eleanor Rogers and E.K. and Jean Wallace and Bill and Julia Cain.

In January 1988, Hampson apologized for his absence at the last vestry meeting saying he had gathered at a diocesan conference center with a small group of conservative and evangelical Episcopal clergy, "all rectors of large influential churches." They would try to put together an effort for the "faith once delivered to the Saints (Jude 3)." Most of these men were old friends.

In February, the senior warden distributed handouts regarding the usher's duties and a new procedure for communion. There was a discussion that most of them did not usher but only gave out programs. The vestry committee, headed by John Paul, was to look into the matter.

In April 1988, a covered dish supper was held in the parish hall for "a night of fun, fellowship and a humorous roast of our friends Terrell and Teresa" celebrating their upcoming wedding. In May, the ECW would host a reception for Terrell and his new bride.

In May 1988, Hampson stated that St. Philip's needed to endorse Chris Huff for ordination to the diaconate. The vestry agreed.

Fire Chief W.E. Guthke, in July 1988, wrote a letter to the vestry concerning the use of candles in the church. After considerable discussion, the vestry decided to prohibit lighted candles in the nave except those that were traditionally a part of the ceremony. No candles were allowed on the window sills or in the pews.

REVEREND ADDISON HART

ASSISTANT RECTOR

SEPTEMBER 1988 – SEPTEMBER 1989

Bishop Allison suggested the church hire Addison Hart through October. He would graduate from the Trinity School of Ministry in May as a deacon. Hart, who would preach both services on June 21, was ordained as a priest in August 1988 and called to St. Philip's for a short stay that ended in September 1989.

Addison Hart and his wife, Janis, and their two children, Addy and Anna, were departing for St. Alban's Church in Kingstree where he was called as rector. His first Sunday there would be October 1, 1989. Hart said that his two years at St. Philip's had been good and eventful and that leaving would be sad. He gave special thanks to Jim and Terrell for all they had done to help a rookie learn the ropes and that he would have an abiding affection for these two Godly men.

Hampson mentioned that Tony Campbell, director of Camp Baskerville, Pawley's Island, would be the guest minister at the 10:00 a.m. service on June 26. 1989. Campbell was the first black to preach at St. Philip's.

In October, Hampson reviewed his first year before the vestry. He mentioned a number of accomplishments but his main thrust was to address two nagging problems: the interpretation of the by-laws and the restoration of the rectory. The by-law issue was basically about whom the rector could hire and fire but Hampson did not want to make an issue of it.

The 200th diocesan convention was held at St. Philip's on February 22 – 23, 1990, with some events at the cathedral. St. Philip's lay delegates were Tempe Parker, Dr. Clay Robertson, Ben Hagood and Winfield Sapp. John Paul was named as parish chairman of the convention. The Venerable John Q. Beckwith III (Jack), archdeacon, wrote a thank you letter on February 28 to Hampson thanking him, his staff and volunteers for making the convention a great success.

REVEREND JAY FOWLER

ASSISTANT RECTOR

AUGUST 6, 1990 – AUGUST 20, 1995

The Rev. Jay Fowler started work at St. Philip's on August 6, 1990. Hampson made him head of a ministerial committee. His duties included: baptisms, hospital visitation, neighborhood groups, college and young adults and marriage counseling.

Fowler was born in Kansas the son of Don and Joyce Fowler. He graduated from the University of Kansas in 1982 with B.S.E. in mathematics and a secondary education degree in mathematics. He graduated from the Virginia Theological Seminar and was ordained deacon in June 1988. Fowler was ordained a priest at St. Michael's Church in Mission, Kansas, on December 26, 1988.

Fowler sent memories to share. "Moving to Charleston from Kansas was a new and wonderful experience and people received me as a young priest very graciously. I had been in the ministry since college but had only been ordained for two years when I came to St. Philip's. I had a lot to learn about being a priest and the people of St. Philip's encouraged me and got involved in ministries and programs with me. My wife, Janine, and I led small groups for young married couples, first at our home, then at the church and we continue to enjoy those friendships today. I started a men's group on Friday mornings at 7 a.m. in the church office where it became time to grab some donuts, do some Bible study and pray for each other." That group continues in 2012.

Fowler continued, "I also led a mid-week service that combined music including guitars, Biblical teaching and Anglican liturgy. About 150 people of all races and economic backgrounds gathered to worship and learn together. I'm thankful for my five years at St. Philip's. The Lord used those years to form me as a priest. I know God has many more years of gospel proclamation ahead for the people and clergy of St. Philip's Church."

Fowler departed St. Philip's on August 20, 1995. In 2012, Fowler continues his ministry at Cambridge Church in Leawood, Kansas.

✣ ✣ ✣

Mike Cooke was hired as director of Christian education on August 6, 1990, replacing Ann Welch who accepted the job of director of Christian education at St. Andrew's Mt. Pleasant.

In September 1991, DeRosset Myers wrote, "after forty years of intense activity at St. Philip's," he was leaving St. Philip's to join St. Stephens Church at 67 Anson Street because that church was involved in a unique and wonderful work in the religious life in the community. He promised he would occasionally attend a service at St. Philip's.

Mrs. Charles Geer (Francie) remembers Hampson very fondly. She called him very late on a Friday night in 1991 to tell him her mother, Frances Waring Voigt, was dying in the hospital and asked if he could come. Even though Hampson was suffering with the flu, he went to the hospital to be with Mrs. Voigt and her family. She died that following Sunday.

The March 1991 issue of *The Spire* called for St. Philippians to pray for those serving in the Middle East, who were members or had some tie with the church. The Gulf War began April 20, 1990, and ended February 28, 1991, but many American service men were still in that area in March. Names included were Lt Cdr. Paul M. Allen, Maj. M. Ball, Maj. John David Brophy M.D., Maj. Sharon DeGrace, Capt. William Griffen, Jr., Master Sgt. John Macmurphy, Cpl. Philip Alston Middleton,[28] Cpl. Woodward Middleton and Staff Sgt. Joseph R. Trott, III,

---

28 In 2011, Alston is a major serving in Afghanistan. In 2012, Col. Middleton has retired and works at SPAWAR.

REVEREND MAURICE LEE

ASSISTANT RECTOR

FEBRUARY 11, 1992 – NOVEMBER 20, 1994

The Rev. Maurice Lee was called to St. Philip's and Lee believed that Hampson's daughter, Anne, a member of the Church of the Apostles, told her father of his availability. Lee wrote in 2011, "And so we came to St. Philip's"

Lee and his wife, Janet, arrived in Charleston in late December 1991. They found a Christmas tree, provided by Jim and Sarah, in the temporary apartment the Hampsons had rented for them. The Hampsons had also furnished the apartment because the Lee's condominium in Atlanta had not been sold.

Lee, who was born in Sydney, Australia, in 1935, studied at Moore Theology College in Newtown near Sydney graduating in 1961. In 2011, the college wrote, "Our focus in all things is Jesus Christ as he is made known to us in the Bible." He was ordained in St. Andrew's Cathedral in Sydney. After ordination, Lee served two cities in Australia, Sabah, Malaysia, in the English diocese of Winchester and briefly as English chaplain in Interlaken, Switzerland.

In the early eighties, Lee married an American widow named Janet and he inherited "three wonderful children." In 2011, their son is a retired Commander in the United States Navy, their son-in-law is a Commodore in the Royal Australian Navy and another son-in-law is a well-established officer of the Coca Cola Company. There are eight grandchildren.

In the late eighties, on one of their visits in the United States they met Dr. Youssef, an Egyptian who also studied at the Moore Theology College and later was given permission by the bishop of Atlanta to plant a parish that grew to 3,000 with another 1,000 listening on the internet. Youssef, the founder of *The New Way*, needed another clergyman and asked Lee to fill the position at the Church of the Apostles. Lee said, "Youssef was one of a select group in this country who would understand me." All went well until the congregation became serious about separating from the Episcopal Church. Lee had a real sympathy with their dilemma but he did not feel it was the time for him to surrender his Anglican orders. "With great regret, my wife and I decided that we could not continue with them and we paid a fairly heavy price for the decision to remain within the Episcopal Church."

The Rev. Maurice Lee's last day at St. Philip's was Sunday, November 20, 1994. A parishioner wrote in June 1995 that Lee left St. Philip's because of the attitude and approach to existing problems and that with the prevailing attitude it would be difficult to replace Lee. Hampson said that Lee has a deep faith in Christ and good theological training and as an Anglican priest he has literally world-wide experience. He developed a keen insight for pastoral matters.

Lee was called to be the rector of St. Barnabas in Havana, Illinois, in the diocese of Springfield. In 2011, the Lees are retired in Atlanta and it is the 50th year of Lee's ordination. In their retirement, they attend "a very fine parish" of the Anglican Church of North America in communion with Nigeria and Uganda. They pray regularly for Bishop Lawrence and the Diocese of South Carolina.

Lee also said that they greatly enjoyed the friendship of Bishop Allison and "that the Lord's blessings outweighed any difficulties; Charleston will always hold a special place in our affections."

In May 1993, Hampson gave the vestry a complete analysis of membership transfers reporting a net gain of forty-three members during the last four years even though ninety-eight members had transferred to St. Andrews in Mt. Pleasant.

St. Philip's Spire reported in the February 1994 issue that the congregational meeting held in January was one of the most pleasant in recent memory. There was no controversy or unpleasantness. Discourse soon popped up. Hampson, with the backing of the vestry, changed the worship schedule: "8:00 a.m. Holy Communion Rite I; 9:30 a.m. Contemporary Worship Holy Communion Rite II (all Sundays) and 11:00 a.m. Traditional Worship Morning Prayer Rite I on the first, third, and fifth Sundays with Holy Communion Rite I second and fourth Sundays." The new schedule began June 19, 1994.

Some parishioners felt the congregation would be divided in two. A newspaper article was published in the *Post & Courier* on Sunday July 3, 1994, entitled "Battles split churches." Hampson quickly replied with a letter to the newspaper's editor, Barbara Williams, and the publisher, Andy Anderson. Hampson stated that there is diversity at St. Philip's and he thanked God for the "traditionalists" who endorse St. Philip's and he praised the "renewalists" who bring joy and vitality to our faith. "As in a family, so in a church, it is painful to face our differences, but necessary to talk about them." Hampson said, "the current 'split' was somewhat exaggerated.

In 1994, the church hired Dr. John Savage from Canal Winchester, Ohio, who founded the LEAD system that has reached more than 100,000 people in fourteen countries working with churches and other organizations. His expertise was in fields of listening dynamics, conflict management, resolution, etc. Information from surveys and other input was received from clergy and parishioners.

There were pro and con letters about and to Hampson. When letters are written, particularly against someone, the writer will most often include a sentence like, "My friends agree with me." or "I know many people who agree with me." That makes it difficult to gauge the mood of the time, but there was so much discord in St. Philip's that Savage was brought in.

Even bringing in Savage irritated one parishioner. "The complete dissatisfaction of a large portion of the congregation in multiple areas was made abundantly clear during the weekend of the Savage workshop." The writer continued that because Savage had been hired, "we are now involved in an expensive, superficial, and in my opinion, futile attempt at a 'quick fix.' There cannot be any remediation in this. The only solution is the replacement of Jim Hampson … Hundreds of former St. Philippians (now) at other churches attest to the damage caused to this church by Hampson."

Reverend Doug Peterson, church business manager, reported that there did not seem to be a higher number of transfers than normal.

Another parishioner wrote to Hampson, "We wish to reinforce you, Bishop Salmon, members of the vestry and others with our wholehearted support of you and your ministry. In a time of watered down morals and chaotic society it is a great blessing to have a strong and Godly rector who teaches us in black and white, not gray. We appreciate your Bible based theology and thank God for it in a time when many church leaders have gone astray."

More than 100 St. Philippians, "traditionalists" and "renewalists," joined together and "gave unselfishly of their time and energy" to make the first steps possible.

In May 1995, Hampson presented the findings of the "Savage Worship Committee on Service Schedule." Barbara Boatwright said it was a turning point when the committee turned to God and asked Him to do His will. The new schedule that was unanimously approved by the vestry was announced.

In 1995, St. Philippian R. Edward Holt III was treasurer of the diocese.

As previously written, Rev. Maurice Lee left St. Philip's in 1994 and Rev. Jay Fowler left in 1995. In January 1996, Hampson reported to the vestry while searching for additional clergy, he had many positive comments about Rev. George F. Weld II. On February 13, the vestry approved Weld and on March 12 he opened the vestry meeting with prayer.

In April 1996, Mike Cooke, as he was departing, presented a brief report on the youth minister position and introduced David Dubay who was the diocesan coordinator for youth ministry. Dubay would become an assistant rector at St. Philip's in 2005.

At the November 1996 vestry meeting, a motion that was made was seconded by Arthur Wilcox and passed unanimously. "When John Haden McCormick completes seminary and ordination, he shall serve as Assistant Rector at the pleasure of the Rector." He was hired as the third minister.

Also in November, the vestry unanimously decided to rehire Canon Samuel T. Cobb who was youthful looking and energetic at age eighty. He was to work twenty hours per week plus three services and special assignments.

Cobb was rehired, at least partially, to douse some of the fires in the congregation. Some parishioners preferred Cobb for baptisms, weddings and burials and he was not welcome to perform these services from 1987 to 1996. Cobb admitted there were differences between himself and Hampson. Cobb said he often tried to change Hampson's mind but he never succeeded. Even so they had a good relationship.

In November, Charlotte McCrady sent a letter to the vestry complimenting McCormick's recent sermon on the Trinity. McCormick was to oversee: assisting, worship support, ushers, readers, chalice bearers, acolytes, altar guild, small groups, hospital and home visits, Stephen's Ministry, recovery, support groups and counseling.

Because Craig Bennett, Jr. felt the church needed to know its attendance for the past five years, he volunteered to do the research and put the figures on a spreadsheet. Bennett did a very thorough job. In 1984, the year Scott arrived, the annual attendance was around 45,000 and by 1985 it shot up to 58,000. After Scott departed, a decline set in going down to around 43,000 from 1989 through 1991. Between 1992 and May 1997, attendance went up and down between 38,000 and 40,000.

At the vestry meeting on October 21, 1997, it was announced that Weld had resigned.

At the January 1998 vestry meeting, Frank Rogers moved that Haden McCormick's position be changed to assistant rector. The motion carried. In June, the vestry agreed for Hampson to take a sabbatical in Cambridge, England, from August 10, 1998, until

January 10, 1999, and gave him a monthly $2,000 housing allowance for his use in Cambridge.

Eight days after Hampson left, Rogers made a motion at the vestry meeting that McCormick should be in charge of the people, programs and the spiritual side of the parish. He was also charged with the responsibility for both the administrative and ministerial staff.

In January 1999, Hampson thanked the vestry for his recent sabbatical and for a financially good year in 1998. While he was on sabbatical, Hampson felt an orderly transition for his retirement should be planned. Bishop Salmon, Hampson and the wardens, Frank Rogers and Steve Graudin, all agreed that his retirement date should be tied to an event such as the completion of the parish house and not a specific time or date. Rogers was appointed transition manager. The bishop and Hampson agreed his "gifts to St. Philip's" should be in counseling, preaching and teaching with administrative duties turned over to others. The vestry agreed. In February, the transition manager and wardens sought to ensure McCormick's continued employment in a significant clergy role until Hampson's retirement.

Lon Burris headed a tremendous effort to take a "census" of St. Philippian's by phone attempting to reach 1,300 people. Ruby Bennett said "DO NOT CALL –old and ill," Mr. and Mrs. Tony Harrigan lived in Washington, D.C., Kingman & Joan Hodgkiss – "she was a Sams," Preston Hipp's wife responded, Lenora Kessler – husband responded, W. Howell Morrison and Kitty and Mike Mullins responded and Dan Russler was a new member.

THE YOUTH, MEN'S MINISTRIES & THE LADIES

Mrs. Jody Anderson was president of the ECW in 1988. At the same time, St. Philip's took over the Little School that was run by Frances Bonsal. Four and five year olds would attend a weekly chapel service and would learn the basic Christian values in personal relationships. In 1990, Mrs. Blount Ellison was president of the ECW.

Some of the 1990 Sunday school teachers were Suzanne Buckley (later McCord), Steve and Tracy Graudin, Kyra Morris, Preston and Laura Hipp, Malcolm and Caroline Rhodes, Creighton and Nina Evans. The Little School was booming with fifty-five students. In 1991, parents of the children at the Little School were very concerned that the construction on the parish house would disrupt the classes and they asked that the school be moved. The restoration committee assured parents no work would begin prior to April 15, 1992, at the earliest. It was suggested Mike Cooke start looking for a new school location.

Louisa Hawkins was president of the ECW in 1992 followed by Jane Hagood. John Kerr advised the vestry that Jody Anderson was chairing the spring tour and needed help with publicity. Gordon Lyle gave the vestry an overview of a prayer ministry which he had been asked to chair.

In August, Mark Phillips reported that even though the Little School was going to move to Grace Church during the renovation, it was still called the St. Philip's Little School. By November 1993, Frannie Bonsal requested that the school be permanently relocated to Grace Church. The vestry approved the concept but had concerns that the school maintain a Christian identity and that St. Philippians children be given preference. The finances were to be turned over to Grace Church on January 1, 1994.

Frances Bonsal, who died November 10, 2011, at age 71, taught for forty-six years at the Little School and was its director. "She left a host of her students who adored her," in addition to many cousins, and Godchildren. The funeral was November 12 at St. Philip's.

Mike Cooke, the DCE, submitted a seven page report in the fall of 1993 concerning the Sunday school and the adult forums. He wrote, "The goal for everyone who participates in the St. Philip's Sunday school must be to know, love and follow Jesus!" Cooke thanked three exceptional ladies, Suzanne Buckley, Mary White and Jane Hagood, who had taken care of the nursery. He wrote, "This year's supervisor, I can report with full confidence, will prove to be another exceptional lady. She is a fantastic mom, a great manager and a credentialed consultant in child development. We will work well together because she is also my best friend – she is my wife, Lynda."

In July 1994, Jane Guerard was president of the ECW. There was a note in the December minutes stating the name ECW had been replaced with the name "Women of St. Philip's." Hampson enthusiastically reported on the recent Cursillo where Joan Hagan was lay rector.

Baptisms in 1996:

April 27 Rufus Calvin Barkley, IV, son of Jessica Henrici Barkley and Rufus Calvin Barkley, III
April 28 Elizabeth Sams Huey, daughter of Elizabeth Hodgkiss Huey and William Crawford Huey
May 12 David Maybank Hagood, Jr., son of Elizabeth McMillan Hagood and David Maybank Hagood
May 12 Madeleine Elise Kennedy, daughter of Elise Rivers Kennedy and Sean Thomas Kennedy
1996 Weddings:

April 27 Martha Izard Middleton to Bradley Ware Wallace
May 4 Rebecca Motte Gilbreth to Daniel Paul Herres
May 11 Nancy Layton Dilks to William Christopher Ravenel

May 18 Eleanor Laurens Hastie to Louis Twells Parker, Jr.
May 25 James Conlon Nimmich to Elizabeth Harris

In October 1998, the vestry passed a motion to discontinue the annual Kanuga weekend in 1999 because of the low attendance during the past three years.

THEOLOGY, EVANGELISM & MISSIONS

Hampson said he felt that $1,500 should be placed in the charity fund to assist the street people who regularly come into the church for assistance. Hampson also asked the vestry for an annual $700 car allowance for business manager Rev. Ball because Hampson had asked him to visit and to take communion to shut-ins. The vestry agreed to both requests.

Mary Anne Hanckel reported in November 1987 the ECW bazaar was a great success raising $13,000. Of that, $10,000 was given to help support the Johnstons' ministry in Haiti where Thomas William Johnston, Jr., former St. Philippian vestryman, would be appointed missionary/administrator on Bishop Garnier's staff for the office of development.

Johnston grew up in Spartanburg, majored in forestry at Sewanee, graduating in 1978. He worked in forestry and later graduated from the law school at Cumberland University in Birmingham where he met and married his wife, Rees Moyler. They moved to Charleston where he took a position in the law firm of Buist, Smythe, Moore and McGee. They bought a downtown house and became involved with St. Philip's. In 1987, there were two children, Welden (2 ½) and Atlee (14 months).

Johnston, who was moving to Haiti, was asked why he was moving there after he had established himself as a successful lawyer. He replied that he wanted to make certain he was called to something and not running from something else. His law firm gave him a leave of absence.

He agreed to stay in Haiti, working with Episcopal priest Pere Valdema on the island of La Gonâve, from 1987 to 1989 even though he had to raise $2,115 each month. But in fifteen days, the fund, that was administered by a committee of St. Philippians, grew from $70.00 to $18,000. Johnston was director of the partnership program of the Episcopal diocese of Haiti where he coordinated all incoming donations to that diocese. Johnston had to learn Creole and Rees took a two-week Episcopal class to acquaint missionaries with alien cultures. They lived in a cinder-block bungalow without air conditioning or potable water but the people were friendly. Johnston traveled a great deal, usually by donkey.

Prior to 1991, St. Philippian's donated money to help build a church on La Gonâve named St. John the Baptist, dedicated in 1991, that became St. Philip's sister church.

After an embargo prevented travel to Haiti from 1992 through 1994, an assessment trip in 1995 was made to Haiti to learn what was needed. At that time, student scholarships were raised through St. Philip's so Haitians on La Gonâve could attend one of the nine Episcopal schools – each school was attached to an Episcopal Church. Other Episcopal dioceses and church denominations also have helped to support the diocese of Haiti.

Pere Valdema has spoken at St. Philip's in the past. In 2002, he was relocated to the main land and he was replaced by Pere Alexendre Soner who has spoken at St. Philip's numerous times.

Gerry and Suzanne McCord have led a mission trip to Haiti virtually every year from 1996 to 2011. They have taken musical instruments, athletic equipment, school supplies and money for nutritional and water needs. These mission trips have made a huge difference in the lives of those people on La Gonâve.

The St. Philip's Mission Trip to Haiti needs your support in many ways. You can donate equipment or money (501(c)3) but best of all actually traveling on the trip that has changed the lives of many participants. The 2012 trip was scheduled for June 20 to 25 and in 2013 from June 21 to June 26. Please visit the web site. www.lagonavepartners.org

Johnston was to return and graduate from Sewanee's seminary and he became an associate rector in 1995 at Grace Church. In 2012 he is a bishop in the AMIA church and rector of St. Peters in Mt. Pleasant.

In February 1988, Hampson and Dr. E.K. Wallace gave a report on their Honduras trip. The trip's goal was to explore forming a relationship with the Society of Anglican Missionaries and Senders (SAMS) and to work near San Pedro Sula. Others on this first trip included Garden Frampton, Frenchie Richards, Ann Welch and Lavinia Thaxton. After the trip was so successful, a commitment was made to send mission trips for eight years. Hampson was on the board of SAMS.

Dr. Wallace brought two children to Charleston for needed surgery and treatment. . Gilberta Pineda (7) had corrections to the urinary system and Nicia Vaquedro (14) suffering from a severe arthritic condition had surgery to correct her hands. Garden Frampton and Frenchie Richards invited Nicia into their homes on a rotating system and doctors Ed Hay and Will Middleton provided medical services pro bono. The St. Philip's Churchwomen provided for the air tickets for the two children and Gilberta's mother. A Honduran doctor wrote a thank you letter to St. Philip's.

In the proposed 1988 budget, $60,000 was to be allotted for missions and ministries.

Bishop Allison gave notice of his resignation which shocked and deeply saddened St. Philip's vestry. The vestry passed a resolution on February 18, 1989, stating that

Allison was alarmed by the direction in which the national church was headed. He was also alarmed about the harmful indoctrination of children, the manipulative methodology used and much more. Allison had repeatedly and forcefully spoken out against the "prevailing winds and strange doctrines without and within the Episcopal Church."

Palmer Gaillard proposed the vestry adopt a resolution supporting Bishop Allison. The vestry agreed and the resolution was written by Gaillard, Glenn and Helen Barkley: It was resolved by the vestry that St. Philip's regretted the bishop's resignation but the vestry would continue to support him in his ministry and they urged him to continue to speak out against such radical teachings which are contrary to scripture. It was further resolved that the vestry call on all Episcopalians to support Bishop Allison.

As previously written, Bishop Allison resigned as bishop so he could have the time to speak out against the national church, its policies and teachings.

At Easter 1989, Hampson sent out a letter to the congregation entitled *He Is Risen*. He wrote, "When you have been raised by Christ, you want to share it with others." It was about 1972 and things were not going badly, at least not outwardly, but he felt inwardly something was missing in his life and he knew it. At that time, after preaching, the Rev. John Stott had dinner at the rectory with the Hampsons and Hampson said "Whatever it was, he had it and I didn't, and I wanted it. No secret about it," he said, "it was the Risen Christ dwelling in the heart."

Later, on a winter night, Hampson "knelt down and opened the doors of my personality and invited Christ to come into my heart. It was a change that I shall never forget. I learned later that my believing wife had been praying especially for me over the past year."

During that summer, his best friend in the seminary, Alden Hathaway, came for a visit with his family, and Hampson told Hathaway what he had done and what a great difference it made in his life and ministry. He said he had always been a churchman but never until then as a <u>decided</u> Christian.

It turned out that Hathaway had been on the verge of leaving the ministry in some sort of spiritual despair. "Instead, he gave his life to Christ and Christ gave him back his ministry and he emerged as a leader for renewal in the Episcopal Church."

Hampson wrote that, "I tell you this to give you hope."

In May 1989, the vestry wholeheartedly endorsed Suzy MCall's interest and calling to the missionary field in Costa Rica under the auspices of SAMS. In July, she told the vestry she would work at St. Philip's one more year and in 1990 she would go to Costa Rica.

The vestry agreed to give the diocese 19% of NDBI[29] in 1990. That translated into $191,618 as opposed to the $150,618 given in 1989. It was about this time that a decision was made by the diocese that no money that was received from churches in the diocese of South Carolina would go to the national church. Yet years later, Episcopalians including St. Philippian's would grumble about all the money that was being sent to the national church. It was a wonderful excuse not to give money to the church.

In June 1991, Hampson and the vestry signed a letter to Bishop Haines of the diocese of Washington, D.C. condemning his ordination of a lesbian. Hampson led a Bible study so the members of the vestry would have Biblical knowledge of the subject. The Bible verses he chose were: Leviticus 20:6,10,13; Genesis 19:1-11; Romans 1:18-27; and First Corinthians 6:9-10. Hampson said, "There is hope for the homosexual who repents."

Hampson's July 9 Bible study for the vestry was about the Lord's Prayer (Matthew 7:9) with respect to "the Fatherhood." Hampson said, "God calls us to call Him Father. It is not passive. This counters the movement within the church to revise the masculine language in the original Biblical texts and in worship services."

At the January 1995 vestry meeting, there was a lengthy discussion about changing the way mission money was spent. The old model saw two kinds of expenses, parish expenses that were spent within the parish and mission expenses for money spent outside of the parish. The new emphasis saw only one kind of expense whether parish, community or foreign. The vestry said the parish itself had become a mission statement and local and foreign mission spending would be allocated and spent according to the church's operating plan. In April, Hampson spoke about the missions the church supported and said they should try and target those with the greatest need rather than give a little to every group. Hampson said to see Mark 12:28-34 for the "Great Commandment" and Matthew 28:10-20 for the Biblical basis for mission outreach.

Gene Lesesne of the foreign mission committee chose the areas they wished to support by praying about the requests and talking with the leaders of those organizations. Bob Ables said the home missions committee chose their areas of interest very much the way foreign missions did.

In 1995, foreign missions expenditures for the year totaled $65,679.48 and home missions spent $44,754.

---

29 NDBI is a diocesan term "Net Disposable Budgeted Income" or another way of saying normal operating income for a given year. Technically it is composed of three items: pledge payments and plate offerings, net operating investment income and other operating income. Thank you Chisolm Leonard for this information. It was in the late 1980s and early 1990s, that the financial reports got more sophisticated and very lengthy. The vestry at that time seemed to use the term NDBI frequently. Leonard said in 2011 the term NDBI is used only to figure out the percentage of St. Philip's funds that would be given to the diocese.

St. Philip's Vision Statement as written in 1996

"By the Grace of God and the power of the Holy Spirit, <u>St. Philip's Church</u> will continue her historical role in this community as a <u>Biblically based, Christ-centered</u> Episcopal Church.

"Our <u>purpose is to glorify God</u> through worship, prayer, fellowship and teaching, and to <u>build up the body of Christ</u> through our sacrifice and <u>care for one another.</u>

"Our mission is to <u>love others as God loved us</u> by spreading the gospel and serving in the Charleston area and beyond, as the Lord Jesus gives us call, inspiration and opportunity."

Thomas C. Reeves wrote in 1997 *The Empty Church: The Suicide of Liberal Christianity*. David Klinghoffer, literary review editor at National Review, reviewed the book and a copy was included in the vestry minutes. Reeves asked why should the Episcopal, Presbyterian and other mainline churches survive? These churches have diverged further and further from Christian orthodoxy while losing parishioners in droves. "The liberals in charge think they know why. In our 'post Christian' era, they maintain old-fashioned Christianity repels potential churchgoers. The solution is to follow the descending path of modern culture to whatever depths it leads. As one Episcopal priest explains, 'Every time that we ordain someone who is not a heterosexual white male, we gain hundreds of new members.'"

Reeves wrote, "Except that it doesn't work that way. The more heterodox – multicultural, multi-doctrinal – the churches become, the more congregants they lose, and yet they keep it up. The United Presbyterians, United Methodists and American Baptists were pro-abortion even before *Roe v Wade*. As early as 1982, at a United Methodist Women's conference, the Greek earth goddess Gaia was called upon for a blessing. A 1993 conference funded by the Presbyterian, Methodist, Lutheran and American Baptist churches 'featured a veneration of Sophia, Creator God' ... and rites from other religions such as the American Indian tobacco ritual."

"Once the Bible and other holy documents have been stripped of their 'necessary offense,' any religion based on those texts is reduced to a mere adjunct of the surrounding culture rather than a challenge to it. The typical congregant at a liberal church finds it increasingly hard to see why he should spend Sunday morning in a place where secular views are simply echoed."

Reeves called for an orthodox revival. "But an orthodox awakening in the pews would have to get past those mainline leaders. In the meantime, serious Christians can take refuge in serious churches, as they already do, swelling the evangelical Protestant groupings." Reeves ended by writing, "Why should the Episcopalians survive?" The reviewer ended, "It is the one question this excellent book cannot answer?"

The Alpha Course was first brought to St. Philip's in 1998 by the Rev. Haden McCormick. The course began September 13 and was followed by another session in the winter/spring quarter of 1999. More than 150 people attended.

Alpha began at Holy Trinity Brompton in London in the late 1970s as a means of presenting the basic principle of the Christian faith to new Christians in a relaxed and informal setting. When former lawyer the Rev. Nicky Gumbel took over the course, he realized it could appeal to non-churchgoers and he adapted it to make all welcome. During the 1990s, the course spread internationally and continues to grow with more than 135,000 courses running in 169 countries including 5,000 courses running in fifty states. The courses are generally ten weeks and provide good food and fellowship. Many come who know nothing about Christianity and participants can ask any questions. Alpha now offers the courses for the youth, college students, young adults, for Catholics, the military, prisoners and those in the workplace and more.

In 2012, Alpha is still offered at St. Philip's four times a year. Why not try it?

In December 1998, McCormick discussed the new "Marriage Preparations at St. Philip's" pamphlet. He also said the church had collected $30,000 for the Honduran Relief and that six water purification machines would soon be sent.

FINANCES & THE VESTRY

Hampson attended his first vestry meeting on October 5, 1987. Also attending were Glenn, Ball and Mary Anne Hanckel, president of the ECW.

In December 1987, Bill Elmore pointed out to the vestry there was a concern. First, the 1987 budget included $70,899 as an expense item for the "Restoration Expenses" but there was no corresponding expense in the 1988 budget. It was noted in the finance committee meeting that the vestry decided some years ago that a significant amount should be included in each year's budget for restoration items. Since the 1988 budget had no provision for restoration expenses, those expenses would have to be paid out of "Trust B."

The 1988 proposed budget was $786,161.

In January 1988, the vestry contacted the Ben Gill of Resource Services, Inc. of Dallas regarding the possibility of that firm assisting the church in a capital fund-raising. There would no charge for the first stage and they were told the firm worked on Biblical principles. In February, the firm estimated it would probably raise one and half to two times of the church's budget with Gill's estimated charge from $40,000 to $70,000. The new vestry in May voted unanimously to enter into a contract with that company because other churches had given them good references.

In February 1988, the vestry called upon church architect Dan Beaman to determine what he had learned about the physical condition of the church. He said that in addition to a thorough inspection of the church, he had spent considerable time reviewing vestry minutes and reviewing information from the church's archives to learn what he could about the building. He regretfully advised the vestry that "the church records were poor at best."

Rev. John C, Ball resigned in April as business manager. Ball would not complete thirty years in the ministry until June 30, 1988, so Hampson suggested his full salary be paid until that date as it would benefit his retirement income. The motion carried.

Hampson complained his personal long distance calls made from his residence were not being paid by the church although he thought the church would pay for them. Tom Myers presumed such calls would be included under utilities but Kitty Holt did not consider those calls as a utility. Hampson said the reason for the high amount of $260 was because his three children were all in other cities. The vestry asked the senior warden, treasurer and the finance committee to make a recommendation. In May, Hampson met with the wardens and the finance chairman and he advised them he had paid the $260 bill and would continue to do so and "that the matter is settled."

The senior warden addressed his concern about rampant rumors, misstatements and half-truths regarding a number of topics that were heard in the congregation. He stated that in his opinion, the gossip was dividing the church and making the work of the vestry much harder. He called on all vestry members to correct any misstatements and above all to make sure that in any discussions in which members were involved, to ensure the truth was known and false statements corrected. He reiterated his concern and called on all members to work together for the growth and progress of St. Philip's.

Nick Zervos, chairman of the "Special Committee," recommended that Mrs. Charles (Jan) Hipp be hired as the new business manager. She would be employed prior to July 1, 1988.

Philip Kassebaum agreed to serve as chairman of the renovation fund drive.

In August, Zervos reported from the "financial advisory subcommittee" that the budget projection would show a year end deficit of $47,000. Several cost cutting suggestions were made: postpone all building maintenance, postpone new choir robes ($2,000), limit newspaper advertising, pass the hat at pot luck suppers, use prudence with any reception, etc. The group realized that the above recommendations would produce nominal savings. A letter would be sent to the parishioners stressing the need for extra funds and the committee urged the vestry to end the year in the black. In December 1988, Zervos said the balance sheet showed the budget was in the black by $264.

Two receptionists were hired, Carolyn Warlick and Barbara Lisle, one to work in the morning and the other in the afternoon.

As previously written, Helen Barkley and her son-in-law, Dr. James Ravenel, served together on a vestry. In 1988, the same thing happened again except her nephew, Dr. Clay Robertson, who was senior warden, made it a family trio.

Office manager, Rhett Barrett, resigned from her long held position on February 28, 1989. A letter was sent to the congregation asking for donations so the vestry could surprise the Barretts with a Caribbean cruise. They had a good time.

Mary Perry, who lived at 2A Ladson Street, resigned her church position on October 7 and the vestry paid her $60.00 a month for the balance of her expected life. She continued to work on the ladies Altar Guild.

In December 1988, the vestry signed the contract with the architect so the renovation fund could continue. The names "restoration fund" and "jubilee fund" had given away to "Fourth Century Fund" by 1989.

There were 850 household units in 1989 capable of pledging at St. Philip's and by March only 37% or 313 pledges had been received. Weekly pledges ranged from $5.21 weekly to $450.

Hampson revived seven "Vestry Standards" written by the Archbishop of Canterbury Rowan Williams in 1954. The standards were actually meant for all Episcopalians:

1. To follow the example of Christ in home and daily life, and to bear personal witness to Him.
2. To be regular in private prayer day by day.
3. To read the Bible carefully.
4. To come to church every Sunday.
5. To receive the Holy Communion faithfully and regularly.
6. To give personal service to church, neighbors and community.
7. To give money for the work of the parish and diocese and for the work of the church at home and overseas.

Jan Hipp proposed hiring someone at a minimum wage to be in the narthex during July and August to sell posters, show video presentations, to lock up, etc. The vestry agreed.

In 1989, Teddy Guerard replaced DeRossett Myers as the church's lawyer. Mrs. John Rivers gave the church stock worth $61,990.75. The total pledges, gifts and memorials received by August 8, 1989, was $1,628,444.

In January 1990, Winfield Sapp was senior warden and Frenchie Richards was junior warden. Scott Hood was elected treasurer and Charles W. Knowlton, Jr. was elected secretary. Newly elected vestry members were George Greene, John Kerr, Bill Warlick and David Maybank. At the same time, it was announced that the 1989 budget ended with a $46,000 surplus. The proposed 1990 budget was $1,023,722 and total assets were $2,200,628.22.

At the same time, Hampson, Glenn and Dr. E.K. Wallace met with Leonard Taylor, sexton, and his assistant, Matthew Sweat, and asked them to resign as of January 9, 1990. Problems with Taylor escalated over the years but the decision to ask Taylor to resign had been postponed to give him an opportunity to improve his performance and attitude. The vestry paid his salary and his medical insurance through February. Taylor had a very disrespectful nick name for Hampson and Hampson may not have even known that. In regard to Sweat, his performance in the light of the necessary requirements for the position made it necessary to relieve him of his duties.

Larry White, the new sexton, was called a facilities assistant and lived at 67 Cumberland Street. He had two assistants, Kristen Kifer and Kenny Stewart. After Nick Zervos said the new sexton's Sunday attire was not appropriate, White improved his dressing but he had to leave St. Philip's because he was running the Redeemer Mission full time and could not do both. He would take homeless and former convicts to Kanuga.

Some people love to grumble about "what's wrong" with the church or any church. One undercurrent was that Hampson was "paid too much money." Andy Anderson discussed Hampson's compensation package with Bishop Allison who was surprised to find out what the total was because of the rumors suggesting Hampson's package was so much higher. Allison said he did not believe the compensation was at all out of line considering the size and *complexity* (italics by author) of St. Philip's.

In May 1990, John Kerr challenged the vestry for a renewal commitment to the church and all of its activities during the time when Hampson was all alone. People forget that Hampson had no permanent assistant for one year.

In June, Mr. and Mrs. John Welch gave eighty-five shares of Delta Air Lines stock as their pledge to the Fourth Century. Their daughter, Ann, resigned from her St. Philip's office job on September 7, 1990, to take a position at St. Andrew's Church in Mt. Pleasant. Rhett Barrett agreed to help out temporarily until a replacement could be found.

In August, Frenchie Richards chastised her fellow vestry members. She stated that "she seemed only to be dealing in crisis management and that the majority had not taken the prayer ministry seriously." She handed out an article by R.C. Sproul, a renowned, orthodox Presbyterian minister, to each vestry member to take home and read, study and to pray about each person's prayer partner. Vestry pray partners were changed monthly.

In 1990, there had been a dispute as to whether the chapel should be turned over to the choir for its use. Many St. Philippian's were against the idea and the vestry waivered. In September, John Kerr made some interesting comments stating the vestry should not have multiple votes on the same issue. He continued, "Instead, we should remember that the <u>Vestry of St. Philip's is never going to please all the people all the time unless we do nothing.</u> We will get into trouble if we try to 'fix it' so every person can be happy. When that happens, get on your knees!" Jay (Fowler) preached a sermon stating that a church that is moving and growing in the Lord is going to have problems but a dead church has no problems. St. Philip's is very much alive as evidenced by the 390 people in attendance at the 10:00 a.m. service on the fourth Sunday in August.

As was standard, Hampson opened the vestry meeting with a prayer and then led a Bible study. In October, he chose Ecclesiastes 5: 18-19 regarding the Protestant work ethic. "Here is what I have seen: It is good and fitting for one to eat and drink, and to enjoy the good of all his labor in which toils under the sun all the days of his life which God gives him; for it is his heritage. As for every man to whom God has given riches and wealth, and given him power to eat of it, to receive his heritage and rejoice in his labor – this is the gift of God."

A memorandum was given to the vestry in December 1990 by Andy Anderson concerning the 1991 budget. "I see us operating at a level our parishioners are unwilling to support, and I don't think we can go on like this. The financial texture of the church is now such that we have zero tolerance for a deficit, because all of our liquid assets, and more, will apparently be required to complete Phase I of the renovation. I can see no other solution other than learning to make do with less – less programs, less administrative overhead, fewer employees, and ultimately a sparse renovation program. I think it's unrealistic to expect any bonanza of financial in-flows during the recession year that 1991 promises to be."

Anderson continued, "I do not believe that we can continue to run St. Philip's in a financially prudent way without a major overhaul and restatement of our priorities. We've been lucky so far, but our luck is running out in the absence of a major commitment to state what is important to us and what is not."

The 1991 proposed budget had been reduced from $1,065,149 to $945,000. The actual 1990 budget was $1,014,480.

New faces on the vestry in 1991 were Jim Broody, Rutledge Coleman and Bill Warlick. Joy Hunter, who was previously a staff writer for the American Bible Society and was very proficient on work processing, replaced Rhett Barrett.

In May 1991, Gerald (Jerry) McCord made a memorial to his late wife, Carol Martin from Andrews. Jerry and Carol were married on June 15, 1984, and the family included her two children Jeff and Laura Wolter from a previous marriage. Carol was confirmed at St. Philip's and six months after the marriage she was diagnosed with a serious illness. After enduring more than three years of treatments, "the Lord took her home" on August 8, 1988. Jeff and Laura were confirmed at St. Philip's on August 30, 1988. The interest from the memorial was intended to go "to the Glory of God and Kingdom Work."

In April 1994, the vestry explored ways of raising the $800,000 to $1,000,000 needed for the addition of the new parish hall. In May, it was reported that as much as $700,000 had been saved during the renovation. He added that he and recent vestries had always seen this as one continuous project and he recommended that they proceed. Andy Anderson offered a prayer of thanksgiving for God's provisions through the entire restoration project. In June, the consensus was to proceed with a fall fund raising $1,000,000 to complete the new construction and renovation of the existing parish house.

Hampson's secretary, Sally Steers resigned to take a position at the Catholic cathedral.

In 1992, George Greene was elected senior warden and Ben Hagood as junior warden. Five of six newly elected members of the vestry were Bob Ables, Foster Gaillard, Ed Holt, Ann Payne and Mark Phillips.

Marvin Powell was hired as the new sexton on March 12, 1992.

At the end of June, the deficit had grown from $29,000 to $54,000 and Andy Anderson projected the deficit at the end of the year could grow as high $127,000 if they continued on the same tack. The vestry made cutbacks of $66,000 and thanked Hampson for offering to take a 10% pay cut, but the vestry declined his offer. By December 1992, the financial situation was better. "Everyone on the vestry agreed that we needed to give continual praise and thanks to God for his blessing on a fantastic turnaround in giving."

In November, "George Greene requested that due to his age, he wondered if the Secretary (John Kerr) could print the minutes in a larger type. In deference to his elder, the Secretary stated he would honor the request."

Perhaps the vestry was getting a little punchy because there were so many issues as the year ended just between finances and property that there were four vestry meetings from November 17 through December 23. The December 15th meeting lasted until 11:00 p.m.

Also, there was humor usually led by John Kerr. Kerr, who was from Dillon, died at home on the Isle of Palms on Wednesday, July 4, 2012, age 66. He was survived by his wife, Rebecca H. Kerr and five children. A Citadel garduate, he served in Vietnam from 1968 to 1970 earning a Bronze Star, an Air Medal and a Purple Heart. He practiced law for thirty-nine years and in 1990 was a founding member of the Charleston Men's Choir. He sang in St. Philip's choir for thirty years. He is buried at St. Philip's.

Benjamin Hagood, Jr. was elected senior warden in 1993 and Joe Land was junior warden. Those elected to the vestry were Preston Hipp, Steve Swanson and Dr. E.K. Wallace for three year terms and Ken Johnson DMD and Joanna Macmurphy for one year term each.

Malcolm Rhodes was stewardship chairman and Richard Moore headed the all member visits. Joe Land personally signed all the letters sent to the 800 plus giving units requesting they respond to the church regarding anticipated giving in 1993.

During this time, the first thirty minutes at the vestry meeting were allotted to the "Open Forum." Any parishioner could ask questions, etc. At the August 10 meeting two parishioners attended. Caroline Rhodes noted the excitement generated by the increase in the number of young adults at St. Philip's and she wanted to encourage the vestry to have more involvement in the adult forum and social gatherings where new members were welcomed. Martha Elizabeth Ferguson spoke supporting Hampson's leadership.

In 1995, Mark Phillips was senior warden and Preston Hipp was junior warden. Gene Lesesne was secretary. Steve Swanson resigned from the vestry due to personal demands. Those new to the vestry were Eugene Foxworth, Maybank Hagood, Richard Hutson, Dorothy Anderson and Edward Morrison.

Donna Hickman was the receptionists/secretary and Mary Anne Hanckel was the assets administrator. Joy Hunter was publicist/secretary.

In 1995, Dot Anderson spearheaded the movement to preserve St. Philip's records and she wanted the records to stay in the church. Some of the vestry thought all of the church's records should be sent to the South Carolina Historical Society but Dot prevailed. She advised the vestry a humidity free area would be required in which to store the records. That area was built and has been called "The Archives" ever since. Prior to that, Dot remembers that all the records were stuffed into a closet along with soft drinks and other items.

In June, Gene Foxworth and Mark Phillips volunteered to attend a workshop on how to write grants. Two grants were received: one for $1,260 was sent on December 18, 1995, from the State Historical Records Advisory Board to the church; The second grant for $2,300 was sent to the church on August 2, 1996. The grants were used to send people to seminars, to learn how to manage the archives, to purchase shelves, to have documents put on microfilm and for other uses. More than twenty volunteers helped put the archives together.

Archive volunteers have included Gordon and Margaret Garrett, Grace Creel and Lenora Kessler, who completed a complete listing of the church wardens from 1725 to the present date.

Many thanks to Dot Anderson and others who made the archives possible.

In June 1995, Hampson said that since the Savage worship committee had been implemented that more surveys would come. Because some people were still uneasy with passing the peace, Fowler explained that we express a peace to one another prior to coming to the communion table. It was recommended that some of the traditional Episcopal observances be taught. In November, Hampson asked Andy Anderson and Barbara Boatwright to stir up the Savage committees to continue the work. He also suggested that they should not deal with any "anonymous rumors or gossip."

The Implementation Steering Committee (ISC) was asked in 1996 to consider seventeen pastoral recommendations that emerged from the Savage process. The committee responded that a high priority was to make an effort to get to know and to respect one another. That would take a "matter of attitude and changed hearts so that the congregation could heal itself."

The top priority was that, "The Rector should focus on the spiritual life and relationships in the parish" with particular emphasis on pastoring and participating in the various activities of the church family life. In short, Hampson needed to know the congregation and to demonstrate his care by spending time with them.

Lon Burris in May 1997 was charged with the closure of the Savage reports. They would be reviewed and recommendations would be made to the vestry concerning actions that should be taken.

The end of year financial report showed a total income for 1995 as $1,131,582.49 of which $844,592.88 were from pledges. Expenses were $1,196.086.51 leaving a deficit of $64,504.02 for 1995. The deficit the previous year was $111,223.21.

The 1996 diocesan pledge report showed the amounts paid to the diocese from each church. The top four were: St. Philip's - $129,052, St. Michael's - $115,000, St. Andrews Mt. Pleasant – $100,000, St. Helena's in Beaufort - $85,000

In 1996, Mark Phillips was senior warden and Eugene Foxworth, Jr. was junior warden. Gene Lesesne was secretary and in August Heyward Harvey was appointed treasurer by the vestry to fill a one year unexpired term to end on June 30, 1997. Harvey served as treasurer until he resigned in July 2002. The delegates to the diocesan convention were the wardens, Helen Barkley and Catherine Jones.

Once again, a question came up about Hampson being overpaid. Business manager Glenn Peterson looked into the matter and found his compensation comparable to rectors at smaller churches such as St. Michael's, Grace and All Saint's. Mary Bissell compiled Hampson's compensation history from 1989 to 1996 and found he had not had a raise since 1990 plus his utility allowances had been decreased. Peterson said, 'It seems to me we are certainly not over paying Hampson."

In February, Arthur Wilcox made a motion that *Robert's Rules of Order* be adopted for the vestry. After much pro and con debate, the motion was defeated seven to six.

By January 1998, *Cannon's Rules* had been adopted by the vestry instead of *Robert's*.

By May 20 1996, Eric Williams was hired as the new sexton on a three month trial. By June, it was reported that Williams was performing well.

In April 1996, Laura Wichmann Hipp wrote "A Note of Thanks to the Body of Christ at St. Philip's." in *The Spire*. Preston and Laura learned in December 1995 that their six month old daughter, Delia, had a heart abnormality that required immediate surgery and the Hipps wanted to thank Jim and Sarah Hampson for being there at a critical time. When things were a bit scary at the hospital, Jim and Sarah would appear. Another unexpected blessing at MUSC was St. Philippian Dr. Ken Holden, a pediatric neurologist. Laura offered special thanks to Lynn Land who organized volunteers to bring them meals. Delia had more surgery, but as we know, she has grown up to be a very attractive young lady.

When rump committees met at the Carolina Yacht Club, it was a sign of dissension at St. Phillip's as occurred during the process of calling Renny Scott as rector. Bishop Salmon said, in effect, that such meetings involving only a portion of the vestry were not helpful.

It was decided vestry meetings would begin at 6:30 p.m. although there were a few morning vestry meetings that began at 6:00 a.m. Because many of the meetings lasted a long time, sometimes five hours that in August 1996 the vestry agreed no meeting would last longer than one and a half hours. In November, a limit of one hour vestry meetings was approved but there was a provision a meeting could be extended if approved by a majority. The vestry began to go into executive sessions during their meetings. Craig Bennett wanted the full vestry minutes to be mailed out with *The Spire*. At one point only one person would agree to run for the vestry because virtually no one wanted to endure the lengthy and loud meetings.

In 1997, Eugene Foxworth was senior warden and Frank D. Rogers, Jr. was junior warden. J. Palmer Gaillard, III, was secretary. Helen Barkley and John Welsh were elected to the vestry. Because church had no requirements or qualifications to run for the vestry, they, instead, used the diocesan requirements: a candidate must be confirmed communicant, who has taken communion at least three times in the year preceding their election and have attained the age of eighteen. Wardens must be at least twenty-one years old. Hampson and the vestry added responsibilities: be a Christian role model to all people, cooperate with the rector in promoting the spiritual welfare of the congregation and others.

In March, Rogers made a motion that the vestry would spend no more than $1,000 for a memorial plaque to be located in the narthex to honor those who donated to the "Fourth Century Fund." The motion passed. In November, the plaque had to be replaced, at a cost of $600, because of spelling errors. The plaque reads:

> "BLESSED ARE THE DEAD WHICH
> DIE IN THE LORD;
> YEA, SAITH THE SPIRIT THAT THEY
> MAY REST FROM THEIR LABOURS;
> AND THEIR WORKS DO FOLLOW THEM.
> REVELATION 14:13
>
> STEEPLE RENOVATION
> COMPLETED OCTOBER 1994
> TO THE GLORY OF GOD
> AND IN LOVING MEMORY OF:
>
> MATTHEW BAIRD BARKELY, KIRK SHERIDAN KESSLER,
> BARBARA ANN HUGUENIN, DUNCAN CHRISTIE MILLEN,
> CORNELIUS HUGUENIN, PHILIP MILLEN,
> COL. AND MRS. EDWARD H. deSAUSSURE,
> MR. AND MRS. DANIEL ELLIOTT HUGER,
> MR. AND MRS. THOMAS HUGUENIN

The first mention of the new sexton, Isaiah (Ike) McPherson, was in the January 1997 vestry minutes although he had arrived in December 1996. He would have pension coverage and medical coverage.

In 1998, Francis D. Rogers, Jr. was senior warden and Steve Graudin was junior warden. Newly elected to the vestry were: Elizabeth Bowles, Henry (Henno) Hutson, Ann Bee Rhett and William (Bill) F. Thompson.

Thompson reported in April that Mrs. Virginia Dwight left the church $10,000. The Clerk of Court, Julie Armstrong, sent a $500 check as a retribution payment from a perpetrator of vandalism back in 1987. Mary Haskell Lemons left $20,000 to the church in memory of her parents.

Miss Miriam Anderson left 75% of her real estate to the church. There is a plaque in the parlor in memorial to her:

> "This room is dedicated
> In memory of
> Miss Miriam Ashley Anderson
> September 30, 1914 – March 15, 1998"

In 2000, the church had received $84,500 from Miss Anderson's bequeath.

In January 1999, Rogers stated that December 1998 was the highest income month ever with total income at $212,603. He added that Peterson agreed to continue to work with the church for another six months. The vestry approved the 1999 budget at $1,131.895.

In 1999, Steven D. Graudin was senior warden and Elizabeth P. Bowles junior warden, and Alonzo A. Burris, III, Lon, secretary. Those elected to the vestry were: Ed Holt, Bob Ables, Lydia Evans and Betsy Harvey.

In 1999, member of the vestry Betsy Harvey would attend vestry meetings together with her husband, Heyward, who was the church treasurer.

In February, Joy Hunter took a position as parish administrator at St. Paul's in Summerville. Burris sent her a letter of thanks, "We know the road has not always been a smooth one, but your diligence and kindness have been a fine example for all." Joy wrote some great articles in *The Spire*.

PROPERTY & MAINTENANCE

In October 1987, St. Philippian Bill Warlick was chosen as the architect for the renovation of the church office building. By November 16, he reported the work was nearly finished.

In 1988, Charles Boykin once again offered $115,000 to pay for the building of the new sacristy. He wanted a three by five inch brass plaque to be suitably located stating "This Sacristy was built to glorify the Lord and in memory of Vivian C. Boykin." The vestry accepted the generous gift, but construction could not begin until the problem of the east wall was solved. The brass plaque remains in the sacristy in 2012.

Previously, the vestry had loaned the portrait of Bishop Gadsden to the Episcopal church home named after Bishop Gadsden. Tom Myers, chairman of the home, passed on a request that the home wanted to keep the portrait longer and hang it over the mantle in their dining room, The Hampsons hoped to hang it in the rectory. It was decided that the home could keep it but it must be returned to St. Philip's with thirty days notice. The home had to have the painting appraised and insured.

In May 1989, Hampson updated the vestry about the all parish banquet at the Omni Hotel, in 2012 called Charleston Place, to raise money for the Fourth Century Fund. In June the church authorized architect Dan Beaman to proceed with plans and specification for phase one that included the church building. The Preservation Society and Historic Charleston Foundation (HCF) took interest in the plans and wanted input.

In May, Lawrence Walker, director of HCF, wrote to senor warden Dr. E.K. Wallace. "I understand that I gave some of your Building Committee members the impression that I felt there was a similarity between what St. Philip's is proposing and the building plans for First Baptist Church. Obviously there are great differences between the two proposals."

In November, Vestryman Palmer Gailllard wrote Lawrence Walker that plans were moving and they were told a model of the property would be helpful but a model would cost $10,000. Gaillard asked HCF for any assistance they could provide. By January 1990, there was no response from HCF so the vestry approved $10,000 to purchase a velcro model that could be changed easier and at less expense.

HURRICANE HUGO

"They ate, they drank, they married wives, they were given in marriage, until the day that Noah entered the ark, and the flood came and destroyed them all." Luke 17:27.This is not to say God sent Hugo to Charleston, but a catastrophe would soon strike and those people in Awendaw and McClellanville certainly could have used a Noah's ark. It was as though most of South Carolina had the wind sucked out of it and it took a long time to fully recover.

Business manager Jan Hipp reported she had been dealing with an insurance company about the rectory's insurance coverage. The property evaluation in April 1986 was $487,000 and the insurance shown on the property was $348,000 plus $32,000 on the contents. Hipp told the insurance company that the rectory had received a major restoration and the house was worth $1,000,000. The insurance company said they would only increase the coverage if an addition had been added. Hipp advised them in this case they might want to reassess to cover a valuable secretary in the rectory with a rider. On August 8, Hipp reported the rectory was covered for 100% replacement cost. (Author – nick-o-time)

On September 12, the vestry discussed what to do with the furniture from the rectory that was being held in storage. Ben Hagood reminded the vestry that two rugs owned by the church had been stored at Shogrys for almost two years. Edward (Ed) Shogry, a member of Grace church, started Rug Masters on St. Philip Street in 1951. In those days, everyone called Shogry in late spring to come and pick up their carpets for cleaning and storing. Then the straw rugs were placed on the empty floors where they remained until fall. When the straw rugs arrived the homeowners would place their white slip covers on the furniture. Shogry later removed the business to Calhoun Street and after Hugo moved to Romney Street and Morrison Drive where in 2012 his daughter, Vicki and her husband, John Kammeyer, still successfully run Rug Masters.

Also on September 12, 1989, Hampson passed out the latest photographs of the "crack meters" (sensors) that showed that the chancel continued to move away from the church.

As the members of the vestry went home that night, a three-day old cluster of rainstorms that were far out in the Atlantic Ocean became Hurricane Hugo. The storm struck Guadeloupe on September 17, St. Croix on the 18th and then Puerto Rico. Between Puerto Rico and Charleston, Hugo intensified into a category four and it entered Charleston Harbor on the evening of Thursday, September 21 with gusts of wind at 108 miles per hour. In addition to the wind, there was a five foot surge of water. The eye of the storm went up the peninsula to North Charleston and beyond. There was a twenty foot water surge at Awendaw and McClellanville and many were trapped in school shelters, barely escaping.

The National Guard moved into the area as soon as Hugo left and a curfew was enforced. The horse lot at Broad and Chisolm streets was the city dump and bricks were stripped away from homes on Murray Boulevard. On the first Sunday after Hugo, St. Philip's was open for a service. About thirty people gathered and Hampson suggested members volunteer to share helpful items with one another. This author learned to warn people from off not to ask about Hugo unless they had three weeks to spare. Let us leave it there.

During this mess, the senior warden was Dr. E. K. Wallace and the junior warden was Winfield Sapp. The first post Hugo vestry meeting was held on September 28 at 5:15 p.m. Jan Hipp gave an inventory of the damage that occurred. Many Charlestonians learned the hard way that some damage would not show up until later and then they would have to hassle with the insurance companies.

The tea garden had no damage and the rectory, other than flooding in the basement, had slight water damage. Twenty-seven Cumberland Street fared well with one broken window and some bricks that fell off the roof. The roof blew off the back part of the parish house and leaked in the front flat area where there was severe water damage to the ceilings, floors, carpets and walls. The chapel's roof came completely off causing water damage to the ceiling, walls, floor and its contents. There was no major flooding under the chapel but there was rain damage that caused part of the sheetrock ceiling to fall.

Chimney vents on the office building opened and let water pour into the third floor damaging ceiling tiles. Two offices on the northeast corner of the building sustained damage to the ceiling, rugs and books.

The storm caused a hole in the church's roof, much of the copper on the steeple came off and the round windows on the north and south sides[30] blew out allowing water to come into the church. The cracks in the recently examined chancel had gotten even big-

---

30 The vestry minutes say "north and east windows" but "east" may not be correct.

ger. The front door blew out causing damage to the narthex ceiling and the rectangular window and semi-circle window in the church blew out.

Secretary Bucky Knowlton wrote, "There being no further business, the vestry meeting was adjourned at 6:45 p.m. in order for all to return home by the 7 p.m. curfew."

In October, Charles Hipp, chairman of the property committee, was the point man for Dan Beaman and his company. More damage was pointed out at the parish house because it is lower than the church and is closer to Market Street making the building more prone to flood. Its air conditioning was subjected to salt water flooding. There was discussion of demolishing the parish house.

Mrs. E.K. (Jean) Wallace announced the bazaar was canceled for 1989 and that the ECW was working with Mary Anne Hanckel to assist the church's needy and to help churches in the Wando/Cainhoy area.

By November 1989, the Church Insurance Company gave a figure of $407,316.91 needed to repair the property excluding the steeple and the playground equipment. The estimate also did not include temporary repairs, churchyard trees and fences and many other items.

The master restoration plan had been drawn and redrawn because there were so many opinions. Some people wanted to build a new parish house in the green space between the church and the old parish house while others wanted to remodel the then current parish house. Another group wanted to tear down the parish house at 67 Cumberland Street but in April 1990 Charleston's Board of Architectural Review rejected St. Philip's plan to demolish the parish house and 67 Cumberland Street. Teddy Guerard opposed the demolition because the construction would take years and the church did not have the money. He said, "The approval of the demolitions is unnecessary and premature ... What the church will finally put up is anybody's guess." Beaman confirmed what Guerard said. Hampson asked the property committee to return to the BAR "as often as it takes to have the needed space approved."

In November, the estimate for all of the restoration work was $4,500,000 including grave site relocations. The church had $2,278,000. With no decision on the different plans, tempers flared and Hampson "suggested" apologies were in order.

A letter went out explaining there were two main reasons why any of the major renovations had not begun. Hugo had a significant impact on the increase of the cost and the discovery of the poor foundation under the sanctuary, including the apse. The estimate for repairing the apse that was built in the 1920s, including additional stabilization of its foundation, and of the sanctuary, was $903,782. One person in the project said the apse never had a proper foundation and it was not fixed in the 1990s. Someday there could be quite a costly expense to build a proper foundation for the apse. Craig Bennett

Jr. and said the preliminary indication is that the northeast end of the church continued to settle at an alarming rate.

The chaos continued in 1991. Charley Hipp resigned as chairman of the property committee in March and was replaced by Richard Powell.

The amount needed for the work was $4,955,948. The steeple was $2,205,648, the sacristy was $1,250,000, HVAC and electrical work $300,000 and the parish house $1,500,000. There was a shortfall of $1,612,548.

At the end of the report, it was written, "Because our needs exceed our resources, we are being forced to trust God to provide. This really should not be surprising. God typically places us in situations where we have an opportunity to place our trust in Him."

Because stucco was falling from the steeple, it had to be wrapped in a debris net at a cost of $29,950. There was a debate whether or not the steeple needed to be straightened and if so how much.

A newly formed Hugo insurance committee was formed. The 1991 vestry minutes contain five pages of restoration activity from fall 1987 to December 1990. One July report said, "Today our buildings are in worse shape than they were three years ago." In August, Mary Anne Hanckel was hired as a liaison with architects, workers, etc. Looking back from 2011, Hanckel said her job was a very positive experience and the Ruscon employees could not have been nicer. They would stop work during a wedding or a funeral and did all they could to keep the church running.

In September, the BAR approved the conceptual plans for both the church building addition and renovation presented by Dan Beaman of Cummings and McCrady and the parish house addition and renovation by Bill Warlick of Warlick & Graudin architects.

In September, Mark Phillips wrote a lengthy letter to Andy Anderson saying he strongly felt that an outside specialized counsel should review the proposed Hugo settlement. He said he was not undermining the work of the Hugo committee but because the amount was so great, outside counsel could compliment the Hugo committee. By November 1991, the church had received a total of $962,079.08 from the Church Insurance Company. Finally in October 1992, the church settled with the insurance company receiving $1,237,920.92 for a grand sum of $2,200,000.

In April 1992, after prayer, the vestry accepted Ruscon for the restoration work. "The vestry had decided to move forward with the restoration knowing there was a one million dollar shortage, trusting the Lord to provide." James Mitchell Stelling (Jim), executive vice-president of Ruscon, saved $200,000 on window repairs.

At the December 8 vestry meeting, Greene reported the chain link fence had gone up around the Church Street side of the building. Although the challenges were great, the excavation work around the church had begun for the steeple scaffolding. Mary Anne Hanckel said she would chastise St. Philippian Jim Stelling if they in anyway damaged Miss Nellie's dogwood tree. He was much relieved when that spring her dogwood tree was, as always, the first in the city to bloom.

After experimenting, Hayward Baker from Tampa suggested minipiles which did not require heavy equipment. The scaffolding rose to the top of the steeple and while preparing to re-guild the cross they found a bullet hole in the cross and also found that someone had carved his or her initials on the cross.

In the 1950s there was a very prominent downtown doctor who on New Year's Eve would stand in the back yard and fire his rifle at St. Michael's and St. Philip's steeples.

The pile driving began December 14, 1992, and ended on February 5, 1993.

On December 15, Greene reported the balance in Trust B was $3,646,142 and the balance expected from the Fourth Century Pledge funds was expected to be $278,537 plus an estimated $80,000 would come from the Dill and Boykin gifts. The total resources to date were $4,004,679.

On December 23 it was written in the vestry minutes that "For historical purposes, it should be noted in the record that a full and wide ranging discussion was held on each of the items prior to voting on the motions."

George Greene was senior warden in 1992 and during the heat of the building situation parishioners felt welcome to call him at any time and many expressed their great displeasure. After one call, Greene's son asked his father if they were going to have to leave St. Philip's. He was assured they did not have to leave. At his vestry meetings, Greene requested one half hour for prayer and unanimity and he added that the vestry was comprised of a great group of people who would stop and pray and sometimes put some things off.

The 1992 vestry, included Greene, Ben Hagood, Jr., as junior warden and: Bob Ables, Jim Broody, Rutledge Coleman, Ed Holt, Foster Gaillard, John Kerr (secretary), Joe Land, David Maybank, Ann Payne and Mark Phillips.

By April 1993, the church was having problems with people, including students, climbing the scaffolding. Jan Hipp put the church's policy in writing and sent it to Lt. Doyle of the police department's team two. The church requested the police not to arrest anyone on the scaffolding but they be sentenced to thirty-two hours of community service that must be completed within sixty days.

In the meantime, the interior of the church was being restored. Stelling said in 2011 that even with the thorough work the interior of the church received most of it remains original. The chancel had to be pulled toward the rear of the church and that was completed by the use of "rebars." Holes were drilled in the wall allowing long metal reinforcing bars to be inserted into the wall so that the chancel and the wall would be "stitched together."

Hank Bauer, of The Ball Corp., was superintendent of the plastering of the interior of the church and the steeple. After the stucco was removed from the steeple, Stelling, who found initials of a former craftsman written inside, gave orders to put the craftsman's initials where they were. Bauer gave the archives an obstructed picture of the writing. All that can be seen to the left that are readable are the letters "G & N" and to the right is the word "England" which could be a surname.

Another inscription was added in the steeple:

> DAN BEAMAN, AIA
> 1993
> RUSCON CONST – JOE WOOTEN
> BALL CORP.
> H. BAUER – J. ACKERMAN

Then the "England" memorial was placed over the above memorial, not to be seen. The stucco, mixed in Birmingham by the Rainbow Co., was matched to meet the same color, sand texture, lime and even the size of the grain that would be used on the steeple.

On the interior, Bauer checked the plaster and found that no more than 30% needed to be replaced. Again, they used an appropriate mixture that would match the remaining plaster and all the plasterers came from South Carolina. Stelling donated to the St. Philip's archives two of the large, custom hand-made plastering, wood tools that were made on site.

At some point in time, damaged cherubs, that had been replaced with paper mache, were sent off and replaced in plaster. Bauer said each cherub had different facial expressions and different wings. Broken ornamental leaves in the chancel were also replaced with plaster.

THE LIGHTING DISCUSSIONS

An example of the passions that St. Philippians have for properly maintaining their church began at the April 20, 1993, vestry meeting. The agenda was altered to allow Joan Algar and Jane Hagood to present a petition concerning the vestry's decision to proceed with recessed lighting in the vaulted ceiling. They wanted to keep the current lighting and or use indirect lighting. A supporting letter from Arthur Wilcox was read. In a closed session, the vestry passed a motion to stay with the original decision to put in the recessed lighting. The motion passed seven to five.

Hampson gave an overview of the events of the last five days at a called vestry meeting to address the lighting issue. Ben Hagood asked Teddy Guerard for the legal procedure of calling a special congregational meeting. One parishioner told a representative of the Ruscon Company that no changes were to be made within the church. Greene suggested not putting any lights in the arched ceiling or any other place where recessed lights were to be used because engineers concluded that the lighting reflected from the ceiling would be sufficient. Jack Jagar wore a green shade to church to protest recessed lights. He said they would be too bright.

At the special congregational meeting held May 9, 1993, Ben Hagood recounted the struggles the vestry had maintaining the historical perspective with the good stewardship of church funds. "Afterwards, Hagood very effectively admonished us all to become one in Christ, bearing with each other in our differences and striving to love one another."

Several parishioners showed up at the May 11 vestry meeting for the "Open Forum" who complained about recessed lights over the balconies. But on June 22, the vestry unanimously agreed at their meeting to remain with their former decision to use recessed lighting under the balconies.

Also on June 22, Dan Beaman presented the vestry his design for the face of the clock that would approximate the clock faces of the mid-1800s "that adorned our steeple." The vestry unanimously accepted the design and accepted the gracious gift of an anonymous donor who paid for the clock face. The BAR also approved the design.

In April 1994, the vestry explored ways of raising the $800,000 to $1,000,000 needed for the addition of the new parish hall. In May, Greene reported that as much as $700,000 had been saved during the renovation. He added that he and recent vestries had always seen this as one continuous project and he recommended that they proceed. The vestry agreed and in June the consensus was to proceed with a fall fund raiser to obtain the money.

The vestry in May 1995, voted to make the final payment to Ruscon for the church construction. The amount was not recorded.

THE DISSENSION OF THE 189, OR WAS IT 190, MEMBERS WHO OPPOSED THE PARKING GARAGE

In 1990, the city had a $25,000,000 bonding authority to build parking garages in certain areas. After the vestry met to discuss a proposal regarding the construction of a parking garage on the northwest corner of Cumberland and Church streets, the vestry rejected the proposal six to two.

Mark Phillips served two terms, 1995 & 1996, as senior warden. The junior wardens were Preston Hipp in 1995 and Eugene Foxworth Jr. in 1996.

On September 6, 1995, Bill Logan, Director of General Services for Charleston County, advised the vestry as to the county's interest in obtaining the church's empty lot on the northwest corner of Cumberland and Church streets. A 360-space parking garage built there would "satisfy the parking requirements for the new judicial complex."

Junior Warden Hipp gave a report on Logan's letter. After a lengthy discussion, the vestry required a ground lease that would permit the church to have input about the façade of the garage instead of selling the property. Hipp felt, "This agreement would be financially beneficial for St. Philip's." Foster Gaillard advised Logan of the vestry's decision.

An appraisal the vestry made for $1,000 showed a value of the lot was $1,428,000. By February 1996, the vestry presented a long draft term sheet for a proposed lease between St. Philip's and the county as lessee. Lengthy negotiations proceeded.

The county offered to purchase the property for $2,000,000 and would offer, free parking, in perpetuity, for church members during scheduled services. Logan said their offer was 41% over the church's appraisal. If the church did not accept the county's offer, "the county has the option to exercise their right of eminent domain."

After a forty-five minute discussion at a March 6, 1996, meeting between county and church representatives, the lease proposed by the church fell through. Church leaders walked out and the county council members voted six to three to discontinue talks with the church.

One St. Philippian reporting on the March 6 meeting between the county and the church stated, "From the tone of last night's meeting, it appears to me that the government operated in bad faith. While we are called to render unto Caesar that which is Caesar's, I will defer to Jim (Hampson), but I do not believe we must roll over and render to Caesar that which is not Caesar's."

Because of previous remarks by the county, the vestry asked if the county could condemn the church's lot. John Kerr said, "As far as I can determine, there has never been a decision by the South Carolina appellate courts passing on the constitutionality of our condemnation statute which appears to allow the taking of church property."

Gaillard emphasized they had been throwing out those words "eminent domain" since day one. "They have a real club over our heads and as a result the church has no choice but to negotiate the lease."

Logan told Gaillard that if by the April 11 county meeting there was no agreement, they would move (the garage) to another site.

At the congregational meeting on April 21, 1996, a petition showed opposition but the vestry quibbled whether 189 or 190 members signed the petition. This issue took up a tremendous amount of the vestry's time and fueled dissension. Gaillard wrote a concise letter on May 17, 1996, to Bishop Salmon explaining what had transpired from the beginning.

The county then renewed its offer to St. Philip's to purchase the parking lot for $2,000,000. At about the same time, an inquiry was received that there was a possibility of a swap of the parking lot for the property on the southwest corner of State and Cumberland streets known as the "Old Charleston Day School Property." Suddenly the county withdrew the $2,000,000 offer to St. Philip's and a proposal was made by the county about swapping the parking lot for 51 State Street.

The city and the county proposed paying $2,000,000 in cash to the associates of Cumberland and State, owners of 51 State Street.[31]

The city put a lot of pressure on the wardens but eventually they decided it was a good deal. After much discussion and comparing, the vestry approved the swap in principle.

In June, Hampson, who wrote in *The Spire* about the gossip concerning the parking lot, heard the most improbable things about the vestry. "I'm amazed at how wrong some 'reports' are." He asked parishioners to call a vestry member to obtain the true facts.

In the same issue, Mark Phillips wrote a "Parking Lot Update." He acknowledged that "about 190" protested the plan and the vestry formally received the petition, thanked the petitioners for their interest and agreed to take the petition under consideration. Phillips said that the proposed swap would occur. He wrote, "Despite the difficulty and the emotion associated with this process, I feel that the vestry made a well-reasoned decision. The Charleston Day property is 20% larger than the parking lot and should conservatively generate $145,000 in yearly income. That was roughly twice what the church received from the parking lot on the northwest corner of Church and Cumberland streets."

The vestry drew up letter of intent outlining principal terms and conditions such as parking privileges. Approval for the swap was given by the standing committee signed by Rev. Terrell Glenn, Jr. There was an affidavit from an attorney representing the Cumberland and State property stating the true value of the property was $2,500,000. All was worked out by July 2.

Frank Brumley wrote in 2012, "The city asked Cumberland and State Associates to participate in a three way transaction in which they were trying to acquire the St. Philip's parking lot. Our partnership sold our building at 51 State Street to the city and they in turn worked out an exchange of 51 State Street to St. Philip's for its parking lot."

---

31 Vestry minutes Jan. 1995 through July 1996 p.118 in July 1996

The *Post & Courier* on July 3, 1996, also wrote, "Last week City Council gave final approval to the complex deal, which involves a four-way property transaction among the city, the county, St. Philip's and the owners of the day school …The day school site's owners are getting $2.5 million, including $2 million in cash from the county and a 15-year, rent free interest in retail space under construction inside the Francis Marion garage."

In 1996, "the County of Charleston, the City of Charleston and St. Philip's entered into an Exchange of like-kind Property Agreement dated June 27, 1996. Cumberland and State Associates sold the property to St. Philip's for $5.00 and other valuable consideration." The deed was recorded July 2, 1996.

The vestry debated what to do with the parish house. Assets available for restoration were $455,000. The intent was to reserve $425,000 for a new parish hall which would be augmented by a third "Fourth Century Fund" campaign. The house at Cumberland Street and Philadelphia Alley was in terrible condition and the roof on the parish hall preceded Hugo. Although ceilings were peeling and carpets were stained and dirty, Mike Cooke cleaned and painted Sunday school rooms himself even though that was not in his job description.

By July 1996, the vestry was interested in legally removing the use of the church home as a place for the needy. It had not been used for that for at least twenty years. It was recommended that a genealogist be hired to see if there were any heirs of Jane M. Rudolph, the lady who conveyed the property to St. Philip's in 1870 leaving the building in trust for the use of the poor at St. Philip's. It was also recommended that a congregational meeting should be called to change usage for church offices, classrooms, etc. The meeting was held on November 8, 1997, with fifty-nine members attending. The resolution for the change was passed by the congregation. Foster Gaillard said, there being no heirs, the judge should approve.

By February 1998, a choice had to be made whether to patch up deteriorating buildings or to, as recommended by the long range committee, make a full renovation. The long range committee made its final suggestions and then ceased to exist as its duties were turned over to two subcommittees.

In January 1999, Jerry Sifford resigned as chairman of the property committee after serving for four years. Graudin sent a letter of thanks, "As junior warden, I saw your dedication month after month in what is often a behind the scenes, thankless job … I believe you may receive a special jewel in your crown for this service, although I'm not sure of the accuracy of this theological point."

In April, Bill Thompson made a motion, seconded by Betsy Harvey, that the parish house should be restored rather than demolished. The motion passed unanimously.

Frank Rogers presented the following datelines provided by the restoration report.

On August 31, 1999, the consultant would give an estimate as to how much money could be raised. September 1 would open the silent campaign that would run through December 31. The consultant said 50% of the money should be raised by the silent campaign. The public campaign would begin January 1, 2000, and run through June 30. Construction would begin on June 1, 2000.

THE RECTORY

The controversy went on and on. The vestry voted to sell the rectory and purchase another one. A majority of the congregation at the meeting voted not to sell the rectory. A committee was formed to find another rectory, but they could not find anything as nice as 92 Church Street. Hampson did not want to live at the rectory. Hampson wrote, "I cannot be the kind of Rector that you need if I have to spend 20% of my energies worrying about the house ... surely you want to resolve this situation as quickly as we do."

In December, the Hampsons said they would live in the rectory if it were properly renovated. Andy Anderson and Palmer Gaillard headed a fund raising drive to raise $250,000 to $300,000 for the rectory's restoration although Hampson said a fund raising consultant should be used in this drive.

Myers, Paul and Zervos could not in good conscience spend so much money on the house because he felt that our rector would be living in a million dollar house. They preferred to sell the house for $600,000. Palmer Gaillard said "We have a responsibility to keep up the property." Dr. Barnwell made a motion, seconded by Helen Barkley, that Beaman could proceed with the plans to restore the rectory. The motion passed ten to one. In June 1988, bids were put out for contractors.

Beaman saved time and money because he found a set of plans for the rectory made in the 1930s when Merritt Williams was rector.

In August 1988, the estimated cost for the rectory renovation was approximately $500,000. Hampson reminded the vestry that the last vestry voted to proceed and that he and his wife did want to live there. The motion was deferred to the next meeting. Vereen Coen, Mrs. Thomas (Mary V.) Huguenin, Charlotte R. McCrady and Mary S. Webb wrote in favor of the rectory. Helen Barkley asked the vestry to take $195,000 from unrestricted church funds and $155,000 from the restricted pledges for a total of $350,000 for a scaled down renovation. Dr. Robertson was encouraged but wanted more discussion before voting. Hampson urged the vestry to support Barkley's motion and after more discussion, Barkley's motion passed with nine votes approving and two against. The vestry signed a contract not to exceed $270,000 including the 10% due the contractor.

In September 1989, Ben Hagood reported on his investigation of placing a plaque in the rectory garden in thanks for funds donated to the rectory restoration fund by the Huguenin family and the ECW. The plaque was to say, "Garden Restoration 1989 in loving memory of Thomas Abram Huguenin and in appreciation of the Episcopal Churchwomen of St. Philip's Church." The plaque remains on the wall in 2012.

MUSIC, THE CHOIR & BELLS

After visiting Charleston, in July, 1987, and prior to becoming rector, Hampson requested six more members be added to the choir. After fifteen years, Bill Oplinger resigned on September 27, 1987. He said it was difficult to give it up but felt someone with more time and energy was needed.

In June, the choir lost two members and Mrs. Yonker, who became ill and was put on a leave of absence, died in 1989.

After George Mims and his wife, Leslie, visited Charleston and St. Philip's that summer, he accepted and was to begin by September 1 as organist and choir director.

In March 1990, when the Mims had been at St. Philip's one year and five months, he issued a seven page report for the vestry. The adult choir had grown from twelve to forty-six, the children's choir grew from zero to thirty-eight and the music team grew from seven to fourteen. The Mims were busy people.

His resignation letter was given to the vestry on April 20, 1993. In 2012, Mims was an organist in a church in Texas.

In July, Richard Powell, chairman of the property committee, submitted a report regarding a proposed addition of fourteen new bells for the steeple. The vestry passed a motion to permit Mrs. Virginia Neyle to begin fundraising. The bell committee wanted to add two more strikers for a cost of $4,995 from the Van Bergen Bell Foundries. The vestry agreed.

In October, the vestry approved the salary package for the new organist/choirmaster, Preston Smith, who began work on November 1, 1993. Smith came from Kingstree and was a graduate of Furman University with a BA in music and was on the Dean's List in 1986.

Dorothy Margaret Bollwinkle, church organist from 1924 to 1968, died on Sunday, June 19, 1994. Bollwinkle, a member of the Huguenot Society, was also the organist at the "KK Beth Elohim Temple" on Hasell Street. She was buried at St. Philip's and had inscribed on her tombstone, "St. Philip's organist."

REV. JAMES EUGENE HAMPSON, JR.

CAPERS CROSS

ORGANIST / CHOIRMASTER

By June 1995, Capers Cross was chosen by the vestry as the new organist-choirmaster. Cross and his twin, Kenneth, were born in Moncks Corner on November 29, 1947, the sons of Herbert, who was a merchant and part time farmer, and Ruth Attaway Cross who taught English in the Cross school. The twins were raised in Cross where they were members of the Friendship Methodist Church and where Capers began playing the organ in the eighth grade. His piano teacher and mentor growing up was Mrs. Frances Law of Moncks Corner with whom he credited as guiding him into music as a profession.

After graduating from Furman University in 1969 with a degree in music, majoring in organ, Cross enlisted in the navy reserve and taught music in the Cross School for a year before going on active duty. He married Nancy Snyder of Greenville after his 1972 discharge from the navy. In 1973, they moved to Dallas where he pursued a masters' degree in sacred music at Southern Methodist University. In 1975, Cross accepted a civil service position as organist-choirmaster at Holy Trinity Chapel at West Point where their two children, Adam and Talley, were born,

In 1982, Cross accepted the position of organist-choirmaster at St. Andrew's in Mt. Pleasant where he remained for thirteen years. While there he was given a sabbatical which he used to take the course requirements and residency of a doctorate in choral conducting at the University of Texas in Austin. Without finishing that degree, he accepted his current position as organist-choirmaster at St. Philip's in 1995. Cross wrote, "I am now (2011) in my sixteenth year and I would not want to be anywhere else."

Craig Bennett spoke about Virginia Neyle's plan to increase the number of bells in the steeple to allow for English change ringing that would cost between $200,000 and $300,000. Neyle would do all the work, supply the material and contact large corporations. The vestry would only supervise the work because church buildings have first priority. By January 1997, the bell fund total rose to $8,200.

Cross in November 1997 proposed bringing sixty-five men, boys and girls choir members and chaperones from All Saint's Church in Northampton, England for a week-long "engagement" May 22 – 31, 1998, at St. Philip's.

In 2011, Cross offered some thoughts on today's church and its music:

"Church music, like the church itself, is in a state of flux. Perhaps that is always true, but never more so than now. We live in an increasingly secular world, where

Christian values are no longer the norm, and where the flow of influence has reversed direction. For most of the last millennium, it has been the church which exerted influence on the culture. In recent decades, however, there has been a decided shift, in which the culture is redefining the church, and a weakened church finds itself unable to wield any meaningful influence on the culture. That phenomenon is seen in the dwindling numbers of professing Christians and in the watered-down version of the Gospel which prevails at the highest levels of our leadership in our national church. In a desperate attempt to become "relevant," in the vain hope that it could recover some of its lost prestige, the modern church has sold its birthright.

"St. Philip's has boldly taken a stand against that incursion and in favor of the unchanging message of the Gospel of Christ as expressed in Scripture and by our church fathers throughout the ages. Ours is an orthodox understanding of the faith and our primary style of worship similarly embraces the best of that tradition. We understand that ours is the not only legitimate style of worship, but it is one that is consistent with whom we are. It connects our past and present.

"St. Philip's Sunday morning worship is a vibrant expression of traditional worship. It eschews the newer Rite II, with its weaker theology, in favor of Rite I which is unflinching in its proclamation of the Gospel. The great treasury of hymns, which is our church's priceless legacy, is gratefully and unapologetically embraced by our congregation in contrast to many churches which today have largely forsaken them. The important role of the traditional choir in the leadership of worship is understood and widely supported by our parishioners.

"Church music, at its best, leads worshipers into a close encounter with God. It nurtures, nourishes and equips them to follow the Great Commission. We endeavor to give God the first fruits of our labors – the best, and only the best, of our art, our music and our language. This is how we honor him and praise Him. Our dress, our demeanor, our music and our pageantry all proclaim God's greatness and our love for Him. This beautiful church where we gather to worship together is not an ordinary place because it has been consecrated and set aside expressly for the worship of God. We can encounter God in other places – in fact, in every place. But this is a special place. This is God's house. Similarly, the time we spend together in common worship is a special and anointed time, unlike any other. It is a time when we summon the best that is within us to commune with God and to join with our brothers and sisters in one united act of worship.

"Music reaches its full potential when it adheres to its supporting role in worship. We embrace art in worship not for art's sake, but for God's sake. We thrill to the sounds of a beautiful anthem beautifully sung, not just because it is lovely music but because it has given flight to the words of our faith and we find ourselves connecting to it on a deeply spiritual level. When a hymn gives voice to our deepest yearnings, we are enriched and renewed. Without music as an aid to our worship, we would be impoverished indeed.

"We have a duty to our children to preserve what is good from our past – to teach them to love and desire it. One of our richest traditions is our music. We all have a role to play in preserving that tradition in this holy and historic place. May St. Philip's Church ever resonate with the joyful sounds of its faithful responding to the psalmist's exhortation, 'O go your way into the gates of thanksgiving, and into His courts with praise.'"

Heritage Sunday 1990's

THE CHURCHYARDS

In 1960, Mary McLeod Armstrong purchased a burial plot in the western churchyard. After she left St. Philip's in 1966, she lost the right to be buried there as the rules state. Mrs. Armstrong still requested to be buried at St. Philip's and in 1987 the vestry waived the rules and let her be buried in lot 4196. No reason for the waiver was given.

In April 1993, there was a continual problem with homeless people jumping the brick wall and sleeping at night in the northwest corner of the western churchyard. Many were still passed out in the morning and the church's grounds people complained about the mess they left behind. Jan Hipp contacted the police and gave them permission to enter the churchyard.

Deaths in 1994 included: Martha Robinson Rivers, February 5; Susan Pringle Barnwell, May 30; Francis Prettyman Rhett, June 14; Hilliard B. Good, June 15; Mary Vereen Huguenin, June 27; F. Johnson Bissell, July 5; Ann Gibbs Leland, August 6; and Randell C. Stoney, September 16.

In 1999 church treasurer, Heyward Harvey, reported Mrs. Marjorie Sullivan left $50,000 in her will to the St. Philip's churchyard fund.

HAMPSON'S DEPARTURE

On March 22, 1999, Hampson sent a letter out to parishioners and friends advising them he decided that staying another two or three years was too long and he announced his retirement as of September 1. At the March 25 vestry meeting Steve Graudin moved, "With profound sadness and deep regret but knowing that God has released Jim from his call from St. Philip's, I move the vestry release Mr. Hampson from his ministry." Elizabeth Bowles seconded the motion that carried unanimously.

"Anything to be done before September 1, Jim will handle and anything to be done after September 1 Haden will handle."

Because Hampson was 62 ½ on September 1, his retirement would be smaller than if he had worked until age 65. A letter from the vestry was mailed on April 1 stating, "In appreciation for Hampson's ministry at St. Philip's, your Vestry unanimously approved, and Jim accepted, a supplementary retirement package designed to make up for the pension fund shortfall at a present value cost up to a certain amount." The church also agreed to pay the church insurance plan until he reached 65 and ccould apply for Medicare.

At the same meeting, Elizabeth Bowles, seconded by Ed Holt, moved that Haden McCormick be appointed as vicar of St. Philip's effective September 2, 1999. The motion passed unanimously. Bishop Salmon asked the vestry not to convene a search committee for a new rector so that an interim period could assure a continuity of leadership following Jim's retirement. The bishop said. "As Vicar, Haden would have authority and responsibility for St. Philip's."

Prior to Hampson's departure, Jim and Sarah attended the Interim Ministry Training Program with the anticipation of doing interim ministry during the next few years.

On July 30, Graudin gave a report on Hampson's last sermon at St. Philip's and said that Bob Ables, Ann Rhett and Betsy Harvey would select Hampson's gift and have it inscribed.

In August, John Welch made a motion to acknowledge Becky Riggs for her work on *The Spire* that featured Hampson. There were many pictures and written goodbye notes. For example, one couple wrote, "From the Thursday morning men's Bible study, and tears in between, we have grown to love them (the Hampsons) and appreciate their ministry, friendship and family in so many ways ... Thank you for faithfully preaching God's word carefully, practically and living it as humble, loving servants among us."

The vestry agreed to Lon Burris' request for a budget of $4,000 for the Hampson farewell reception.

In 2012, Jim and Sarah are in Tallahassee where he is the rector St. Peter's Anglican Church.

THE REV. JOHN HADEN McCORMICK

HIRED AS ASSOCIATE 1996

ORDAINED AS A TRANSITIONAL DEACONATE

MARCH 1997

ORDAINED AS PRIEST AT ST. PHILIP'S

ASSISTANT TO THE RECTOR

SEPTEMBER 22, 1997

PRIEST IN CHARGE AND VICAR

SEPTEMBER 2, 1999 – JUNE 10, 2000

RECTOR

JUNE 11, 2000, TO PRESENT AND BEYOND

John Haden McCormick was born March 28, 1946, in Jacksonville, Florida, the son of John Townsend McCormick and his wife, Jean Haden. There were two older sisters and two younger brothers, one of whom is an Episcopal priest in Alabama. He was raised in Jacksonville Beach where he was baptized in St. Paul's by the Sea Episcopal Church. McCormick attended public schools and graduated from Princeton University in 1968 with a BA in economics and a minor in civil engineering. He attended the Harvard Business School, graduating from the Advanced Management Program.

Upon graduation, he joined the family heavy construction business, B.B. McCormick & Sons that specialized in clearing, earth moving, etc. They performed work in the United States, Brazil, Guyana, the Bahama Islands and South Viet Nam.

Haden and Lynn's romance began with a literal "love at first sight" across a crowded room in the summer of 1967. On October 19, 1968, McCormick married Lynn Edrington Fant.

Haden thought their family was complete upon having three children. Lynn thought differently and she told Haden she felt God had three more children in mind for the McCormicks. In 2012, their daughter Courtney is married to Baron Fain and they have a son, Tradd. Brooks is divorced and has three children – Josephine, Sophia and Ashlyn. Their son, the Rev. Matthew McCormick, is married to Lisa. John is a lawyer, Stephen is a doctor and daughter Katherine is a banker in Columbia.

In 1975, McCormick left the family company and assumed operational control as President and CEO of the Clement Brothers Co. in Hickory, North Carolina. It also specialized in large earth moving. He turned the company around with an annual dollar volume of approximately $50 million and then sold his interest back to the Clements.

In 1978, McCormick was the owner and president of McCormick Machinery, Inc. in Jacksonville that specialized in the acquisition, refurbishment, leasing and export of Caterpillar construction equipment. The annual income was approximately $20 million but in 1985 they liquidated the business due to a prolonged industry downturn. He returned to the family business where he liquidated $6 million worth of construction equipment.

In 1988 he entered into the retail food business in Jacksonville. Because McCormick was trying to keep his aged uncle Hugh, who had lost his appetite, alive, he resurrected his uncle's receipts for smoking ham, bacon, sausage and pork shoulders. This led to the opening of Haden Ham Café and Gourmet Foods with two stores, one with a restaurant.

A long road led McCormick to enter seminary. His Catholic father and his Methodist mother compromised on the Episcopal Church and church attendance was regular. McCormick was an acolyte at age twelve. McCormick said, "Serving at the altar was a special time for me and I cherished the moments." As he grew older, his orthodox priest was followed by a series of non-orthodox priests causing his theology to grow more confused under their teaching and influence. This continued into his married life so that he developed a dualistic view of the world, with religion being viewed as mostly a vague attempt by man to give meaning to life. He said, "My belief system was neither well defined nor defensible."

Haden wrote, "I was doing great! I had a big house, three terrific kids, a wonderful wife and an airplane that took me any where I wanted to go at any time. My life had all the signs of success. I was active in community affairs and attended church regularly. You may not believe this, but I was not very happy. I had all the 'things' that many of us dream of having and yet I was empty inside.

In December 1980, McCormick had a road to Damascus experience that "could best be described as an Epiphany." Life just didn't make any sense. "I was a deeply troubled person. When I believed life was not worth living, I called a good friend who listened and then asked McCormick if he believed in Jesus. I said yes, but honestly I was not sure then Jesus was the Son of God." His friend then prayed for him but McCormick could not remember what he prayed. Jesus revealed Himself to Haden, and he acknowledged His Lordship as revealed in Holy Scripture.

The result was that I had an encounter with the Living God that left me joyfully aware of His presence and reality. It was the beginning of the most exciting part of my life, which is still going on. Within a few weeks, Lynn had a similar experience and we have continued in our walk together seeking to know God, to love God and to serve God. The best description of my belief system is the Nicene Creed. I recite it without crossing my fingers."

The McCormicks were spiritually active in the Jacksonville and Georgia areas from 1980 until 1994. He was a lay preacher, made home visitations, was active in street evangelism, visited prisoners, he was a featured speaker for the Full Gospel Business Men's Fellowship and more. Haden and Lynn have been and remain strong supporters of prayer. In 1994, he entered the Trinity School of Ministry in Ambridge, Pennsylvania, at age forty-eight. In December 1996, the McCormicks moved into 2 ½ on Orange Street in a garage apartment and by June 1997 the family settled in to 1160 Harbor View Road on James Island.

J. HADEN McCORMICK'S COMMENTS ON THEOLOGY

Written in 2012

In the 1930s, H. Richard Niebuhr defined theological liberalism with the following brilliant insight: "A God without wrath brought men without sin into a kingdom without judgment through the ministrations of a Christ without a cross."

This, of course, is the opposite of bedrock Anglican theology that was purchased with the blood of our martyrs. Jesus Christ gave his sinless life to provide for us, "one oblation of Himself once offered, a full, perfect and sufficient, oblation and satisfaction for the sins of the whole world … (BCP p. 334). It is upon the foundation of Jesus Christ that St. Philip's is built.

CHURCH SERVICES, MEMBERSHIP & CLERGY

A special service: "The Celebration of a New Ministry, The Celebration and Induction of John Haden McCormick as rector of St. Philip's Episcopal Church on Sunday June Eleventh, Two Thousand, Five O' Clock P.M. at St. Philip's." The sermon was given by The Very Rev. John B. Burwell. Communion was offered and the Prayer of Humble Access was included in the service.

Henrietta Gaillard asked McCormick if he were planning to have female ushers and chalice bearers in the church. He said he was deciding how to implement this.

McCormick in March reported the need for more clergy support. There had already been twelve deaths that year within the congregation as well as two other deaths that impacted the church. He said that in light of Sam Cobb's recent health problems the need was more urgent. The bishop had referred two candidates, both ordained clergy, for McCormick to consider.

In August, McCormick was having a "fabulous" time off that summer enjoying Waynesville, North Carolina, Blue Hill, Maine and James Island. In November, McCormick reported he had been asked to serve on the board of the Porter-Gaud School where he has served through 2013.

In March 2003, three hundred copies of *The Purpose Driven Life* were sold at St. Philip's. The book ranked third on a best seller list. one hundred forty parishioners participated in Sunday school, forty to fifty participated in the Wednesday night school and four to six participated at Wednesday Noon. The book ranked third on a Best Seller List.

Kathy Ravenel would head a "host of volunteers" to collect and edit membership data including addresses, phone numbers, etc. They expected to finish within six to eight weeks. Don Evans and Baron Fain took an inventory of prayer books and hymnals and those in disrepair would be thrown away. It was recommended that the 1940 hymnal be purchased rather than the 1982 hymnal. Blue hymnals over red were preferred because the blue ones last much longer.

Hamilton Smith, a former lawyer from Summerville who received "the call," arrived in mid-June 2004 at St. Philip's to work as a summer intern. He was attending seminary in England at Winthrop Hall. McCormick said Smith arrived at a most opportune time, especially with the absence of Sam Cobb. In 2012, Smith is an associate rector at St. Michael's.

Al Philips reported there was a discussion concerning the appropriate time to pass the peace during the service. McCormick explained that passing the peace was moved to the end of the service to minimize interruption and distraction. The point was also raised that the time to greet one another in the Lord was after communion as a celebration of forgiveness and reconciliation. St. Philip's is St. Philip's. We love one another but there is no physical passing the peace.

By December 2004, Rev. Andrew Hayler was at St. Philip's, part time. It was understood that Hayler would leave by May 2005 when the Rev. David Dubay would come. Hayler, an Englishman, was well received by the congregation. He later became a United States Navy Chaplain.

McCormick announced that The Rev. Henry (Hank) Avent would come to St. Philip's in January 2005.

REVEREND HENRY (HANK) ELBERT AVENT, JR.

ASSISTANT RECTOR

JANUARY 2005 -

Henry Elbert Avent, Jr. was born in Columbia on March 20, 1951. When he was six months old, his father, a World War II pilot, was called back into active duty during the Korean War and was sent to Patrick Air Force Base at Cocoa Beach, Florida. They lived there until Hank was two.

At the conclusion of the war, Avent and his family moved to Bennettsville where he grew up, graduating from Bennettsville High School in 1969. In the same year, Avent entered Clemson University, studying architecture and graduating in 1973. From 1973 to 1993 Avent progressed from intern to licensed architect. He practiced in Columbia.

During his time there, he and Gloria (Glo) Van De Water were married in Trinity Cathedral in Columbia on August 7, 1976. Their three children, all born in Columbia, are Emily Hope Avent, June 25, 1981, Courtney Lee Avent, December 10, 1983 and Andrew Clark Avent, July 19, 1989.

Because Avent answered a call in 1993 to the ministry through the Diocese of South Carolina, he and his family moved to Sewickley, Pennsylvania. Avent graduated from the Trinity School for Ministry in nearby Ambridge with a Masters of Divinity degree in 1997.

The Rev. Henry E. Avent, Jr. was ordained and assigned as vicar to Holy Apostles Church in Barnwell in June 1997. After almost eight years in Barnwell, he arrived at St. Philip's in January 2005.

From the beginning, Avent was interested in men's ministries and that has brought forth great fruit at St. Philip's. For the past few years, Avent has organized a monthly men's lunch, presenting some very inspiring speakers from St. Philip's and other churches. The focus of these talks is to touch men with the reality that God is with them in their daily lives.

Avent served almost six years on a ministry board that organizes the annual "Diocesan Men's Conference" at Camp St. Christopher. He also served one term on the "Diocesan Ecclesiastical Court" as well as a term with the diocesan council. He has been a clergy spiritual advisor for several Cursillo weekends.

World Missions has always been another passion for Avent and he has served as the clergy representative on St. Philip's very active world mission committee. He traveled with other St. Philippians on a mission trip to Honduras through the Lamb Institute. Since seminary, Avent has been a board member of the Society of Anglican Missionaries and Senders (SAMS) and has gone to Costa Rica with that group.

Flying is his hobby and his unfulfilled dream is to fly a Spitfire.

HANK AVENT'S COMMENTS ON ST. PHILIP'S THEOLGY

"Currently, we are experiencing a faithful, biblical, orthodox theology: that all humanity has sinned, rebelling against God, and fallen from our original love relation with God. In response, God has not abandoned us to our tragic alienation from Himself, which results in our spiritual death. And we are powerless to undo this death.

"Rather, He has reached out to rescue us, sending his Son, Jesus Christ, to pay the penalty that redeems us from our sins, through His death on the cross.

"Jesus came as the 'great physician' to heal our souls of their sin-sickness and free us from our bondage in sin and death. By His resurrection, He shows us the promised inheritance that, after our physical death, we shall be resurrected to life eternal in loving fellowship with God and all His redeemed people."

In April 2005, McCormick advised the vestry he had been elected to the diocesan convention's standing committee. He said this was important because the election of a bishop to replace Bishop Salmon had become entangled in some political maneuvering and the standing committee has significant control over the process of electing a new bishop.

Bob Nuttall, Donna Stouffer and Riley Watson explained in May 2005 the working of greeters on Sunday mornings. They had enlisted nine married couples, who prior to the

10:30 a.m. service, handed out bulletins, a welcome brochure and a visitor card to the visitors. After the service, Nuttall took the visitor cards from the offertory and personally called each local visitor that day. He would mail a letter to those who did not want a phone call.

In 2008, a very nice brochure called *Our Doors are Open* was printed promoting St. Philip's and its theology. When the brochures arrived, everyone realized the picture of St. Philip's showed the door as being closed. They were reprinted with the south door open. The brochure is a valuable tool and it has frequently helped people to decide to come to St. Philip's.

Stouffer said that in the second phase each newcomer was also sent the *Our Doors are Open* brochure. In addition, a booklet filled with information and contacts for all committees was included. Watson reported on the third phase for the newcomer. They were encouraged to take the Alpha course, headed by Harold Holt, and offered twice a year. Avent and Watson offered a four part inquirers course that featured Avent teaching on worship, baptism and Episcopal worship. It was also suggested that there be two new member dinners each year.

THE REVEREND DAVID DuBAY

ASSISTANT RECTOR

JUNE 1, 2005 - 2008

The Rev. David Dubay arrived as an associate at St. Philip's on June 1, 2005. He graduated from the College of Charleston in 1989 with a degree in music. Dubay served in the diocese of South Carolina as a youth minister for more than fifteen years, five years of which he was "Coordinator of Youth Ministries for the Diocese." He graduated from Suwanee in 2005, was ordained deacon on June 23 at Holy Trinity and was ordained as priest was in December 2005. His wife, Lisa, a middle school teacher, took time off to care for their three children: Joseph (11), Sadie (6) and Julia Grace who was eight weeks old. They lived in Canterbury Woods west of the Ashley.

Dubay said in 2005, "since arriving at St. Philip's I have been learning how to be a priest. I have been practicing my sacramental ministry and sharing in the leadership of the Sunday and Wednesday services. I was involved almost immediately with the Wednesday contemporary service".

As previously written, Dubay left St. Philip's in 2008 and went to Holy Trinity on Folly Road.

THE REVEREND JACK RAYMOND OWENS

ASSISTANT RECTOR

JUNE 2006 – DECEMBER 30, 2012

Rev. Jack Raymond Owens was born in Steubenville, Ohio, on May 4, 1954. At the age of three, he and his family moved Follansbee, West Virginia, where he attended grammar school. In 1972, he graduated from Brooke High School in Wellsburg, West Virginia.

Even though Follansbee was a "Catholic church town, Owens became friends with the Rev. William Jesse Redmond, rector of the Episcopal Church of the Good Shepherd. Redmond, newly out of seminary, went to their house to evangelize his parents but only Owens attended Redmond's church and that was when he was twelve and thirteen. After that, Owens said, "I became too cool to attend church, and it would be many years until I would pause to hear God calling me back into the fold."

Owens left home in 1972 and worked as a steel worker at the Weirton Steel Company located in Weirton and two years later he married his high school sweetheart. In 1984, Owens received a two year associate degree in nursing from the Virginia Northern Community College. In 1985, he left the steel mill and he and his wife moved to Mt. Pleasant where their son, Max Michael Owens, was born on December 25, 1987. In 1988 he and his wife divorced. Owens graduated from the Medical University of South Carolina in 1992 with a Master's degree in nurse anesthesia. His second wife, Betty, and Jack have a son Jeffrey Michael Owens, born in 1997. They thought by giving each of his sons the same middle name, it would bring them closer together.

Owens had just finished three hard years of anesthesia school but his life was in turmoil. He said, "I felt God calling me back to church and I began attending, on the periphery, at

Holy Cross on Sullivan's Island" where he later took Alpha. One Christmas Eve, Owens knew, indeed, "God wanted him back." He was elected to the vestry and Betty was became director of adult Christian education. Betty is also a nurse and also has a Master's Degree in Missions and Evangelism from the Trinity School for Ministry.

Owens enrolled at Trinity in 2003 and after graduating in 2006 came to St. Philip's. He was ordained priest by the Right Reverend Edward L. Salmon, Jr. on Saturday, January 13, 2007, at St. Philip's. In 2012, Owens worked as a nurse anesthesia four ten hour days. On Wednesdays, he often conducted the 8 a.m. and 10 a.m. services and afterwards is a pastoral minister visiting hospital patients, shut-ins and residents of Bishop Gadsden. He also preached at St. Philip's.

In late December, after receiving a call to the Church of the Good Shepherd west of the Ashley, he left St. Philip's. He is missed.

REV. JACK OWENS' THEOLOGY

"I believe that we are saved by Grace through Faith, but we are saved by God in order to do good works that he has pre-planned for us. That is what discipleship means."

After twenty-two years, Clifton Orvin retired in March 2006 from the praise team. A letter was sent to recognize his efforts and thanking him for his service. Update – fortunately, Clifton returned to the praise team in 2011.

Concern was expressed about small children leaving the church to go to the parish hall during the 10:30 a.m. service. There was no supervision at that time. McCormick said there would be articles in the *inSPIRE* about this and it was the vestry's opinion that a small group should be formed to make certain our buildings were being watched. John Blincow offered to oversee this committee.

Charlotte Williams in June 2006 reminded the vestry a vote was needed on the clergy sabbatical leave regulations. Bishop Salmon informed McCormick that each cleric should have two weeks of annual continuing education that could not be accrued. After six years of service, the rector is entitled to three months of paid sabbatical leave which does not include vacation time. Assistant clerics to the rector may have a leave of absence at the rector's recommendation, not to exceed six weeks. The vestry passed the motion.

Karen Phillips said that the *inSPIRE* was mailed to 950 families each week.

Nancy and Dubose Blakeney, who visited Nancy Cobb and Mary Louis Webb at Bishop Gadsden, said how much they both enjoyed Jack Owens' visits.

THE REV. HAZEL WILKINSON

PRAYER MINISTER
AUGUST 2007 – 2009

By August 2007, the Rev. Hazel Wilkinson, who was working at St. Philip's two days a week, primarily with prayer, was lauded in 2008 for fine healing prayer. Previously, Wilkinson had been with the Centers for Disease Control and Prevention in Atlanta. Her soaking prayer was held on the first Tuesday morning of each month. Six or eight cots were brought into the nave in front of the chancel and people, who wanted prayer, were invited to lie down while the prayer team prayed over those needing prayer. One member of the church was horrified to see cots in the church, but the prayer sessions were highly praised. Wilkinson left St. Philip's to go to Holy Cross.

Former senior warden, Brian McGreevy, was ordained deacon in September 2007 at the cathedral. The same month, McGreevy came to the church on staff part time as deacon and would work with David Dubay in Christian education.

In June 2008, St. Philip's vestry requested permission from Holy Cross to allow Rev. Matthew McCormick, son of J. Haden McCormick, to preach and assist at St. Philip's for a few months.

REV. MATTHEW WRIGHT McCORMICK

ASSISANT RECTOR

2008 –

Matt was born April 9, 1978, in Hickory, North Carolina, where his father had a business. At age two, his family returned to Jacksonville where he attended St. Mark's Episcopal Day School from kindergarten through age six.

When his father entered the Trinity School for Ministry, they moved to Sewickley, Pennsylvania, where he attended Quaker Valley High School from grades ten through twelve. During his time at the College of Charleston from 1997 to 2001, he had a double major, history and theater.

A pilot for a television show *Not Just Another Show* was being filmed in the Charleston area. Matt got a job in the program, but it turned out to be a flop. After that he became a licensed tour guide. Then he worked for two or three years in sales and marketing at Charleston Golf, Inc.

On September 9, 2004, Matt married Lisa Christian, the year after he enrolled at the Trinity Episcopal School for Ministry, where his father had attended. Lisa had a terrible allergic reaction to the air pollutants in Pennsylvania so Matt graduated in two and half years in December 2007. He worked from January 2008 at Holy Cross as a transitional deacon until June 2008 when he was ordained priest on June 1. Matt was the first deacon ordained as priest by Bishop Lawrence.

In June 2009, Bishop Lawrence spoke to the vestry about staffing issues at St. Philip's as well as those within the diocese of South Carolina. There was a difficulty because so many clergy wanted to come to this diocese because it is an orthodox diocese. He added that on the flip side there was little movement of clergy from this diocese. He said, "We were fortunate to have Matt McCormick available to move to a position at St. Philip's last year when David Dubay was called to be rector at Holy Trinity on Folly Road."

MATT McCORMICK'S COMMENTS ON THEOLOGY

"I believe that the unconditional and lavish grace, mercy, love and promises of Jesus Christ are everything. His unconditional mercy and forgiveness for broken and sinful people is the center of God Himself. The merciful resurrected Christ is God. God loves you without reservation or condition. There is no grave too deep, no burden too big, and no life too dark for God to touch. Christ will find you, pick you up with His resurrected pierced hands, place you gently on His shoulders and carry you home."

In February 2010, McCormick reported St. Philip's was reaching out and the congregation was growing. There were 126 new members reported in 2009, twenty-eight people baptized, thirty-five adults confirmed, fifty-six youth confirmed, thirty-seven transfer in, sixteen deaths, and fourteen members transferred out – some to out of town churches.

Dan Russler reported in March 2010 that the newcomers lunch was a great success with forty-five new members in attendance.

St. Philip's enrollment in 2013 is more than 2,700.

YOUTH, LAYMEN & THE LADIES

Mike Cooke, director of Christian education, gave notice in March 2000 that he would be leaving St. Philip's in six months. Jim Algar was the part time youth music minister. Dorothy Hanckel Lancaster was hired as the Christian education director for sixth graders and younger. In November, Gregory, her husband, who works for SPAWAR, was sent to Germany to work for two years in their Stuttgart office. During that time, Dorothy and Gregg visited twenty countries.

Caroline Rhodes and Julia Arnold were commended for their hard work with the 150 children who participated in "Vacation Bible School." Some people complained that the program the Bible school children put on prior to the 10:30 a.m. service "disturbed those who wished to pray and contemplate prior to the service. It was suggested next year there be a shorter program."

In April 2000, Caroline Rhodes gave the vestry the ECW report. Doug Peterson asked the vestry if they objected to female chalice bearers for the Wednesday evening services. There were no objections. Hampson never permitted female acolytes.

By September, a youth minister had not been found. The program was carried on by Doug Peterson, Al Dasberg and McCormick.

THE REVEREND MARC ROBERT PAUL BOUTAN

ASSISTANT RECTOR

JANUARY 2001 – MAY 2006

The Reverend Marc Robert Paul Boutan was born January 8, 1953, in Watertown, South Dakota, the son of an American mother, Marilyn Guddal, and a French father Pierre Jean Boutan, who had a degree in chemistry. Boutan spent his early childhood in Paris and studied in the French school system through grammar school. His parents moved to Manhattan and Boutan studied at the Lycée Français de New York. After two years in high school in North and South Dakota each, he graduated from the University of Iowa in Iowa City. Always curious about the meaning of life, he committed his life to Jesus Christ during his senior year.

While Boutan was in Lyon, France, in 1975 working for his dad's company as a translator, he visited a nearby seminary, trying to discern if he should go into the ministry. Its director advised him to not go seminary before he had work experience.

He returned to the United States and went to work for IBM. During that time he married Patricia (Trish) Marie Hartman at the Old Greenwich Presbyterian Church in 1977. They later attended St. Paul's Episcopal Church in Darien, Connecticut, that had a strong emphasis on Bible teaching and preaching. This is where Renny Scott had previously been assistant rector. The Boutans have two children: daughter Renée and son, Christian, married to Mattie, parents of Calvin born in September 2010.

In 1980, Boutan left IBM and he and Trish moved from Connecticut to Maine where their children were born. There his interest took him into construction work, in the old style craft of post and beam construction. They joined St. Matthew's Episcopal Church in Lisbon Falls, Maine where Boutan became involved in every facet of the church. He became so passionate he took copious notes on the rector's Biblical sermons – critiquing the message. Boutan would send those notes to the minister every week. When the minister and his wife received these letters, they would say to themselves, "Oh, no. Not another letter from Marc Boutan." A false rumor circulated saying his rector urged him to go to seminary so he would not have to read more of Boutan's critiques.

In 1987, they moved to California where Boutan earned his MDiv Degree from interdenominational Fuller Theological Seminary in Pasadena but the bishop of Maine told Boutan that if he wanted to be ordained in the Episcopal Church, he would have to take an extra year of Anglican studies at Virginia Theological Seminary. In 1991, Terrell Glenn, who was at St. Andrew's in Mount Pleasant, called Boutan to that church. He was ordained priest on March 18, 1992, by Bishop Salmon,

Through St. Philippian Louise Des Francs, Boutan was called to Belgium and served from 1996 to 1999 at Holy Trinity Anglican Church in Brussels. Boutan said, "It was wonderful to speak French fluently and regularly and to practice it in liturgical settings including bilingual weddings, baptisms and funerals."

Boutan's church and other Anglican churches in Europe and North Africa are overseen by the Intercontinental Church Society (ICS) headquartered in Coventry, England. ICS is also a mission agency of the Church of England. enquiries@ics-uk-org

Their mission statement is, "We make known the good news of Jesus Christ to English speaking people who find themselves living, studying, working or 'holidaying' away from home in countries where English is not the main language." Visitors touring Europe are also welcome.

The Boutans returned to Charleston, and after one year as assistant at St. James on James Island, with the Bishop's permission, Boutan started a home repair business called Hands On, Inc. It was through a serendipitous meeting at the Lowes check-out that McCormick found Boutan. McCormick wanted help with Boutan's musical gifts for the Wednesday night service.

In Elizabeth Hagood's pastoral care committee report in December 2002 she said, "Marc Boutan is extremely effective in the pastoral role. His heart and passion are in pastoral care." By this time he had trained lay Eucharistic ministers and they were ready to "deploy."

Boutan left St. Philip's in May 2006. "We pray for his success and joy in his work." He became priest-in-charge of St. Mary's Church in Goose Creek under the oversight of St. Andrew's in Mt. Pleasant. In June 2007, Marc and Trish moved to Maine where he is employed at Timberwolf Tools. Boutan has acted as a supply minister and teaches Bible studies in Maine.

Good news. Marc and Trish are returning to Charleston. The Rev. Marc Boutan begins his work at St. Philip's during Holy Week in 2013.

THE REVEREND ARIEL KENNETH WELDON

ASSISTANT RECTOR

JULY 2001 – SEPTEMBER 2004

At the same time, Doug Peterson and McCormick interviewed a Sewanee seminarian who would become a deacon in this diocese in June 2001. Ariel Kenneth Weldon was born November 11, 1967, who grew up in Sumter with his parents attending Holy Comforter Church. They moved in 1980 where he graduated from the Fort Mill High School in 1986. During high school, Weldon was a volunteer each summer at Camp St. Christopher as a counselor and continued working there each summer in college as paid staff.

Weldon attended Suwanee for three semesters and then transferred to the College of Charleston where he graduated in May 1991 with a double major in philosophy and English. That fall he was called to be the youth minister at the Church of the Redeemer for one year. In 1992, Weldon went to St. Anne's Church in Atlanta as youth minister.

Weldon met Mary ("Boo") Lovejoy at Camp St. Christopher when they were in high school. "Boo," from Orangeburg, was an acolyte at the Church of Redeemer. She would later receive a bachelor of science/nursing (BSN) degree from MUSC where she worked for several years.

Ken and "Boo" were married in Orangeburg on May 22, 1993, and they have two daughters – Mary Matthews Weldon, born January 2, 1997 and Evelyn Mims Weldon, January 24, 2000.

In 1994, Weldon was called back to the diocese of South Carolina by the Rev. Charles D. Cooper to serve as youth minister at St. John's in Florence. He remained there until 1998 when St. John's sponsored him to the seminary at Suwanee. Weldon said his theology was strong when he entered Suwanee. He believed the Nicene Creed and believed Christ is the only way. Some of the professors were orthodox and some non-orthodox but he enjoyed debating with the non-orthodox. He graduated in May 2001 and was ordained priest at St. John's in Florence in June 2001.

When Weldon visited St. Philip's in 2001, he was impressed with the number of young families in the parish. McCormick said, he thought this young man was "terrific." Weldon was ordained priest at St. Philip's on Saturday December 8.

For the first six months Weldon worked with young couples, youth, singles, etc. preparing a youth ministry for a permanent person to be hired in 2002. Weldon would head the committee to search for the new youth minister.

He said that St. Philip's was a fantastic first job for someone just out of seminary. "St. Philippians were an encouraging, and a very forgiving congregation for a first time priest."

In Weldon's last sermon he talked about the three mentors at St. Philip's that meant most to him. They were Haden McCormick, Ike McPherson, the sexton, and Sam Cobb. Weldon left in September 2004 to accept the position of Porter Gaud's chaplain. Weldon would continue to participate at St. Philip's by giving sermons, communion, baptisms and funerals. He and "Boo" would also be involved in youth ministries and with the young adults.

Later, in 2008 Weldon left Porter Gaud to take a call from St. John's, the church in Florence that sponsored him for the seminary. He remains there in 2012.

It was reported that the compassion committee was operating very effectively guided by Charlotte Hartsock. Later Nancy McGown and Charlotte Williams would take delicious meals to St. Philippians who were ill or having other problems.

By April 2002, Chris Thompson had been hired as youth minister and Riley Watson was hired in July to replace Laura Snedecker, who worked with children's programs. Watson was hired as full time. Everyone acknowledged Watson was excellent for the position.

Miles Barkley at the July vestry meeting handed out a copy of the newly revised St. Philip's hand book. "The revision was a massive effort."

A note was sent in April 2003 by the vestry to thank Betsy Grimball for "her tireless job at the Tea Room." It was a roaring success and all other participants were congratulated. Because the "Tea Room" work is so intensive, the "Tea Room" had to cut down from two weeks to one week. Everyone loved the delicious food, the piano music as played by Bill and Dottie Rhett, Capers Cross and others. Parishioners were needed to deliver meals, to be waiters, cooks, cleanup people, waitresses and busboys, who also serve the drinks. Delicious desserts need to be placed on a table and many ladies bring in the famous okra soup. Most of the profit is given to home and foreign missions.

In 2004, the co-chairs were Betsy Grimball, Neyse Barkley and Caroline Rhodes.

The first Wednesday night program was a huge success thanks to Gene Lesesne's cooking. It was decided in the future to prepare for up to 140 people.

In April 2003, some issues with the ECW came up. When McCormick heard of this, he immediately called a meeting with Helen Trask to show concern and resolve them. Hagood commended McCormick who said he would attend ECW's monthly board meetings.

Four St. Philippian ladies have been president of the Episcopal national ECW: Helen Barkley, Lydia Evans, Catherine Jones and Mary Trott. Trott, at one time, was the head of the Episcopal United Thank Offering.

Charlotte Hartsock reported Anne Jennings would have a program on recovery on June 7. In June, Stephanie McDonald was introduced to the vestry as the new ECW president.

In 2004, Sheryl O'Neal was president of the ECW. Marsee Lee reported the tea room produced about $22,000 in net profit, $4,000 more than last year. Bonnie Schrimpf took over the committee to greet visitors that Mac Anderson held that for many years.

Ric Webb of the worship council reported that more volunteers were needed on the altar guild. He said the wedding guild was going well, although photography was still a problem at some weddings and baptisms.

St. Michael's and St. Philip's had vacation Bible school together in June 2005 at St. Philip's because St. Michael's parish hall was being renovated.

In August 2005, Riley Watson began a "Mother's Morning Out" on Tuesdays and Thursdays. She reported in September that the program was full with thirty-five children divided into four classes.

In March 2006, Liz Marr was president of the ECW and Charlotte Hartsock was vice-president.

Charlotte Williams reported the youth were going to Long Beach, Mississippi, in early July 2006 to help the area come back. Hurricane Katrina struck on August 29, 2005.

Over a period time the following wrote notes to the sick and bereaved: Sally Fine, Eleanor Jenkins, Jane Martin, Suzanne McIntosh and Renee Merriam. Thomas Boulware said the Kanuga weekend looked good for the last weekend in October.

MRS. MATTHEW BAIRD BARKLEY, JR.

The vestry in February 2007 passed a resolution of condolence to the family of Mrs. Helen Lebby Barkley. "Mrs. Barkley was a deeply committed Christian and a leader among the women of St. Philip's and of the diocese."

Helen Barkley née Lebby was born August 25, 1914, in Greenville, the daughter of William Lebby and Ross Haddon Lebby. She was a graduate of St. Mary's Junior College in Raleigh and of the women's college of the University of North Carolina in Greensboro. Helen came to work in Charleston where she lived at a boarding house at 11 King Street run by Mrs. Caroline H. (Carrie) Douglas, a widow. She found a job as a stenographer in an office on the top floor of the People's Building. On September 29, 1938, she nearly died. A tornado struck downtown Charleston that morning and wrecked havoc with the top floor. Helen survived because she sat under her desk.

On March 30, 1940, she married Matthew Baird Barkley, Jr. (February 20, 1906 – March 31, 1987) at St. Philip's with the Rev. Merritt F. Williams officiating and Miss Dorothy Bollwinkle, organist. The matron of honor was her sister, Mrs. Henry Clay Robertson née Lebby. After a honeymoon in Nassau, they would reside at 130 South Battery.

Matt Barkley graduated from Woodberry Forest and Yale University. He was vice-president of the Cameron and Barkley Co. and later president of the Southern Corporation, a paper mill supply company. He and his wife also lived at 7 Legare Street and 83 South Battery. Later Helen resided at Bishop Gadsden until her death.

She loved people and people loved her. Helen enjoyed working with the Junior League, Colonial Dames and the Ladies Benevolent Society. Her main interest was St. Philip's and the diocese of South Carolina.

Helen joined St. Philip's Church in 1937 and remained a member until her death sixty-nine years later. She was chair of the prayer room and the Wednesday morning Bible study group. In 1969, she was the first lady to run for the vestry but she was not elected until 1975. She was re-elected to the vestry in 1988 and again in 1997. Helen was president of St. Philip's ECW and she held several diocesan offices. She was president of the diocesan ECW, first lady deputy to the general convention (1976), first lady elected to the standing committee and she was recognized as Honored Woman of the diocese for her Christian leadership. She was the head of the national Episcopal ECW.

When Helen ran for vestry in 1997 she was asked two questions.

Q. Why do you desire to serve on St. Philip's vestry?
A. To assist our rectors in glorifying God through worship, prayer, fellowship and teaching.

Q. What gifts or talents do you have that would be an asset to St. Philip's vestry?
A. I love Jesus Christ and I love His body at St. Philip's.

She was survived by her daughter, Elizabeth Barkley Ravenel, her husband, Dr. James Morris Ravenel and their children – Helen Barkley Hammond née Ravenel and James Morris Ravenel, Jr. Helen was predeceased by her granddaughter, Elizabeth Ross Ravenel. Helen was also survived by her son, Matthew Baird Barkley, his wife, Eve Barkley and their daughter Rachel Auserman Barkley. Helen Barkley died Monday, February 26, 2007, buried at St. Philip's.

On August 23, 2007, it was reported that Jack Owens wife, Betty, was hired part-time to organize a Stephen Ministry at St. Philip's. Betty and Sheryl O'Neal went to training in Pittsburg.

The Stephen Ministry was founded in 1975 in St. Louis by Rev. C. Haugh PhD, a pastor and a clinical psychologist. Since then more than 11,000 worldwide congregations have implemented a Stephen Ministry.

The completion of a fifty hour course is required for lay people to provide one-on-one Christian care to people who hurt. Stephen Ministry provides high quality, <u>confidential</u> Christ centered care to support people experiencing grief, divorce, cancer, job loss, loneliness, disability, relocation and other life difficulties.

The first leaders of the group were Betty Owens, Sheryl O'Neal and Clay Robertson. The first eleven graduates were: Preston Hipp, Chloe Huddleston, Catherine Jones, Al Katz, Gerry and Suzanne McCord, Bill McIntosh, James and Celia Rembert and Don and Mary Wilbur. Later Don Wilbur would become the group leader.

Clay Robertson died Sunday, February 12, 2012, at age seventy-two. The burial was in the western churchyard.

By October 2007, McCormick hired a "chef," Connie Stahl. He said food brings people in and it was time to give the volunteers a break. In October and November, Stahl prepared food for forty-nine events. Everyone enjoyed Stahl's cooking and her chocolate chip cookies are fantastic. With the "Great Recession," Stahl's job had to be scaled back.

In June 2008, Sheryl O'Neal reported the funeral of Kitty Holt was a wonderful expression of the love the congregation had for Kitty and the Holt family.

Buzz Morris in October 2010 accepted the position of "Senior Acolyte Master" and Thomas Boulware accepted the position of "Chairman of the Ushers Guild."

In 2012, St. Philip's children's ministries are doing well under the leadership of Angela Clark and Lee Moore. Angela, who was born at Fort Dix, New Jersey, grew up in Charleston. She attended Middleton High School and graduated from the College of Charleston in 1986. Her family lived at The Citadel and most Sundays they rode their bicycles from there to St. Philip's.

Clark started working at St. Philip's in 1995 as nursery coordinator and worked with Kirk Middleton and Susan Cale and later Lee Moore, Becky Riggs and Dottie Leonard. Moore was from Columbia and a graduate of the College of Charleston. In 2007, McCormick hired Clark as "Director of the Children's Ministry" and Moore was hired as her assistant. In 2010, they took responsibility for the "St. Philip's Pre-school."

In 2012, the pre-school serves seventy-four students from eight weeks old through three years on Mondays through Fridays from 9:00 a.m. to Noon – also offering a "lunch bunch." There are sixteen teachers and Clark and Moore.

The number of children in the Sunday school, who are from sixth through twelfth grades, has been steady at 125 for the past few years. They attend prior to the 10:30 a.m. service. The children from three years old through sixth grade attend the "Children's Church." during the 10:30 a.m. sermon. A nursery is also available on Sunday mornings. Clark added that sexton Ben Singleton helps a great deal with the pre-school.

DR. AND MRS. MAXWELL ANDERSON

Dorothy (Dot) Middleton was born in Charleston August 3, 1920, the daughter of Charles Francis Middleton, born 1889, and Jane Margaret Simons. Dot attended Craft elementary school on Legare Street and graduated from the all-girls Memminger High School in 1938. After taking a year off from school, she graduated from the College of Charleston in 1942.

Maxwell Anderson, who was born in Charleston on February 10, 1921, never liked the name Max or Maxwell so he called himself "Mac." Mac and Dot became friends, the friendship blossomed and they were married two years after Mac graduated second in his class from The Citadel in 1942. The wedding was held on September 22, 1944, at St. Michael's where Dot had grown up.

After having taken pre-med, Mac enlisted in 1944 in an "Army Special Training Program" for an advance medical program. He served at Boca Raton, Biloxi and Augusta and left the service as a captain in the army air corps. Dot was with Mac at all these places. Afterwards, while Mac took his internship and residency at Bowman Grey in Winston-Salem, Dot would wash, iron and starch his hospital whites to save money.

The Andersons returned to Charleston and moved into 5 Council Street because it was the only apartment they could find for $50.00 per month. Mac, a cardiologist, opened a private practice and cared for his patients for more than forty years.

Mac had grown up at the Citadel Square Baptist Church so Dot tried really hard to be a Baptist. The sermon on every second Sunday would be against alcohol and the sermon every fourth Sunday would be anti-Catholic. One Easter, Dot arrived in her "beautiful homemade dress" to hear a resurrection sermon. However, that Easter fell on the second Sunday and the sermon was against alcohol and not a resurrection sermon. She was incensed and said all her family and friends would have drinks after church. Dot also loves to dance.

After looking at several churches, they settled in at St. Philip's.

They were able to purchase a home in Avondale at 7 Oak Hill Place and then moved to 3 Johnson Road, where Rev. Marshal Travers at 95 Folly Road, tried to recruit Dot to run the Sunday school at his new church. She declined but remained friends with Travers who she always liked so much. Her aunt, Annie Baynard Simons Hasell, told Dot that by living west of the Ashley she would lose her heritage. In 1991, Dot and Mac moved into her parent's former downtown home at 24 New Street.

They had four children: Dr. Robert Maxwell Anderson, Jr., Lois Anderson Ganner, Dr. Charles Middleton Anderson, DMD and Thomas Randolph Anderson. There are eleven grandchildren and five great-grandchildren.

Many St. Philippian's, who go un-thanked, have run the race for a long time but

Mac, who died in 2005, and Dot have run many extra miles. Dot has taught her Monday morning Bible class for more than forty years, Mac and Dot worked hard in the Sunday school and Dot organized the archives from scratch. Most St. Philippians have never seen the archives but it is complete with a large, walk-in vault. Dot said that it was a miracle that any of the records exist. There was a hole on the ground floor of the ministries hall where a large Bible was placed over the hole to keep the rats out. Dot was responsible for the Heritage Sundays, lectures about the church's history, and dramatizations performed in the church to teach "our members" about the history of the church.

God bless you, Dot.

✢ ✢ ✢

Covell Rogers, Travis Dew and Lee Otis were co-chairs for the 2012 Tea Room that was open from Monday April 23 thru Friday the 27th. More than 200 members volunteered, many working more than one shift.

"Vacation Bible School was fantastic this year." In 2012, Joshua 1:9, "Have I not commanded you to be strong and courageous," was the Bible verse on which they focused. The 115 children raised $202.00 for Water Missions and collected school supplies for the Haiti Mission trip. Each of the fifty-five volunteers "deserved a gold medal for their great performance."

THEOLOGY, EVANGELISM & MISSIONS

By December 1999, St. Philip's mission statement was changed. It remains in 2012:

"Building up the body for the work of the Gospel"

✢ ✢ ✢

In 1981, George and Molly Greene moved to Charleston and started General Engineering Laboratories (GEL), an environmental testing lab and engineering consulting company. The Greenes began working on water projects in developing countries in 1998, and formed Water Missions International (WMI), a 501(c)3 Christian engineering ministry, in 2001. That same year they sold GEL to their COO, Jim Stelling, also a member of St. Philip's.

Greene grew up in Ocala, Florida, and graduated from the University of Florida with a chemical engineering degree when he was twenty-three. After graduation, he ventured out of Florida for the first time and headed to Columbia University where he received an MS in chemical engineering. From 1969 to 1973, Greene received a PhD with a major in chemical engineering from Tulane University.

Molly and George were married in Tupelo, Mississippi, in 1970. Their three children are Jeni (who has four lovely young children), George IV, (who has two lovely children) and John Christian who sadly drowned on December 28, 1984.

Two weeks after John died friends invited the Greenes to come to the St. Philip's Wednesday evening service which they continued to attend for many years. They were

Christian at that time, but the services and a sermon taken from the Book of Job enhanced their spiritual growth. They felt "embraced" from the first day they walked into St. Philip's. Molly and George remain faithful members of St. Philip's in 2012.

WMI is a Christian, nonprofit organization that provides clean, safe water and sanitation to people in developing countries and disaster areas through a variety of technologies. Their goal is to provide sustainable access to safe water so that no person should perish for a lack of drinking water.

Equally as important, "A part of WMI's goal is to share the Living Water message with all who receive safe water ... WMI is effectively integrating Biblical principles for healthy living as well as providing opportunities for sharing the truth of the Gospel."

More than forty-nine countries have been served around the world. WMI could use a donation. – www.watermissions.org

In September 2000, it was announced there would be a tenth anniversary banquet for Suzy McCall. It was to be a celebration, not a fund raiser, of her work in Honduras.

In July 2002, Gene Lesesne reported the Haiti trip had just returned and it had been very successful. Ken Holden traveled to Beijing to lecture on folic acid and spinabifida. John and Sharon Dubois were in Panama for language school and then three years in the field.

In February 2003, McCormick reported the *Charleston City Paper* named St. Philip's as the "Best Church and Best Steeple."

When the general convention met in Minneapolis July 28 through August 8, 2003, a controversial action was passed: "Consenting to the election of Rev. Gene Robinson, a man engaged in sexual activity outside the bonds of Holy Matrimony, as bishop of New Hampshire."

The diocese of South Carolina called a special convention for October 2. The first emergency meeting ever called in the history of the Anglican Church, would take place that October. Many of the thirty-eight primates were outraged.

The media, of course, had a field day reporting the Episcopal Church had been torn asunder because of the ordination of Bishop Robinson. That is not true. Robinson is the tip of the iceberg or the straw that broke the camel's back. The national church has been separating from the Word of God for decades, if not longer. Non-orthodox Episcopalians would tell people that it is just a political issue blown up by conservatives. It is not political. It is a theological schism as pointed out by Bishop James M.

Stanton of the diocese of Dallas, who spoke at St. Philip's at the adult forum on August 17, 2003.

Maybank Hagood put Stanton's opening paragraph in the vestry minutes. "In the days before us, you will hear a lot about 'schism' in the church and how awful it would be. But I believe schism has already been committed but it is not the so-called conservatives who have committed the schism. Instead, it is the 2003 general convention of the Episcopal Church which has done so."

In July, it was suggested that St. Philip's join the American Anglican Council (AAC), a group founded in 1995 to reaffirm the Episcopal liturgy. One could join as a member either as an individual or as a parish as two churches in the diocese of South Carolina had already joined. McCormick read aloud the AAC parish affiliation agreement and its covenant. The vestry discussed joining but preferred to learn more about the AAC.

At the August vestry meeting, Jim Stelling made a motion, seconded by Maybank Hagood, for St. Philip's to join the AAC. The motion passed unanimously and it was also voted to send the AAC $1,500 for 2003 and to plan an amount for the 2004 budget. Gaillard asked each vestry member if she or he were in support of the church's conservative position. The members were voluntarily polled with unanimous support. As we know, St. Philip's has not joined with the AAC.

The AAC held a meeting in Plano, Texas, October 7 - 9 in response to the decisions made at the general convention. Senior Warden Henrietta Gaillard, Junior Warden Miles Barkley and Ken Weldon attended. Lydia Evans was there as the province's ECW president. Gaillard said it was a "powerful meeting – Great Peace."

In October, McCormick and all the clergy in the diocese spent three days with former Archbishop of Canterbury George Carey who said the actions by the general convention are an abandonment of scripture, not an interpretation. Archbishop of Canterbury Rowan Williams said he would not recognize Gene Robinson as a bishop when he was consecrated on November 2 and added Robinson would not even be able to preach in England much less be a bishop.

Robinson decided to retire seven years early at age sixty-five in 2013. In a newspaper interview, Robinson said, "The storm had proved too much ... world wide controversy and death threats caused him to resign."

Gene Lesesne in January 2004, compared the 2002 percentages with the 2003 percentages. While giving had gone up, percentages of total outreach funds had declined. His statement that more funds were needed to go to missions and outreach ensued in a lengthy discussion. A motion was approved to withdraw $2,000 each from the vestry's contingency fund for foreign missions and home missions.

In 2004, the details of the amount of money going to missions and outreach were: diocesan outreach $133,000, home missions $38,000 and foreign missions $38,500.

Bishop Salmon informed McCormick that as a result of the redirection of St. Philip's $130,000 diocesan pledge, a check for $10,000 was sent to Bishop Pye and the diocese of Burundi. McCormick emphasized that this was the true definition of outreach and that at least 70% of the diocesan pledge was for helping churches.

In March 2004, each vestry member was asked to provide a roadmap of goals over the coming years. Vestry member Carol McLaren voiced a basic conflict with the concept. She stated that God works from the top down. McLaren did not feel certain "that we can develop a roadmap because the Lord keeps us off balance to make sure we listen to Him and respond to His roadmap." She encouraged the members not to adopt a secular roadmap, but to be open to hear the Lord and pray about it.

The issue of fundraising came up because there were three fundraisers listed in a recent issue of the *inSPIRE*. Jim Stelling said there needed to be some controls to keep things from getting out of control. McCormick said, "We want St. Philip's to be known for fellowship, not to be known as a fundraising church.

Bob Nuttall and Carol Burk developed a new welcome card in July 2004 to be placed in hotel lobbies. Good ideas keep popping up. St. Philip's welcome cards, as previously written, were distributed to hotels in 1924 and 1939.

McCormick loves collects. At the August vestry meeting, McCormick emphasized the importance of understanding collects and their Biblical basis. Archbishop of Canterbury Thomas Crammer put together the first prayer book in 1549. Then, people went to church twice daily and they knew the Bible front and back. By definition, Anglicans should know the Bible. This is something that is largely lost today. McCormick said, "We are a people of the Book."

By April 2005, Marc Boutan began holding contemplative prayer in the church at noon on Wednesdays as this evolved into also handing out gospels of John to our visitors. Eventually, the name of the committee to greet visitors was changed to the "Church Street Mission" (CSM) and in 2011 approximately 2,000 Gospels of John had been handed to our visitors by our CSM members. The church also offers other tracks in foreign languages. These dedicated volunteers are fulfilling Christ's "Great Commission."

Bob Ables in June resigned as head of the home missions committee after many years of dedicated service. Jane McGreevy served temporarily as chair. In 2012, Preston Hipp is chair.

About fourteen St. Philippians volunteer on Fridays at the Tri-County Ministry in North Charleston. St. Philip's home mission committee financially helps to support the organization that prepares and serves lunch and deliveries groceries to various homes. In March 2006, the vestry voted to move the 2005 $18,000 budget surplus to foreign missions.

In February 2007 the Alpha class was packed, some participants would be confirmed on April 1 and several couples were participating. In May, Bill McIntosh took over the Church Street Mission from Bonnie Schrimpf. Ryan Graudin told about the three weeks she spent in Cambodia with Campus Crusade living with a family in the poverty of their everyday lives.

In October, Georgia Bell, a member of the vestry, began a new outreach. She read the "Real Estate Transactions" each Sunday and sent a letter to those listed welcoming them to St. Philip's. The letters were signed by McCormick.

Another outreach was the distribution of copies of *How to Pray* written by R.A. Torry. Although the book was written in the 19th century, it is as fresh as if it were written today. About 300 copies were placed in the pews of St. Philip's on Easter Day 2008.

McCormick reminded his congregation that in 2003, a majority of his parishioners signed a petition disassociating this parish from certain actions at the 2003 general convention, and a resolution to that effect was passed at the following diocesan convention. Those actions still stand in effect today. "Additionally, since my tenure as Rector that began June 10, 2000, no money of St. Philip's has gone to TEC. In 1999, the diocese gave the churches in the diocese the option of redirecting our funds to necessary missionary funds, spent at the bishop's discretion."

✢ ✢ ✢

In 2010, Suzy McCall was interviewed by the *Post & Courier* about her work in Honduras. McCall grew up in a small Episcopal Church (Holy Apostle) in Barnwell with compassionate parents who often responded to community needs. She had never heard a missionary prior to her senior year at the College of Charleston. She attended a festival in Orlando called "Jesus 79" when Tony Campolo gave a stirring sermon in which he said there were many places that had no Christian presence. An altar call followed, she went forward. She definitely knew the Holy Spirit spoke to her that night and that she was called to be a missionary. McCall said she never doubted that He led me to Honduras.

Her home church, St. Philip's, had previously sent mission groups to Honduras and the mission agency that sponsored her was the South American Missionary Society (SAMS). It seemed to her that the Lord was opening doors for Honduras, so she simply walked through. Her LAMB Institute (www.lambinstitute.org), opened in 2000, sought to minister "to the least of these." The Institute opened in an inner-city home to 50,000 people with numerous gangs and a large percentage of households with single mothers.

They began with day care and then added a school and later outreach programs of food banks, vocational training and later a ministry to young children and young people as an alternative to gangs. There is also a residential home for sixty-five children, a short distance from Tegucigalpa. McCall tries to save children and women from human trafficking which is a huge and lucrative business in Honduras. There are now sixty-five employees at LAMB and 220 students in the school. St. Philip's World Mission committee helps to support McCall and several St. Philippians have been on the Lamb Institute Board: Addison (Guv) and Tammy Barnes Gottshalk, Steve Graudin, Jini Greene, Ken and Pat Holden, Kent and Susan Clarkson Keller and Joanna Macmurphy. The Rev. Hank Avent has been chaplain to the ministry.

McCall has turned over The Institute, as she had planned, for the Hondurans to run. She is their primary spiritual advisor.

Dr. Ken Holden and his wife, Pat, faithfully lead an annual mission trip to McCall's organization. Because pills were given to McCall that had to be repackaged into smaller bottles, the Holdens each year invite St. Philippians to join their "pill packing party. Join them next year.

A GLORIOUS GIFT HAS BEEN GIVEN TO ST. PHILIP'S

BY

CHARLES DuPRE DeANTONIO

The dedication of a painting by DeAntonio of the presentation of Jesus in the Temple was held after the 10:30 a.m. service in the parish house on February 5, 2012. There was standing room only.

DeAntonio was born in 1968, the eldest son of artist Charles de Antonio. After studying art at the College of Charleston and the Savannah College of Art & Design, Charles lived in Belize and Philadelphia before returning home to McClellanville.

The introduction was made by Capers Cross, director of music. Capers said, "Charles DeAntonio's grandmother, Katherine Morrison DuPre, was a dear friend and spiritual mentor of mine from my years at St. Andrew's Church in Mt. Pleasant where I served for thirteen years prior to coming to St. Philip's. Charles was just a child at that time, but he remembered me as a friend of his grandmother.

"A couple of years ago, out of the blue, I got a call from Charles. When he told me his name, I knew immediately who he was. He called to ask if his two young daughters could participate in St. Philip's choir program, even though they were members of the Church Creek Presbyterian Church. I told him they certainly could join us and that there have been numerous children from other churches, and that it would be a particular honor and privilege to have in our choir program the grandchildren of my old friend Katherine.

"Over the course of the last two years, I have come to know Charles as a young man of tremendous faith and vision. One day he shared with me a deep desire he had to revive a dying tradition of what he called 'biblical narrative painting,' which had held center stage throughout the history of western art – until the last century, when art, reflecting at times, forsook the sacred and embraced the secular. The work you see before you today is Charles' first salvo in his fight to reclaim a place for the sacred in today's art world. To tell you in his own words the story of how this painting came to be, I give you the artist himself, Charles DuPre DeAntonio."

Charles DeAntonio's speech

DeAntonio thanked everyone here at St. Philip's – particularly Capers Cross and Bill Warlick for all their hard work and trust. He said, "Our work together and friendship have been a great blessing to me.

"There are three things I think that an artist ought to concern himself with his (or her) work, whatever art he practices, and they are the Good, the True and the Beautiful. These things, seen together, are far too often missing from the art of today.

"To have purpose, Beauty needs a connection with the Good, and the Good is meaningless without Truth. In contemporary art there is much focus on beauty – or ugliness as its contrast – but many contemporary artists are unsure about what a standard of beauty might be – just as many might be unsure about a standard of the good and it's this uncertainty which leads Pilate to ask Jesus, 'What is truth?'

"The answer comes from God in the whole Canon of Scripture and the person of Jesus who proclaims, 'I am the Way, the Truth and the Life,' whose *actions* made Truth, Goodness and Beauty Visible.

"We are here to dedicate this painting of what was once a popular subject among European painters – and I have several slides to show how other artists have treated this subject..."

DeAntonio showed three slides of three different paintings of "Presentation in the Temple:" Ambrogio Lorenzetti painted one in 1342, Raphael in 1503 and Paolo Veronese in 1560. "Notice they are all set in European buildings."

"It is depictions like these to which Sir Joshua Reynolds refers when he calls history painting the highest and noblest form of the art. But this discipline, this highest calling, has been largely ignored among practicing artists for the better part of the last century, and it is this neglect that I seek to address in my work.

"Where better in our great country to revive the noble art of history painting than in Charleston with its distinguished history, its men and women and virtuous action, its great beauty, and – its truth – since this is, as they say, 'The Holy City.'

"As all of this was becoming clear in my mind, the question became what *should I paint?* I was thinking about this one Sunday morning when who should walk up to greet me but Charlie Luce. Looking into his face, I began to run through the list of fitting Bible characters and after a time I settled upon Simeon. A depiction of Simeon not only suited Mr. Luce, but because the story takes place at the temple it allows the use of a local church as the backdrop, thus clearly distinguishing it as an American painting. So, I set about finding models and a location, building the painting around the central figure of Simeon.[32]

"Of course, I eventually settled on St. Philip's as ironically Charleston, which is important to me because not only is this not Europe, it is a recognizable, familiar setting – the ancient story has been brought into our world, suggesting that Simeon's story is also our story, that the significance of the scene is *living* and *active* in our own lives.

"My children sing in the choir here and through them and my wife, Carrie, I was reintroduced to Capers Cross. Hoping to learn from his perspective as an artist working in the church, I took him to lunch one day. As it happened, Mr. Cross ended up asking all the questions, and the conversation turned to my work and my ideas about History. Before long, we were discussing the possibility one day of owning this painting.

"Throughout our association, I have been impressed with St. Philip's faithfulness to the gospel, which is exactly what this painting is about, so what better place for it than a church which faithfully upholds that gospel, proclaiming it through the spoken word, thought its music, even through its architecture. This painting is meant to proclaim that same gospel visually.

"I am a professional artist. Painting is how I make a living for my family, and I have no problem with being paid for what I do. But, as an offering of thanks for the many gifts I have been given – among them the ability to make a painting like this – I wanted to give this particular work to the church as a gift for the glory of God. And so here we are."

Unveiling of the picture

St. Philippians gasped and there was a long standing ovation. The portrait's beauty is indescribable.

---

32 Mr. Luce is about ninety and lives at Bishop Gadsden. Mary is De Antonio's first cousin Alexa DeAntonio. Joseph is David Gilbert, St. Philip's youth pastor and Bill Warlick's son-in-law. Jesus is Charlotte Dixon. Simeon's prayer robe belongs to Haden McCormick

De Antonio continued, "Most of us were in the service this morning and heard the full text, I'll just read Luke 2: 2 – 28" Simeon took him in his arms and praised God, saying:

> "Sovereign Lord, as you have promised,
> You now dismiss your servant in peace.
> For my eyes have seen your salvation,
> Which you have prepared in the sight of all people,
> a light for revelation to the Gentiles
> and for glory to your people Israel."

"The moment depicted in the painting is this moment in the story. Simeon stands with the baby in his arms, his eyes and his hand raised to heaven.

"Mary stands serenely in a pose reminiscent of the annunciation from the previous chapter, Luke 1 verse 38 – 'I am the Lord's servant. May it be to me as you have said.'

"Her quietness contrasts Joseph's alarm, which is apparent in his furrowed brow and his raised hand. He brackets the action and his gesture and gaze direct our attention back to the central figure of Simeon holding the child, the heart of the story and of the painting.

"Simeon, dressed in white and blue, represents faithful Israel and, by extension, us. As he stands in front of the open doors, the story, the gospel, has come down out of the church, the gate is open, the way inside can be seen and that way is through faith – through Christ.

"I could certainly say much more – about the light, the colors and the clothing – but if you have seen this much, I am satisfied. It is my hope that the painting will be a blessing to you all now and to generations of St. Philippians to come.

Thank You."

Thank you Charles DuPre DeAntonio and may God bless you.

The painting's permanent home is in the narthex above the main entry to the nave.

FINANCES, THE VESTRY & THE SEXTONS

In 2000, Elizabeth Bowles was senior warden and Ed Holt junior warden. Elizabeth Hagood was secretary and Heyward Harvey was treasurer. Brian K. McGreevy and Malcolm Rhodes were new to the vestry.

The vestry voted to direct all undesignated gifts and bequests into the 5th century fund. In June, Elizabeth Bowles reported that a communications committee would inform the congregation biweekly on the progress of the restoration project. Lydia Evans suggested that prayer be encouraged from both the congregation and individuals.

In July 2000, Mary Bissell announced her retirement. In July 2001, Ann Burris resigned. In August, Becky Riggs resigned to take a position at Holy Cross and Mary Anne Hanckel retired on October 31, 2001.

Heyward Harvey said in October that the Haig fund was to be used for medical expenses for the needy and it was not only for St. Philippians. He also presented the final draft of the "Permanent Endowment Fund." The document was unanimously approved by the vestry.

In 2001, Ed Holt was senior warden and Brian McGreevy, junior warden. Malcolm Rhodes was secretary

McGreevy had earlier expressed concern that there might be a drop off of attendance because of construction but by October there were record numbers of attendees at Sunday school and at services. In fall 2001, McGreevy reported the administrative staff was in place with two newly hired people Donna Stouffer and Juli Garland.

Donna L. Stouffer was born in Okinawa while her father was stationed there in the United States military. He was eventually stationed at Fort Jackson and Stouffer attended schools in Columbia where she was raised in St. Andrews Church of Christ. She came to Charleston in 1976 where she worked at the Medical University of South Carolina in the pharmacology and later the psychiatric departments. Stouffer was a member of Grace United Methodist Church west of the Ashley where she worked for twenty years before coming to St. Philip's on November 2, 2001. She began in publications and two years later became the clergy administrator, a position she still holds in 2012. She is recognized as "Queen of the second floor on Fridays." Her two sons are Ted (41) and Seth (37).

Juli Garland née Bass was born in Williamsburg, Virginia. Her father was in the navy and they also lived in Scotland before arriving in Charleston when Juli was five. After graduating from Garrett High School, she attended the College of Charleston and received a bachelor of science in dental hygiene from the Medical University of South Carolina. Juli and Norman married December 30, 1977, and they have two daughters – Heather born in 1984 and Tiffany born in 1986, both in Charleston. Juli had always been a Lutheran, until 1986 when the family moved to Jacksonville where they joined St. David's Episcopal Church. Juli did church volunteer work and had a part time job in finances. Much of the congregation left St. David's to organize the Church of the Messiah Charismatic Episcopal Church where Juli obtained a full time job working with the church's finances. In 2001, they moved back to Charleston and Juli obtained a job on October 16, 2001 at St. Philip's as the finance administrator, a position she continues to hold in 2012.

Doug Peterson, who announced his retirement in November 2001, was employed by the Citadel in March 2002 "and was happy in that ministry."

In 2002, Brian McGreevy was senior warden and Henrietta F. Gaillard was junior warden. Malcolm Rhodes was secretary. New members on the vestry included Susan Cale, Gerry McCord, Bill Phillipps and Jim Stelling.

In March of the same year, Elizabeth Bonner left $10,000 to St. Philip's endowment fund and Mary Vereen Huguenin left $5,000 toward the church's "Fifth Century Fund." In September, DeRosset Myers left the church $1,000.

A plan was devised so that vestry members could learn more about what was happening in the church and pass on that information to the congregation. The ten vestry members were each responsible for one of these areas: buildings and grounds, membership, pastoral care, parish life, liturgy, outreach, stewardship, communications, Christian education and youth. Each vestry member was to meet at least quarterly with his or her "area" and furnish minutes to the secretary. It is a system that continues to work well.

Also in March, McCormick sadly reported that Carolyn Moseley would be leaving because she and her husband, Tom, decided to move back to Greenville. Carolyn worked "tirelessly" as McCormick's secretary, as vestry secretary with baptisms, wedding schedules and much more.

Carol Burk was hired at St. Philip's on June 1, 2002. In 2012, her title is director of publications and communications. Her grandfather, married to Camille Jachens, was a fireman for the City of Charleston as was his son, Harry Burk, Jr. who married Anne Mizell. After thirty-nine years, her father retired in 1986 as an assistant chief.

Carol was born was born in Charleston on May 17, 1949, and graduated from St. Andrew's High School. She attended Winthrop College for two years, married briefly and worked full time in a hospital while studying full time at the College of Charleston from which she graduated in 1974. Burk taught middle school for three years and then entered the Lutheran Southern Seminary in Columbia from which she graduated in 1980 and in 1981 she was consecrated as a deaconess. After living in several cities working in Christian Education, she became an editor in a publishing house in Minneapolis. Burk left Columbia after her father died to be nearer to her mother.

She started looking for a job and saw an advertisement in the paper by an unknown downtown church. She had to reply to a mail box. After McCormick interviewed her, she had a second interview with the wardens and was hired after they saw her very impressive portfolio.

Carol attends St. Barnabas Lutheran Church. The minister and his secretary recently left the church where Carol volunteered to put out its weekly bulletin in addition to putting out the *inSPIRE*, bulletins and other St. Philip's printed matter. Carol reminds everyone that she is the editor of the *inSPIRE* and that she is not responsible for gathering the material. Some unnamed St. Philippians have been guilty of turning in articles after the deadline. Please remember that the deadline is the Friday before Tuesday.

Burk said she loves her job, the people with whom she works and St. Philippians. "Sometimes I feel more at home at church than at home."

In July 2002, Henrietta Gaillard reported a "Ministries Fair" would be held on August 25 with displays from each area of ministry. This was a chance to not only attract members to our areas of ministry and service but to also showcase the new facilities. The fair was well received. Miles Barkley also reported that the first edition of the handbook would be available there. In 2002, yearly giving totaled $962,000. In 2003, Henrietta Gaillard was senior warden and Miles Barkley, junior warden. Jim Stelling was secretary. Newly elected to the vestry were: Maybank Hagood, Charlotte Hartsock, Carol McLaren and Harry Gregorie III.

Malcolm Rhodes in January 2003 wrote his reminiscents of three years on the vestry. "Uncertainty would have been the prevailing sentiment faced by the vestry three short years ago having just lost our rector (Hampson). By the grace of God, Bishop Salmon was in place to guide the vestry as to what course of action had to be taken very quickly. These weekend sessions with the bishop led to the calling of J. Haden McCormick as rector. Haden prayerfully (mercifully?) accepted.

"In a leap of faith, we decided to restore **both** the ministry and parish buildings. The 'experts' gave no hope of fundraising success. Like Nehemiah, our trust was in the Lord. Maybank Hagood and his (fund raising) committee were steadfast in this task and God honored their work and prayer.

"Through the construction process, the congregation became more excited. Temporary facilities on State Street, the parking garage, the Dock Street Theater and the Footlight Players did not dampen the enthusiasm for the Gospel. Jim Stelling and George Greene were tireless in their work with our contractor. God was gracious when we discovered the second floor of the Parish Building was held up by one half course of bricks,

"St. Philip's has been filled with faithful clergy. Haden, Marc (Boutan) and Ken (Weldon) possess differing talents, passions and gifts but all love the Lord. Chris (Thompson) and Riley (Watson) provide phenomenal services for our children and youth. Our cup overfloweth!

"St. Philip's has faced difficult times over these last three years but now seems to be in a Spirit led communion with God. We are members of a prayer-led, program driven church that ministers to her own flock and is reaching outside of her borders to others both in the community and overseas. You are bearers of a sacred trust. Stay committed to prayer. Lift up Haden, Marc, Ken, Chris and Riley daily. Pray protection for Chsiolm Leonard and the staff who work for promotion of the Gospel. Finally commit to one another in prayer. God has placed you in this position at this time.

"And this I pray, that your love may abound still more and more in knowledge and all discernment, that you may approve the things that are excellent, that you may be sincere and without offense till the day of Christ, being filled with the fruits of righteousness which are by Jesus Christ, to the glory of God. I love you all and commit your work to the Lord. Malcolm"

Marc Boutan and Juanita Orvin led the March vestry meeting's opening prayer. "Prayer does not prepare us to do greater works; prayer is the greater work." Both prayed for the individual vestry members.

In 2004, Vestryman William H. Phillipps nominated J. Miles Barkley as senior warden and D. Maybank Hagood as junior warden. The secretary was Jim Stelling. All were elected. New faces on the vestry were: Tracy Graudin, Marsee Lee, Al Phillips and Charlotte Williams. The members of the finance committee were: Henrietta Gaillard, Betsy Harvey, Richard Hutson, Mark Phillips, Jim Stelling, Terry Trimble, John Welch and the two wardens. Henrietta Gaillard was warden emeritus. St. Philip's definition of "emeritus" for wardens is one year.

It would appear that secretary Jim Stelling had not been typing the vestry minutes himself. It seems his assistant, Marcy Woodsome, has been doing the work. Thank you Marcy.

In January 2004, outgoing senior warden Miles Barkley thanked everyone for their involvement, team work and patience in 2004. "The Lord has blessed us in so many ways and has positioned us for future growth."

Maybank Hagood was senior warden in 2005 and Tracy Graudin junior warden. Harry Gregorie was treasurer and John Blincow, Jr. was secretary. New faces on the vestry were Mary Ables, Dubose Blakeney, John Blincow and Bill McIntosh.

Hagood said starting in November 2005 vestry terms would begin thirty days after Easter because it was to difficult to have the finiancial reports prepared by Janaury. The next congregational meeting would be April 30, 2006.

Andy Anderson said 2004 was the best year the church had financially in a long time. The church's 2005 budget was set at approximately $1,789.000. Barkley thanked Mccormick and Chisolm Leonard for their leadership and budget discipline.

The vestry approved a plaque, and its location in the narthex, for a memorial honoring Sam Cobb. The plaque was funded privately by his friends. It was a "big secret" as they did not want his widow, Nancy, to find out before it was unveiled. In 2012 the memorial reads:

> To the memory of
> THE REVEREND CANON
> SAMUEL T. COBB
> May 14, 1916 – November 29, 2003
> Rector and Rector Emeritus
> of St. Philip's Church
> 1965 – 2003
> This tablet is erected by Members of
> his grateful and loving congregation.
> Faithful Pastor
> Kind Counselor
> Quick Wit
> Music Teacher
> Clergy Mentor
> Ready Friend
> "Be strong and of good courage' be not
> Frightened, neither be dismayed; for
> The Lord your God is with you
> Wherever you go." Joshua 1:9

Cobb's portrait hangs in the parlor at St. Martin in the Fields in Atlanta.

In March 2006, John Welch left a bequest of $100,000 that was restricted to be used solely for the interior of the chapel.

Because of health problems, Tracy Graudin decided she would not accept the senior warden position. Alton C. Phillips was the new senior warden and Bill McIntosh, junior warden. Charlotte Williams was secretary. The four new members to the vestry were: Thomas Boulware, Clay Hershey, Karen Phillips and Jill Stevenson. The vestry year ran from April 2006 to April 2007.

Chisolm Leonard announced in April 2006 an unrestricted $10,000 gift from the estate of W.B. Johnson of Shelby County, Kentucky, would go toward the 5th Century debt reduction. When Johnson, an attorney in Louisville and not a member of St. Philip's, attended a Spoleto event he was so moved to see the interior of the church, he left the gift. Anderson said a healthly church receives surprise, random gifts such as Johnson's bequest.

Andy Anderson said in April 2006, another sign of a healthy church receiving gifts was a bequest left by Margaret Camp Robertson of $81,000 plus a $52,000 gift designated for the bell fund.

At the same time, Anderson observed that the mainline churches were declining, but the fundamentalist churches seem to be growing. St. Philip's was growing as well and he believed the reason for the growth was its orothodoxy. "We believe what we pray!" There had been four years of solid growth. The previous year's congregation had grown by 15%. The church owed $1,500.000 toward the 5th Century debt. Anderson said St. Philip's "is steaming as before."

Maybank Hagood reported that the number of families who pledged increased from 450 in 2001 to 600 in 2005. Al Phillips said in August 2006 the three big expenses would be the bells, 5th Century fund and capital needs of the church, including the organ.

In January 2007, Senior Warden Al Phillips reminded the vestry that "we are spiritual leaders of the church as well as financially responsible for the parish.

The new senior warden was Bill McIntosh and Clay H. Hershey, junior warden. Chase A. Wood was secretary. Others on that vestry were: Mary Ables, DuBose Blakeney, Georgia Bell, John Blincow, Thomas Boulware, Harry Gregorie, Karen Phillips, Dan Russler and George Wilson.

In April 2008, Clay Hershey was senior warden and Daniel T. Russler, Jr., junior warden. Clay Hershey and his wife, Emmie, hosted a party at their house on Montagu Street for the outgoing and the incoming vestry members. A good time was had by all.

By September 2008, when the economy was collapsing, Hershey made a motion to suspend the church's monthly contribution to the diocese and to place a temporary hold on funding for home and world missions. The motion passed unanimously. Other budget items would also be cut back. Maybank Hagood was chair of the 2008 stewardship campaign. In October, Hershey reminded the vestry of the power of prayer especially entering into the stewardship season.

Anderson reported that even though giving was better in October and November, the church was losing income from rental properties. When the stock market collapsed, many parishioners were hard hit. In December 2008, the vestry voted to release the remaining funds that had been budgeted in 2008 to the home and world mission committees. In January 2009, McCormick reported 2008 ended with a $50,000 deficit for the year. There would have been an even greater deficit except for pro-active cuts that saved $127,000.

Daniel T. Russler was the new senior warden and Elaine Pendarvis, junior warden. Roberta O'Shea and Sheryl O'Neal were co-scribes. Those elected as delegates to the diocesan convention were the wardens, Miles Barkley and Ann Harrington. Alternates were Bill Thompson, Gerry McCord, Suzanne McCord and Buzz Morris.

The finance committee reported in January 2010 that "giving was flat." Maybank Hagood would chair the stewardship drive.

At the same time, Dan Russler hosted a lunch for all senior wardens from the past twenty years. It was well attended, including Bishop Salmon. They discussed the need for transparency within any church, working on discipleship in all age groups and focusing on how well the St. Philip's youth programs were doing.

In May 2010, the incoming wardens were Elaine B. Pendarvis as senior warden and Robert H. Nuttall, junior warden. The four new vestry members were Lydia Evans, Elizabeth Hagood, Myron Harrington and John Kerrrison.

ISAIAH McPHERSON

St. Philip's beloved sexton, Isaiah (Ike) McPherson, who died in 2010, arrived at St. Philip's in December 1996. McPherson was born August 27, 1953, the son of Charles and Viola McPherson who gave him two other nicknames – "Ickey" and "Duke" He was a 1971 graduate of Charles A. Brown High School and also attended Denmark Technical College in Denmark. He worked for more than twenty years with the George A.Z. Johnson Survey Company and from there he came to St. Philip's.

As a young man, McPherson played football and baseball. He was on the 1980 Shriner's baseball team when their record was thirty to zero. He had five children: Tyra Shawnté, Isaiah, Derrell, Cyrus and LaTasha and two adoped children, Michelle and Patrice.

Rev. Ken Weldon said, " McPherson taught him more about being a priest and being a man of God than any other single person." McPherson also told Weldon, "You can either work the work or the work will work you." Weldon said McPherson was right. "You can't let the work work you. You gotta work the work."

Sometimes McPherson would sing to the ladies in the ministries hall.

McCormick wrote, " Ike was hunble, soft spoken and always eager to help. Every event held at the church ... Each of us had a special relationship with Ike that transcended anything typically developed in the work place. Our relationships were personal and we will desperately miss him. He was our colleague in ministry, an essential member of our team, a true brother. We have lost a friend that helped define who we are. Ike loved us and we loved him." His last words were, "Lord Have Mercy On Me." He died as the day was beginning on Saturday, July 3, 2010.

There were two viewings, the latter at the Reformed Episcopal Church, 90 Anson Street from 6:00 p.m. to 8:00 p.m. Laura Wichmann Hipp wrote a wonderful letter to the *Post & Courier* about McPherson's funeral held on Saturday, July 10, 2010, at noon at the Mother Emanuel African Methodist Episcopal Church at 110 Calhoun Street. It is located opposite Buist School where McPherson attended elementary school.

Hipp wrote: "The funeral was memorable. It began in one large church with more than 600 people seated, including at least twenty to thirty per cent of them being St. Philippians. McCormick was to be a part of the funeral. The funeral had begun at Noon and ten minutes later as Rev. Ron Sadderfield was reading the Scriptures, firemen entered the church and announced the church must be evacuated because of a fire." Power lines leading into the church began to "arc and spark" during the funeral. The fire department decided it was a bird's nest on the power lines that caused the problem.

Because it was a slow very hot evacuation, everyone was trying to find shade on Calhoun Street. McCormick offfered to move the funeral to St. Philip's but that did not work. The funeral director brought Ike's casket and the mourners moved back around the corner to The Reformed Episcopal Church where seating was much more limited. Weldon offered prayers in the front of the church with those who could not get into the church. To those who got in the church, it was a very moving ceremony.

Ben Singleton, who was hired as the new sexton by August 30, 2010, grew up on James Island where as a twelve year old, he started a flower business. He would pick the wildflowers from James Island, put a rubber band around the stems of each bunch of flowers and charge twenty-five cents each. Singleton said it was a good business albeit it was seasonal and that he grew up on a farm learning how to work.

Later, Singleton, who worked for Middleton Gardens, came to the church from a local beverage distributor after he was recommended by Pastor Herman Robinson. His wife, Kisha, who grew up in Summerville, works for the Charleston Police Department. They live with their eleven year old daughter, Samamtha, in Ladson. Singleton, who works 8:00 a.m to 5 p.m. Monday through Friday, is doing a great job.

Richard Washington serves as sexton and church support person on Saturdays and Sundays.

In January 2011, a non restrictive bequest from the estate of Mrs. Virginia Neyle of $7,500 was received. The money was put in the general fund.

To cut back the 2011 budget, no new staff positions were added in 2010 and there were no new financial increases for staff or clergy. "Home" and "Foreign Missions" budgets were reduced by $10,000 each. The overall music budget was decreased to $226,000 including the elimination of four salaried singers.

The new wardens, who served from May 2011 to April 2012, were Robert H. Nuttall, senior warden and Myron Harrington, junior warden. Harry Gregorie was again elected as treasurer.

St. Philip's by-laws were updated in 2011 for the first time since the 1940s. The by-laws committee, consisting of Miles Barkley, Foster Gaillard, Chisolm Leonard, McCormick and Bob Nuttall held regular meetings from the fall of 2010 to April 2011. The by-laws were presented to the congregation at the annual meeting on May 15 where the feeling was the vote should be postponed until the next congregational meeting so people would have time to digest the contents. Copies of the proposed by-laws had been available prior to May 15. There was agreement that the next meeting would be held a week later on May 22. The by-laws were then overwhelmingly accepted.

With tongue-in cheek, the by-laws declared the pews were free. One item that would be nice to have in the by-law was omitted. From the *Vestry Handbook* of the Episcopal Diocese of South Carolina 2002, 2nd Edition, Part One, section II, page 7, "The Canons of the church give exclusive authority over the fiscal affairs of the parish to the vestry. Vestry members are also spiritual leaders who are committed to building up the Body of Christ so that it can be an effective instrument of mission and ministry in the world."

"The church received a bequest in the amount of $25,000 from the Estate of J. Palmer Gaillard, Jr. for the beautification and upkeep of the church 'cemetery.' In 2010, the vestry, with the approval of the Gaillard family, created 'The Gaillard Cemetery Fund' for purposes of investing and using these funds in accordance with the provisions set forth in Mr. Gaillard's Will." Written by Foster Gaillard.

The 2011 - 2012 wardens were Robert H. Nuttall, senior and Myron Harrington, junior.

The 2011 - 2012 vestry council heads were: Al Katz, fellowship, Catherine Jones, outreach, Guv Gottshalk, pastoral care, Roberta O'Shea, Christian education, Pettigrew Clare, worship, Jay Davis, parish life, Lydia Evans, communications, John Kerrison, youth, David Grubbs, financial resources and Elizabeth Hagood, buildings/grounds.

Andy Anderson in July 2011 informed the vestry of an extraordinary, unrestricted gift of more than $129,000 the church received in June from the estate of a deceased parishioner, Mrs. Constance Rose Pultz who lived in Mt. Pleasant.

In October 2011, Mrs. Renee Flint née Fox resigned to go to nursing school.

Mrs. Felicia Lescow née Erdmann, who was hired as receptionist/volunteer coordinator, was born in Nebraska. When she was three she and her family moved to Arizona where she later graduated from Arizona State Unversity with a bachelors degree in health science. After she married the Rev. John Lescow, a Missouri Synod Lutheran minister in 1999, they moved to Wisconsin where he was called to a church. Eleven years later, they chose to retire in Charleston because they felt it was the best place in the world. They visited many churches but felt most at home at St. Philip's. John Lescow sings in the choir and their daughter, Monet, is eleven.

In 2012/2013, Myron Harrington was senior warden, David Grubbs as junior warden.

Budgets: 2010 actual $1,916.764.14,
2011 actual $2,332.345.82
The 2012 actual budget was $2,469,314 with a projeted surplus of $25,695.

PROPERTY & MAINTENCE

After a roofer said the roof would last another three to five years, Steve Graudin suggested the vestry spend $1,000 a year for maintenance and allow at least $35,000 in the future for a new roof.

In December 1999, Ables advised Craig Bennett, Jr. about the cracks in the sanctuary caused by the county parking lot construction. Elizabeth Bowles requested the church spend $11,500 to restore the six narthex doors. The motion carried and thirteen years later the doors look great.

In January 2000, a committee recommended hiring a parish administrator. Bowles said they took the opportunity to hire Chisolm Leonard who had returned to Charleston with his family. Leonard was on board by April 18, 2000. For the past twelve years, Leonard has lovingly and efficiently looked after St. Philip's property and finances. Mary Anne Hanckel was promoted to assistant parish administrator.

In December, Holt said the vestry needed to convey to the congregation that the 4th century funds were still segregated in the "Trust Fund B" and that the money was being invested wisely in bonds. Maybank Hagood reporting on the 5th century fund stated that $2,845.000 was on hand representing 114 families. One very generous donor gave $500,000. It was projected that work on the ministries hall would take nine to ten months and work on the parish hall would take eleven months.

After all this time, there had never been a ruling that would allow the former church home to be used for multiple purposes. The church petitioned the court in light of the extensive renovations that were planned for the building. Foster Gaillard volunteered his time and efforts to bring this complicated issue to a conclusion. On September 14, 2000, Judge Victor A. Rawl, Sr. ruled in favor of St. Philip's allowing the building to be used for church offices and other uses.

On December 1, Preston Hipp, Craig Bennett, Chisolm Leonard and Foster Gaillard went up to the roof to examine the steeple where they found that drilling for the county parking garage caused cracks in the steeple and in other nearby properties. Eleven months later on November 7, 2001, the vestry voted to hire attorney Allen Gibson, who recommended a suit be filed immediately because the statute of limitations for filing against Charleston County was November 8. The church could drop the suit at any time. Also, the Church Insurance Company sent an appraiser who did extensive work evaluating the damage.

In January, a copy of Bishop Gadsden's portrait and plaque was taken to Bishop Gadsden and swapped for the original which today hangs on church property.

By February 2001, there was about $3.2 million in the 5th Century Fund. In September, the amount rose to $4,450,000, a figure that represented 89% per cent of the total needed. In March, teams of two vestry members wearing hard hats went to each adult Sunday class giving a talk about the 5th Century Fund. Pledge cards were available. 5th Century offering boxes were handed to the children during Sunday school. In November, a fundraiser held at Robert Dixon's restaurant, Robert's, was a "spectacular success." The dinner was to be repeated as there was a waiting list. In 2002, an anonymous person donated $250,000 to the "5th Century Fund."

The ministries hall was scheduled for demolition in July followed by the parish house on September 15 with both projects taking about twelve months. Laurie Snedeker needed help in removing and storing years' worth of items from the parish hall. Classes would be conducted at the Dock Street Theater, the Footlight Players Workshop and a third Sunday service was considered.

Chisolm Leonard reported that on January 1, 2002, the church would begin a 5.5 year lease from Mrs. Ursula Kaiser for the parking lot on the northwest corner of State and Cumberland streets. In 2012, the lot is for sale.

In February 2002, Henrietta Gaillard reported the irreparable church boiler finally broke. A replacement would cost between twelve and fifteen thousand dollars.

Attorney Alan Gibson reported on the litigation concerning the steeple cracks. The church was currently suing Case Atlantic, J.A. Jones and Charleston County for cracks possibly caused during the placement of pilings (caissons) for the new garage. Two repair estimates had been quoted. The Church Insurance Company

agreed to pay $92,500 to cover the cost of repairs and St. Philip's would subrogate its suit right to the insurance company. The vestry voted unanimously to accept the payment from the insurance company.

Chisolm Leonard reported in March 2002 that the move into the ministries hall went exceptionally smoothly with all the staff doing "yeoman's work." The new phone system and LAN network were both working well. New awnings, reception furniture and blinds were ordered.

After much discussion, the vestry in June 2002 voted to authorize $35,000 for furnishing the parish hall and $125,000 for the "courtyard" adjacent to the south side of the building. The courtyard would have three main foci: playground areas for toddlers, infants and children, garden area and a sports/basketball course.

Leonard showed the vestry bags of artifacts from the construction site that included old bottles, coins and an unexploded artillery shell that was detonated. As previously written, two or more artillery shells on church property were detonated in 1949. Perhaps, there are more.

By October 2002, the cost of construction was $5,619,000, leaving an estimated maximum shortfall of $1,124,000 through 2006 unless more gifts were forthcoming.

Jim Stelling said the parish hall was nearly complete. The buildings were rededicated on November 15.

Bill Phillipps said the property committee made a proposal that McCormick had to approve any usage of the parish house and that only programs that promote the Gospel would be permitted. The guidelines were approved with one exception – dancing was allowed.

In February 2003, Jerry Sifford was working hard with the BAR to have awnings and signs put back on the parish hall. An electric fire in the parish house raised issues of fire alarms. The ministries building won a Carolopolis Award from the Preservation Society in 2002. D. Dubose Egleston, Jr. (who in 2010 became headmaster of Porter Gaud from which he graduated in 1993) put together the church's website and in April 2003, Luke McBee was made chair of the website committee. Bob Nuttall joined the communications committee and would be proofing the handbook and other publications.

The property committee received a request for six Charleston battery benches so parents could sit and watch their children. The cost would have been $1,557, but Harry Gregorie offered six teak benches as a contribution to the churchyard. He was graciously thanked by all.

Henrietta Gaillard thanked Dot Anderson for her help for keeping the archives in such good shape over the years. In October 2003, Dot asked Bill McIntosh to be the co-chair of the archives.

Jim Stelling in February 2004 reported that the insurance claim for the steeple was on hold as the contractor's parent company was in bankruptcy protection but Stelling was hopeful that the insurance proceeds would cover all of the repair costs. The steel scaffolding was still in place as they were trying to figure out the best way to approach the necessary steeple maintenance. The engineer, Eddie Porcher, and the subcontractor were trying to track down specifications for the stucco mix from the restoration in the early 90s. The largest cost, between $80,000 and $100,000, was the access to the steeple. Work would not begin until spring or early summer. Because the staircases had been replaced, Chisolm Leonard could only offer to take two members of the vestry at a time up the steeple.

Fungi on the organ made it evident there was a humidity problem in the church and the complaints went on – the flower guild complained about fleas in the chapel and there was speculation that there might be a rat, squirrel or other rodent residing there as well..

Harry Gregorie and Palmer Gaillard, Sr., were constructing some attractive racks for the narthex that would hold information about the church and the Gospel.

In August 2004, the interior work was progressing. The walls had been scraped and some painting had begun. Both corners of the north balcony were fixed and the scaffolding was down. In September, the north balcony was re-opened since the weather was cooler. The air conditioning had not been repaired. Marc Boutan installed additional pew racks. The steeple repairs were to start in mid-September to the end of October. Major and minor work continued.

Carol McLaren reported it would cost $5,329 to clean the very dirty stained glass window.

Dubose Blakeney reported in April 2006 they were trying to fix the moisture issues in the narthex. Because paint continued to peel due to "sweating" around the cool water pipes, the vestry agreed to pay Morelli $11,350 to remove the pipes, insulate them and put them back. The pipes would be monitored during the hot and humid months and then the plaster and paint would be repaired when the problem was solved. Blakeney in October declared the narthex moisture issue solved.

In February 2007, Dubose Blakeney said the scaffolding in the church would come down in a couple of weeks.

Bill Thompson reported in January 2008 that, hopefully, the narthex leakage problems were solved. Three independent fail-safe control systems were installed that would shut off if a high condensate level was detected. In June, Clark Hanger reported in the south narthex there was a small leak developing, the cause of which was undetermined.

Hanger reported new wrought iron hand railings were installed on the north and south (middle doors), and the west door where railings had not previously been installed.

In June 2010, Bob Nuttall asked the vestry for $6,013 to re-carpet the church's balcony aisles to minimize the noise created by children returning from children's chapel. The vestry agreed.

THE RECTORY

In February 2000, the finance committee recommended the vestry allocate up to $75,000 to be spent on making the rectory habitable. The motion passed. Lead based paint was removed, the heating and air conditioning systems were updated and there were interior painting and repairs.

Bill Thompson said in November an additional $30,000 was required to finish the rectory repairs. In addition to the removal of the lead paint, there were extensive wiring problems, window work and a need to bring everything up to code. The vestry allocated the money.

An estimate was received in July 2005 of $46,658 from Palmetto Craftsmen to repair and repaint weather damaged wood at the rectory. The vestry voted to pay for the repairs from Fund C.

MUSIC, THE CHOIR & BELLS

Virginia Neyle in April 2000 wanted to continue raising money for additional bells. She asked only for stationary and postage and would not solicit members. The amount needed would be between $200,000 and $250,000.

In September 2004, the antiphonal organ was placed back in the church.

Catharine Jones asked that the noise in the narthex be controlled better during the prelude. In December 2001, she praised Capers Cross and Jean Breza for doing an outstanding job with the music.

Jones reported the youth choirs on their next tour would sing in Chartres Cathedral, Strasburg Cathedral and at Canterbury. The children's choir sang with the Charleston Symphony in November 2003.

Capers Cross asked parishioners for a list of their favorite hymns and carols for use in the services. Ten years later, this author votes for *The Song of Isaiah* and *Venite Adoremus*.

To celebrate their thirty-fourth year anniversary, Haden and Lynn had a service for a renewal of their wedding vows on November 24, 2002. Both choirs sang and McCormick asked all offerings be given to the children's choir for their European trip.

In August 2006, the amount needed for the bell fund was $900,000. The vestry agreed if 60% of money was raised, the finance committee would recommend taking on the "Bell Fund Project." Craig Bennett, Jr. made an informative presentation about installing "English Change Ringing Bells." The balance in the bell fund in 2010 was $150,902.

CHURCHYARDS

Kay Bartlett, a member of St. Philip's, has completed a wonderful job posting on the computer all those who are buried at St. Philip's. Most listed show date of burial including other comments and the numbers of the burial plot. It has been a long, tedious and thankless job for her but we and future generations thank her.

The carriage drivers love to tell the story that only those born in Charleston are buried in the eastern churchyard and "those from off" are buried in the western churchyard. That is absolutely not true. In the 18th century a section of ground in the western churchyard grave sites were supposedly set aside for strangers such as sailors. DuBose Heyward, who was born in Charleston, is in the western churchyard and John F. Schmidt, born in Germany, is buried in the eastern churchyard, proving this fable false.

In the 21st century, there are many tour guides in Charleston who offer ghost tours. They stand outside the church fences in droves hearing stories about the so-called ghosts in the churchyards. Ghost stories can be fun, but there is no theological information that ghosts exist. In 2007, the church put up a sign just behind the fence on the north side of the eastern churchyard that says:

**THE ONLY GHOST AT ST. PHILIP'S
IS THE HOLY GHOST
COME JOIN US TO LEARN MORE ABOUT
THE TRINITY INCLUDING THE HOLY GHOST
SUNDAY 8:15 a.m. and 10:30 a.m., Wed. 5:30 p.m.**

The sign has been proven very popular.

In 2009, a tombstone was uncovered in the western church yard that had been buried perhaps for centuries.

> Here lieth The Remains of
> LAURENCE SOUTHEY
> Who
> Departed This Life
> December 4 Anno Domini
> 1770 Aged 29 years
> Come Hither Mortals Cast
> Then Go Way PrePare to Die
> Repent In Time\Make No delay
> Least yorr Like Me Be Snatched Away
> Life How Short
> Eternity How Long

In July 2011, McCormick reviewed plans for a Columbarium in the tea garden annex, a project that was first proposed in 2008. The church desired to move forward with required municipal approvals. McCormick requested that the vestry approve $4,500 for possible permitting expenses leading to the final approval by the city. Guv Gottshalk made an amendment to approve up to $4,500. The motion passed.

THE MOST REV. DR. KATHERINE JEFFERTS SCHORI
PRESIDING BISHOP OF THE EPISCOPAL CHURCH (TEC)
and
THE RT. REV. MARK JOSEPH LAWRENCE
BISHOP OF THE DIOCESE OF SOUTH CAROLINA
AND THE TRIALS AND PERSECUTIONS HE IS ENDURING

Katherine Jefferts Schori was born on March 26, 1954, in Pensacola and raised a Roman Catholic until age eight when her parents joined St. Andrews Episcopal Church in New Providence, New Jersey. Later they moved to Seattle. She received a bachelor of science in biology from Stanford in 1974, a master of science in oceanography in 1977 and a PhD in oceanography in 1983 from Oregon State University. In 1979, she married Richard Schori, an Oregon State professor of topology.

Jefferts Schori's parents were pilots. Jefferts Schori is an instrument rated pilot and their daughter, Katherine, a third generation pilot, serves as a captain in the United States Air Force.

In 1994, Jefferts Schori graduated with a master of divinity from the only Episcopal seminary on the west coast, The Church Divinity School of the Pacific, located in Berkeley, California. She served as an associate rector at the Church of the Good Samaritan in Corvallis, Oregon, where she had a pastoral ministry with Hispanics as she is fluent in Spanish. She was also in charge of adult education. In 2001, she was consecrated as bishop of Nevada. In an email sent to this author from the office of the diocese of Nevada, there was no knowledge of who consecrated Jefferts Schori as priest or who consecrated her as the bishop of Nevada.

The seventy-fifth national convention of The Episcopal Church (TEC) met in Columbus, Ohio, June 13-21, 2006, where Jefferts Schori was elected presiding bishop on June 18 on the fifth ballot with ninety-five of the 188 votes cast. She was the first woman primate in the worldwide Anglican Communion and the twenty-sixth presiding bishop of the Episcopal Church.

The Rev. Haden McCormick opened the June 15, 2006, vestry meeting with the collect for the second Sunday after Pentecost. It was a fitting collect and our prayers were sent to those who were making decisions at the national convention concerning the next presiding bishop. The vestry also prayed for the policies of the national church to be in communion with Canterbury with participants voting for a moratorium on the election of bishops or other ministers in a same sex relationship and also a moratorium on blessing same sex "marriages."

In addition to debating same sex relationships and same sex "marriages," one of the issues, discussed at length, was "bible numerology" that some non-orthodox Episcopalians "say has deep spiritual and prophetic significance. The numbers in the old and new Testaments reveal the hidden meaning and concept often not understood by the common man or casual readers ... many great thinkers, achievers and scientists have shown great interest in understanding the hidden code in the numbers in bible numerology and using them for their own interest."

The *inSPIRE* of July 2, 2006, carried a pastoral letter from Bishop Salmon about the convention in Columbus. He said that worship often just focused on God with only occasional references to the Trinity. He said that of the seven candidates for presiding bishop, Jefferts Schori was in the deepest disagreement with the theology of the Anglican Communion and she with her whole diocese in 2003 approved same sex blessings. There were many other disappointments during the convention.

In 2006, Bishop Salmon, who had been bishop for seventeen years, reached seventy-two which was the mandatory retirement age. The process began to find a new bishop and three candidates came forth: Rev. Canon Ellis Brust, chief operating officer of the American Anglican Council, with its headquarters in Atlanta; Rev. Mark Lawrence, rector of St. Paul's church in Bakersfield, California, and Rev. Steve Wood, rector of St. Andrew's in Mt. Pleasant.

Rev. Dow Sanderson, president of the diocese's standing committee, resigned his position and McCormick was elected president. Sanderson said, "We have three conservative candidates in a conservative diocese." Those who could vote were: every priest in the diocese, four lay representatives from each parish and two lay representatives from each mission.

On Saturday, September 9 a "walkabout" was held at St. Philip's where clergy and lay delegates could ask questions directed to the three candidates. Even though Lawrence had only four hours sleep the previous evening, after hearing some of Lawrence's great responses, some asked what would he say if he had had eight hours sleep? A member of a non-orthodox church asked, "We are just a small church. Can't we stay the same?" Without hesitation, Lawrence replied, "No you can't. All churches must change."

Lawrence was quoted in the newspaper, "We don't want to walk apart from the Anglican Communion. Many Episcopalians are comfortable living with ambiguity because they think culturally, not theologically ... I look at the leadership of the Episcopal Church and they are stuck with their heads in the sand."

Again from the newspaper, "Liberals (non-orthodox) are a minority in the diocese of South Carolina, and they worry how alternate oversight and a new bishop might affect their spiritual lives." One non-orthodox church was "crafting questions" for the three candidates.

On Saturday, September 16, Lawrence was elected in a landslide by the clergy and lay delegates of the diocese. He would also need a majority approval from the church's house of bishops as well as a majority approval from the standing committee members from each diocese. McCormick spent countless hours working for Lawrence's election. Among other contacts, there were many phone calls to bishops. Lawrence sent out letters to standing committee members affirming his intention to abide by canon law and remain part of TEC.

Lawrence had 120 days from June 16 (to March 9, 2007) to gather the necessary votes. He needed fifty-six affirmative votes from the dioceses to be elected and he received fifty-seven. The bishops also responded favorably. It was not until Thursday, March 14, 2007, six months after the election, that the presiding bishop called McCormick to say she was declaring Lawrence's election null and void because some dioceses voted by email or fax. That was against canon law. Several dioceses, both on or off American soil, did not realize that at the 2006 general convention the use of electronic permission ended.

McCormick wrote in a March 14, 2007, letter, "I hope that this tragic outcome will be a wakeup call to clergy and lay throughout TEC as to the conditions in our church." Rev. Dr. Kendall Harmon, canon theologian for the diocese, said "This is very big. For the first time in at least sixty years, a bishop is in real danger of not getting consent."

Even though Bishop Salmon had turned seventy-two, he agreed to stay until Lawrence was consecrated although Salmon had no authority from TEC. The diocese's standing committee granted Salmon full authority to act, except for calling a diocesan convention. Salmon carried on full steam and did a magnificent job. He would not be able to retire until late January 2008.

Lawrence expressed disappointment in the state of the church and called on Episcopalians to pick one side or the other. He said, "that in one camp are those who emphasize the church's 'broad tent' tradition. In the other are those who believe a broadening tent has caused the church to stray too far from doctrine." Lawrence believes "the instruments of unity – Scripture, the Creed, the Book of Common Prayer and articles of religion – constitute the rock upon which All Anglicans must rely."

Lawrence continued, "It's astonishing, the way people have flung mud. It's ludicrous what is being portrayed here". He said "he has been portrayed as a candidate willing to split the church."

Lawrence said, "I shall commit myself to work at least as hard at keeping the Diocese of South Carolina in the Episcopal Church as my sister and brother bishops work at keeping TEC in covenanted relationship with the worldwide Anglican Communion." He continued, "People went berserk, people went apoplectic." Yet all Lawrence said was that the church cannot function unilaterally. He acknowledged the world has changed and that church practices have become a global issue with global consequences.

Lawrence and his wife, Allison, returned to his parish church in California. Lawrence said, "My heart has been tied to the people of South Carolina. I'm not sure it's over. The ball is in the court of the diocese. If they desire that I stand for election once again, then we would look at that. In four months of often acrimonious debate and 'mud flinging,' many people have learned a great deal. Perhaps it would make more sense to 'play the second half.'"

The vast majority of the delegates did, indeed, want Lawrence to run again. In fairness, McCormick made certain that others could have the opportunity to oppose Lawrence. No one else stepped forward.

Bishops and members of standing committees sent Lawrence a set of questions. They were concerned about his intentions of having an alternative primatial relationship, meaning he did not want to answer to Jefferts Schori, and they wanted to know in what ways he would work to keep this diocese in TEC. Lawrence replied that he might as well have been asked while he was engaged to my wife, "In what ways will you work to keep your wife from leaving her commitments?" And he informed his interrogators Jefferts Schori would not be welcome at his consecration.

On Saturday, August 4, 2007, the clergy and lay delegates reconvened the 2006 annual convention. They overwhelmingly approved two measures to suspend normal bylaws and convene a special "electing convention." The mood at the convention, held at St. James on James Island, was "spirited," reflecting the consensus in the room. Bishop Salmon often joked with attendees who burst into applause when Lawrence was re-nominated. By October 29, 2007, Lawrence received the necessary consents.

Mark Joseph Lawrence was consecrated as the fourteenth bishop of the diocese of South Carolina at the Cathedral Church of St. Luke and St. Paul on Saturday, January 26, 2008. Lawrence said, "It's a joyous celebration of God's faithfulness."

Bishop Salmon retired happily to St. Louis.

One month after Lawrence's consecration, Jefferts Schori arrived in the diocese of South Carolina for a two day visit on Monday and Tuesday February 25 and 26. It is required that a presiding bishop visit each diocese in TEC at least once during her or his nine year tenure. She participated at St. Philip's in evensong in which there is no sermon. Non-orthodox Episcopalians came in droves, filling St. Philip's, showing their support of her with loud applause.

Afterwards, there was a reception in the parish hall honoring Jefferts Schori where she made some brief remarks explaining that she was developing a guide line for all churches in TEC. As she put it, "How will we engage in God's reconciling mission – by sharing the good news, healing the world, and caring (or 'greening') for all of God's creation." There were other guidelines as well. It sounded good until the very end when she said, "but, of course, no church can undertake all of these guidelines." "Sharing the good news" would be optional.

On Sunday, November 30, 2008, Lawrence presided at the diocese's annual HIV/AIDS healing service at St. Stephens at 67 Anson Street in Charleston. The 6 p.m. service included laying-on hands and Holy Communion. The service commemorated World AIDS Day, December 1.

RT. REV. MARK JOSEPH LAWRENCE

Mark Joseph Lawrence was born March 19, 1950, in Bakersfield, California. His father was from Arkansas and his mother, a fifth generation Californian. "His progress toward Christianity and toward the ministry was incremental, growing more solid in several stages, and when it set, it set hard. He had read much philosophy and literature, especially poetry of the 17th and 20th centuries, enjoyed wrestling in high school and college, backpacking in the High Sierra, folk music and his guitar."[33]

Lawrence was educated at California State University in Bakersfield, graduating in 1976 with a BA. While in college, he married Allison Kathleen Taylor in 1973. They have five children: Chadwick (Chad) who in 2012 is headmaster of the St. Helena's Christian Church in Beaufort and married to Wendy with three children; Adelia married to Stephen Matson with three children; Emily married to Jacob Jefferis; Joseph married to Joette with one child and Chelsea who was twenty-three in 2012.

After graduating from the Trinity School for Ministry in 1980 with a M. DIV., he returned to California where he served at two churches. From 1984 to 1997 he served at St. Stephen's in McKeesport, Pennsylvania, a steel mill region. Even though the area faced decline, with Lawrence as rector, the parish grew by more than fifty percent. He returned to Bakersfield where he served as rector at St. Paul's from 1997 to 2007. In 2003, Lawrence for the first time attended an Episcopal national convention as a clerical deputy from the diocese of San Joaquin. He returned to the 2006 national convention as a clerical deputy.

---

33 *Charleston Mercury* January 31, 2008, by Dr. James Rembert

He was known for being a dedicated pastor-teacher. It was Alden Hathaway, retired bishop of Pittsburg, who encouraged Lawrence to become a candidate for the bishop of the diocese of South Carolina. Hathaway preached at Lawrence's consecration.

McCormick, who was a clerical deputy, and lay deputy Lydia Evans attended the 76th general convention held in 2009 in Anaheim. Lawrence was at the convention as a deputy in the "House of Bishops."

In Jefferts Schori's opening speech, she talked about crisis and said the general convention was at a critical juncture in making decisions and she rehashed moments of past general conventions. She said, "Our mission is to keep traveling, bearing the good news of Jesus and working to transform the world." Continuing she added, "The crisis of this moment has several parts, and like Episcopalians, particularly ones in Mississippi, they're all related. The overarching connection in all these crises has to do with the great Western heresy – that we can be saved as individuals, that any of us alone can be in a right relationship with God. It's caricatured in some quarters by insisting that salvation depends on reciting a specific formula about Jesus. That individualist focus is a form of idolatry, for it puts me and my words in the place only God can occupy … That heresy is one reason for the theme of the Convention."

Jefferts Schori continued, "Ubuntu - That word doesn't have any 'I's in it. The 'I' only emerges as we connect – and that is what the word means. I am because we are, and I can only become in relationship with others. There is no 'I' without 'you,' and in our context, you and I are known only as we reflect the image of the one who created us … Ubuntu implies that selfishness and self-centeredness cannot long survive." She closed, "Will our words imitate God's effective word, speaking shalom to creation? That's our decision, individually and collectively – that is our opportunity to live Ubuntu."

The general convention voted to declare gays and lesbians eligible for any ordained ministry. Lay people voted 78 – 21, clergy voted 77 – 19 to approve the measure and the House of Bishops voted 99 – 45 to approve.

The Rev. Todd Wetzel from Dallas said, "It is time to shake off the gloom of the 2009 convention and get back to prayer, proclamation of the Apostolic faith and stabilizing our parishes."

On his return from the convention, McCormick gave a synopsis of Bishop Lawrence's ten page address to the clergy on August 13 about the 2009 general convention. Lawrence said, "In my opinion the current Presiding Bishop has repeatedly been irresponsible with her comments regarding the doctrine of the Uniqueness and Universality of Christ. This will not surprise you, for I said as much to her when she visited us shortly after my consecration. In answering questions, about the Uniqueness and

Universality of Christ, she has repeatedly suggested that it is not up to her to decide what the mechanism is God uses to save people. Lawrence continued, "quite to the contrary, it is her responsibility as a bishop of the Church to proclaim the saving work of Jesus Christ and to teach what it is the Scriptures and the Church teach. Anything less from us who are bishops is an abdication of our teaching office."

The following issues were identified by the bishop and the standing committee for the convention to consider on October 24, 2009:

1. A resolution that at every ordination in this diocese, prior to the candidates' spoken vows, sign the document of conformity – explicating what the BCP means by loyalty. Loyalty means to the doctrine, discipline and worship of Christ as this Church has received them.
2. A resolution that this diocese begin withdrawing from all bodies of governance of TEC that have asserted to actions contrary to Holy Scripture; until such bodies show a willingness to repent of such actions.
3. A resolution to promote the formation of "missional relationships" with other dioceses and orthodox congregations isolated across North America.
4. A resolution for the diocese to endorse a draft of the Anglican Covenant, a proposed document that would unify orthodox Anglicans worldwide.

These four resolutions were passed overwhelmingly. A fifth resolution stated "that the diocese will not condone prejudice or deny the dignity of any person, including but not limited to, those who believe themselves to be gay, lesbian, bisexual or transgendered, but will speak the truth in love as Holy Scripture comments to the amendment (change) of life required of disciples of Christ." The fifth resolution was postponed to the next convention.

Bishop Lawrence wrote the following in the March, 2010 issue of *The Anglican Voice*:

"The chancellor of the diocese, Wade Logan, was informed in December, 2009 that a local attorney had been retained by the presiding bishop's chancellor to represent the Episcopal Church in some local matters. Beginning in January, 2010 a series of letters requesting various documents from the diocesan records were to be sent sequentially to the presiding bishop's chancellor. These actions led the diocese of South Carolina to believe the presiding bishop's chancellor, if not the presiding bishop herself, is seeking to build a case against … the diocese including the bishop and standing committee and some local parishes.

"The documents that were sought were: lists of all persons ordained since October, 24, 2009, (the date the diocesan convention was held) all parish by-laws and amendments since 2006, all standing committee minutes since the episcopacy of Bishop Salmon, parish charters, parish founding documents, parish deeds, parish mortgages, documents evidencing parish participation in diocesan programs and others. In some cases, the stated reason for the information requested is the assertion that these parishes have left the diocese of South Carolina because of changes made to their respective by-laws. However, these parishes have not made these changes with the intention of leaving the diocese of South Carolina, nor have they left. The standing committee and I (Lawrence) believe this action is an unjust intrusion into the spiritual and jurisdictional affairs of this sovereign diocese of the Episcopal Church.

"This provocative interference has been pursued without the presiding bishop having communicated with me. This is not a time for precipitous action. Faithfully yours, the Right Rev. Mark Lawrence, Bishop of South Carolina."

In September 2010, a group of anonymous non-orthodox Episcopalians called on the presiding bishop to launch an investigation of the diocese. Bishop Lawrence said, "this group was resorting to fear tactics. With this latest attack this group continues its weary institutional approach to God, as if you can keep people in a church by fear." Lawrence added, "What we are trying to do in the diocese of South Carolina is to hold fast to the best of our Episcopal heritage while sharing Christ's transforming freedom to the needs of the people today."

The diocesan convention of October 24, 2009, was not adjourned but was to reconvene on March 4, 2010. Because more time was needed to draw up resolutions to protect the diocese, the convention did not reconvene until Friday, October 15, 2010, at St. Paul's in Summerville. Headlines in the *Post & Courier* harked, "Convention takes issue with leader" and "Episcopalians assert authority."

Four resolutions were overwhelmingly approved at the convention:

Resolution 1 states that Jesus came into the world to save the lost, that those who do not know Christ need to be brought into a personal and saving relationship with Him and affirms long-held doctrine which some argue has been subverted by the presiding bishop Jefferts Schori.

Resolution 2 affirms the diocese's sovereignty within the Episcopal Church and its legal and ecclesiastical authority. It also states that the presiding bishop has no authority to retain attorneys in this diocese that present themselves as the legal counsel in South Carolina.

Resolution 3 states that the bishop and, in his absence, the standing committee has sole authority with respect to any dispute concerning the interpretation of the constitution and canons of this diocese.

Resolution 4 prohibits the desecration of consecrated buildings and the alienation of church property without the consent of the ecclesiastical authority and the standing committee. And it adds the following to Canon 30 – It is within the power of the ecclesiastical authority of this diocese to provide a generous pastoral response to parishes in conflict with the diocese or province of the Episcopal Church as the ecclesiastical authority judges necessary to preserve the unity and integrity of the diocese.

The above resolutions were passed on October 15, 2010, because the national church had several new resolutions that would take effect on July 1, 2011. After that date the diocese of South Carolina could not have passed their resolutions. Diocesan officials said the national church's resolutions were unconstitutional intrusions into the corporate life in South Carolina.

The Rt. Rev. David C. Anderson Sr., AAC president and CEO, wrote in the *Encompass* in the October/November 2010 issue about the adoption of the national church's new resolutions. "We will now see kangaroo courts, or as some of you remember from the days of McCarthyism, 'Are you now or have you ever refused to bless the partnership of any gay couples?'" Four retired bishops, Rt. Rev. C. Fitzsimons Allison, Rt. Rev. Alex D. Dickson, Rt. Rev. Alden M. Hathaway and Rt. Rev. Edward Haynsworth, living in the diocese of South Carolina wrote a letter supporting the actions of Bishop Lawrence and the diocesan convention.

The Rev. Paul C. Fuener of Prince George Winyah at Georgetown, president of the diocese's standing committee, received a letter dated September 30, 2011, from Josephine H. Hicks, national church attorney to the disciplinary board. A copy was sent to The Rt. Rev. Dorsey Henderson, disciplinary board president.

Hicks announced the national church's disciplinary board wished to review allegations that The Rt. Rev. Mark Lawrence had abandoned TEC and in that capacity she wrote to request the diocese's standing committee provide the following documents:

1. Concerning the ordination of the Rev. Chadwick E. Lawrence (the bishop's son) to the diaconate and/or priest, they accused Chad of not having been ordained a deacon in an Episcopal Church.
2. They wanted copies of the standing committee's minutes and any and all other documents reflecting votes by standing committee members concerning resolutions sponsored or submitted to diocesan conventions, etc. from October 2009 through February 2011.

According to TEC rules, those accusing the bishop and his family do not have to be identified until the process moves on much further. It is known that the accusers are the anonymous, non-orthodox Episcopalians.

Bishop Lawrence wrote, "In order to understand the possible implications and to engage in corporate prayer for the diocese, I, as bishop, have called a meeting of all our active and canonically resident clergy for this coming Tuesday, October 11, 2011, from

10 a.m. to noon at St. James Church on James Island. Rest assured we will do all in our power to defend gospel truth and catholic order. We ask for your prayers."

The vestry of St. Philip's sent a resolution:

> "Resolution of Support
>
> We the members of the Vestry of St. Philip's Church, Charleston, SC unanimously approve the following:
>
> Be it resolved that the Vestry of St. Philip's Church, Charleston SC unanimously and enthusiastically support our Diocesan Bishop, The Rt. Reverend Lawrence, as he defends the charges from TEC that he has 'abandoned' his church. We herewith prayerfully pledge to continue that support as Bishop Lawrence fights to defend these attacks from TEC on our traditional orthodox theology.
>
> Unanimously approved this 25th day of October, 2011.
>
> Robert H. Nuttall, Sr.
> Senior Warden
> Myron C. Harrington, Jr.
> Junior Warden and secretary."

After TEC's disciplinary committee read sixty-three pages, it was decided on Monday, November 28, 2011, that Lawrence was "innocent." The retired bishop of upper South Carolina, Dorsey Henderson, head of the committee said, "Applied strictly to the information under study, none of these three provisions was deemed applicable by a majority of the board." Henderson said it was significant that Lawrence has said repeatedly that he does not intend to lead the diocese of South Carolina out of the Episcopal Church. Henderson said he believed Lawrence.

While TEC's disciplinary committee was deciding Lawrence's fate, the diocese of South Carolina took a proactive action. A quitclaim deed was issued on November 16, 2011, to St. Philip's and all the churches in the diocese. This meant the diocese relinquished any claim it had on the real estate of any church in the diocese. St. Philip's accepted the quitclaim. The non-orthodox Episcopalians rejected the quit claim deeds.

The 77th general convention convened in Indianapolis July 5 – 12, 2012. Prior to the opening, a declaration was issued on June 15 by the diocese's standing committee stating, "We view with dismay and great sadness what appears to be the official approval of a rite for blessing of same-gender unions. We will instead continue to partner with Anglican entities here and abroad to further the spread of the Good News of salvation for sinners through Jesus Christ." Even as late as this, Lawrence said again the diocese of South Carolina will remain in TEC.

On Monday, July 9 in a separate vote, the full convention approved new anti-discrimination language for transgendered people that cleared their way to become clergy. The same sex blessing vote took place on Tuesday, July 10 with the house of bishops voting 111 in favor, 44 against and 3 abstentions. About 80% of lay delegates supported the proposal to authorize a provisional rite for same-sex unions for the next three years.

Supporters of the same-sex blessings insisted it was not a marriage ceremony despite any similarities called "The Witnessing and Blessing of a Lifelong Covenant." The ceremony includes prayers and an exchange of vows and rings. Same-sex couples must complete counseling before having their unions blessed by the church.

Included is a three year option that permits each bishop to decide whether or not to allow same-sex blessings using the "conscience clause" that bars any penalties for those who oppose the resolution.

On Wednesday July 11, 2012, Lawrence requested and received a private session with the house of bishops in which he was grateful for "intentional engagement in honesty and collegiality with fellow bishops." He expressed his grievous concern with the two resolutions that passed and told the bishops he then would leave the convention as did five of the diocese of South Carolina deputies who also returned home that day. Rev. John B. Burwell and Lonnie Hamilton volunteered to stay and monitor the remainder of the convention.

Lawrence agreed with the diocesan canon theologian, Rev. Kendall Harmon, who said the convention was "unbiblical, unchristian, unanglican and unseemly."

THE NATIONAL CHURCH ATTACKS BISHOP LAWRENCE AND THE DIOCESE

On August 27, 2012, Lawrence, Bishop W. Andrew Waldo (upper South Carolina) and Chancellor Belton Zeigler began a discussion with both South Carolina dioceses to find solutions between TEC and the diocese of South Carolina. Waldo asked the Presiding Bishop Katherine Jefferts Schori (PB) for a meeting on August 30. The PB replied on September 5 that she could meet on September 6 or not until October 3 which was confirmed. At that meeting, the PB met with Waldo and Lawrence and she agreed that "creative solutions" were desirable to avoid total war. The PB focused on how long Lawrence planned to remain bishop and she asked if five years were a reasonable assumption. On October 9, PB asked Lawrence to meet her in Atlanta on October 13, but he could not meet her that day. The PB wanted a phone call together with Lawrence and Zeigler. She suggested October 15, 16 or 17.

While Presiding Bishop Katherine Jefferts Schori was "negotiating" with Lawrence in October, the Disciplinary Board for Bishops (DBB) met in Salt Lake City on September 17, 18 and 19, 2012. Apparently the DBB certified abandonment on three charges, two of which had been previously dismissed on November 22, 2011.

On October 15, 2012, the PB called Lawrence and advised him that she had received certification of abandonment from the DBB on October 10. She sent Lawrence a restriction of ministry. Later that afternoon, Logan received an unsigned copy of the DBB's certificate of abandonment with attachments and a letter from the PB regarding a restriction of ministry.

There is a similarity between this scenario and 1941 when the Japanese diplomats pretended to negotiate in Washington D.C. all the way until December 7 and then let their bombs loose on Pearl Harbor.

Fortunately, the leadership of the diocese was ever mindful of protecting the diocese and its parishes. They had resolutions in place that would become effective upon any action by TEC.

On Monday October 15, 2012, when the bishop and the diocese learned of the attack against our bishop, the diocese of South Carolina was no longer part of TEC as a result of its actions. The diocese's accession to the TEC constitution and its membership in TEC had been withdrawn.

Rev. Kendall Harmon wrote, "We are still the diocese of South Carolina, holding the faith of the apostles that was handed down to us." The name of the diocese remains The Protestant Episcopal Church in the Diocese of South Carolina (PEC). More is written below.

In 2012, prior to October 15, there were more than 30,000 baptized Episcopalians in the diocese of South Carolina in twenty-four counties with seventy congregations served by 107 active clergy. It was announced on November 11, that "at least twelve or more parishes and mission churches would remain with TEC" bringing, perhaps, 10% of baptized Episcopalians. Those churches in Charleston remaining with TEC are Grace, St. Stephens, Holy Communion, St. Marks and Calvary. Others were spread around the diocese.

Three thousand members of TEC in this diocese are trying to keep the 27,000 members of PEC from worshiping in their churches.

On Thursday October 18, the *Post and Courier's* "religious" reporter wrote, "The Rt. Rev. Mark J. Lawrence, bishop of the Episcopal Diocese of South Carolina, has abandoned the church according to the Church's Disciplinary Board for Bishops." This triggered a headline, "Bishop abandons church."

Bishop Allison made it very clear in an October 24 letter to the *Post and Courier* that Lawrence did not leave the Episcopal Church. He wrote, "Bishop Mark Lawrence and this diocese have not abandoned The Episcopal Church. TEC leadership has abandoned not only Bishop Lawrence and this diocese but its own heritage and the Christian faith itself." He included a litany of examples of TEC ignoring the Gospel.

Finally, the fourteen[34] names of the non-orthodox Episcopalians, who brought charges of abandonment against Bishop Lawrence, released their names. They said they did so voluntarily but Rev. Canon James B. Lewis said it was because canon laws required it. Lewis wrote, "For the forum to claim it is not responsible for these actions is disingenuous at best."

The names are: Robert R. Black, Mr. and Mrs. Charles G. Carpenter (Margaret), Frances L. Elmore, Eleanor Horres, Mr. and Mrs. John Kwist (Margaret), Mr. and Mrs. David W. Mann (Barbara), Warren M. Mersereau, Delores J. Miller, Robert B. Pinkerton, M. Jaquelin Simons, Mrs. Benjamin Bosworth Smith, Mr. and Mrs. John L. Wilder and two clergy – Rev. Colton M. Smith and Rev. Roger W. Smith.

All of the fourteen in 2012 are presently members of The Episcopal Forum of South Carolina (formerly written here as the anonymous non-orthodox Episcopalians in South Carolina). Of the twenty-one forum board members, six of the signers are on the list. Others came from five parishes, one unaffiliated congregation, with half of the lay members indicating they are parishioners of Grace Church.

MORE SKULDUGGERY?

On Wednesday, November 7, 2012, a majority of the diocese's clergy received an email with the diocese of South Carolina's seal from the "Domain Discreet Privacy Service" from Florida. The email was an invitation to a "Clergy Day for the Diocese" to be held at Holy Communion and presided over by the retired bishop of east Tennessee, Charles von Rosenberg, now living on Daniel Island.

PEC wrote "Bishop von Rosenberg would have no authority to convene or preside at any meeting in this diocese and to do so would put him in violation to TEC's canons." The meeting was canceled.

The meeting was reinstated. It was held, Thursday, November 15 at St. Mark's church. Bishop von Rosenberg, a parishioner of Grace church, was invited to perform the Eucharist and all the clergy were invited to attend the information session.

PEC objected in strong terms to the plans of the "Clergy Day for the Diocese." "Whoever called such a meeting had no authority to do so or to use the diocesan seal

---

34 The four married couples were counted as one entity each.

in any fashion. All of this is further evidence of the necessity for the precautions this diocese has taken during the past several years. It seems TEC does not follow its own canons, repeatedly insisting in the past that the diocese of South Carolina do so."

In early November, non-orthodox Episcopalians placed half a page advertisement assuring the "Episcopal Church in the Diocese of South Carolina is continuing." They formed a steering committee headed by Hillery P. Douglas from Charleston and secretary Erin E. Bailey from Mt. Pleasant. There were twelve other steering committee members. Advisors were Bishop John Clark Buchanan from Mt. Pleasant and Bishop Charles von Rosenberg. This group will meet on March 8, 2013, to hold their "diocesan convention" and begin the process of selecting a bishop.

On November 15, 2012, PEC ran a full page notice in the *Post and Courier* entitled, "A MESSSAGE TO THE PEOPLE OF TH DIOCESE OF SOUTH CAROLINA."

Bishop Lawrence wrote, "You need to know that the national leadership of TEC is taking steps to undermine this diocese. We are faced with an intentional effort by the ill-advised TEC organization to assume our identity, one that we have had since 1785.

Bishop Lawrence continued, "This misuse of the diocesan seal and the diocesan name is a denial of the good faith and fair dealing expected of all institutions engaging either in public communication or commerce. It is especially disconcerting for those who profess and call themselves Christians. Not only is it morally questionable; it is something for which they can be held accountable."

He closed by saying. "We are still here and by God's grace we shall not only endure we shall prevail."

Thirty-four churches, including St. Philip's, stated in the November 15 newspaper notice, "We, the following rectors in the Diocese of South Carolina affirm our Support of and stand with our Bishop, The Rt. Rev. Mark J. Lawrence." The list is being updated.

McCormick was quoted in the November 15 *Charleston Mercury.* "The church growth in the USA is among churches that are conservative in that they believe that Jesus is the Christ, the Son of God sent to save the world. The groups that do not embrace Jesus' divinity slowly die on the vine. I mean, what's the point in engaging in some religious charade if Jesus is not who He claims to be? So to the point, the Diocese under Mark Lawrence will continue to thrive and flourish."

Charles Waring III wrote in the *Charleston Mercury,* "We have seen TEC behaving in ways unimaginable to the faithful a decade ago and earlier. The way they have treated the Bishop of the Diocese of South Carolina the last several years parallels the worst of power politics in the U.S. Congress. As all know TEC is using law suits around the country to grab the church properties of dioceses, even individual parishes."

As of November 15, 2012, according to TEC, "neither Lawrence nor the standing committee has been informed that they have been removed as the ecclesiastical authority." PEC wondered if they had been removed without being notified..

With perfect timing, Presiding Bishop Jefferts Schori placed an article in the *News and Courier* on Saturday, November 17 threatening PEC that they could not leave TEC of its own accord. It was the same day that PEC held its diocesan convention.

The conventioneers were quiet and determined but full of optimism and trusting in God. Bishop Lawrence said, with God's help, PEC would grow. He made it clear any churches could remain with TEC. And that, for now, PEC was not joining another entity

At the convention, there were seventy-six active clergy and 170 lay. There were fourteen missions and forty-one parishes for a total of fifty-five.

Three resolutions were proposed:

1. "The Ecclesiastical Authority of the Diocese hereby declares that we concur on the decision of the Standing Committee that we are no longer in any relationship with TEC, including union or association with in any capacity and we declare him rightful Bishop to be the Rt. Rev. Mark J. Lawrence. By stating this, we declare that as God has sent Bishop Lawrence to be our Bishop, only her has the authority to declare otherwise, and be it."
2. A Standing Committee amendment to the diocese's constitution
3. A Standing Committee amendment to the Canons of the Diocese of South Carolina.

The first resolution also protected the name of the diocese and its seal. "The Protestant Episcopal Church in the Diocese of South Carolina (Diocese) has been in existence since 1785 and from time to time additionally called herself, and has been known variously as The Protestant Episcopal Church in South Carolina, The Protestant Episcopal Diocese of South Carolina, The Protestant Episcopal Church in the state of South Carolina, The Episcopal Diocese of South Carolina and the Diocese of South Carolina."

"The Diocese continues to be additionally called and known today as the Diocese of South Carolina."

"The Protestant Episcopal Church in the Diocese of South Carolina and such additional names are immediately set forth above and its seal have been recognized by the South Carolina Secretary of State as protected marks of this Diocese."

The necessary three resolutions were made to the constitution and canons with only four churches abstaining.

MORE HARRASSMENT

On December 5, 2012, Bishop Lawrence received a "Renunciation of Ordained Ministry and Declaration of Removal and Release." The former PB of the diocese of South Carolina "called Lawrence that afternoon to inform him that she and her council had accepted his renunciation of ordained ministry." Lawrence listened quietly, asked a question or two and told her it was good to hear from her. He left it like that. Lawrence said, "Quite simply I have not renounced my orders as a deacon, priest or bishop any more than I have abandoned the Church of Jesus Christ."

A special St. Philip's congregational meeting was called for January 13, 2013. Senior Warden Myron Harrington gave a thorough talk at the meeting.

Excerpts from Harrington's talk, "I would like to take a minute to recognize the vestry and thank them for all their hard work, dedication and determination to do the right thing for St. Philips. Over the fall and early winter we have had almost weekly meetings in order to keep up with the ever changing dynamics that litigation brings and ensure that St. Philip's is in the very best position to preserve not only our property but the historic faith as handed down by the apostles. They deserve your thanks."

Harrington continued, "In reaching the decisions we had to make, I can attest that much prayer, discussion and deliberate processing of all the pros and cons of an issue went on before any decision was made, and on several occasions we would discuss and debate the issues and then adjourn for a time to pray, digest information and consider the impact of the parish before taking a vote." He reported that all their votes were unanimous.

The dedicated members of this vestry are the senior warden, Junior Warden David Grubbs and vestry members Miles Barkley, Lydia Evans, Guv Gottshalk, Elizabeth Hagood, Catherine Jones, John Kerrison, Sarah Phillips Marshall, James Rembert and Dexter Rumsey.

Harrington said, "Should TEC take over, Bishop Lawrence, Haden, and the rest of the orthodox clergy in the diocese, will be gone. In their place will be a bishop and clergy who will bring a degree of liberalism and unorthodox teachings and liturgy which most of us will not be able to support. To ensure religious freedom for the next generation of St. Philippians, we must stand with our bishop and do everything in our power to not only preserve and protect our historic properties but ensure our clergy will not be constrained from bringing us Holy Scripture as it was meant to be."

As of January 23, 2013, there were thirty one PEC congregations joining in with the January 4 lawsuit.

At the request of the Diocese of South Carolina, South Carolina Circuit Court Judge Diane S. Goodstein on January 23, 2013, issued a temporary restraining order lasting to February 1 that prevented TEC from assuming the identity of the Diocese of South Carolina. The order took place immediately. TEC opted to forgo court so the judge replaced the temporary restraining order with a temporary injunction.

TEC only agreed to honor the restraining order because it benefited both sides since the church had not yet responded in court on the original complaint from January 4. The diocese had filed a lawsuit to defend more than $500 million in property from a "blatant land grab" as TEC seeks control. In the past TEC has spent twenty-two million dollars grabbing orthodox churches.

The end of January 2013 was busy. There was the injunction and the former PB of the diocese of South Carolina, again with her perfect timing, decided she would come to Charleston on January 25 and 26 as the annual Mere Anglicanism Conference was being held at St. Philip's.

Jefferts Schori was quoted in the *Beaufort Gazette* January 26 saying "Our task, when people decide to leave, is to bless their journey and pray they find a fruitful place to pursue their relationship with God." Then she added, "In the meantime, we are going to do what we feel called to do in the Episcopal Church."

For some reason the *Post & Courier* chose not to print her sermon. Fortunately, there were observers such as Dr. Peter T. Mitchell of Georgetown. Comments –

"I was saddened and appalled, but not surprised, by the vindictive and mean spirited language Jefferts Schori used in her sermon on January 26." Her allusion to Bishop Mark Lawrence as a "tyrant" and comparing him to citizens' militias deciding to patrol … the Mexican border for unwelcome visitors was unconscionable." Mitchell said, "The language used by Jefferts Schori from the pulpit is as unloving and un-Christian it gets."

As of February 28, 2013, there were thirty four PEC congregations joining in with the January 4 lawsuit. An additional thirteen congregations decided to stay with PEC and are considering their own participation in joining the litigation at a later time.

As of March 3, 2013, TEC has nine parishes and seven missions staying. Sadly, the charming, small church St. James in McClellanville chose TEC.

Five missions and two parishes are undecided.

PEC has forty seven parishes and churches which is 80% of the 30,000 members of this diocese.

On Wednesday March 6, TEC announced it had filed suit in federal court in a counter-offensive meant to resolve an identity dispute.

Lawrence said he has lashed himself to Christ's mast and trusts where Christ will lead him (and us). He said the road may not be easy. Let us all pray for PEC and St. Philip's as we are part of this entity.

Lawrence wrote, "Many speak to me of the difficult task I have at this time. They wonder how I am dealing with the stresses and pressure on me. I respond by saying I draw strength from God's call, and from the people of this diocese and from our history. For we have faced far more grievous challenges than the ones we face today; and as God was sufficient then He shall be so now."

Mark Joseph Lawrence walks in the Light and lives in the Word. Let us all pray for our bishop, his family and God's orthodox Diocese of South Carolina.

AMEN

APPENDIX

Pew holders c. 1922

Most pews accommodate six people. But a pew could be sold into multi units. A number behind a name or behind an address indicates how many seats were purchased.

Odd numbers on the south side of the main aisle headed toward the chancel.

1 Unassigned (unas)

3 Mrs. W.B. Sanders (4)

5 Dr. R.B. Rhett (52 Legare St.) (3)

   E.S.N (illegible) (3)

7 W.G.H. R(illegible) (3)

   G.H. (illegible) (3)

   Mrs. S. Tupper (1)

9 Mrs. Helen Warley (6)

11 W. F. Gray (6)

   Elizabeth A. Brown (21 Logan St.)

13 Ashmead F. and Agnes Pringle (29 Legare St.)(6)

15 Estate Wm. Aiken

17 Theodore D. Jervey (71 Rutledge Ave.) (6)

19 William G. Mazyck (56 Montagu St.) (6)

21 J.T. Leonard, Jr. (97 Tradd St.) (2)

    Walter Pringle, Jr. (99 Tradd St.) (2)

    W. States Lee (57 Legare St.) (2)

23 John and Edith Poppenheim (8 Ashe St.)

    Miss Mary Poppenheim (4 Ashe St.) (6)

    Misses Louisa and (illegible) Poppenheim (31 Meeting St.)

25 Daniell E., Louisa C. Huger and Daniell Huger, Jr. (36 Meeting St.)

    Elizabeth P. Huger (widow of W.E. Huger) (36 Meeting St.) (6)

27 Walter and Agnes B. Pringle (104 Tradd St.)

29 W.W(illegible and R (illegible) (3)

    Mrs. Celia McGowan (widow of W.C. McGowan) (5 St. Michael Place) (3)

31 Henry C. and Langdon McC. Cheves (47 South Battery) (6)

33 Mrs. Louisa Smythe (widow of A.T. Smythe) (31 Legare St.) (1)

    Mrs. E.W. L(illegible) (2)

    Mrs. Gourdin (Annie) (43 South Battery) (1)

    Mrs. Washington (3)

35 Henry A. M. and Emma R. Smith (26 Meeting St.) (6)

37 Alexander E. Gadsden (40 Henrietta St.) (3)

APPENDIX

   Mrs. DeSaussure (2)

39 Mrs. Mason Smith (6)

41 – 57 unas

Pews on the south aisle leading from the chancel to the narthex

59 Estate Dewar Bacot (widow of Sarah C. Bacot) (57 Tradd St.) (6)

61 B.R. Burnet (169 Queen St.) (4)

   Frank P and Rosalee Wish (104 Church St.) (2)

63 Mrs. Wilson Walker (2)

   Paul M. McMillan (49 Gibbes St. (2)

   William Heyward (2)

65 Mrs. Martha Frost (widow of Thomas Frost) 27 King St. (3)

   Miss Mazyck (1)

67 Mrs. (illegible) (3)

   Walker (3)

69 Rev. Robert Wilson (2)

   Mrs. Epps H. Mazyck (widow of Arthur Mazyck (68 Broad St.) (1)

   Mrs. Julia R. Mazyck (widow of Isaac Mazyck) (75 Tradd St.) (1)

   Julia Mazyck (1)

71 Rev. Cary Beckwith (92 Church St) Did Beckwith have to pay a fee for his family pew? (6)

73 Mrs. Wm. Stoney (2)

75 Mrs. Gracie Murdock (widow of J. H. Murdock) (69 Meeting St.) (6)

77 Estate J.G. Dill (6)

79 Christopher G. and Martha Howe (5 Limehouse St.) (3)

81 Miss Julia Chapman (1 Atlantic St.) (3)

83 W. Huger and Annie P. Fitzsimons (65 Legare St.) (6)

85 Thomas W. & Louisa deB. Bacot (22 Water St.) (6)

87 William Butler and Gertrude Minott Jr. (97 Church St.) (3)

   Miss P … (1)

   C.C. Pinckney (2)

89 Dr. Robert S. and Kathrine Cathcart, Misses Kathrine M. Cathcart and Mary Frances Cathcart (2 Water St.) (6)

91 Mrs. T. Waring (3)

   Mrs. George G. Martin (3)

93 J. G. Snowden (2)

95 and 97 unas

99 and 101 don't exist.

Even numbers from the north mail aisle from the narthex to the chancel.

2 and 4 unas

6 Miss Heyward (6)

8 Miss Simmons) (3)

   Mrs. B… Simons (3)

10 Mr. R. H. Gilchrist (3)

   Misses Kate, Marie and Virginia T. Price (22 Water St.) (3)

APPENDIX

12 J. Campbell and Mariam Bissell (95 Rutledge Ave.) (6)

14 Estate R. M. Marshall (6)

16 Arthur M. Manigault, Edward Manigault, Robert S. Manigault, Miss Harriott Manigault and Miss Mary H. Manigault (all at 131 Tradd St.) (6)

18 R. Bee and Hess W. Lebby (38 Church St.) (6)

20 Frederic G. Margaret M. Davies and Carlton G. Davies (11 Legare St.) (6)

22 William H, Louisa Barnwell and William H. Barnwell, Jr.(6)

24 Gibbs (6)

26 Nicholson (6)

28 George T. Pringle, Jr., Robert a. Pringle, Miss Washington G. Pringle and Miss Lucy G. Pringle. (All at 27 New St.) (6)

30 Edward P. and Alice Guerard (1 Logan St.) (3)

    Misses Alice, Elise and Ellen Hayne (26 New St.) (3)

32 Mrs. Westmoreland (1)

    Miss Hayden (5)

34 unas

36 Mrs. T.G.S. Lucas (3)

38 W. Gordon and Frances McCabe (50 S. Battery) (6)

40 Mrs. Claudia Tucker (widow of J. R. Tucker) (36 Meeting St.) (2)

42 – 50 don't exist

52 Mrs. DeSaussure (?)

54 Miss Bragg (3)

56 & 58 unas

60 Dr. Franklin F and Elizabeth Sams

    Annie, Donald, Elizabeth, James and Lily Sams (All at 37 New St. (6)

62 Estate R.T. Walker (6)

    Miss Mary Geddings and Miss O'Hear (The Church Home at 142 Church St.)

64 Watson (6)

66 Willis W. and Susan M. Shackleford (16 Lamboll St.) (6)

68 John and Madge H. McCrady (56 South Battery) (2)

    O. Russell and Ada G. Locke (93 Church St.) (2)

70 M. deLisle Haig and Miss Mary Haig (30 Meeting St.) (2)

72 J.W.S. (illegible), (2)

    Miss H. Walker (1)

    Miss Thurston (3)

    Miss O'Bryan

74 Philip P. Mazyck and Misses Margaret K., Arabella S. and Frances K.

    (All at 116 Church St.) (4)

76 Illegible

78 Porteous R. and Ella Paine (57 Charlotte St.) (3)

    Harry J. and Adelaide P. O'Neill (177 Tradd St.) (3)

80 Miss Henrietta Heyward (169 Queen St.) (2)

    Miss (illegible) (3)

82 Mrs. H. Bryan (4)

84 J. Palmer and Eleanor B. Gaillard (8 Weims Court) (3)

    Miss Bellinger (1)

APPENDIX

   Miss O'Brian (1)

   (illegible) McCrady (1)

86 Isaac G. and Jane H. Ball (129 Bull St.) (3)

   Dr. Edward & Lily W. Rutledge (44 South Battery) (3)

88 Jeffords (6)

90 J.S. Sinkler (6)

92 M.T. Hay (3)

   C. P. Cuthbert (3)

94 Edward H. and Kate B McIver (23 Meeting St.) (3)

   J. H. & Belle Furman (48 Savage St.) (3)

96 unas

98 Mrs. Baker (1)

   Mrs. Sams (1)

   Mrs. E.D. Clement (Mamie) (119B Beaufain St.) (?)

100 & 102 unas

PARTIAL INDEX

If a name is mentioned more than one time on a page, the name will only be indexed one time. There are 775 individuals indexed.

A

Ables, Bob 298, 303, 314, 345

Ables, Mary 354, 356

Ackerman, J. 304

Albrecht, Rev. Fleetwod 161, 162

Alston, Edward 144

Algar, Jim 332

Algar, Joan 304

Allen, Charles L. 264

Allen, Martha 127

Allen, Paul 276

Allen, Sam III 127

Allison, Bishop C. Fitzsimons 88, 135, 270, 284, 285, 291, 374, 378

Allston, Edward F. 106

Anderson, Andy 187, 224, 249, 259, 264, 265, 267, 268, 279, 291, 292, 295, 302, 309, 354, 355, 356, 362

Anderson, Dorothy M. 38, 39, 181, 190, 198, 207, 244, 267, 294

Anderson, Florence 264

Anderson, Mrs. Jody 281

Anderson, Miss Miriam A. 297

Anderson, Dr. R. Maxwell (Mac) 117, 131, 135, 140, 157, 193, 209, 239, 249, 337, 340

Andreas, Anthony 126, 127

Andrews, Miss Sarah A. 29

Archer, H.P. 36

Avent, Rev. Hank 321, 322, 347

B

Bacot, R. Dewar 40

Bacot, Robert 18

Bacot, Thomas W. 26

Baker, Hayward 303

Baldin, Kim 264

Ball, Edward R. 120, 128, 136, 208

Ball Elias, 24

Ball, Nat 139

Ball, Rev. John 251, 263, 265, 289

Ball, Robert Jr. 127

Barclay, Wm. 189

Barkley, Calvin IV 282

Barkley, Helen 96, 170, 178, 185, 194, 197, 229, 230, 267, 290, 295, 309, 337, 338, 339

Barkley, Matthew B. 297

Barkley, Miles 336, 344, 353, 354, 356, 359, 381

Barkley, Neyse 337

Barkley, Rufus 80, 151, 152, 153, 157

Barkley, Mrs. Rufus 130

Barnes, Read 205

Barnwell, W.H. 95, 229, 249

Barnwell, Wm. 160, 169, 199, 259, 296

Barrett, Lawrence 71

Barrett, Rhett 151, 152, 245, 250, 252, 259, 264, 290

Bartell, J. 19

Bauer, Hank 304

Beaman, Dan 202, 250, 253, 289, 301, 302, 304, 305, 309

Beckwith, Rev. Cary 1-45, 48, 49, 116

Beckwith, Rev. John Q. 274

Behrens, L. 20

Bell, Georgia 346, 356

Bennett, Craig Jr. 280, 301, 360, 364

Bennett, Craig Sr. 127, 199, 214, 229, 230, 253

Bennett, Edward 246, 247

Bennett, Mary Lily 129, 181, 186, 188, 194, 199, 208

Bessinger, Charles 201

Bevan, Miss Caroline 101

Bishops from St. Philip's 238

Bissell, James Campbell 89, 10, 18, 19, 21, 26, 39, 53

Bissell, Johnson 183

Bissell, Mary 295, 315, 351

Blakeney, DuBose III 74, 328, 354, 356, 363

Blakeney, Mrs. E. DuBose 82, 83

Blincow, John 354, 356

Boatwright, Barbara 279, 295

Bollwinkle, Dorothy 11, 34, 58, 70, 104, 105, 106, 107, 145, 205, 208, 310

Bolt, Mrs. M.A. 129

Booker, Mrs. Jo Ann 124, 185

Bonnoitt, Albert Jr. 127

Bonsal, Frances 281, 282

Boykin, Charles 204, 227, 228, 229, 240, 251, 266, 298

Boykin, Mrs. Charles 224

Boulware, Thomas 338, 355, 356

Boutan, Rev. Marc 333, 334

Dr. and Mrs. Robert Bowles 219, 297, 298, 314, 350, 351

Boyette, Albert 127

Brannan, C.B. 100, 196, 229

Breza, Jean 364

Briggs, Loutrel 144, 202, 214

Broody, Jim 292, 303

Brooks, Ham 112, 127, 134, 135, 193

Bruns, Miss Annabel 93

Buck, Lee 241

Bullock, Edward 85

Burk, Carol p. iii 345, 352, 353, 354, 356

Burkette, Alice Gaillard 104

Burnet, Jane 264

Burris, Lon 295, 298, 351

Burrows, Mr. and Mrs. John 186, 198, 199

Burton, E. Milby 135

Burwell, Rev. John B. 376

Byrd, Rev. Ralph 165, 166, 167, 184

C

Cabell, Jean 183

Cain, Dr. Frank 55, 90

Cain, Dr. Wm 182, 196, 270

Cale, Susan 340

Camp St. Christopher 49

Campbell, Tony 273

Canfield, Mrs. G.D. 55

Caper, Bishop Ellison 4

Cart, William Porter 75, 166

Carter, Dr. Wm 224, 239, 240, 242, 243, 245

Carpenter, Miss Carolyn 84

Carruthers, Ewing 118

Carruthers, Bishop Thomas 71, 77, 78, 89, 106, 111, 113, 119

Cathcart, Bobby and Mimi 270

Cathcart, Dr. Robert S. 30

Causey, Vicki 130

Cave, Morris and Cinda 127

Cheves, Henry C. 14, 22, 25, 34, 35

Cheves, Mrs. Henry C. 21

Cheves, L. Mc 7

Chicken wings resting on the organ 228

Childs, Ernest 129

Childs, Mrs. St. Julien 110, 111

Chisolm, Caspar 33, 36

Chisolm E.N.

Christenings: 1973, p. 167; 1976, p.170; 1977, p.175; 1978, p/175; 1980, p.180

Churchyards – Those forgotten and humble souls 41, 42

Clare, Pettigrew 359

Clark, Angela 340

Clark, Harry 246

Clary, Rev. Sidney 119, 139, 149, 150, 158

Claypoole, Mrs. Barbara 239, 240, 243, 249

Cobb, Rev. Sam 153, 156, – 159, 160, 280, 320, 355

Coen, Mrs. Richard 92, 309

Coen, Mr. Richard 121, 182, 193, 203

Coffin, Miss Harriet (Hallie) 48

Cohoeb, Mrs. Blulma 25

Coming, John and Affra 22-24

Cone, Mrs. Douglas S. 104

Conklin, Otis 180, 198, 206

Coleman, Parker 247

Coleman, Rutledge 292, 303, 308

Cooke, Mike 276, 280, 281, 282, 332

Cotillion 81

Coventry, Dr. Frank 124-126, 143, 156, 157

Cox, Mrs. Eliza S. 41

Cox, Jane 185

Cram, Ralph A. 20, 57

Creel, Grace p. iii 242, 294

Cross, Capers 311-313, 337, 347, 364

Crosse, Mary Fisher Bayly 155, 156

Culp, F, Bartow 80-85, 135, 138, 142, 184, 193, 205, 217

Culp, Mrs. F. Bartow 80, 86

Cutler, Mary 264

D

Daniell, Mrs. Eliz. H 127

Daniell, E. Roy 135, 136

Daniell, Gov. Robert 41

Daniell, Teddy 127

Dashberg, Al 332

Davies, Carlton 15, 55, 74, 91\

Davies, Frederick, 14-16, 21, 26, 30, 32, 36, 40, 41, 43, 44

Davies, Mrs. Margaret 55

Davis, Jay 359

Dawson, Louis Y. 95

DeAntonio, Charles p. iii 347-350

De Costa, Herbert 98, 140

Deas, Col. Alston 95

DeGrace, Sharon 267

deForest, G.S. 32

Dehon, Bishop Theodore 52

Dehon, William Russell 35, 36

Dent, Annie 26

DeSaussure, Col. and Mrs. Edward 297

DeSaussure, Henry W. 34

DeSaussure, Mary 99, 134

Devereux, J.H. (Mrs.) 12, 58

Dew, Travis 342

Dickinson, Mrs. Dorothy 266

Dickson, Bishop Paul C. 374

Dilkes, Nancy L. 282

Dill, Miss Charlotte 226

Dill, Miss Pauline 129

Dockstader, Mrs. D.M. 101, 106, 141, 142

Dority, Rev. Richard 88

Dotterer, Gillie 157

Dotterer, Harold G. 96

Dotterer, Miss Nathalie 92, 152

Dotterer, Mrs. W 85

Dougherty, Francis 137, 138, 144, 197, 204, 211

Drake, Joanne 267

Drake, Miss Mary 107

Dwight, Charles S. 54, 91, 95

Dubay, Rev. David 115, 280, 281, 325

E

Egleston, D. DuBose, Jr. 362

Elmore, Bill 265, 267, 288

PARTIAL INDEX

Elliott, Cam 246

Ellison, Mrs. Blount 281

Ellison, Joanna 245, 259, 264

Ellison, Wm. B 85, 92, 93, 94, 113, 204, 207, 224

Eubanks, Miss Nana 209

Evans, Don 320

Evans, Lydia 298, 337, 344, 351, 357, 359, 371381

Evans, Nina 281

F

Fain, Baron 320

Farrow, Mrs. E. Ravenel 109, 184

Ferguson, Martha E. 294

Fine, Sally 338

First nine ladies on the vestry 194

Fishburne, Rev. Charles 67

Flint, Jim 157

Flint, (Fox) Renee 359

Ford, Frank Jt. 182, 194, 196

Fosbroke, Hughell 52

Foster, Robert 127

Fowler, Rev. Jay 275, 276

Foxworth, Col. 197, 198, 206, 294, 296, 306

Foxworth, Mrs. 225

Frampton, Garden 284

Frost, Eugenia 57, 101

Frost, Frances 59

Frost, Thomas and Martha 57

Furman, J.H 18, 32, 65, 75, 79, 81, 92, 96, 117

G

Gadsden, Mrs. Dwight 207

Gadsden, Mrs. Julia 25, 48

Gadsden, Miss Mary Trapier 102

Gaillard, Foster 303, 306, 308, 359, 360

Gaillard, Henrietta 320, 344, 353, 354, 366, 362

Gaillard, J.P. Jr. 92, 100, 199, 217, 224, 267, 285, 309, 359, 363

Gaillard, Lucas 127

Garden, Alexander 64

Garland, Juli 331

Garrett, Gordon and Margaret 294

Geddings, Miss Mary 37

Geer, B. Owen 142, 205

Geer, Gene 182, 164, 209

Geer, Helen 228

Gibbs, Affra 24

Gibbs, Coming B. 24, 29, 55, 64, 91, 92, 102, 103, 136, 140

Gibbs, Mrs. Coming B. 81

Gibbs, Charles H. 54, 144

Gibbs, Charles, Jr. 128

Gibbs, Gendron and Helen 24

Gibbs, James 3, 14

Gibbs, James Gendron 54, 91

Gibbs, Mrs. James (Martha) 107, 211

Gibbs, Jenks 182

Gibbs, John E. Jr, 54, 83
Gibbs, John E. Sr. 18, 54
Gibbs, Mrs. Wilmot 194, 204, 247
Gilbreth, Frank 195
Gilbreth, Rebecca M. 282
Gillingham, Canon Peter 263, 264, 265
Glenn, Dr. James 178, 179
Glenn, Mrs. Lucy 199, 225
Glenn, Rev. Terrell 237, 238
Gottshalk, Guv 26, 347, 357, 366, 381
Graudin, Ryan 346
Graudin, Steve 281, 297, 298, 302, 308, 314, 347, 360
Graudin, Tracy 253, 264, 281, 354, 355
Gray, Wm. F. 14
Green, F.L. 3
Green, Lola L. 97
Greene, George 228, 267, 270, 291, 292, 303, 305, 342, 343
Greene, Jini 347
Gregorie, Becky 224
Gregorie, Dr. Harry 187, 192, 199, 208, 247, 249, 259
Gregorie, Harry III 353, 354, 356, 358, 363
Gregorie, Jane 267
Gribbin, Bishop R.E. 151
Grimball, Betsy 337
Grimball, Miss Mary 48
Grubbs, David 359, 381
Guerard, E.P. 14, 25, 26, 42, 45
Guerard, Jane 282
Guerard, Julius 181
Guerard, Theo. 138, 153, 154, 157, 208, 229, 244, 249, 290, 301, 305
Guerry, Mrs. Roderick 210, 211
Guerry, Bishop W.A. 4, 11, 29-32, 43
Guthke, W.E. 271

H

Hagan, Joan 282
Hagood, Ben Jr. 294
Hagood, Ben Sr. 185, 193, 196, 198, 201, 267, 276, 299
Hagood, David 282
Hagood, Elizabeth 357, 359, 381
Hagood, Jane 282
Hagood, Jimmy 224, 244, 249, 259, 264
Hagood, Maybank 294, 303, 344, 353, 354, 356
Haesloop, F.J.H. 35
Haidet, Peter 75
Haig, Isaac Motte 91
Hanahan, Alida 240
Hanahan, Betty 250
Hanahan, J. Ross Jr. 92, 94, 98, 108, 111, 114, 136, 138, 140, 142
Hanahan, Maria 243
Hamilton, James (sexton) 83, 138
Hamilton, Lonnie 376
Hampson, Rev. James 269-270, 276, 296
Hanckel, Miss Anne 25
Hanckel family 130
Hanckel, Mary Anne 185, 244, 283, 288, 294, 301-303, 305, 351, 360

PARTIAL INDEX

Hanckel, Richard W. 95, 98, 108, 125, 137, 251, 252

Hanger, Clark 363

Harmon, Rev. Kendall 377

Harrigan, Miss Chardon 186

Harrigan, Tony 131, 138, 155, 162, 204

Harrington, Ann 131, 138, 155, 162, 204

Harrington, Myron 357, 358, 359, 375, 381

Harris, Eliz. 283

Hart, Rev. Addison 273

Hartsock, Charlotte 336, 337, 353

Harvey, Betsy 298, 308, 314, 354

Harvey, Heyward, Jr. 162, 298, 314, 350, 351

Hastie, Eleanor R. 283

Hathaway, Bishop Alden 285, 374

Haven, Malcolm 90, 94, 100, 107, 111, 112, 116, 120

Hawkins, Louisa 245, 246, 281

Hay, Dr. Ed 284

Hayler, Rev. Andrew 22

Hayne, Miss E.F 8, 16, 38, 39

Hayne, Miss Ellen 53

Hayne, Miss Nellie 101

Haynsworth, Bishop Edward H. 374

Heaton, Clement 21

Helms, WM. 225

Hepworth, Thomas 64, 92

Herrin, Mrs. Ray 107, 181, 182

Hershey, Clay 355, 356

Hershey, Emmie 356

Heyward, DuBose 33, 50, 365

Heyward, Eliz. Middleton 35

Heyward, Miss Henrietta 19

Heyward, Miss J. 35

Heyward, Mrs. J.S. 8

Hills, Billy 214

Hipp, Charles 301, 302

Hipp Jan 289, 290, 299, 300, 303, 313

Hipp Laura 281, 296, 357

Hitt, Jack 184

Hitt, Robert M. 92, 113, 114, 193

Holden, Dr. Ken 296, 343, 344, 353

Holt, Ed 198, 199, 229, 243, 267, 298, 303, 314, 351, 360

Holt, Kitty 184, 249, 253, 259, 263, 270, 289, 340

Holt W.I. 84, 92, 98

Hood, Miss Sarah Barley 81

Hopke, W.G. 39

Howard, Bevo 65

Howard, Langhorne 65

Howe, Mrs. Christopher G. 80

Howe, Bishop W.B. H. 4, 28

Huey, Elizabeth 282

Huff, 271, 239

Huddleston, Chloe 339

Huger, D.E. 297

Huger, Daniel 64

Huguenin, Barbara 297

Huguenin, Cornelius 92, 100, 297

Huguenin, Mary V. 314, 352

Huguenin, Thomas A. and Mrs. 34, 88, 90, 310

Huguenot Church 56, 156, 157, 227, 228

Hume, Wm. Pringle 84, 102

Humphreys, David Jr. 128

Hunter, Charles 124

Hunter, Joy 292, 294, 298

Hutcheson, Josephine (Humphrey) 187

Hutson, Henno 297

Hutson, Richard 294, 354

Hyde, John 138

I

Izard, Dr. Edward 209

J

Jackson, Original p.vi

Jackson the cat 215

Jagar, Jack 305

Jefferts Schori, Katherine 366, 369, 370, 371, 376, 377, 380, 382

Jenkins, Eleanor 338

Jenkins, Mrs. John T. 52

Jennings, Anne 337

Jervey, Ellen Hume 65

Jervey, Miss Henrietta 29-32

Jervey, T.B. 3, 14, 34, 41

Johnson, Rev. John 2, 4, 110

Johnson, Mitchell 131

Johnson, Ken 294

Johnston, Thomas 259, 264, 265, 283

Jones, Cadwallader 82, 88, 134, 137

Jones, Catherine & Harry D. 85, 155, 183, 295, 337, 339, 359, 364, 381

Jones, Monti 185

K

Kammeyer, John 299

Kassebaum, Philip 289

Katz, Al 339, 359

Kaufman, Col. R.C. 9, (Trust)

Keller, Kent 347

Kennedy, Madeleine Elise 282

Kerr, John 198, 240, 242, 244, 248, 249, 257, 258, 259, 261, 263, 264, 267, 281, 291, 293, 294, 303

Kerrison, Dottie 264

Kerrison, Horry 182

Kerrison, John 357, 359, 381

Kessler, Kirk S. 297

Kessler, Lenore 183, 281

King, DeWitt 105

Kinloch, Joseph (sexton) 83

Knowlton, Charles 291, 301

Kops, W. deBryn 32

L

LaBruce, George 107

Lancaster, Gregg & Dorothy 332

Land, Joe 294, 303

Land, Lynn 296

LaRoach Dr. J.J. 30

Larsen, Rev. Kal 221-222

Laurens, John 18, 56, 70, 91, 98

Lawrence, Bishop Mark 366, – 383

Lebby, Robert Bee 29

Lee, Marsee 337, 354

Lee, Rev. Maurice 277, 278

Legge, Dorothy 214

Leland, Ann Gibbs 314

Lemacks, Candy 183

Leonard, Dottie 340

Leonard, W.B. Chisolm 197, 354, 355, 359-362

Lescow, Mrs. Felicia 359

Lesesne, Gene 286, 294, 337, 343, 344

Lesesne, H.D. 29

Lewis, Charles R. (sexton) 153, 171, 197-199, 204, 206

Lewis, Rev. Canon James 378

Lilienthal, F.J. 98, 140, 205

Linton, Mrs. I. Grier 106

Lisle, Barbara 290

Locke, Mrs. William G. 39, 40

Lonck, E.L. 29

Lyle, Gordon 282

M

Manigault, Arthur 26

Manigault, Miss Mary Huger 63

Manigault, Peter 64

Manigault, Robert Smith 64

Marr, Liz 337

Marshall, Miss Mary O. 21

Marshall, Rev. Samuel 24

Marshall, Sarah Phillips 381

Martin, Jane 338

Martin, Miss May 129

Mathew, J.D. 32

Matthews, Matty 83, 105

Matthews, Rev. Stuart 198

Maybank, David H. 167, 182, 303

Maybank, Mrs. David 86

Mayers, Rev. W. Herbert 63, 67

Mazyck, A. 3, 14, 17, 34, 41

Mazyck, I. 3, 6, 14, 17

Mazyck, Dr. McMillan 14, 18, 36

Means, Cotesworth P. 32, 58, 78, 88, 90, 104, 106, 107, 142, 143

Merriam, Renee 338

Middleton, J. Blake 214

Middleton, Martha 282

Middleton, Phillip A. 185, 197, 276

Middleton, Dr. Will 284

Middleton, Woodward 276

Miller, Philip 297

Millford, Mrs. Carl E. 92

Millford, Carl Jr. 128

Mims, George 310

Minott, Mrs. Frances S. 129, 205, 206, 207

Mollegen, Dr. Albert T. 131-133

Momeier, Robert C. 121

Momeier, Rudolph 80, 86, 185

Moore, Mrs. Elfrida 208

Moore, Lee 340

Moore, Rev. Moultrie 261

Moore, North 80, 86, 185

Moore, Rev. Peter 268

Moreland, E. 3, 14

Morris, Buzz 340, 356

Morris, Kyra 281

Morrison, Edward 294

Morrison, Henrietta 99

Morrison, Nan 187

Morrison, Tom 199

Morrison, W. Howell 281

Mortimer 42

Moseley, Carolyn 352

Muller, Kruse 97

Mullins, Mike 281

Munnerlyn, R. Baron 54, 90

Murdaugh, Marvin Jr. 128

Murdoch, Henrietta 17

Murdock, James 13, 14

Murphy, Mr. and Mrs. Jesse 78

Myers, Archie Baker 26, 57

Myers, Thomas (Sr. & Jr.) 12, 14, 40, 44, 54, 64, 78, 79, 91, 92, 94, 108, 140, 178, 193, 194, 206, 219, 229, 245, 298, 309

Myers, DeRosset 92, 139, 170, 171, 197, 198, 276

Mc

Macmurphy, Joanna 294, 347

Macmurphy, John 276

McBee, Luke 362

McCall, Suzy 346

McCord, Suzanne (Buckley) 282, 284

McCord, Gerry & Suzanne 292, 339, 352, 356

McCormick, Rev. J. Haden p. iii 155, 216, 248, 280, 281, 288, 314, 317-319, 346-347, 364, 366, 368, 371, 379

McCormick, Rev. Matthew 329, 331, 332

McCrady, Charlotte 130, 183, 280, 309

McCrady, Edward 195

McCrady, John 210, 250

McCrady, Lewis deB. 55

McDonald, Stephanie 337

McGown, Nancy 336

McGreevy, Rev. Brian 329, 350, 351, 352

McGreevy, Jane 345

McIntosh, Bill 270, 339, 346, 354, 355, 356, 362

McIntosh, Hayden 190

McIntosh, Suzanne p. iii 126, 338, (and also her hard work alphabetizing most of this index)

McIver, F.H 92

McKnight, G.G. 53, 137

McLaren, 345, 353, 363

McManus, Dick 128

McPherson, Ike (Sexton) 357-358

N

New members: 1978, 175; 1980, 176; and 1981, 186.

Newton, A.C. 32

Neyle, Mrs. Virginia 209, 310, 311, 358, 364

Nicholson, Francis 64

Nuttall, Bob 322, 323, 345, 357, 358, 359, 362, 375

O

Oliveros, Mrs. L.L 129, 207

Oliveros, Robert L. 74, 79, 171

Oliveros, Rev. Robert 171, 231

O'Neal, Sheryl 337, 339, 340, 356

O'Neil, F.Q. 35

Oplinger, Wm. 210, 310

Orvin, Clifton 139, 328

Orvin, George and Rosalie 96, 124, 125, 130, 181

Orvin, Juanita 354

O'Shea, Brendan 203

O'Shea, Roberta 356, 359

Otis, Lee 342

Owens, Betty 339

Owens, Rev. Jack 327, 328

P

Palmer, Frances 210

Parker, Tempe 274

Parris, Alexander 64

Parsley, Rev. Henry 169

Paul, John 271

Payne, Ann 303

Pearce, Christopher C. 167, 196

Peeler, Homer 202

Pendarvis, Elaine 356, 357

Perry, Chester 91, 92

Perry, Louise 239

Perry, Mary 253, 290

Peterson, Rev. Doug 279, 298, 332, 352

Phillips, Al 320, 354, 355, 356

Phillips, Ashton 208

Phillips, Karen 328, 355, 356

Phillips, LaVonne 185, 192, 208

Phillips, Mark 282, 294, 295, 302, 303

Phillipps, Bill 306, 307, 354, 352, 362

Pigott, Mrs. Patsy 92

Pinckney, Alfred 127, 128, 167, 178, 187, 196, 197, 199, 224, 229, 244, 264, 266

Pinckney, Mrs. Alfred 196

Pinckney, Anne 247

Pinckney, Elise 195

Pine, W. Morton 225

Pogson, Rev. Milward 41

Porcher, Caroline 81

Porcher, Eddie 362

Porcher, Ellen 29

Porcher, Jennie Rose 187

Porcher, Margaret 109

Powell, Marvin (sexton) 293

Powell, Richard 302, 310

Pratt, Dr. Edward W. 96, 97, 98

Pratt-Thomas, Dr. and Mrs. Rawling 108

Pringle, Ashmead 85, 95

Pringle, Drexel 187

Pringle, Ernest 14, 73, 91

Pringle, Godfrey 128

Pringle, Walter 5, 14, 34

Pringle, Mrs. Walter Jr. 81

Pringle, Walter IV 128

Pringle, Washington Green 216, 217

Prioleau, Dr. W.H. 26

Pritchard, Boopa 185, 225, 249, 252, 259, 264, 265

Pritchard, Mrs. E.K, (Julia) 52, 181, 182, 210

Pritchard, Edward K Sr. 54, 92, 181, 188

Pultz, Constance 359

Q

Quakers 155, 156

R

Ravenel, Anne Stevens 108, 109

Ravenel, Daniel 199

Ravenel, Dr. James 170, 171, 185, 194, 247, 290

Ravenel, Kathy 320

Read, Fran 183

Read, I. Mayo Jr. 181, 195, 225, 243, 245, 249

Read, I. Mayo Sr. 76, 90, 95

Read, Peter 167, 188, 196, 203, 204, 205, 229

Rees, Miss Julia 52

Reeves, Dick 71, 72, 92, 96, 120, 203

Rembert, James and Celia 339, 381

Richards, Frenchie 235, 258, 284, 291

Richards, Robert 198, 204, 249, 250, 258, 259, 267, 268, 270

Riggs, Becky 243, 315, 340, 351

Riley, Francis Marion 55

Rhett, Miss Alicia 214

Rhett, Ann Bee 297, 319

Rhett, Mrs. F.H. Dill 250

Rhett, I'On L. 91, 96

Rhett, R.C. 36

Rhett, Rev. Wm. 61, 154, 174, 337

Rhodes, Caroline 294, 332, 337

Rhodes, Malcolm 281, 294, 350, 351, 353, 354

Robertson, Edgar R. 181

Robertson, Dr. Henry C. Jr. 55, 74, 75, 83, 92

Robertson, Dr. H. Clay III 199, 200, 229, 231, 248, 274, 290, 309, 339

Robey, Rev. Waddell 79, 104, 107, – 116

Robson, Franklin E. Jr. 58, 104

Robson, Franklin E. III 128, 171, 198

Rogers, Corvell 342

Rogers, Edwin 50

Rogers, Frank 167, 183, 197, 203, 204, 206, 267, 270, 281, 297, 309

Rowe, Sister 182

Rudulph, Jane M. 29

Rutledge, Anna Wells 135, 184, 195

Rumsey, Dexter 381

Russler, Dan 281, 332, 351, 357

S

Saint Michael's Church - 66+ items on St. Michael's including:

Belser, Rev. Rick 229, 242, 259

Candlelight tour 208

Coleman, Rev. Ed 242

Fire rifle at steeple 303

Kershaw, Rev. John 5, 74

Kirkland, Dr. Tommy 246, 263

Moore, Rev. Peter 268

Parker, Coleman 247

Smith, Hamilton 320

Stuart, Dr. A.R. 50, 98

Williams, George 145

Salley, A.S. 195, 200

Salmon, Bishop Edward 270, 279, 281, 296, 307, 367, 368

Salvo, Mrs. May 130

Sapp, Winfield 185, 199, 223, 225, 226, 229, 274, 300

Sanders, Miss Sue 202

Schmidt, John F. 365

Schrimpf, Bonnie 337, 346

Scott, Rev. Henry, Jr. 168, 171, 190, 230, 231, 233-235, 253-260, 296

Scott, Henry, Sr. 168, 185, 197, 198, 225

Seabrook, Baynard 128

Settle, John 182

Shackelford, W.W. 28, 43

Sifford, Jerry 308, 362

Simons & Lapham 20

Simons, Lucas 208

Simmons, Philip 228

Simmons, Theodore 121, 136, 196

Singleton, Ben (sexton) 340, 358

Sinkler, Alida 130

Sinkler, Huger 3, 13, 25, 34, 66

Sinkler, Robert L. (sexton) 18

Skilton, Bishop Wm. 270

Smith, Mrs. Burgh 134

Smith, Miss Charlotte 213

Smith, Erin 57

Smith, Frank C. 246

Smith, Mrs. H.A.M. 6, 28

Smith, Mrs. Isabel 10

Smith, Dr. Josiah 113

Smith, J.J. Pringle 6, 14, 28, 29, 141

Snedecker, Laura 336, 361

Sosnowski, Rev. Frederick 163, 164, 168, 181, 264

Spong, Bishop John 134, 135, 188

Staats, Henry 95, 105

Stahl, Connie 339

Steers, Sally 293

Stelling, Jim 302, 303, 344, 345, 352, 354, 362

Stender, Herbert 153, 239, 240, 250, 267

Stender, Molly 251

Stevens, J.S. 18, 32, 60, 70, 80, 81, 91, 96, 98, 99, 139

Stevens, W.S. 91, 135

Stevenson, Jill 355

Stoney, Rev. James 77

Stoney, Randell C. 98, 140, 181, 264
Stoney, Mrs. Thomas 129
Stott, Rev. John 285
Stouffer, Donna 322, 323, 351
Streaker 216
Sunday, Billy 12
Surratt, Tim 264
Swanson, Steve 294

T

Tassin, Richard, 128
Taylor, Leonard (sexton) 198, 199, 200
Taylor, Miss Nellie 214
Temple, Bishop Gray 120
Tezza, Betsy 242, 247, 299, 259
Todd, Jack 137, 152, 153
Todd, Mrs. 144
Thaxton, Lavinia 266, 288
Thomas, Bishop A.S. 48, 71, 89
Thompson, Bill 297, 308, 356, 363, 365
Thompson, Chris 336, 353
Trapier, Mrs. Aida 195
Trask, Son 245
Travers, Rev. Marshall 67, 69, 115
Trimble, Terry 354
Trott, Joseph R 106
Trott, Joseph R. III 276
Trott, Mary 100, 170, 184, 185, 198, 337
Trumbull, Mrs. Maria 26
Tucker, Rev. A. Campbell 2, 73-75
Tucker, Miss Belle 33
Tucker, Mrs. Cornelia 147
Turnage, Rev. Ben W. 99, 173-174
Tyler, Dr. Lyon 225

U

Uzzell, Mrs. T.M. (Marjere) 128

V

Valdiva, Mrs. Charlotte Dozier 78
Valk, Marguerite Sinkler 96, 217
Van Ness, Legare 128
Verner, Elizabeth O'Neil 43, 94, 158
Vetter, Martha 244
Vincent, Edward 250
Voigt, Frances W. 239, 276
Voigt, Richard J. 106, 210
Von Kolnitz, A.H 18, 44

W

Wagner, W.H. 25
Walker, E.M. 120
Walker, Mrs. Henry 52
Walker, Julian 181
Walker, Larry 128
Walker, Lawrence 299
Walker, Patience 15, 40, 55
Walker, Wallace 86

PARTIAL INDEX

Walsh, Miss Pressley 51, 54, 63, 71, 95

Wallace, Dr. E.K. 259, 267, 270, 284, 294, 299, 300

Wallace, Jean 301

Wallace, Nancy 130

Waller, Adelaide 194, 199, 229, 230

Wardlaw, Pat 130, 264

Waring, Charles III 372

Waring, Leila 43

Waring, Louisa 195

Waring, May 43

Warley, W.H. 3, 16, 17

Warlick, Bill 291, 292, 298, 302, 348, (and for all his work at Christmas Eve)

Warlick, Carolyn 290

Washington, Mrs. M.B. 130, 264

Washington, Richard (sexton) 358

Watson, Riley 323, 336, 337, 357

Webb, Mary L 49, 309

Webb, Ric 337, (in seminary in 2013)

Webb, Rutledge 49

Weil, Julius 95

Welch, Ann 276

Welch, John T. 94, 110, 133, 137, 138, 148, 152, 153, 157, 196, 198, 209, 212, 291, 297, 354

Welch, Mrs. John T. 89

Welch, Mrs. Norman 52

Weld, Rev. Geo. 280

Weldon, Rev. Ken 335, 336, 357

Wells, Capt. E.L. 7

Westmoreland, Mrs. W.C. 186

Whaley, Ben Scott 67, 75, 80, 95, 111

Whaley, Mrs. Emily

Whipple, Mrs. Grant 81

White, Larry (sexton) 291

White, Mary 282

White, Thos. P. 92, 133, 137, 142

White, Mrs. Thos. P. 78

Whitmore, Rev. Bruce 177

Whitney, John J. (sexton) 3

Widney, Rev. Charles 123, 124, 151

Wilbur, Don and Mary 339

Wilcox, Arthur M. 64, 116, 120, 130, 131, 135, 156, 196, 199, 207, 229, 296, 304

Wilcox, Mrs. A.M. (Katharine) 199

Wiles, Julian 184

Wilson, George 356

Wilson, Gwynn 65

Wilson, John 125, 130, 131, 152, 153, 154, 155, 157, 182, 191, 193, 194

Wilson, Dr. Robert 30

Wilson, Sally 130

Wilson, Winnie 185

Wilkinson, Douglas 83, 92, 93

Wilkinson, Rev. Hazel 329

Willcox, E. Lloyd 55

Williams, Charlotte, 328, 336, 337, 354, 355

Williams, Eric (sexton) 296

Williams, Rev. Merritt 47-49, 60, 309

Williamson, Rev. Atkin 47

Williman, C. 29

Witte, Franz 100

Wood, Chase 356

Woodsome, Marcy 354

Woodward, Rev. James Herbert 29-31

Wooten, Joe 304

Wooten, Roy 84

World War II Roll of Honor, 80+ names 65, 66

Y

Yarborough, Mrs. Harriet Travers p. iv 69, 103

Yonker, Mrs. Sarah 211, 252, 310

Z

Zabriskie, Alexander 88, 89

Zervos, Nick 247, 264, 289, 291, 309

Made in the USA
Charleston, SC
27 April 2013